ALL'S FAIR

SIMON & SCHUSTER

NEW YORK   LONDON   TORONTO   SYDNEY   TOKYO   SINGAPORE

ALL'S FAIR

LOVE, WAR, AND
RUNNING FOR PRESIDENT

MARY MATALIN
AND JAMES CARVILLE

WITH PETER KNOBLER

RANDOM HOUSE

NEW YORK

Copyright © 1994 by Mary Matalin and James Carville

All rights reserved under International
and Pan-American Copyright Conventions. Published
in the United States by Random House, Inc., New York,
and Simon & Schuster, Inc., New York, and simultaneously
in Canada by Random House of Canada Limited, Toronto.

A leatherbound, signed first edition of this book
has been published by The Easton Press.

Library of Congress Cataloging-in-Publication Data
Matalin, Mary.
All's fair : love, war, and running for president / Mary Matalin
and James Carville, with Peter Knobler.
p.   cm.
ISBN 0-679-43103-9
1. Presidents—United States—Election—1992.   2. Bush, George,
1924–   . 3. Clinton, Bill, 1946–   . 4. United States—Politics
and government—1989–1993.   I. Carville, James.   II. Knobler,
Peter.   III. Title.
E884.M38   1994
324.973'0928—dc20   94-10606

Manufactured in the United States of America
24689753
First Trade Edition

Designed by Oksana Kushnir

To Eileen Emerson Matalin and Chester James Carville

—M.M. and J.C.

To Jane and Daniel

—P.K.

Follow me if I advance
Kill me if I retreat
Avenge me if I die.

> —Vietnamese battle cry,
> embraced by Mary Matalin

When your opponent is drowning, throw the son of a bitch an anvil.

> —the CEO of a large corporation to James Carville,
> on what he perceived to be their common strategic philosophy

ACKNOWLEDGMENTS

In my years of political consulting, one piece of advice that I continually give to candidates—which, I might add, they never take—is to not recognize the dignitaries at county or state party functions, because inevitably you end up mildly pleasing fifteen people and thoroughly dissing another three. As difficult as it is, this is one instance where I'm going to follow the advice I give my candidates and not make any public acknowledgments of the people who helped me with this book or my career. Each of you knows who you are, and if in my own way I've failed to acknowledge you in a person-to-person manner, please don't blame my parents—they raised me better than that. Blame me.

I will take this opportunity to depart slightly from my counsel and acknowledge one person, and that is President Bill Clinton, without whose tenacity, hard work, vision, and trust in me this book and a lot of other things that have happened would not have been possible.

—JAMES CARVILLE

As is often the case, while he might be right, from my vantage point he's wrong. At the risk of annoying someone, the following people really do deserve special thanks.

To George and Barbara Bush, who taught us all grace, dignity, and honor.

To all of the campaign foxhole comrades . . .

First and foremost, to the special friends who had the guts to read the first draft and the grace not to laugh out loud: Grace Moe and Torie Clarke, honest editors and dear pals.

To the queen organizers, linear thinkers, sanity keepers: Dalit Toledano and Rhonda Keenum.

To the story collectors and tellers: Mary Lukens, Dave Carney, Margaret Tutwiler, Janet Mullins, Ann Devroy, Steve Provost, David Tell, Jim Cicconi, Stan Huckaby, Bobby Burchfield, Gary Foster, Chris Dube.

To Carville's Clintonista helpers: Paul Begala, George Stephanopoulos, Mandy Grunwald, Stan Greenberg.

Special thanks to hand-holders: Caroline Critchfield, Camilla Montgomery, Ann Klenk, Gus Weill.

To the miracle workers:

Our friend, referee, life and legal counsel, a real Renaissance Man: Bob Barnett. To David Rosenthal and Alice Mayhew, who envisioned and styled what we could not. To Harry Evans and Carolyn Reidy, whose commitment never wavered.

Mostly, endlessly, to Peter Knobler, who made a silk purse of a sow's ear; who overcame his extraordinary knee-jerk, fuzzy-headed, bleeding-heart liberalism to craft a balanced story—although he refused to make a happy-ending GOP victory. It's no picnic to live with either of us, let alone both of us. And to his great family, Jane and Daniel, for sharing their guy for weeks at a time.

To Barb Matalin for our gift of family.

Finally, to the guardian angels Maria Cino and Renie O'Brien for daily life sustenance.

—MARY MATALIN

James

Like most honest people in the political consulting business, we've both had losses and we've both had wins. The losses are much easier to recall. They stick with you. I was so relieved not to have lost the 1992 presidential campaign that it didn't really dawn on me that we'd actually won.

Mary

The glory of a campaign is that, winning or losing, when you recall it, even in its worst moments, you recall it in a positive light. You remember the funny stories, the wonderful people, the esprit de corps. And that's what this book is. It's not a day-to-day blow-by-blow, because that's not how you live campaigns. You live campaigns event by event. As my early mentor Rich Bond once said, "The thing about it is, you know every day you're alive."

James

But you also remember how you did it. There are things you do that make you win. You want to remember them. And you want to do them again.

The intensity of not just the endeavor but the relationships is what lasts. You spend literally every waking moment with the same people, you're at their houses, in their kitchens, talking about the same thing, and you do it all in public. When you win it feels great. When you lose you feel awful for your candidate and all your friends.

Mary

 Didn't you feel bad for me?

James

I felt bad for you. I felt terrible. It was difficult to see you go through it.

Mary

 Did you feel worse for me than good for yourself?

James

On many occasions, yes, for sure.

Mary

 Well, I felt worse for me than good for you, to tell you the truth. And worse for the country.

James

 I felt good for the country but I felt bad for you.

ALL'S FAIR

CHAPTER 1

James

It was another lost day, another disaster. We had a message to get out, to tell the good people of the state of New Hampshire who Governor Bill Clinton was, what he stood for, and why they should vote for him in this leadoff primary. But were we doing it? No. We'd spent almost a month dogged by Gennifer Flowers and the press hounds on the trail of the smoking bimbo. The Republican party had played no small part in that parade of trash and now, when we had almost put it to rest, all of a sudden ABC News shows up with this twenty-two-year-old letter from Bill Clinton to the head of the University of Arkansas ROTC program. Now how the hell did they get that?

Mark Halperin of ABC said, "We have this letter that Clinton wrote to Colonel Eugene Holmes in 1969. We want to show the letter to the governor, do an interview, and get his comments."

It was the Thank-you-for-saving-me-from-the-draft letter. When George Stephanopoulos read it he said, "That's it, we're out of the race, we'll never survive." But that's George, he has a strong streak of pessimism that he's got to run through before he kicks into gear.

I read it and said, "Partner, this is a hell of a letter. This letter is our friend, this letter will save us. This is a torn man. People will understand this.

"We have to *want* questions on this letter," I said. "We're going to publish this letter. We are going to be very aggressive about it—"

"Oh, man . . ."

"Look, I'm telling you, if you let them take excerpts out of this thing it'll kill us. If you read this letter in its totality you say, 'Geez, I want a president who could write a letter like that when he was twenty-one years old.' "

ABC didn't go with the story on Monday, which was fine with us. We had spent the night in western New Hampshire, away from our headquarters in Manchester. Tuesday morning on our way back I was driving on a highway with George and my partner, Paul Begala, and we got beeped.

Our van was cruising in a major-league hurry for a telephone. We passed the Hillbrook Motel in Bedford, New Hampshire, but it didn't have a pay phone. We needed privacy. "Look, just give us a phone. How much is a room? Ninety bucks? Here's the money, here's the credit card, just give us the room, I don't care what it costs." This was a phone call worth the price of a motel room. Ted Koppel had gotten the letter from another source and was talking about going with it on *Nightline*.

The governor called Koppel the next morning and they had a discussion about the letter. Nothing got resolved. We weren't sure what Koppel was going to do.

But each of us knew what the results would be. Very soon that letter would get out and all hell was going to break loose. Was the media going to tell the voters about Bill Clinton's position on health care or what he could do to strengthen the economy? Of course not. All the networks and local stations would lead with another take on "Slick Willie." That was all you'd be reading about in the papers or hearing on talk radio. It would be another day, couple of days, or a week off message. If things kept on the way they were going we'd never get our message out; we'd never talk about anything important or anything that could help Bill Clinton get elected president.

Governor Clinton asked, of course, but Koppel wouldn't say where he'd gotten the letter. He wasn't going to reveal his sources. But Koppel did tell the governor that he was under the impression the letter had come from somebody at the Pentagon.

All right. Now we had some evidence that they were monkeying with the election here. Now I had an enemy. Something out of his files? They'd taken something out of Bill Clinton's files? Those are confidential. I called Koppel and said, "We've got to blow this damn thing up about the Republicans using the Pentagon."

Nightline didn't go with the letter on Tuesday, which was a big break for us. We wanted to be there with the news first.

So Wednesday at noon we held a press event in an airport hangar in Manchester and released the letter ourselves. After it was over there was a spin session and the media just went crazy. So did I.

"What is the Pentagon doing leaking something— Lemme finish! The larger question here is, What in the world business does the Pentagon have in the middle of a political campaign?"

"Why did the Pentagon release the letter?" a reporter asked.

"Let's try a case of rocket science," I told him. "Here's an article in *The Wall Street Journal* on Friday and here's a story that looks like it might be going away. And somebody says, 'Aha! Look, we have something that can kick this story an extra day. Because if Clinton is talking about the draft, he's not talking about the fact that we've had the lowest GNP growth under this administration than we've had under any administration in the history of this country; he is not talking about the fact that George Bush has had four different positions on the civil rights bill in two months; he is not talking about the fact that taxes have gone up for the middle class while services have gone down. . . . So, what we will do is we will leak this to the press and we will get the microphone in Bill Clinton's face talking about something that is not particularly advantageous to him . . . and we will block him out from talking about the things that made him the leading candidate.' You understand? That's what's going on here. And if nobody can see that, I can't explain it to you."

Of course, as it turned out, I was wrong; the letter came from somewhere else. But, hell, I was angry. And it made the evening news. In fact, as disruptive as that letter was, it kind of turned a corner for us in New Hampshire. It lit a fire, raised the bloodlust, gave us something to fight.

Mary

In various corners and offices of campaign headquarters, campaign chairman Bob Teeter, chief strategist Charlie Black, director of research David Tell, field director David Carney, and press secretary Torie Clarke had all been watching CNN. The TVs were on pretty much all day. Not mine. I was on the phone, preoccupied with endless catastrophes. The campaign hierarchy stampeded through my office door like wild elephants.

"Mary, Mary, hang up, get off the phone. Look, you have to see this!"

"What? What's going on?"

"Your boyfriend has lost his mind! He's having a nuclear meltdown! Turn on CNN!" They flicked on the television that was perched on top of the little icebox I moved from campaign to campaign.

Of course by the time they got in there we'd missed it, so we had to wait for the replay, which, on CNN, wasn't very long in coming. All the while they were trying to describe this bizarre scene to me. Finally it reappeared.

They were screaming, "There it is! There it is!"

That was James, all right, in the middle of a ferocious media feeding frenzy. Unshaven. Hair, such as it was, askew. Standing in this ripped-up ratty old Burberry with the torn collar and Frankenstein stitching. Wearing some goofy T-shirt. There were huge dark circles under his eyes and he had the hollow-eyed look he gets when he's in full rant. His long arms flailing, he was screaming demonically into their faces.

The reporters were all yelling questions at the same time and his head was snapping from side to side like he was getting smacked. David Gergen was leading the inquisition. NBC's Andrea Mitchell asked him a question and he screamed at her. Syndicated columnist Ben Wattenberg and all these big-time network and political reporters were after him.

"If you let the Pentagon dictate the course of a presidential election," he told them, "you are missing something big."

And from all sides of me my GOP sisters and brothers were laughing. "See him? Oh, my God." "This man has lost his mind. He's in meltdown." "Mary, we love you but your boyfriend's imploding!"

Now, Teeter and Carney and Torie and Charlie and Tell had never met James. It was early February 1992; he was just some political consultant I was consorting with that they'd heard about. My assistants, who had come with me to the campaign from the Republican National Committee and who had just run into my office to see what all the shouting was about, knew him better. He was the guy who was in and out of the RNC every day bringing me tuna sandwiches, doting on me, keeping my office stocked with a fresh supply of flowers.

Everybody was standing there huddled around my little TV and I just had to laugh. It had never occurred to me that he could be perceived as a crazy person.

"Look at that face," said the new guys. "He's a madman. He's demonic. He's a serpenthead!"

Okay, as media guru Roger Ailes put it, sometimes Carville does look like a fish who's swum too close to a nuclear reactor. But he was my man.

I had seen it all before. I had seen James fake a heart attack to get a good table at a chichi restaurant. He can be a little theatrical.

The three women who worked with me at the RNC kept waiting for what it was these guys were seeing as unusual behavior.

"Yeah," they said. "So?"

"That's how he always is," I said. "But forget how he's acting, listen to what he's saying."

We weren't paying much attention to the Democrats at this point; we had enough trouble dealing with Pat Buchanan and figured we'd just let Clinton and Kerrey and Harkin and Tsongas and Brown beat each other up for a while. We'd get involved when the time came.

But I could see where Carville was going with this outburst. This was a preemptive strike. He was going to charge the Republicans and the entire government with dirty tricks. Ever since Nixon it's been a charge that's worked against Republicans. We had taken a lot of heat for our paid media in the 1988 presidential campaign, and now here was my boyfriend trying to create another smokescreen and cut into our ability to hit Bill Clinton hard. It was a winner's tactic. For all of his seeming lunacy, you had to admire his technique.

But the campaign was so freaked out over his appearance, they missed the content. They thought he was a total nut case and dismissed the possibility that he could do anything sane or productive. Inside the campaign, it became a joke. People would make fun of me because James was so crazy. They kept creating names for him and trashing him when he showed up on TV.

"Serpenthead" stuck.

Torie Clarke, who was my good friend, would always talk to her mother about characters on the campaign. Her mom called up one day and said, "I'm very concerned about your little friend Mary. Every time I see that man on TV he just . . . sweetheart, he looks like he eats small children."

From then on, in Republican campaign lore James was the Man Who Eats Small Children.

James

I wasn't so sure I wanted to do a presidential race. I had lost consistently, didn't win my first statewide campaign until I was forty-two years old. Now I had a pretty fair winning streak going in the states: Bob Casey had won governor of Pennsylvania; Wallace Wilkinson, governor of Kentucky; Frank Lautenberg, senator from New Jersey; Zell Miller, governor of Georgia; and now Harris Wofford had beat Richard Thornburgh to become senator from Pennsylvania. I knew how to do it. I liked the hands-on way you could run a state, the fact that you could talk to everyone who needed to be talked to, that if something really needed to be dealt with you could jump on a plane and get anywhere you wanted in a couple of hours. I like to control a campaign, and you lose touch when it gets too big. Too many Washington insiders get their fingers in the pie until there's nothing left of substance or political nutrition.

Paul Begala and I weren't saying, "Gee, if we win this we can get in the presidential race and go up the ladder and some day get on *Good Morning America*." I wasn't looking for flight attendants to know who I was, or for strangers to get up from their meals to come shake my hand. Just professionally, I wanted people in the political consultant business to know that I was good.

I always felt that because I was from Louisiana and didn't go to a prestigious school, and was older, and my candidates were not glamorous or high-visibility national figures, somehow or other I was being professionally slighted.

I'm a runner. I run hard for a half hour every day, rain or shine, on the campaign trail or in the mountains. And any runner will tell you: When you run you dream.

I'm giving a talk to a bunch of political professionals and they're milling around out in the hallways, and they say, "Carville is speaking, let's go in and see what he's got to say." I'd dream about that. That was a big dream for me.

There's a great old Fats Domino, New Orleans rhythm-and-blues song that goes,

> *I'm gonna be a wheel someday*
> *I'm gonna be somebody*
> *I'm gonna be a real gone cat*
> *Then I won't need you.*

When you're toiling out there, particularly when you're not winning, you dream of being a wheel someday, dream of being somebody.

When Harris Wofford came from 47 points back to beat George Bush's cabinet member Dick Thornburgh, candidates came calling. Paul and I talked with Bob Kerrey, Tom Harkin, and Bill Clinton. It was there if we wanted it.

I knew Mary didn't want me to run a presidential; it takes all of your time. She should know, she'd worked for Reagan in 1984 and been pretty high up in Bush's 1988 campaign, which she never let me forget.

By November 1991 we'd been going out for about a year, but with one campaign after another, I hadn't been home much and we'd never really got settled in. She would come visit me at campaign headquarters in Pennsylvania; I'd disrupt her day at the Republican National Committee. We didn't see each other a lot but we thought about each other all the time. We were neither of us youngsters; this wasn't puppy love.

It was like I told Mary: I wasn't that interested in running the race. I liked what I was doing; Paul's wife, Diane, was going to have a baby, and Paul didn't want to be an absentee husband or a telephone daddy; I had a girlfriend who seemed like the real deal.

But Paul and I had a hard time saying no. Neither of us felt any sense of destiny about hooking up with Bill Clinton. He just seemed like a good guy, someone we could work for. In the end I went to work for a presidential candidate for the same reason that I went to law school: I never really wanted to but it was sort of expected of me. It was the next stage. I was a political professional, and that's what political professionals are supposed to do, run their guys for president.

Mary

When Harris Wofford beat Dick Thornburgh in November 1991 lots of people in the Republican party started wringing their hands. When our polls showed that only 41 percent of Americans thought George Bush deserved to be reelected, it got worse.

"We've got to start the reelection campaign now. We can't wait another minute."

President Bush didn't really want to start. He liked to govern and he wasn't interested in disrupting the important work of his administration until it was absolutely necessary.

This was my dream job, to be political director of the campaign, to help put a man I totally respected and really did love back in the most important position in the world.

But meanwhile here was James Carville—to Republicans he was pretty much the devil—and I was big-time smitten with him.

We hadn't seen half enough of each other almost since we'd begun going out. First he'd been in Georgia running a governor's race; then he'd been in Pennsylvania "discovering the health care issue" and kicking the bejeezus out of a good Republican who deserved to be in office. He had this really annoying string of successes, putting Democrats in places that without him would probably have gone to Republicans. If we talked politics we'd just have these screaming fights, so we avoided the obvious areas of conflict and found that just about everywhere else we were simpatico.

It was the beginning of Thanksgiving weekend and I was supposed to meet James at i Ricchi, this loud, to-be-seen kind of Washington restaurant. I hated this kind of scene. We never got to see each other and now we were having a group dinner with Joe Klein and Mandy Grunwald.

I had met Mandy through James. She is a very tough Democratic media consultant. Joe Klein is a good reporter, a New Paradigm kind of guy, what's now called a New Democrat. He's very hip, a lot of fun to banter with, Lee Atwater liked him and I think he liked Lee. He was just sort of a pal, not the kind of reporter you have to watch every little wiseass remark you make or it'll show up in a headline and cause trouble.

I walked in and started cringing. The three of them were sitting at the most visible, most embarrassing front table, the kind powerful people barter for, and it seemed like everybody in the place was fawning over James after his Pennsylvania upset victory. I wished that just once we could go out to dinner alone instead of with reporters or his Democratic friends or some liberal sycophants who wanted to tell James how wonderful he is.

The conversation went on and the clock was ticking.

Klein asked me whether I'd seen his latest column, a mock strategy memo from the recently deceased Lee Atwater to President Bush about how Lee would handle this election if Lee were still alive.

Lee Atwater was a genius, a best friend, and one of the most wonderful people the world has known. He had died of brain cancer that March. I had been thinking a lot about what Lee would have done, and every time anybody brought up his name that entire year I'd get teary-eyed. Talking about his column, Joe brought Lee back to life for me for a second. I was really moved.

Maybe he saw me get a little choked up. So Joe gracefully changed the subject.

"So, James," he said, "when do you officially start the Clinton campaign?"

If I'd had something in my hand I would have dropped it. I felt like I'd been kicked in the chest. I couldn't catch my breath.

Maybe it was a fake. Joe wasn't one of those guys who go fishing for a story over a friendly dinner, but he *was* a reporter, and nothing was impossible. Presidential candidates had been calling the house since the first weekend James had gotten home from Pennsylvania.

I looked at James and expected something to the contrary to come out of his mouth. "I'm not doing a presidential campaign" would have been good, especially since that was the last thing he'd told me on the subject. Instead he had a sheepish, guilty, I-meant-to-tell-you, there's-more-to-it-than-this kind of look.

I excused myself, got up. I thought, I'm not going to make it to the bathroom.

I got there and leaned against the sink. In my pretty little blue silk picked-out-for-Carville Anne Klein dress, I caught my breath and then threw up.

It took me a good ten minutes to get it back together.

I must not have done such a good job, because when I returned to the table Carville gave me a once-over.

"You okay, honey?"

"I'm fine."

Every once in a while it would just wave over me that he was going to do this race and I would start to tear up, then I'd blow my nose and Joe and Mandy would wonder what was the matter. Klein thought I was crying over his Atwater column.

I didn't say much for the rest of the dinner. James felt very guilty, which was manifested by his yakking on and on. I couldn't wait to get out of there.

In the car I couldn't even speak at first, but in short order I was screaming at him.

"How could you do this? I can't believe this! Why didn't you tell me? You don't know what this is like, you've never done a presidential race, it's not like a state race. You don't know what this is going to do to us. You don't know what it's going to do to you!"

He tried to calm me down. "Well, you know, we'll probably lose the primary or something. You don't know what's going to happen— it might not be a whole year."

I said, "This guy is going to win the primary. You're going to be running against us. We're going to be working against each other!"

"You don't know that."

"*Yes,* I know it!"

And before me flashed the whole next year. Something that had never happened in the annals of presidential politics: a boyfriend and girlfriend working against each other. We were just starting the campaigns; he's on one side, I'm on the other. In a couple of weeks we're going to be at each other's throats.

On top of that, this was the weekend the Republican boys were going to the mountain to make their choices on the key jobs for the reelection campaign.

"If this story gets out, that you're running Clinton's campaign, before they make their decision—I will not get my job." They could leave me as chief of staff at the RNC, where no Bush loyalist could complain about my "traitorous" relationship. It was a good job; it just wasn't the one I wanted. "You call Klein and you tell him that if he's writing, he can't write this until after they make the campaign assignments. If this gets out I've got no chance."

"Oh, that's not true. You're so good, and everybody knows you're so good."

"Look," I told him, "there are a lot of good people without the baggage of you. I wouldn't pick me to work in the job I want on the campaign knowing that you were going to go work for Clinton. I wouldn't!"

This was Thanksgiving weekend and we were visiting his mother and family in Baton Rouge. So James was going to call Klein from Louisiana. I said, "I want to hear every word of this conversation."

James picked up the phone. "Hey, it's Carville. Can you hold off writing about me and Clinton for a while? Mary feels it might cause a problem for her. Can you not break this story till we get back?" Klein agreed.

The whole weekend I was a wreck—(a) there was no time to be alone in the one and only last opportunity we were going to have to be together before the campaign started, and (b) I was waiting to find out if I got *the* job of my life. I could really have shot him between the eyes.

There was also the issue of whether James had lied to me. A bad omen.

James

I said I never *wanted* to do a presidential. I didn't say I *wasn't* going to do one. I never said that. I only said that I didn't want to do one and I could see all the problems with doing one, but I never said I *wasn't* going to do one.

Mary

You can spin *The New York Times* but you clearly left me with the impression that you weren't going to do one. For weeks you'd been saying you and Paul don't want to do one, and these candidates are calling and you've met with them and you don't like them, or "This is all Washington hype, I don't want to go to a bunch of meetings and hang out with a bunch of people who don't know what they're doing."

And plus, you never told me. I had to hear it from Joe Klein!

So then James went into his customary second-phase defense: "That's my story and I'm sticking to it. You're wrong."

And his third phase: "I don't want you to work in a presidential. I want you to stay at the Republican National Committee."

"What? *What?!* You get to work on a— I've worked my whole life for this job and you're going to do one and I'm not? *Get out of here!*"

"You've worked on one. You've worked on *two*! Why shouldn't I work on one? You're the one who should stay at the RNC. You love Clayton Yeutter and that's a perfectly good job you can do and be just as involved from there." (And, P.S., pay attention to me.)

I was disgusted. "You must be out of your mind."

I got the big spin.

The next week I got the big job, political director of the campaign to reelect President George Bush. And we were off.

CHAPTER 2

James

There was one road sign in Carville, Louisiana, when I was growing up in the 1950s. It said STOP on one side of the road, nothing on the other. There's nothing in Carville but my daddy's store with the post office attached to it. My family had run the post office for generations and when the town was named, it was named after the postmaster.

In Carville, Louisiana, it got hot in the summer and not very cold in the winter, you did things together as a family, and you played and you rode horses. Whites and blacks may have done the same things, but we did them separately. The town was segregated. That's the way it was, you just didn't think about it, that was the natural order of things.

But after *Brown v. Topeka, Kansas, Board of Education* in 1954 and the Montgomery bus boycott of 1956, that all changed. From then on all conversation about baseball or sports or geography or books or family or anything ceased. The single source of conversation was race.

The town of Carville was about 85 percent black. My father's store was a typical country operation where people bought on credit. He had a black man who worked there, which was a big deal; that a black person could get around a cash register was unheard of.

My parents, Chester and Lucille (everyone called her Miss Nippy), never allowed us to use racial epithets. They weren't prejudiced and there wasn't a racial flash point in Carville. Actually, aside from the

school, there was no facility to segregate. There wasn't a movie theater, a swimming pool, nothing. As for the Mississippi River, anybody
that wanted could swim in it. We didn't swim together, but we were
all there.

But every conversation I heard outside my family was "The niggers
this" or "The niggers that." It became a white Southern obsession and
went on for years, and after a while I just felt, "Can't we please just
talk about something else?" I wanted to have a life other than worrying about who was going to school with me or who was going to ride
in my bus or were all the white women going to get raped.

I sometimes would wish that if the blacks just didn't push so hard,
we could go back to talking about other things.

Then I read *To Kill a Mockingbird*.

I put it inside another book and read it under my desk during
school. I attacked that book with a vengeance, and when I got to the
last page I closed it and said, "They're right and we're wrong."

Of course, I was already a Democrat. Everyone in Louisiana was a
Democrat. But one of the reasons that I became an *enthusiastic*
Democrat was that Democrats believe in the power of the federal
government to do good, and on the one burning persuasive issue in
the formative years of my life, the federal government was one hundred percent right and everybody else was wrong.

The federal government was for integration. When a group of black
kids was trying to integrate Central High School in Little Rock and
fell under siege, it was federal agents who kept the mob off them.
When James Meredith was integrating the University of Mississippi it
was always federal agents who were protecting him. What this did
was make me one of the few people in the country that maybe *over*-
believes that the federal government can do some good.

Politicians, to me, were larger than life. If a kid grows up in New
York City and sees some big star on the street, maybe he gets fascinated with the theater and gets a ticket to a show or sneaks in to see
a rehearsal. It was that way with me and politics. These were all big
stars and the legislature was a big theater and there was a big drama
being played out.

Carville was about a half-hour ride from Baton Rouge and I com-
muted to parochial school for sixth and seventh grades. The state
capitol was about two blocks away. Then I went to Catholic high
school in Donaldsonville. One summer I had a job as a runner for one
of the local Baton Rouge banks, picking up and dropping off checks
from the state treasury. Whenever the legislature was in session I

would always go sit in the gallery and watch it for ten or fifteen minutes, much like a kid would go and look through a knot hole to see a baseball game.

There was a great clamor to the Louisiana legislature. Bells would ring. The combination of stale cigar smoke and the fresh ink used to print up the bills gave the place a very specific odor that meant power and action.

Earl Long, a progressive by Louisiana standards, was governor when I was growing up. I saw him one time only. There was a commotion in the capitol halls, hard shoe leather on marble, echoing, and it was coming right at me. The governor was walking through the capitol, kicking up a wake, cops around him, a couple of reporters. I just looked up and he was there. To be governor was such a big thing, it was unimaginable that you would ever see one. It took my breath away. Am I supposed to be here? Should I look? What does he really look like? I was fifteen, and it was like I was staring at a naked woman.

That same year, 1959, I started my career in politics. It was a race for the state legislature between Price LeBlanc and a guy named Boisee Jumonville. Price was a car dealer, called himself the Trading Country Boy, and his name recognition was probably 95 percent. His campaign slogan was "I Want You, I Need You, and I'll Work for You." I had just gotten my driver's license and I would go up to the northern part of Iberville Parish, Maringouin, Grosse Tete, Ramah, Shady Grove, and knock on doors for LeBlanc. That was a lot of responsibility, that was really like leaving home.

There was a ferryboat that went from one side of the Mississippi to the other and I would sit out there for half a day and pass out literature to people waiting in line. I'd say, "I know this guy and he's a good guy." I spent a lot of time putting our signs up and tearing the other guy's signs down.

It broke my heart the night we lost.

I graduated high school in 1962 and entered Louisiana State University. After all those years at an all-boys Catholic school there were girls everywhere and bars open every night. Me and the guys would drive down to Laredo, Texas, about every weekend, which is probably six hundred miles, and party in Mexico. They had some unique attractions down there in the border town. I was something less than an attentive scholar.

I had fifty-six hours' worth of F's before LSU finally threw me out. I remember going home to tell my folks. They started crying and apologizing, like it was their fault that I was a bum and didn't go to class and slept through everything and got drunk every night. It would have been way less torture if they'd just started screaming at me.

As I've always been a cultural Catholic, I had to have some punishment quick. I joined the Marines in 1966 and was fortunate to get stationed in San Diego and not go to Vietnam. When I got out of the service in 1968, I went back and graduated from LSU at night. I taught junior high school science for a while (which I knew nothing about) and didn't know what the hell to do with my life. Everybody else assumed I was going to be a lawyer. People were always saying, "You can talk, that's what a lawyer does, he gets paid to talk." Well, why not? I didn't have anything approaching the money to go to law school. My uncle Lloyd, my father's brother, paid my way.

I joined the firm of McKernnan, Beychok, Screen and Pierson in 1973 and started practicing law, but I was always more interested in politics. Jerry McKernnan, a friend of mine at the firm, was running for the public service commission and I went and helped him in his race. He lost. I worked for a woman in the firm, Mary Olive Pierson, who ran for city judge in Baton Rouge. She lost. In 1979 I worked in the governor's race for a guy named E. L. "Bubba" Henry. Lost.

Still, I knew I liked it. I liked the excitement. I liked that there was a definite date to fix on, that there was a winner or a loser. And I always wanted to be a winner.

Which wasn't happening in the campaign *or* in the courtroom. My law career ended one day in 1980 when I looked up from my desk and said, "If I had to hire a lawyer, I wouldn't hire me." And I quit.

I hooked on with a political consulting agency called Weill and Strother. We ran a congressional race for a guy named Billy Tauzin and he actually won. I was not *the* player in the campaign, but I had a medium-to-large role. I freelanced a campaign for Pat Screen, who ran for mayor of Baton Rouge. He won and made me the number two guy in the mayor's office. There's nothing like a substantial job to give a guy some self-esteem. I liked the responsibility, but the more I worked the more I found that I wasn't really cut out to be a city government professional. By spring of 1981 I had to make another choice with my career. I left the mayor's office without a job.

I called Peter Hart, a pollster I'd worked with on the Bubba Henry and Mayor Screen races. He said, "What you ought to do is run a campaign. If something comes up I'll see if I can get you an interview."

To avoid an internecine battle within the Virginia Democratic party, the state's recently elected lieutenant governor, Dick Davis, was prevailed upon to make a last-minute bid for the party's U.S. Senate nomination. Davis needed a campaign manager and needed one quick. Peter Hart was the pollster and he recommended me. I went up, did a meeting, left my number. They called me back and gave me the job.

Dick Davis was the former mayor of Portsmouth, Virginia, a mortgage banker, a businessman Democrat. He had a way of saying things that, shall we say, could have been phrased better. If you liked him, he was refreshing; if you didn't, his language was an easy target. One time he was asked what he thought about the West Bank and the Middle East peace initiative, and he said, "Look, those folks have been fighting over there for the last three thousand years. I'm not sure there is much that I can do as a senator to stop them." There may be more than a grain of truth in what Davis said, but voters elect officials because they want things done; they don't want to be told that the powerful don't have power.

Still, with about a week to go we had a little lead. A fragile one, but a lead. We planned an event at a senior citizens' center around our biggest issue, Social Security, which we were accusing President Reagan and the Republicans of trying to destroy. Everything was fine until Davis was asked whether Social Security was owed to the older generation. He told a group of elderly voters that the younger generation owed them Social Security and if the young folks didn't like it that was just tough luck. The next day's headlines were essentially "Davis to Young People: Drop Dead."

The opposition seized on it and I very timidly—very stupidly—backed off. I got cautious and tried to sit on a lead.

It was a major mistake. In a state that had elected a lot of Republican officeholders, I discarded our best issue because the candidate had made one gaffe and I was worried that he might make some more. And in the last week, when undecided voters make up their minds, I let the opposition be more aggressive than me. We sat back and hoped the voters would know enough about us to vote us in.

With virtually no money to spend on advertising, we lost by 1 percent among a lot of votes cast.

There are three things you can do with defeat: You can try to blame everybody else for it; you can ascribe it to luck; or you can really try to learn from it. This was a bad loss and it taught me two valuable lessons.

First, don't let the other guy outraise you by two to one, no matter what. Money talks.

Second, you cannot ever lay back, particularly in the last ten days of a campaign. From day ten to election day you have to be there all the time with everything you've got.

There are only anywhere from 3 to 7 percent of the voters in any election that really decide the outcome. Most people out there are going to vote a certain way, and you know who they are and how they're going to vote before the campaign begins. A majority of people do basically vote the party, not the person. I'm not talking about a 10- to 12-point runaway, where it's already a done deal, but in a close race it comes down to the 3 to 7 percent available undecided, and you'd better be there with your best at the exact moment they're making up their minds. If you're not, you might as well not even start.

To lose a race you know you could have won takes a long time to get over. If you're paying attention, the lesson will stay with you even longer. I played that race over and over in my mind and came to the inescapable conclusion that we would have won if we'd been aggressive.

So in the late fall of 1982 I was thirty-eight years old, no job, a loser the first time around. I didn't feel too good.

Mary

My grandparents met on the boat coming to America from Yugoslavia in the early 1920s. He had fifty cents, she had a loaf of bread. They didn't speak English, they were teenagers, somehow they made it to Chicago, rooted into the Croatian community, and made a life for themselves. He became a pipefitter, they married, bought a house, had my father, struggled through the Depression.

My grandfather never did speak very good English but he put all three of his kids through college, which was unheard of among his circle of Croatian immigrants. He even served in the Marines. At every family gathering that I can remember, the women would wait on the men endlessly, and after dinner Poppy, as we called him, would always sing the "United States Marine Hymn" and start crying.

Their South Chicago neighborhood was an ethnic enclave of Croatians, Italians, Poles, and Serbs. On the nice side of town, called the Hill, were the Irish. My mother, Eileen, came from an Irish family, and her parents were devastated when she told them she was going to marry her sweetheart from kindergarten, a Croatian. They said Steve would make her wash his feet, which is some sort of Irish impression of what Eastern European men require of their women.

My middle name is Joe. My father was a first son, my father's father was a first son, and since I was Steve and Eileen's first child everybody was certain I was going to be a boy.

My grandparents lived a stone's throw from the steel mills. United States Steel, Bethlehem Steel, and Wisconsin Steel ran for miles, and whatever ethnicity you were, everybody worked at one of them. At the end of the last mill they started building row houses. When they filled those up they started building developments. When I was six years old we moved to a new development called Burnham.

It was a collection of newly built row houses, each one separated by a dirt patch that eventually became, decades later, a driveway. There were only three blocks of houses and a gas station.

Having a house was a big deal. All of the families in Burnham had come from flats, so to have a house all your own was a tremendous step up. Burnham was overflow from South Chicago—which was itself overflow of *the* city, Chicago—and it was a little minicosm. Next to us was a Polish family; there were German, Italian, and other immigrants on the block.

All the men in Burnham worked at the steel mills or some spin-off of the steel mills. All the women would get up in the morning with them, pack their lunch pails, and kiss them good-bye. Then they'd pour a cup of coffee, light up a cigarette—all the women smoked— and get on the phone.

This was an ongoing conversation; it would go for years, like a soap opera. They'd talk, finish the cigarette, hang up, go downstairs, throw in a load of wash, run it through the hand wringer, then go in the backyard, hang it up—no one could afford an electric dryer—and talk again outside. Then they'd go in and make some lunch and start that night's dinner. In the afternoon they'd go to each other's houses with their kids in tow and smoke cigarettes, drink coffee, and talk. Today's woman would call it a support group; back then it was just coffee talk.

And then their husbands came home and the center of the universe would shift.

When I was eight my mother decided she wanted more, so she went to beauty school at night. When she graduated she had my father turn our basement into a beauty shop. Now, instead of making the daily rounds from kitchen to kitchen, all these women and their kids would come and hang out in our basement. We had a shampoo bowl and a dryer, and even the boys would come down there and get their hair cut.

My mom was a terrible hairdresser. She even turned her own hair bright orange. But it turned out she had other skills. She became a beauty-school teacher, then an administrator, and in time she owned beauty schools.

I was so proud of her. It was so glamorous. The beauty schools were always fun, but what was so adventurous was the fact that she was running the show. Starting when I was eleven I would go with her summers to the beauty school in our neighboring town, Calumet City, also known as Sin City. It had a whole row of strip joints and real bad bars, which besmirched the reputation of what was otherwise a town of good, solid, blue-collar working families. My mom would have me sit at the front desk and check in the customers.

It was weird that my mom would put an eleven-year-old girl out there to be the public face of the place and schmooze with these people. When you go get your hair done at a beauty school you're getting it for half price because you're letting the students experiment on you, so you're worried about getting your hair ruined. Plus there was always a long wait, which made the women even more cranky. Maybe she thought the ladies would be less demanding with a kid, or maybe she was saving money since I worked for my allowance. All I know for sure is we loved being together all the time. We were always kidding around with each other like pals.

When I was in sixth grade my teacher called my mom and told her that I was a problem, I was boy crazy. Maybe I was. I always wanted to hang out with boys because they *did* things. And I did boy things. When I was about eleven I used to steal my father's car. He had an old red convertible Chevy bomber for work and I started sneaking out of my room at night after everybody had gone to sleep and driving the three miles to Calumet City.

My dad had this incredible work ethic. He could never not work. At the steel mill he was on swing shift in perpetuity, and he'd go to school. He spent weekends for years locked in a room getting his B.S. in mechanical engineering. After that he got his M.B.A. at Purdue. He worked his way up at the steel mill from mechanic to superintendent. The guy just never quit, he was always on the rise. He used to say things like, "It's good to be selfish. If everybody was selfish and took care of themselves, the world would be all right. By being selfish you're really being *un*selfish, you're not imposing yourself on anybody. Do it yourself." So I shifted from hanging out with the boys to being my father's shadow.

In high school our little three-block town of ethnics was isolated from the in crowd; we were the outcasts. All the hip kids lived in Calumet City and had gone to these private Catholic grade schools and all knew each other and were instantly cliquish. They were either more well-off Catholics than we were, or WASPs with blond hair and blue eyes. I wasn't part of that clique, didn't expect to be, and didn't really want to be.

But by junior year I was going out with an older guy and somehow I got nominated for homecoming queen. The five other nominees were just what you'd expect homecoming queens to be—perfectly coiffed, well-dressed good girls. I was the weird one of the bunch.

But here's how politics works. My sister was a freshman and, without my knowledge, she went crazy campaigning for me. Here was one of their own with a stake in the race, so I got all the freshman vote. My boyfriend, who was a senior and good-looking and pretty popular, got a bunch of his friends to vote for me. My outcast group, the fringe element who usually never got involved in this stuff, saw a chance to take the stage and turned out in force.

The five good girls split the cute-girl vote and next thing I knew I was homecoming queen. My sister thought I was really cool. I was eternally embarrassed.

This was 1970. The Midwest was light-years behind everybody else and we went from *Leave It to Beaver* to hippiedom overnight. The school split between "socialites," "greasers," and this new group of ill-informed, ridiculously naïve, liberal Flower Power hippies. Like me. We had an underground newspaper and we'd sit around writing poems, listening to Cream and the Jefferson Airplane. We all grew our hair, quit wearing bras, and thought we were really cool. We'd read Camus and, like, hurt, man.

We all smoked pot, and we inhaled.

Smoking pot then was not about drugs, it was a statement, a culture, an attitude: motorcycles, cutting class, marching for Earth Day, marching against the war, overnight stints in jail; the police were pigs, adults were the enemy, capitalists were imperialists, socialism was utopia; the traditional family was anachronistic—people should live in open marriages in communes; God was out, meditation was in; competition was retro, collectivism was civilized.

It was all so hip and exciting . . . and totally phony and self-indulgent. All these socialist utopian kids had parents who were picking up the tab. The marches and drugs were really counterculture sock hops. I'm sure some people must have understood the issues, but everyone I knew went along to party. Free thinking was really group-thought, and our group-thought was a fuzzy-headed drug talk.

Even before I went away to college, the whole scene was beginning to get on my nerves. Then my uncle came home from Vietnam.

He was a late-life baby and my mom had raised him since he was five years old. Back from the war, he moved into our basement, and boy was he screwed up from the Vietnam experience. I loved my uncle, and here were all my oh-so-cool friends trashing the war and the vets, and every single one of their candy butts had a student deferment.

My mom babied her brother. For weeks he hung out all day drinking beer and not looking for a job. My father, a veteran himself, finally kicked him out, after which he lived in his car. My mother was beside herself, but my father said it was character development, time for my uncle to take personal responsibility. (To this day, my uncle credits my father with getting his life on track.)

By the time I got to college, flower children weren't a clique, they were running the joint. We were always marching over something or storming the administration building. During a march on the county courthouse, I turned to a fellow long-hair. "What are we protesting?"

"I don't know, man," he said. "Nixon did something."

I was really homesick. I was always close to my family and spoke to them every other day, to my mom for hours on Sundays. I began having long discussions with my dad about politics and current events. He would just laugh at me when I'd regale him with the virtues of socialism and communism, a hip thing to think at the time.

I'd say, "From each according to his ability, to each according to his need." Then we'd look at my personal environment. I was working full-time to help pay for school—cocktail waitress, library assistant, clerk in a day-old-bread store. He'd say, "Don't you work harder in school because you're paying for it? Would you want to give part of your earnings to another, nonworking student because they didn't want to work? What if your earnings were confiscated by the government to support nonworkers—would you work harder for less money?"

I didn't go anywhere near directly through college. I dropped out and got a job at a steel mill. In those days women didn't get the good jobs in the mill, so I grudgingly returned to school. It took me a long time to finish because I always worked full-time. I wanted to help pay my way since my parents by then were putting my sister and brother through college, too.

I took a graduate class in modern American thought. There was only one assignment, one paper, for the whole semester. I chose the topic "Is There a Trend Toward Conservatism in the United States?" I was still clinging to my lefty, liberal, bleeding-heart group-thought and wanted the paper to answer in the negative.

Writing this paper, answering this question, became an obsession. I lived in the library. I'd lock myself up for days and work on nothing else. I couldn't find one scintilla of evidence that liberal ideas, or the big-government programs such thinking spawned, worked. By the time I turned in my thesis I was a full-fledged conservative. My professor laughed at me. He said, "She's found Jesus."

This was 1978 (I took a *long* time getting through school). Taxpayers were revolting in California, housing projects were being imploded in St. Louis, welfare programs were splitting families and creating disincentives for individuals. On my own campus the big-government jobs program, the Comprehensive Education and Training Act (CETA), was a joke; all you had to do was show up and collect a check. Kids who could have worked were somehow getting food stamps. Kids who had worked were collecting unemployment benefits.

Back on the home front, both my mother's and father's businesses were suffering from big-government intrusion. At the steel mill the Occupational Safety and Health Administration (OSHA) and affirmative action were decreasing the quantity and quality of the work that got done; in the beauty-parlor business, my mother was spending more of her time filling out forms and preparing for inspectors than actually satisfying her customers and teaching her students.

Not only was government inept, it was a disencentive; it was like my mom coddling her little brother . . . well intended but ultimately self-defeating.

I had grown up a Chicago Democrat surrounded by the big-city machine. My mother was a Kennedy Democrat. She worshiped Jackie; she wore a pillbox hat. I voted for Carter in '76. I didn't even know what a Republican looked like.

But I was an unthinking Democrat, and when I started thinking, it was hard to remain a Democrat. Finally I had to admit that my friends and my hippie-commune thinking just didn't track right. Most of it was a cop-out. It devalued individual merit and glorified group rights; it defended irresponsible, anti-social behavior as the result of an unjust society; it naïvely minimized self-interest, and depended on selfless altruism.

My friends were all die-hard liberals and couldn't understand my conversion, and I wasn't well enough grounded in my new ideas to articulate it persuasively. To them if you were a Republican you were Nixon, you were for the Vietnam War, you were Goldwater, you were all these horrible things. They were unthinking and closed-minded and weren't interested in going back and questioning their knee-jerk beliefs.

There was also a certain rebelliousness that I liked. Teenagers and people in their early twenties don't like anyone butting into their business or telling them what to do. Getting government off our back is a grown-up version.

I got an A on the paper. I found myself with a new worldview, a fervent passion, and nowhere to go. I was neither a philosopher nor an intellectual. I loved studying politics and theory, but it had no practical application.

Then, another stroke of luck.

In my final semester I took a class called "Campaigns and Elections," taught by my political science adviser, Burt Southard. You actually had to go and work on campaigns to get credit. (In my first political action, in 1976, I was the butt end of an elephant in a Lincoln Day parade in Macomb, Illinois.) I stuffed envelopes, handed out flyers, called people to say, "Have you voted today?" and then dragged them to the polls if they hadn't. And whatever job they put me on, I loved it.

I finally graduated, came home, and, like every other kid, didn't know what the hell I was going to do with my life. I was helping my mom run her beauty school and it occurred to me that maybe I'd become a beautician. I didn't want to go to her school—it would have been uncool to be the boss's daughter—so I went to one on the east side of Chicago.

All my classmates were Mexican or black. Most of them were unmarried mothers, most had more than one kid, and they'd go to beauty school during the day and go home at night and take care of their families. It was a real struggle. Each of these women made my Republican point. They were working hard, they weren't looking for handouts from the government, and they were going to make a life for themselves and their kids and end up fine.

I was right in the middle of getting my beautician's license when Burt Southard called. He had given up his professorship to head the field organization in Chicago for a U.S. Senate race, and wanted me to come work on the campaign.

I was there the next day.

The candidate's name was Dave O'Neal. He was the Illinois lieutenant governor and had won the primary in an upset. He was running against Al "the Pal" Dixon; I started out processing fund-raising mail and worked my way up.

I moved to the city and shared a tiny one-bedroom apartment with two other campaign workers a couple of blocks from the headquarters. What girl fresh out of college (so what if college took seven years?) jumps right into a statewide race? I was working day and night, learning politics on a real campaign, when my father called in the middle of Labor Day weekend.

"Mary, you should come home. Your mother isn't feeling well." This was really bizarre; my mother never got sick.

I had seen her on her birthday, which was two days after mine in August. Her color had been terrible but she was, as always, sitting at the kitchen table smoking a cigarette and coffee-klatching with the girls. I had bought her these little sandals with half-inch heels and hadn't thought much of it. But one day she stepped down off these sandals and her ankle just cracked in half. She'd had cancer for two years and hadn't said a word. The doctor had told her, "Eileen, you've got to tell your family," but she never did. Her mother had died a slow death of cancer and my mom had had to live through taking care of her. She didn't want to put us through that.

By the time I got home, the same day, my mother was already in the hospital in Hammond, Indiana. For the whole month of September, the beginning of the general election, I would work all day long in Chicago and then drive an hour and a half in rush hour down to Hammond, take a sleeping bag and sleep on the floor and spend some time with her. She'd sit up in her oxygen tent and say, "Just take a cigarette out and let me see what it looks like. Bring a bottle of wine and have a drink and sit here and talk to me." Every day I would tell her about the campaign. She was so excited I had found something that I really loved.

My mother died on Sunday, September 28, 1980. I went back to work on Monday morning. I helped my dad with the funeral and then finished off the campaign.

But God works in mysterious ways. That campaign was run by a woman who did not let me fall apart. She just refused.

Maxene Fernstrom, Dave O'Neal's campaign manager, was taking care of her own mother, sister, and daughter by herself, and she would not let me cave in. Illinois is a tough state and Chicago is a tough city and it was odd for a woman to have that kind of political leadership position, but she had earned it. She was as tough as the men were. And so much smarter.

She brought unique management skills to the campaign, female management skills. The campaign ran like a family. There was none of this Men-are-pigs, men-are-the-enemy feminism to her, just a sense that "Men can be dopey and we know that, and we know that we can be smarter than they are, and here's how you act in that world." She loved men, but she was magnificent to women. Maxene was my idea of what feminism could and should be: women helping other women without hating men or aspiring to be men.

She was petite, with beautiful big greenish-brownish eyes and shiny black hair. She'd wear hip outfits like pants suits and a fur coat. She just swooshed into a room and was a presence, always the center of attention.

There was no hierarchical structure to Maxene's campaign. She regularly encouraged input from the entire staff, including the lowliest of the low, which was me. I went from opening fund-raising mail to being deputy finance director.

Maxene wouldn't ask you, she'd tell you. We would have a fund-raising event and she would say, "Go find the chairman of Revlon and tell him this is what we need from his people." And of course everybody would think to herself, "I can't do this, I can't talk to him." But she presumed that you could do anything, and when you tried it you found that things you thought you could never do, you did.

She could also be tough. If you weren't doing your job she'd find a way to ax you. Anybody left standing at the end of the campaign was really working.

There was a wonderfully eccentric guy on the campaign named Bill Greener. He was all energy, talked a mile a minute, had fifty good ideas at once. The trick was to harness him; he used to literally do cartwheels from one end of the campaign headquarters to the other. He and Maxene were very close, knew each other for a long time, had done campaigns together. But one afternoon Greener went too far. He pulled some stunt that even Maxene couldn't forgive. She fired him. No hand-wringing; fired him on the spot.

I was fascinated to watch a woman make a tough decision without all the normal female agonizing: "Oh, he's my best friend. Oh, should I do it?" She just knew that firing Greener was the right thing to do for the campaign, she did it, and she never looked back. (When he came groveling on his hands and knees she tortured him for a while and then eventually rehired him.)

I got her attention, maybe because she knew everything that was going on around her. I was going through the stage where it was very uncool to care about your appearance. You were supposed to have straight, stringy hair and not wear makeup. That political fashion statement was slow in coming to the Midwest but it had finally made it. Well, being ill-groomed was a sin to Maxene Fernstrom. In the real world you looked your best.

She would slap me with a litany of orders:

"Take off that hippie skirt. Get rid of those boots. Cut that hair. Put on some lipstick. Get with it, Mary." She had her own fashion sense. It wasn't conservative, it was personal. I took her advice, and my days as a Republican hippie earth mother were over. It took me all day in Marshall Field's to find a grown-up suit, but it was worth it to get Max's nod of approval.

Unfortunately, Dave O'Neal got shot down. He was lieutenant governor and someone in the campaign did not understand the political impact of using a taxpayer-funded state plane to fly him around for campaign events. The week before the election the Chicago papers ran front-page banner headline stories about this unauthorized use of taxpayer property for political benefit. It was 1980, the Reagan Revolution landslide. We dropped like a lead balloon and lost.

After the election Maxene went back to Washington to work as head of redistricting at the Republican National Committee. I called her.

"I can't stay here anymore," I said. "There's nothing to stay for."

Without even an interview at the RNC, Maxene got me a job as project officer in political education. A few months later she made me her executive assistant.

Maxene got me to Washington, she got me a job, she put me up in her house until I found my own place. And when I found my own place she gave me furniture and blankets and dishes. She never asked for anything.

Of course I was grateful. I was effusive. "How could I ever thank you for this?"

Maxene was not a gushy woman. She said, "Just do it for somebody else."

I thought it was a very Republican thing to say.

CHAPTER 3

James

Late fall, 1982, I was sleeping on a rollaway bed at my girl-friend's house in Richmond, Virginia, in a pretty good state of depression. When most people lose their first race they're twenty-six or so. I was thirty-eight and I had just left home, no job, no prospects. I hung out in the public library every day just to have a place to go.

In December I got a call from Wilson Goode, who was going to be running for mayor of Philadelphia. I took a train up and interviewed with him. I waited by the phone like a schoolboy but never got called back.

Even though the 1984 presidential race was two years off, the Democrats were starting early. I started calling around and got an interview with the John Glenn campaign. Nothing. I heard of an opening for the job of scheduler on the Mondale campaign and went through this long and exhaustive interview. I never heard back from them. A friend of mine got me an appointment with some people in Senator Gary Hart's campaign, and in April they offered me a job. It had been five months, but I was working again.

I liked Hart. I only ran into him twice but he was pretty nice to me. There weren't many Southern guys in his organization and I kind of got pigeonholed as "Well, this guy can do the South." The only problem, they told me, was "Look, you can't run up any expenses because we're out of money."

I was making $2,000 a month, which I would have been happy to make if I ever could have gotten paid. In a campaign it's one thing to say what you're making, it's another thing to actually pull a paycheck. I made one trip and couldn't get reimbursed.

The Hart headquarters in Washington, D.C., was at Fourth Street and Maryland Avenue, and I was up there getting my marching orders. It was cold, maybe forty degrees, and drizzling. I never shivered in Louisiana, and my unlined raincoat wasn't doing the trick so far north. This was the first time in my life that I had ever been cold in April, and my feet were getting wet. I had $47 to my name and I'd found a hotel room in Silver Spring, Maryland, for $41, tax included. That was six bucks left, which was enough to buy a Metro ticket and a breakfast.

I was carrying all of what I owned in a garment bag that hung from me like everything I'd ever worried about. I was walking down to Union Station to catch the train to Silver Spring to stay at this hotel that was going to take all the money I had, when the strap broke and the garment bag and all my possessions fell straight into the mud.

I just stood there near the curb on Massachusetts Avenue between Third and Fourth streets and began to cry. Not some private tears. Big-time crying. Sobbing. "I'm thirty-eight years old and I don't know when I'm going to get paid, I don't have any health insurance, I don't have a winner, I don't have any money. I can't live like this anymore!" It took me a while even to move.

I found a phone booth and, standing in the rain, called a good friend of mine named Jim D'Spain in Baton Rouge. I said, "Jim, this is the most embarrassing thing I have ever had to do in my life, but I'm at the end of my rope. I can't . . . I'm basically scraping money together for a train ticket to go to Richmond. Can you send me some money?"

He said, "I'll send you five thousand dollars. Go to Western Union, I'll send it there."

I worked for Hart through July. A senior adviser in the campaign by the name of Billy Shore saw to it that I got most of my money, but when we both decided it would be hard for them to keep paying me, we parted amicably. I went home in August for my brother Steve's wedding and didn't do much of anything.

The $5,000 I'd gotten in April had sort of run its course when I got a call saying that there was a guy, Lloyd Doggett, running for U.S. Senate in Texas who was looking for a campaign manager. He was kind of a liberal, running in the Democratic primary against this guy

Bob Krueger, who was way ahead. Could I come for a meeting? Sounded all right to me.

I walked into the meeting in Austin and there was Doggett and six or seven people around a table. When you're a freelance worker and you haven't worked in a while the temptation is to jump at whatever's out there. It's better to play and lose than to just sit it out. Doggett was about a gazillion points back in the polls and didn't have many prospects, but I wasn't about to turn down a job that was offered to me, even if it was a loser.

But this felt different. Better. Sometimes you just know, and within about twenty minutes I was saying to myself, "God, I really want this job. I like the place, I like the people. I hope they take me."

They called back and said that the job was mine.

I started on Labor Day, 1983, and we worked our butts off.

During the early days of the Doggett campaign there were thousands of meetings, where people would discuss the schedule and what the candidate would say when he got there. These meetings would go on for two, sometimes three hours. And I noticed there was this reddish-blond-haired kid who, while everyone else was pontificating, would just sit there at a word processor banging out statements and putting stuff together that the candidate would need to actually do the event. He was way more into the practicalities of putting together a press packet, or a statement, or a speech for the candidate than he was into meeting and theorizing about the state of world politics. I asked who this kid was, and he was Paul Begala. I said, "This guy's a keeper. I'm gonna want to work with him again."

You'll find a hundred people in a campaign headquarters who, among them, have a thousand different theories. But you'll only find a handful who actually have an idea *and* the ability to implement it. Paul was one of those, and one of the best. I made it a point to get to know him.

Paul had just graduated from the University of Texas, and it was clear that he had a lot of talent. He could get stuff out. He'd write a complete speech, full of substance and great turns of phrase, while the rest of the crew was trying to figure out what we were trying to say. He and I came up with a basic political philosophy, which states: "Those that can, do. Those that can't, meet."

There were three men in the race: Lloyd Doggett, Congressman Kent Hance, and the front-runner, Bob Krueger. One of the basic political axioms is that when you're behind you go after the lead dog, and Krueger was way ahead. I was hungry and I would read news clips and just look for things to bite him with. I found one quote where Krueger said that Lloyd Doggett was a Little Leaguer. Bob Krueger was a Texas state senator and had been in Congress and used to be dean of one of the colleges at Duke University, and he'd gone to Oxford and been ambassador to Mexico. He was a big guy. Krueger said, "Texas needs a Big Leaguer in Washington and Lloyd Doggett is a Little Leaguer."

So we would go into these small towns in Texas and go out to the baseball diamond—there's always a baseball diamond in the small towns of Texas—and hold these press conferences. And Lloyd Doggett would gather the townspeople and their Little League teams together and say, "You know, I *am* a Little Leaguer. And it's the Little Leaguers of Texas that need a senator, because 'Big League' Bob Krueger and the Big League insurance companies and the Big League banks and the Big League utilities got all the senators in the world."

It was a great photo op, the candidate with kids in baseball uniforms saying that he's for the Little League—for the people that brand their own cattle and plant their own crops and call the players by their first names and take their kids fishing on Saturday—not for the lobbyists golfing on Wednesday. It always made the local papers and the local news.

One of the worst things you can say about a Texan is that he doesn't stand for anything. We wanted to attack Krueger for being wishy-washy. Paul Begala wrote a stump speech for Doggett that said, "In the end it all comes down to guts. The guts to stand up to the special interests. The guts to fight for schoolchildren. The guts to be for civil rights." He brought it in for me to read. I said, "That's a good idea, but it's the wrong imagery. Your listener is going to be sitting there thinking about a bucket of intestines. You can't say 'guts,' it's gross. You need something you can wave around. How about 'backbone'?"

Lloyd Doggett had been a trial lawyer, and one of the props that they use in whiplash cases is a plastic replica of a human spine. That was all we needed. We held a press conference, and at just the right moment Lloyd Doggett pulled this life-sized skeleton out of its velvet sack and held it up to the cameras. "This is what I have that Bob Krueger doesn't have: a backbone. I'm going to take this backbone to Washington so I can stand up for the voters of Texas."

Some people loved it, some were offended, but it became a point of controversy, and Lloyd Doggett dragged that skeleton around from one stump speech to another until pretty much the whole state had gotten the message.

We edged by Krueger. Now we had a runoff against Hance.

Hance's issue was amnesty for aliens. Thousands of Mexicans were coming across the Texas border and he held that the Border Patrol should be beefed up, but that immigrants who were already here should be granted amnesty. Hance was riding that issue and it was working for him.

At first we made the same mistake everybody else makes: We tried to argue emotion with intellect. That didn't make a dent. The head has never beaten the gut in a political argument yet, and I doubt if it ever will. Finally I said, "Go find every bill that Kent Hance has introduced on the question of immigration, aliens, whatever." The research staff came back and said, "Nothing."

"Nothing?"

"Nothing."

Then I said, "Find out every word that he has said on the floor of the House on the subject."

They came back and said, "None. Zip. Nada."

So we had this press conference and had a big easel draped in velvet, like we were unveiling a painting. We said, "Now we are going to show you everything, every word, that Kent Hance has ever said about the question of immigration until his pollster found it in a poll eight weeks ago." With all the cameras running we made a great show of dropping the veil to reveal . . . a blank slate.

"The truth of the matter," we said, "is that Kent Hance is a single-issue candidate on a single issue that he has never done a single thing about."

We never let up. I had learned my lesson and down the stretch we didn't give them a whole day without trying to get in their story or have them respond to ours.

We won the runoff by about four hundred votes.

Of course, the payoff to these primary victories was the privilege of running in the general election against Phil Gramm.

I was sitting at my desk one day when somebody said, "I don't know what this is. I got a call from a reporter saying here is a script of a radio ad that Gramm is running around the state. In it a woman's voice says, 'Sometimes in campaigns we have to discuss difficult things, things that we would rather not bring up that say a lot about a candidate.' " On—and they gave a date—there was an all-male nude fund-raiser for Lloyd Doggett in a gay club in San Antonio, featuring Frankie the Banana Queen and Mr. Gay Apollo from New Orleans. Lloyd Doggett did raise $354, they said. Doggett accepted the money.

He also opposes capital punishment, prayer in schools, and a balanced budget amendment, and we have to ask ourselves, Is this the kind of man . . .

"What is this, some kind of joke? Who's this guy in San Antonio?"

I called the host of the fund-raiser, Tony Zule, in San Antonio and said, "Look, there is a kind of joke going around here . . ."

"Oh, no, man," he said, "it ain't no joke. [A dancer even] put the tips in his G-string and took off. He was going to try and keep the money but we tackled him because they were campaign contributions."

Of course it got to be a big story. The national press got ahold of it, Reuters called, *Der Spiegel* called, it was breaking out all over. I said to one reporter, "Look, I mean everybody that knows Doggett knows that he is so straight he probably bathes with his clothes on."

It was about that time I kind of saw everything unravel in front of me.

We were running a liberal Democrat in 1984 in the teeth of the Reagan landslide and we got what could charitably be called soundly defeated. I was forty years old and still a stone-ass loser.

I scratched out a living in Louisiana for a couple of years doing some part-time lawyering and consulting work. In 1986, David Doak, who was a well-known political consultant and had a powerhouse business concern with Bob Shrum, called me and said, "There is a guy by the name of Bob Casey who is running for governor of Pennsylvania. He was a state auditor, he's a good guy, I think you can do this. We're doing the media. There's one problem: He's run three times before and he's lost all three."

Doak had worked the Hance campaign, and he and I had gotten to know each other under battlefield conditions. A soldier's respect. I said, "Look, man, I don't have a winner and I'm gonna go with this guy who lost three times? I mean, I could carry a lot of stuff, David, but I don't know about this."

"James, they really do want to hire somebody and I recommended you."

I didn't have any money and my phone wasn't ringing off the hook. I said, "All right," and caught a plane to Pennsylvania.

Bob Casey had run for governor of Pennsylvania in 1966, 1970, and 1978. Across the state he was known as the Three-Time Loss from Holy Cross. It was now 1986 and his chances didn't seem a whole lot brighter.

We won the primary handily. But Bob Casey had never lost a primary. He just had never won a general.

The general election was against William Scranton III, a Democratic consultant's worst nightmare. Scranton was a moderate, pro-choice Republican. Casey was pro-life. Scranton was the Pennsylvania lieutenant governor, good-looking, kind of a matinee idol. Casey was old news. The Scranton campaign had a million and a half dollars in the bank; we had to borrow money to make our payroll. Scranton's daddy was the very popular former governor of Pennsylvania who, it was an article of faith at the time, sat on more boards of Fortune 500 companies than any person in America. Their blood wasn't red, it was purple. Our guy had none of the advantages.

We had to keep them off guard and off message, and it wasn't going to be easy. Richard Thornburgh was the sitting governor and he was pretty popular, so there was no anti-incumbent sentiment to work off of. The first polls we took showed us 15 to 18 points down. But I was totally invested in this race.

I had to win.

I was broke.

In my mind Casey versus Scranton was larger than just the candidates' different stands on the issues; it made a lot of big statements about Pennsylvania. To me the campaign turned into this heroic struggle between the son of a coal miner and the son of a coal-mine owner, between people who were tenacious and resilient and those who had had everything given to them. Holy Cross versus Yale. This was a race of significance. Everything got viewed through that filter, and anything that didn't fit I just defined as information that the elites and the privileged class were trying to force-feed the populace.

We went right at them. We looked at the research and found that Scranton had a big name and a poor attendance record. Doak and Shrum produced this spot with a devastating tag line: "We gave him the job because of his father's name. The least he could do is show up for work." It played into working people's resentment of the rich, and it had the ring of truth.

In campaign politics an idea is like a fruitcake at Christmas—there's not but one, and everybody keeps passing it around. I had used that line in a race in New Orleans years before.

From Labor Day to mid-October things were looking pretty good. We'd closed the gap and maybe even forged ahead a couple of points, and the talk was that the Casey people were really aggressive and had kept Scranton off balance for most of the race.

I was sitting at my desk when the phone rang and one of our operatives said, "Scranton just held a press conference saying that he is ending all negative campaigning. Doesn't even matter what Casey does, this is an election about who can do what and that's what he's going to focus on. He, Scranton, is going to talk about positive things."

Clearly what had happened was that the Scranton people had gotten into a pissing contest with a skunk and saw that they couldn't win. It was the Persian cat against the alley cat. So they did a smart thing: They changed the rules.

The press loved it, and Scranton got a lot of stories about what a courageous step he had taken.

It threw us. We had gotten pretty good at savaging Scranton, and didn't really know what else to do. We were stumped, and that gave them even more of a lift.

At about the same time the candidates had a debate in Philadelphia. Scranton had a pretty good night and we didn't. The debate was about all the things we didn't want to discuss. Casey was pro-life, which was not a winning position. There was an unpopular state liquor monopoly that Scranton wanted to change and we didn't. He was for so-called judicial reform, we weren't. Scranton had a very effective message about how it was a New Pennsylvania, a butterfly emerging from a moth, and how we couldn't go back to the old ways. The whole coverage of the debate was framed so that Scranton was the progressive, modern, fresh, young new Republican, and Casey was the old, aging, longtime-politician three-time-loser Democrat.

We lost 8 points in a night and you could feel it. People were calling saying, "You guys are going to lose." Reporters were saying, "Scranton really pulled a slick one on you. You just got outsmarted."

October 25 was my birthday. There's no such thing as me having a happy birthday. I never get a good poll, I always take a nosedive. It was a Saturday and Paul Begala and I walked out of the headquarters and went to the movies. Saw *Peggy Sue Got Married*. Once the lights went down and the picture started, I told Paul, "I'm forty-two years old and we are not only going to lose, we are going to lose in disgrace. This is going to be number three, I'll never get a job, I can't go home, I don't know what I'm going to do. This is awful."

We walked back to the office after the show and I was totally devastated. I didn't think we had a chance to win, all I was really thinking about was how I could make it through the next nine days. I kind of plunked myself down in my chair.

"James," said our comptroller, Tommy Brier, "you heard about this piece of mail that Scranton sent out about Casey being a crook?"

"What are you talking about?"

"Somebody in Scranton got this piece of mail—"

"What is this person's name?" He gave me the name. I called the guy immediately and he read me the flyer that he had just received that morning about how Bob Casey was part of the people who ran Pennsylvania into a ditch, and how he was a crook.

Now there is one thing about Bob Casey: His honesty is above reproach. Not even his worst political enemy would ever say that he is anything but impeccably honest.

I got the full adrenaline jolt. "Sit right where you are," I told him. "Do not move." I told Tommy, "Do not send one, send *three* people over to that house and get that piece of mail and fax one copy down here and have someone else *drive* another copy from Scranton to Philadelphia in case it gets lost in the fax line some kind of way. But under no conditions is anything going to happen to this piece of paper."

The thing arrived and, as I hoped, it was ugly. And it had "Paid for by Bill Scranton for Governor Campaign" right on the bottom. I couldn't have been happier.

The research people were swinging into action. The piece had a bulk-rate stamp on it so we could figure out how many had been mailed and when it had been distributed. We had people in the post office. "Go in there, find somebody, do what you've got to do, get all the records, get this information, we need everything, I mean right now!"

"Get Tom Ferrick on the phone." Ferrick was the political reporter for *The Philadelphia Inquirer.* He was a good journalist—if he covered a story you knew the story was going to go.

"Tom, how big of a story do you think this is?" I read him the piece of mail. He said, "I'll be right over to you boys."

On Sunday the thing hit.

The same day, we came up with a counter-story to goose the headlines even more. A lot of people in the campaign were saying that we had to run a spot attacking Scranton for admitting he had smoked pot in the sixties. Casey had promised he wouldn't. I said, "We will get slaughtered if we do that. They'll say that Casey broke his word. With all of this negative campaigning stuff, we can't have Bob Casey breaking his word."

Between pollster Pat Caddell, Bob Shrum, David Doak, myself, Bill Batoff, Paul Begala, Governor Casey, and two or three of Casey's kids, we had one of the toughest, most rancorous political meetings I've ever been in. We were 8 points down with ten days to go. We knew we had to get Scranton some bad headlines, get him out of his message, shake him. So I told Batoff, "We can't run a drug spot, but we have got to put out that we are getting ready to run a drug spot, okay? But it can't come from us."

Batoff had supported Ed Rendell in the primaries and then come over to us when we'd won. Without Casey ever knowing, I said, "Look, call Rendell and just say, 'The Cajun's lost his mind. He's going to put this drug spot up on Scranton. Casey knows nothing about this. You saw what Carville did to you, he's a wild man.' "

Rendell is now the wildly popular mayor of Philadelphia and one of my better friends in politics. Then, he was a defeated primary opponent. Just like we figured he would, Rendell started calling reporters and saying that the Casey campaign and that asshole Carville were getting ready to run a drug spot. Our people were at an event in South Philly, where Casey was supposed to show up; they called to say that the press were screaming that we're about to run a killer ad.

"Just hold them off," I said.

There must have been fifteen reporters there when I ran over, which is a lot for a statewide race. I didn't want to subject the candidate to this frenzy—what was he going to say?—so I did it alone.

"Is there a drug spot?" they all wanted to know.

"Let me tell you something," I said. "Mr. Casey said no, that he'd given his word. There are some people that wanted to do it but he said that he was a person of his word. *So we are not going to run a spot attacking Bill Scranton for using drugs.*"

Well, of course, bingo, all over TV we are there saying that the campaign strategist wanted to do it but the candidate didn't. I gladly took that heat. The damage was being done—"drugs" and "Scranton" were in the same sentence in people's minds—and we had gotten the story out through a Democrat. If we had called the press and told them we were even considering the possibility, we would have looked like crap. Now I was the only one who looked like crap, and I didn't mind.

Meanwhile Scranton still had to face the dirty-campaigning issue. One thing about the media: If you say you are going to do something and you do something else, they will hand you your head. Scranton had promised to abandon all negative campaigning and now here he was caught trying to sneak one over. He was getting hit pretty hard, and then he got stupid. He did the same thing I'd done in Virginia— he read his poll numbers and froze.

Instead of being aggressive in defending himself, Scranton issued a statement that he had not sent out that piece of mail, didn't know what was in it, that he obviously wouldn't have sent it out, that it was to his political detriment. It was a cold rebuttal. No apology, no remorse, no responsibility. If I'd been working for him I'd have advised him to say, "Whether I knew about it or not doesn't matter; I'm running for governor and I should have known about it. It wasn't the right thing to do and I apologize." People will accept an apology, they'll distrust a stonewall.

Well, just some paper statement wasn't good enough. We were offended, by God, and we made sure that the people of Pennsylvania were, too. The next day there was supposed to be a debate between the candidates. It had been scheduled weeks before, to take place at the editorial offices of the Pittsburgh *Post-Gazette*, a very pro-Scranton paper.

I said, "Nope, I ain't doing this. We are kicking this story one more day." Lesson in Virginia learned: Be on the offensive going into the stretch.

The *Post-Gazette* editors and reporters were fanned out around a conference table, loaded for bear. Bill Scranton and his people were there. We refused to show. We put together a written statement from Bob Casey, and Paul went over to read it. He stood in front of the assembled editorial multitude and said: "Given the fact that Bill Scranton has broken his word to the people of Pennsylvania, won't assume responsibility for his campaign, and is sending out malicious, false, unsubstantiated claims about me *and has refused to renounce them*, I will not appear and dignify this in any form."

It blew up again. That night and the next morning the TV and newspapers led with "Casey Refuses to Debate Scranton." They retold the story of the negative campaign piece and Scranton's breaking of his word.

The next morning I was sitting behind my desk saying, "We got to kick this thing another day." We'd cut the lead from 8 points to 4 but it looked like it was a solid 4. I had to get some more blood out of this turnip.

We needed a visual. I called Casey's son-in-law, Billy McGrath, who worked for a printer. "Billy, can you have six hundred thousand envelopes on the corner of Washington and Third streets in Scranton, Pennsylvania, tomorrow morning at about ten-thirty?"

His answer was unbelievable. He said, "What color?"

"Oh, off-white is fine."

So the next morning an eighteen-wheel truck pulled up and these forklifts piled a mountain of envelopes on the ground in front of Scranton's campaign headquarters, and we held a press conference.

Bob Casey stood in front of this wall of stationery and said, to the best of my recollection, "This is six hundred thousand envelopes, the same number that Bill Scranton mailed out about me. You'd think that if you sent out this many wedding invitations or thank-you notes you would know what was in them. But Bill Scranton wants you to believe that he sent out six hundred thousand of these and had no idea what was going on. Now, how is he going to know when the state sends out six hundred thousand checks? Is he going to deny responsibility for that too?"

The cameras were just eating it up.

By Friday the polls were down to one point. We had made up 7 points in a week and were heading for the close.

We created what we called the "guru" spot. We got a picture of Bill Scranton in college, long hair, beard, scruffy-looking sixties clothes. Also one of the Maharishi Mahesh Yogi. Sitar music twanged in the background. If we could've filmed it in Smell-o-rama there would have been at least incense in the air. The voice-over quoted Bill Scranton saying his "goal was to bring transcendental meditation to state government." The ad never said the word "marijuana." What it said, though not in so many words, was that Scranton was a hippie.

Bill Scranton had been a college student in the sixties and had admitted to doing his share of experimenting in the culture. He was an adherent of transcendental meditation, and when he arrived in state government he suggested bringing it along with him, having the state pay to have employees do TM. Our source for that information was *Time* magazine. Pennsylvania is a culturally conservative state—I suspected there were a lot of people who would think that was pretty weird behavior.

Doak and Shrum made the spot, then we had a day-long decision-making grind over whether to put it out. I was part of the decision-making process and I was all for it. Caddell was also hot to run it. "It could keep Scranton's vote down in the central part of the state. It's a close race and we will probably still lose, but we have to run it. We are selling Scranton's cultural flakiness."

The downside was that we were going to get knocked out of the negative-campaigning story, but that would be okay because the guru spot would be the last thing voters remembered, going into the polling booth. When we came to a consensus I called the candidate.

Casey wasn't wild about it, but we had very specifically not mentioned drugs, which was his promise, and ultimately he gave us the okay.

We didn't have the money to run the spot all over the state. We ran it briefly outside Philadelphia and assumed it would be so controversial that it would make the news cycle and we'd get a ton of free airtime. The chances that someone would see the ad over the weekend, we figured, were not good. The chances that they would see a media story on it were very good.

The "guru" spot is now part of Pennsylvania political legend and lore, and got me a reputation as a brass-knuckles kind of guy. To be honest, it didn't matter one way or the other. It probably did move some of the more conservative voters not to go for Scranton. It also worked against us. Many Democrats were angry over what they thought was the ad's low blow. I thought it was a pretty clever way for us to hold the focus. Very little else got talked about the weekend before the election, and every time the story got written or aired the whole cultural argument had to be rehashed.

Election day I was scrambling, calling a county chair here, a legislative person there, row officers, the clerk in some courthouse. "Can we win? Do you think we can win?" I'd ask reporters, "What do you think? What do you hear around the pressroom?" As if they would know. I used to think that inside a campaign there was some sort of grand knowledge that nobody else had. Of course we didn't have any. Everybody just said, "It's gonna be close."

Down by 8, we won by 2. We made up 10 points in a week.

Finally.

What I felt was not in any way the ecstasy of victory, it was just the sheer relief that I could go home Christmas and not be embarrassed. I called my mother. "Mama, we did it! We did it!" Governor of Pennsylvania, that was big. It dawned on me that I wasn't always going to be a failure.

Mary

When I got there in early 1981 the chairman of the RNC was Ronald Reagan's hand-picked man, Dick Richards. By that fall everyone was calling him Dick Dick and he was supplanted in all but title by Jim Baker's man, Rich Bond, who was installed as deputy chairman.

Before Bond was even on board he jolted the complacent RNC worker bees by strolling into their offices at all hours, unannounced. He was doing "commitment checks." He wanted to see who was working and who was sloughing off. He was scary but exhilarating, a real campaign commando with a five-star reputation.

Rich Bond was a terrorist. He had a tough mouth, a quick brain, and took no prisoners. He got famous in Republican circles by winning the Iowa presidential caucuses for George Bush in 1980, which enabled Bush to remain in the race, which enabled him to get the vice-presidential nomination and ultimately get elected president. When Reagan chose Bush at the convention, so I'm told, all the Reagan operatives beat down the door of their political director and quit. They didn't want Bush, they wanted Reagan's best friend, Senator Paul Laxalt. They hated Bush and all the Bushies. Primaries can do that to you.

Primary fights are a lot more emotional, corrosive, and painful than general elections. It's easy to hate Democrats, but brother-against-brother in the primaries gets really ugly. It's like the Civil War. Reagan Revolutionaries thought George Bush was a regular old Republican, not worthy to be on the great man's ticket. Not only was Bond an ideological adversary, he had duked it out with them personally in vicious fights. Lee Atwater and the Young Turks on the Reagan side were battling with him on a very personal level to become the preeminent political star.

When Reagan-Bush was elected, Bond joined the White House as Bush's deputy chief of staff with a reputation as a real hardball player. He was the only guy there with a partisan political perspective; most operatives stayed outside the White House operation, and those who came inside were more the conservative intellectual types.

Bond is Irish-Italian with a very black emotional side. He grew up in one of the last Republican political machine operations, in Nassau and Suffolk counties on Long Island, New York. He's got a real macho approach; everything is a battle. He is always gracious, but he leaves no leeway for weakness. I learned this firsthand when he made me his executive assistant, which was a fancy title for political side-kick. I really didn't have enough experience for the job, but he was like Maxene—Figure it out, kid.

Bond was a strict disciplinarian who turned the RNC into a campaign machine. You couldn't talk to the press, you learned the law and how to handle it, you learned the mechanics of voter contact.

We were getting ready for congressional midterms, the elections that are historically painful for the party in power. There were new campaign-reform laws limiting individual contributions, which meant no more walking around with briefcases full of money, and it was important that the RNC learn how to work within them.

Under Bond we began using computers and building, enhancing, and segmenting voter lists so we could individualize our message. What the labor unions do for the Democratic party—get mail in people's hands, get people to the polls—Bond, an expert technician, made the RNC and state parties do for Republicans. He set about teaching and defining a whole new generation of Republican operatives by putting us around a table and making us think of creative ways to use the party and every resource available.

The downside was that none of us was trained in strategy or message. We were trained in voter contact, phones, mail, computers, satellite, video. This worked in the Reagan years because there was a big Reagan message. Jim Baker and Ed Meese and Michael Deaver and the rest would sit around divining it, and over at the RNC was warehoused this army of Bond techno-twits who could raise money and get the message out to the hinterlands.

Bond used the RNC's power as far as he could push it. The committee could give direct cash contributions of up to $5,000 to individual congressional candidates, and during the negotiations over the Reagan tax overhaul, Bond went to Capitol Hill and told congressmen that if they didn't vote with Reagan he was not going to fund their campaigns. This, in itself, was nothing unheard of. This, in fact, is the way things work. But Bond made the mistake of admitting as much, off the record, to a reporter for *The Wall Street Journal*, who went back and told his editor, who said it was just too juicy to withhold, and printed it.

The White House, the congressmen, and the rest of the media went absolutely nuts. Here was a policy vote being dictated by political power. It was a big story.

A confluence of forces from the White House convened to decide Bond's fate. Ed Rollins, the White House political boss, delivered the news. Before they'd even tell him if he still had a job, Rich Bond had to go back to the Hill and give every congressman a letter of apology. As he was walking out the door with his sheaf of letters he turned around and told me, "Remember this, kid. The higher up the flagpole you go, the more your ass hangs out."

Bond didn't lose his job, and when he kissed everybody's butt he got major points for loyalty. That's the way it works.

Bond had a running feud with Lee Atwater. They hated each other. Atwater spent all his time at the White House cutting deals, collecting chits, and making a name for himself. During the 1982 midterm elections he called Bond and said he wanted money for a candidate in

South Carolina. Lee was from South Carolina and was looking to take care of his own; everybody always takes care of their home state.

Bond said, "That guy's going to lose. I'm not giving you any money." Ed Rollins and others in the party tried to intercede but Bond wasn't moving. It was his checkbook, and he alone was going to write out those checks. From that point on it was open warfare and everyone was forced to choose sides; you were an Atwaterite or a Bondite. I worked directly for Bond. After Maxene he was my first political boss. I was a Bondite of the first order. Politics is a profession that you can really only learn through mentors and experience. Rich Bond was my "lord and master" and was teaching me the ropes.

Bond may have bridled at Atwater helping out in South Carolina but he made sure to take care of his boys on Long Island. He made me go to New York and hand out money—"You'll figure it out. Here's your checks, now go ingratiate yourself"—to all these thugs. Well, not thugs, actually. Republicans. But they did talk funny.

It was a symbolic act of power for Bond to send his chief aide with these checks. It sent the message "I am no longer a local. I am Mr. National and I can pick and choose whom I give money to and whom I don't."

I drove my putt-putt Chevy Monza up from Washington. I was the tender age of twenty-eight and you have to be from the Midwest to understand what it was like to come over the George Washington Bridge into the city. This was Broadway, this was lights, energy, places that were open all night. It was so adult, so overpowering, so incredibly scary.

After getting totally lost and driving around Long Island for nine hours I finally found my way to these guys' offices, and one by one delivered my envelopes.

I could barely understand the New York accent and thought all of these guys worked on the docks. But I presumed they were deserving candidates, so I'd introduce myself and say, "Rich Bond wanted you to have this contribution for your campaign. The party wishes you well and please call us if there's anything we can do to help."

These men on Long Island in 1982 did not deal with women. The feeling I got was "Thanks for the dough, little girl, you can go home now." I didn't tawk like them and I was an assertiveness-training dropout. "Thank you, sir. Thank you. Of course, I'll be happy to tell him that. He'll be delighted to hear that you asked about his wife."

What a nerd. But I had a check in my hand, and the patronage of Rich Bond, so . . . welcome to the world of real politics.

At night I'd report back to Bond. "Yes, I delivered the check to Mr. So-and-So. He was very grateful. Very grateful." This was Bond's way of torturing me into political adulthood, having me deal with real career politicians.

Nineteen eighty-two was the middle of the Reagan recession and after all the techno-battle we ended up losing twenty-six congressional seats. Reagan unappointed Dick Richards as RNC chairman and put in Nevada state chairman Frank Fahrenkopf, who politely axed all of us to make room for his own team.

Bond went and started his own political consulting business and I went to law school.

It was a nightmare. Most of my professors were crazy libs and one of them used to start his lecture every morning with a tirade on the Reagan administration. I couldn't take much of that. In the summer of 1984, I came back to Washington and ran the RNC voter contact program.

There wasn't a doubt in anybody's mind who was going to win the election, and everyone got to learn a lot and have fun at it.

In 1988 there was going to be some turnover. The Reagan team was disbanding and the battle to succeed him was pretty hot. Bob Dole wanted to be president, Jack Kemp could be perceived as being Reagan's ideological heir, Pat Robertson came out of nowhere, and George Bush was vice president.

Politics is about winning—there are no Pyrrhic victories or honorable defeats. Participating in a presidential campaign full-time, as a professional, is very emotional and very draining. You don't want to put that much effort into a race unless you have a real chance. Unless you're an ideological nut, which very few political professionals are, you don't want to run a race with a dog candidate just to prove a point. It takes too much out of you.

In the culture of campaigns it's not ideological. Most of us have a philosophical grounding—we're working for Republicans only—but in terms of issues the differences between candidates are often pretty small. There's usually one candidate who represents the fringe or extreme element, and then everybody else is fanned out by degrees around the center of your party, wherever that center happens to be. Everybody I knew wanted to be on the Bush team. In the 1988 culture, Bush was the winner.

He was already in the White House, for one thing. He had hands-on experience and a national I.D. He had tons of friends and supporters, and his organization was a cast of superstars. We started the 1988 George Bush presidential campaign in 1986 and technically opened our doors in January '87.

In the culture of campaigns, it is very important who the campaign manager is and who gets hired to be the chief honchos; it sends a message to the troops that you have presence, gravity. It attracts the best.

Lee Atwater was going to work for Bush.

So was Rich Bond.

This was a Collusion of the Titans. Atwater and Bond on the same campaign—every child operative, every budding hack wanted to work with those guys. Bond made quick work of sucking them all into the organization.

In Republican operative circles Lee Atwater was a rock star. He had a long record of winning campaigns and a repertoire of legendary feats he'd pulled off. He also had a following. Political groupies.

I thought there was something a little offbeat about people being so enamored of a political guru, but wherever he went they went gaga over him; they would line up for his autograph. Me, in college I had hung out and tried to meet the Rolling Stones, Jefferson Airplane, Eric Clapton, the Kinks. Those were my ideas of stars. To Republicans, Lee Atwater had that kind of charisma.

I started the '88 campaign as Bond's deputy. Since Bond hated Atwater and Atwater hated Bond, Atwater hated me. My early objective was to stay out of his line of sight.

Our job was to set up the national field organization. Bond threw me into Iowa, the first caucus state, so he could keep his hands on it. This was where he had made his reputation in 1980, and as his personal emissary I had the pressure on to win. The first thing I did was lose.

The first major Iowa event was a straw poll. The way the rules were written, in order to vote you had to buy a $25 ticket. The theory was that a candidate's supporters would buy the ticket because they wanted to vote for him. That's in a perfect world. All parties know that campaigns wanting to win are going to figure a way to buy more tickets than they have supporters and then give them out to live bodies like college kids. The real work was not so much in raising the money but in finding bodies to attach the tickets to and have them go to Ames, Iowa, on a Saturday night and drop them into a voting booth.

When I got out there I found there were a couple of problems. First, there was no way to poll or accurately estimate the evangelical, below-the-radar activity of the Pat Robertson forces. Then there was Dole's influence as a farmer advocate and neighboring Kansan; the voters who had gone for us in 1980 did not like Reagan's farm policies and took it out on Bush. The upshot of it was that we were going to lose.

I tried telling this to Bond and Atwater about two weeks before the event, but it was unacceptable to either of them. What's so hard about buying tickets and hooking them onto bodies? they wanted to know. I tried to tell them but I wasn't getting through.

Straw poll day was awful. We sent out special mailers and brought in all kinds of operatives, and got buses and box lunches, and set up phone banks and an ironclad ticket distribution system. But it was a beautiful Saturday afternoon in the middle of football season and everyone knew the whole process was a sham, and nobody wanted to come.

You walked into the gym where the straw poll was being held and you could feel disaster. Each candidate was supposed to give a speech before the vote, and Robertson had all these people he'd packed onto buses and pickups and flatbed trucks and had driven there. They showed up in matching white shirts and white straw hats, yelling and screaming and playing the theme to *Rocky*. When Robertson came onstage it was their own personal revival meeting.

Not only did we lose, we were humiliated. Robertson won, Dole came in second, we pulled up the rear.

Atwater and Bond looked like they'd just been kicked in the face. I wasn't in shock because I'd been expecting to lose, but they looked close to death. As the event was breaking up I was summoned into Atwater's presence.

He was sitting at the top of the bleachers and he just looked at me—didn't even speak—and then dispatched me. They sent for me again a little later and called me into this holding room and he looked at me again and sent me away. The next day he called me at my hotel just to hang up on me. Then he called me back and fired me. Then he called me back with all the other regional political directors on the line to yell at me in their presence and say how if this ever happened to them they'd all be toast.

The next day I was supposed to meet Vice President Bush in Wisconsin. I'd been fired but it was my event, I was the only one who knew what the gig was, so I had to go. The day after that I went to the office and said to the field director, Janet Mullins, "Atwater's fired me."

She said, "I know. Just don't let him see you and he'll never know the difference. He'll forget about it."

I was exiled to Michigan, where it looked like we were going to lose again. We were running neck and neck with Robertson, with Jack Kemp behind us both. Kemp and Robertson represented the right wing of the party and they struck a loose alliance to push Bush to last place. But at the last minute we negotiated a deal with the Kemp campaign to shift his votes to a new alliance with us, allowing Bush to win and Kemp to come in second. Both of us moved up one place; Robertson dropped two. It was old-time political dealing, and not everyone could deal with it. I had most of the facts, and Atwater insisted that I argue my case directly to Vice President Bush. Some of our advisory staff didn't think the deal was any good, and we had a top-of-the-lungs screaming match in Mr. Bush's front room about whether or not to make it.

Atwater supported me. It was high risk, but the only way to win. Atwater wanted to win. So, finally, did the Vice President. He made the decision.

We won. Atwater instantly forgave me for Iowa. He called me in the middle of the night and drawled, "I'm happy you had the opportunity to redeem yourself," and from then on gave me one great assignment after another.

After we had the nomination in hand, Atwater and Bond took me out of the field and sent me to the RNC to pull all the warring factions of the party together. In the tiny world of operatives this was a great job. I knew what was going on in every state. The guys in the field are kings of the mountain and I was central control.

The press kind of got faked into thinking I was pretty smart. I wasn't; I just had the information they needed, and I could decipher it for them.

Atwater's main talent was that he understood the pulse of the press. He described it as being able to "see around corners." He knew what the press would think was a story and where they would go with it. He knew how to create a story and keep focus on it. He knew how to do damage control and when to get off it. He did not sit around the campaign and run things, he sat around the campaign tracking and spinning the press.

Atwater was always working against the grain. At a time when everyone was saying that the Republicans were sexist pigs and we had these six gray-hairs running the campaign, Lee trotted out all the campaign women. There was me, Janet Mullins, Debbie Steelman, Ede

Holiday, Alixe Glen, Ceci Cole McInturff, and Margaret Tutwiler—
and he created a big press spin about us. We had always been around,
but through his hard work the press began writing about the Bush juggernaut and all the smart young Republican technicians, spearheaded
by women. He'd give the same story with a different twist to enough
different reporters that he'd start a little echo chamber. Then he'd
build the story into an article of faith, fact or no.

Atwater always had a three-cushion shot. There was always something in it for the candidate, something in it for Atwater, and something in it for somebody else so they would be loyal to Atwater. It was
quite a technique.

At the end of the campaign, when we won the election, Lee got his
choice of jobs. He wanted chairman of the Republican National
Committee, the operative's top post. He said to Bond, "Ask Mary if
she wants to be political director." I said, "No, I want to be chief of
staff." And so I was.

Everyone else wanted to work in the White House; the stature and
trappings attendant to even the lowest White House job were addic-
tive. One really gross guy used to brag how he could pick up girls with
his White House baggage tag. Working in that environment could turn
even humble people into pompous, officious jerks. The perks *were*
impressive: seats in the President's Box at the Kennedy Center; private
tours of the White House, President's residence, and Oval Office; por-
tal-to-portal transportation; White House mess privileges; White
House operators placing your phone calls; everyone fawning over anyone wearing the readily identifiable White House pass.

White House trinkets were a particular favorite. Inscribed golf
balls, cuff links, tie clips, stick pins, key chains, and pens were pur-
chased (not with taxpayer money) for the President to dispense, but
it was a status symbol to have your own drawerful. You would trade
up: One box of golf balls was worth two boxes of pens; cuff links beat
key chains. Lee never went anywhere without a pocketful, which he
would pass out to volunteer drivers and other young Republicans
with the solemn, if untruthful, promise, "Top of the line; this here's
top of the line."

The allure was tempting for a nanosecond, but I knew the White
House would suffocate me. Too much protocol, too formal, too
bureaucratic. There's also a lot of motion masquerading as progress in
White Houses. People work from pre-dawn till nine, ten, eleven
o'clock at night; most of the time they're pushing papers around in
circles.

Teeter told Atwater during the transition that President-elect Bush wanted me to work in the White House. But Lee had his own plans for me and never passed the message along. (I only found out about it years later.) I love a guy who sticks to his own agenda.

I wouldn't have gone in anyway. Working with Atwater and running the RNC was a dream job for a political junkie. Because Bush had been an RNC chairman under Nixon, the national committee was going to serve as his own political arm, and Atwater was his political guy.

It turned out to be a better adventure than I had any right to hope for. First off, Atwater was interested in the bigger picture and had little inclination to run the day-to-day operation; he gave me carte blanche and free rein to set it up however I wanted. Second, he loved to pass on his wisdom, and would hold staff meetings every morning just to tell us stories. His goal was to retire from daily politics and teach, and we were his guinea-pig class.

Lee was competitive in all things. He always said that losing made him physically ill. The maddest he ever got at me—and I'm including the times he fired me—was when I failed to line up any ringers for our annual RNC-DNC softball game. When someone on our team let a grounder go through his legs, Lee just lost it. Silly me, I thought it was a game.

I learned more from Lee in that job than I did on the entire campaign.

And then, in March 1990, Lee got sick.

At first he denied it. He said they didn't know what he had. Then he said it was a nonmalignant growth.

This was so Atwater. He wanted to portray to the media that he had nothing, to get attention back on the Republican party. But reporters would stake us out at the hospital. They had moles at the hospital who told them what the real diagnosis was. And though for months he denied he was sick, what Lee had was a galloping grade-four brain tumor.

The disease was ever changing, ever evolving, ever getting worse, but Lee was still hanging on to the reins of the party. He was advising the President but he was becoming increasingly incapacitated.

The minute Lee got sick the political power was sucked back into the White House by the President's chief of staff, John Sununu. The entire RNC was increasingly out of the loop. It was a naked power grab.

Without Lee, the party was floundering. Sununu was negotiating the budget deal with the Democrats, which led to the revocation of one of the great political lines of the century—"Read my lips: No new taxes." Sununu didn't talk to Atwater, didn't understand the disastrous effects of backing off that pledge. The President's press secretary, Marlin Fitzwater, told him it would be a political disaster, but Sununu ignored him.

This was the beginning of the recession, and Democratic Senate Majority Leader George Mitchell and Democratic House Speaker Tom Foley led an attack on all the years of Republicanism with the charge that "the rich got richer and the poor got poorer." They'd distorted that piece of trash rhetoric from a Congressional Budget Office study, which could be manipulated every which way.

Had Atwater had a stronger voice he would have made clear the absolute necessity to combat that piece of class-warfare mumbo-jumbo. He told me repeatedly from his hospital bed that we were doing a terrible job. He knew that in politics you couldn't let a charge hang without disputing it, otherwise it becomes an article of faith, as if it were actually true. But without him the White House, à la Michael Dukakis, never refuted it and the phrase went into the country's vernacular.

The White House said there was no recession. There was a post–Cold War global economic restructuring under way. American industry was streamlining, downsizing, struggling to reemerge competitive. Some industries didn't make it, and unlike in previous cyclical recessions, white-collar workers were being laid off. Which, for the media, made it a more dramatic story. Despite 1991 data showing the economy stabilizing, the Democrats and media kept pounding away, but we never effectively refuted the initial attack. Our response was, "It's all manipulated data. Technically there is no recession, and people won't believe there is, so they won't listen to the Democrats." Atwater would not have stood for that. He understood the power of a hanging charge.

But Lee wasn't physically capable of doing his job anymore.

When he first got sick and they put him on morphine, he would just talk endlessly. We'd wheel him out on his sun deck and he'd tell stories from when he was in sixth grade. How he had been the class comic and kind of an outcast, and because he had this gift of wackiness had found that he could move and persuade people.

Until that time Lee had always seemed to me to be a wary person; there was always an angle with him. You were never quite certain in any conversation if he was trying to get a vulnerable, personal response out of you, which he could ever after hold against you. I was always quite confident that he wasn't revealing anything about himself. Once I figured that out we'd always hit it off.

Never having let a lot of people into his life made this illness even more difficult, more scary for him.

He ran his illness like he ran a campaign. He made me, his wife, Sally, and the rest of the people who cared about him research the best doctors and the treatments with the highest possible chance of success.

He chose the most radical, the most risky. Lee was famous for jiggling his foot all the time, he was always fidgeting and in constant motion. This operation required that, with only a local anesthetic, he lie stone still on a gurney all day long and have ten holes drilled into his skull, right into the tumor, into which was placed a surgical straw the size of a Bic pen through which they dropped pellets of radioactive material. If he moved they'd drill a hole in his brain.

Lee got so much radiation that to visit him after the operation you had to stand behind a lead shield. He was literally radioactive. Only the nurses could touch him, and they had to wear lead gloves. For days after, no one could come in and hug him.

Lee was in and out of the hospital. If the cancer wasn't eating away at his brain, the radiation was. His whole head would swell up. He couldn't walk, he could hardly move. At first he had been able to listen to books on tape and watch TV—he watched the Three Stooges all the time. But after a while the pain was too overwhelming.

In the middle of this, John Sununu removed him as chairman of the Republican National Committee and put Bill Bennett in his place. Nobody in the White House had the courtesy to call and tell him. I had to do it, after the deed was done.

This was going to be devastating to Lee. His doctors and everyone around him all knew that what was keeping him alive was the inspiration of having to do some kind of work every day on the RNC. I'd go over there every morning, barring some medical emergency during the night, and we'd work on projects. It would be fake work; we'd review decisions and talk about things that were already in the pipeline, but the notion and façade that he was still at his job kept him going.

And now I had to go over there and pull this rug out from under him.

I went to Lee's house and said, "I think you need to call Governor Sununu and tell him that you think it's time that you become general chairman and that a day-to-day chairman be put in there. That you can't focus on it the way you would like to." Which was code language for: "They have screwed you."

He broke the code and was devastated. Being RNC chairman had been his lifelong dream, he didn't want to give it up. But he knew I was saying it was already done, I just wanted him to save face.

The first thing he said was, "Who did they pick?" He wanted me to tell him that he had misread the signal. I couldn't.

"Bill Bennett."

Lee called Sununu. Then he had the nurses pick him up and put him in his wheelchair, which was a horror. They carried him downstairs, got him in the car, got the wheelchair in the car, and then we drove over to Bill Bennett's office. Two minutes of physical activity would knock him out, Lee was breathless, but we made this trek to Bennett's office and wheeled him up there and he pulled his physical and mental resources together and had a half-hour private meeting with Bennett to congratulate him and give him his best advice. We got back in the car and Lee burst into tears.

There were many people who wanted to pay their respects, and Lee would gather himself. One day President Nixon came to visit and Lee had himself pumped full of morphine to get through the conversation; it was important to him to be Lee Atwater.

When you're trying to crash your way through a political career, you don't have the time, the wherewithal, or you can't expend the emotion needed to develop deep and caring relationships. You don't have casual friends, you've got people you're loyal to, people you want to be in a foxhole with. You're very myopic. What counts is your candidate, your campaign. Personal relationships, family relationships—they are secondary to winning. Lee began writing letters to everyone he could think of who had ever meant anything in his life.

As you would expect people to do as they're staring death in the face, Lee stopped and looked around and tried to get his priorities straight. People don't go through their lives remembering every day how important the people around them are and where their relationships fit into the scheme of things. Now, because Lee's race was pretty much over, he did. With his increasing physical incapacitation Lee had only irregular periods of lucidity. What began as a book turned into an article for *Life* magazine. I was there for most of the sessions.

Everybody has made a lot of Lee's apology to Michael Dukakis, which appeared in the *Life* article. Lee apologized for anything that would have hurt Dukakis personally. Specifically, for calling him a "little bastard"; for some reason that stuck in his mind as an especially mean-spirited thing to have done.

Lee's condition was degenerative, and talking to him was sometimes like talking to a child. But some of us could hit the buttons
that, for a short while, would make him focus. I specifically asked
him, "Lee, you're not apologizing for the *campaign* against Dukakis,
are you?"

He said, "No, I'm apologizing personally to Michael Dukakis for
any mean-spirited, inhumane things I might have said to him as one
human being to another."

A lot has been made of his supposed deathbed recantation. The press
interpreted the *Life* magazine article as a vindication of their own sen-
timents, as an admission that the campaign was shallow and needed
apologizing for. As he was giving me his final advice, Lee said, "Never
let them redefine the '88 campaign. You guys cannot be squishes about
that."

The *Life* writer, who was a non-political guy, was trying to capture
the drama of the deathbed, and a recantation fits nicely in a romantic
curtain-closer. But the fact is, it didn't happen. Lee was making personal peace. It's a nightmare to me that people would use his death as
the basis for ongoing political debates. Let me say this very plainly:
There was no deathbed recantation.

The guy just wouldn't die. He never quit wanting to live. He fought
it and fought it and fought it until the very end.

James

In 1987 I managed Wallace Wilkinson's campaign for governor
of Kentucky, and went from there to New Jersey senator Frank Lautenberg's reelection run, and we won both. On December 1, 1988, I
moved to Washington, D.C.

I think at some point if you are a country-music singer you end up
in Nashville; if you are a playwright or a stockbroker you end up in
New York; if you're an actor you end up in L.A. If you're a political
consultant, sooner or later you wash up in Washington.

I found a little place on the ground floor of a brownstone on the
300 block of Maryland Avenue. Mostly when I was on a campaign I
would live in a hotel room near the headquarters. I hadn't had an
actual place that I lived in for more than two years.

The apartment was a couple of steps below ground level. It had a
front room with some bookshelves and a Murphy bed, plus a kitchen
in the back, and shared a backyard with the upstairs neighbors, my

landlords. If I really wanted to seclude myself I could close the shutters and the place would be pitch-black. I called it the Bat Cave.

Probably the most asked question I get is, How do you decide who to work for? The answer is generally, when you're coming up, you don't decide. You don't choose candidates, you choose to answer the phone and hope somebody on the other end is offering you the chance for a job. Not a job, the *chance* to get a job. You're not out making great ethical/moral decisions; the phone doesn't ring a lot. And when it does you pick it up and hope it's somebody you can pitch. You talk to three or four people and you hope one hires you.

Political consulting is a profession and a calling, it's what I do for a living. You're not paid every month, only the months you're working, the high season, if you will. For most political consultants it's not a particularly easy or profitable way to make a living. There are not a lot of jobs that pay decent money in odd-numbered years.

There seems to be an infinite amount of curiosity in the standards that political consultants use in deciding on clients. Lawyers may know their clients are guilty but still do everything in their power within the law to get them off. Some people think you are a mercenary if you work for a candidate with whom you disagree. It's not a hard thing for me to rationalize but I am aware that it's a hard thing for people to understand. I'll try to explain.

People have lots of beliefs; some you share, some you don't. I don't expect anyone to agree with me on every issue and I don't expect to fit entirely with anyone else either. I have worked for candidates who have been pro-choice; I have worked for a candidate who was pro-life. I have worked for candidates who have been for the death penalty and others who are against the death penalty. I have worked for candidates who have been for the right-to-work law and others who were against it. But I have never worked for a Republican and I have never worked in a campaign that has engaged in any kind of racial appeal.

If you ask me if I have ever been in a situation where I worked for a candidate who I may not have voted for, I would demur on answering. Working with people, you get to know their faults, you get to have doubts; no one is perfect. I will work for a Democrat who I can get along with who is neither a bigot nor a crook.

But let's say there is a smart, well-meaning person who I agree with on the issues who is running for office and can pay me $5,000 a month. There is also a tough, sort of cynical but not dishonest Washington insider who has raised a lot of PAC money and can pay me $20,000 a month. I'm going to work for the second guy. I mean, this is what I do for a living. If you ask me who would I stay up nights licking stamps for or who would I write a check to, that's another question.

From July through election day in November 1989 I did a Houston mayoral race for Fred Hofheinz and got hammered. Paul had also come to Washington and been working for Representative Dick Gephardt. He and I formed our consulting firm, Carville & Begala. In 1990 Paul and I did Governor Casey's reelection campaign in Pennsylvania and Zell Miller's primary and general election races for governor of Georgia. Our guys won.

We were getting all the work we could handle.

CHAPTER 4

Mary

In the May 11, 1990, *Wall Street Journal* there was this article about the meaner and tougher "new breed" of political consultants, hardball players like Frank Greer, Don Sipple, and James Carville. The article was mostly war stories from these guys' recent campaigns. I knew Don Sipple, he was a superior Republican strategist. I had heard of Greer from when he'd run Doug Wilder's Virginia governor's race. But this guy Carville was new to me. His credentials were good, but what made the biggest impression on me was the way he talked. He was quoted as saying, "It's hard for somebody to hit you when you've got your fist in their face." I thought that was really different and irreverent and smart-assed.

James

It was what my daddy told me when he taught me how to fight.

Mary

There were two reasons I figured this Carville guy might be someone I'd like to know: (a) Being sort of Miss Know-It-All, I prided myself on knowing who our Democratic competitors were. Which wasn't that hard, because the guys who win races are usually so full of themselves they spend all of their time tooting their own horns. My curiosity was piqued because I'd never even heard of Carville. And (b) he was so funny. I mean, nobody lets a profile in *The Wall Street Journal* show his goofy side.

That same evening I was having dinner at the home of *U.S. News* columnist Michael Barone, and NBC *Meet the Press* producer Colette Rhoney was there. I said to Colette, "Have you ever heard of this guy James Carville?"

She said, "Have I? I worked on a campaign with him." I didn't know she had been a Democratic campaign operative.

I like to know people who do politics for a living. There's a special camaraderie to every profession, but campaign politics is really close-knit. It's so intense, and there are so few people who do it well, that sooner or later we all get to know each other. I had a boyfriend at the time, Lee Atwater was in the throes of his illness, the RNC was about to get a new chairman—I didn't need any complications. More for dinner conversation than anything else I said, "I'd like to meet him." I thought I made it pretty clear that I wasn't looking for a date.

She said, "He's so cool! I'll call him for you." I don't know exactly what she said to James.

James

 Colette was my assistant on the Doggett race down in Texas. She knew I liked to meet women. She gave me the lowdown. Said there was this Republican, Mary, that "you'd be surprised. She is a lot better-looking than you'd think."

Mary

What does that mean? "For a Republican"?

James

I don't know. I guess it seems like political women are not as good-looking as in other professions.

Mary

 Well, I can understand that, knowing your political women.

James

 I wasn't just going to take Colette's word for it. I wasn't going to go out with some zealot, so I asked around. Who's this Mary? People knew her. Everybody I talked to went to pains to say that she's not an uptight Republican . . . basically that she was not a wing nut.

Mary

So the ultimate compliment a Democrat can pay is the absence of wing nuttiness?

James

It would be important information to have.

Mary

So that's what they said? Didn't one person say anything affirmative, like "She's good at her job"? Nobody said I was smart?

James

Yeah, very. Very. They said, "She's talented, she's good-looking, she's funny and irreverent and she likes to have fun and she's real smart and real cute." It was a very high tout.

I called a couple of times but our schedules never coincided. That happens a lot. "Well, I gotta go to this thing tonight. You can't go? What about dinner next week. Don't know. Okay, I'll call you." I was seeing a couple of people but I kept calling back. She was kind of fun on the phone. Even though we hadn't met, we kind of got the sense of what the other was like.

Mary

This went on for weeks, and the further I got from that article the less compelling the whole thing became. But Colette is a real little Miss Matchmaker and she kept following up on it. I bumped into her at Tim Russert's Christmas party and she said, "Have you talked to James yet?" I told her we'd been playing phone tag. She and I had both had a couple of drinks and she said, "Let's give him a call right now."

We went into the kitchen and giggled like high school girls calling a football player.

We got his answering machine. By the time he called back it was two days later and I no longer had the giggling urge to meet him. He was going off on vacation to Italy with some woman. When he got back he started back in calling. On January 6 or 7 . . .

James

Eighth . . .

Mary

January 8, 1991, is the night we actually met. You called and said, "Do you want to go to a dinner party at the Shrums' house tomorrow night? Dick Gephardt will be there, and Bob Novak." Bob Shrum was a well-known, big-time Democratic operative whom I had never met. That would be interesting. I could think of plenty of ways to spend an evening rather than talking things over with Dick Gephardt, but I loved Bob Novak. There was really no reason to meet this Carville guy but I said yes because Novak is always good for a few yucks.

"What do you look like?" he asked.

"What do I look like?"

"Don't you think we should lay eyes on each other before we go to that house?"

"Uh, okay."

"Why don't you come over to my apartment beforehand, let's have a drink."

"I'm not coming to your apartment." By this time we had horsed around on the phone so much that it was almost like we had gone out. I wasn't anything like polite to him. "I do want to go to this thing, I do want to see Novak, but I'm not coming to your apartment. No way." I thought it was a little inappropriate to join you at your apartment for a drink. Honey.

James

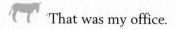 That was my office.

Mary

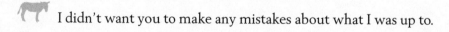 Well, that's not how it was proposed. It was definitely proposed with a little innuendo in your voice.

James

I didn't want you to make any mistakes about what I was up to.

Mary

He was the most unabashed flirt I'd ever met in my life. I said, "I'll meet you halfway."

James

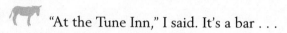 "At the Tune Inn," I said. It's a bar . . .

Mary

A Democratic hang-out bar . . .

James

. . . on Pennsylvania Avenue Southeast. "How're you gonna find me?" I said. "I'm a squinty-eyed, bald-headed, skinny guy. That oughta be easy."

Mary

I didn't want to go in there in the first place, it was crowded and noisy and full of Democrats. I was carting around this giant purse loaded with all my daily paperwork. It weighed a ton. As soon as we found each other I walked outside and dropped it on the ground. He said, "Follow me," and just turned and headed down the street. Whoa! "Please carry my bag," I told him, and walked on ahead.

James

If I ever had a chance of dominating this relationship it ended right there.

Mary

We walked down to the Hawk and Dove and he started force-feeding me vodka on the rocks.

James

Like it took a lot of effort.

Mary

I took a look at him. He was, in fact, a squinty-eyed, bald-headed, skinny guy. He was wearing skin-tight jeans and a little mus-cle-man shirt with a green turtleneck collar. I'll bet any amount of money that he doesn't remember what I was wearing.

James

 I know she had her hair the way I don't like it.

Mary

 I had on black boots and a black skirt and a white tucked-in blouse and a big black belt.

James

 That's right.

Mary

 Perhaps he can envision this because he kept staring lecherously at me. Some men are just mischievous, and they're my favorite kind. He was clearly a bad boy, and funny.

And interesting. We agreed on practically nothing but we had a good time barking at each other. He had a way of speaking that was all his own.

We sat at the bar and ate greasy fried zucchini and french fries for dinner. It didn't take long before we were fighting. We'd known each other for a half hour and we were screaming at each other in public.

I don't remember what we were shouting about, just that he was so intense. Some of his intensity, I have learned since, is shtick. But in real life he's like that too, so much energy, so opinionated. He has these opinions and they are *the* opinions. And that night, just for argument's sake, I kept taking the opposite side of whatever it was he was so certain about. With him it was not that hard, but he made me want to disagree on general principles. That level of "I'm so sure this is right" just makes me want to smack him.

He wasn't arrogant about it, just completely convinced. It looked like the game was to see if I could keep up with him. I took the challenge.

I really liked him.

James

We stayed up late. She didn't come to my place, she drove me home. We were so excited because we really did like each other.

The next day we went through this whole song and dance about how she wouldn't meet me at the Shrums' for dinner. She insisted that I pick her up at the Republican National Committee. I knew what that was about. Okay, so I picked her up.

I walked past her cabal of Republican cronies, swung into her office, and said pretty loudly, "You always have to have the upper hand. You always have to control everything. We're going to leave from *your* office so *you* can be in charge."

Mary

Of course, he was right. Yes, I wanted him to come see my office and see what a big shot I was, and see people waiting on me and answering my phone and fawning over me. So he'd get the drift: "Mary's in charge."

They split you up at these Washington dinner parties. They sat him at one end of the table and me at the other, and I kept looking at him the whole night. He talked in bursts of machine-gun English and I watched all of them, the Shrums, Mr. and Mrs. Gephardt, the Novaks, sit there and take the barrage. Whatever James was saying was all very pointed and profound and interesting, definitely a different point of view than most people in the room were used to getting. But not necessarily appropriate to the conversation. Iconoclastically charming.

My original attraction to James was that he was a guy doing something that I loved in a way that was different than I'd ever seen it done. Politics is a passion, an intricate and demanding line of work that you don't just take off like a business suit at the end of the day. It's not a job, it's a lifestyle. And your mate has to get it, because it's all you've got and all you care about. It's hard to be companionable and compatible with somebody who's not in the business.

Political dating is tough. You don't have time, you don't have energy, you don't have a life—and it's hard to get one. Politics is filled with obsessive-compulsives, and there are such weird personality traits attendant to what we do that even if you meet people, you're not sure you want to have that much to do with them.

The lifestyle and terrain are just not conducive to dating. If you're tied to your desk fourteen hours a day, or you're out being an operative and constantly moving from one state to another, from race to race, how would you get close to people? It's a small community and you've got no time or opportunity to go outside it to find a soul mate. You're going to meet what's put in front of you. In politics you hang out with your guys—there's no way to meet Democrats—which means that already about half the eligible men are no longer eligible.

James

It's unusual in politics, but look at it statistically, it was bound to happen. You've had an explosion in the number of women in the workplace, clearly in some couples somebody's working for Coke and somebody's working for Pepsi, somebody's working for Visa and somebody's working for MasterCard. It happens a lot in journalism, where, for instance, one person is working for *The Washington Post* and the other is at the Baltimore *Sun*.

If you talk to a couple who are lawyers, if one of them is in a big trial and one isn't, it's probably harder on them both than if they're both in a big trial.

If they're both in a big trial against each other, well, that's a different story.

Mary

About three months after we started going out James invited me home to Carville, Louisiana. We made this precipitous leap from "Who are we and what are we doing here?" to "Let's go meet my mom."

We had it planned for Easter. At six in the morning the day we're flying down I got a call at home from Lee Atwater's doctor. Lee had died.

I immediately kicked into operative overdrive. I had calls to make to Lee's friends and to the press. Some media genius called me "the campaign manager of the brain tumor." I wouldn't cry or get upset. In between calls I told James, "I can't go. You go."

James started shouting. "You are really a pig. This is the most selfish thing I've ever seen, that you will not let people help you. It just makes me sick. And you *are* going to go. I'm going to change the tickets and you will get all of this done by whatever is the next flight."

Then he made me cry. He just made me get it out.

I made the calls and we made the flight.

Easter is James's mother's holiday; you cannot not go to Miss Nippy's for Easter. The whole family and extended family gathers and they love their James. And James was bringing home a new girl.

This was my first introduction to Southern belle–ism and to men who are politically incorrect enough to demand that you look a certain way. It's always very important to James how I look, which of course is politically incorrect, but very flattering.

It's inspiring to meet men who actually admit that they're checking you out and take an interest in what you've got on. Although I must say, James's idea of proper attire and grooming is of another age. I must have long hair, it can never be in a bun. And I must wear dresses. So I brought down three different dresses and he picked out the one he wanted. He was *so* un-PC, so unusual, it was amusing. It was extremely funny that he wanted to make this presentation to his family. Actually, it was just very weird.

Unbeknownst to me, it had been a while since he had brought anybody home who was even a little more than postpubescent. The last girlfriend he'd shown around was so young that his sister thought she was his nephew's date. He will deny this but his sisters swear they'd never seen James with anybody over the age of eighteen, so they were kind of shocked that I was actually over thirty.

James

That isn't even remotely true. Mary has the most exalted status possible in my life and she's still got to embellish it even more.

Mary

James picked out this pink dress for me to wear with white lace pantyhose and little pink moccasins. I was thinking, "Who am I? Where did I get this dress?" He had on tight white Levi's and this pink shirt. We looked like a couple of Easter eggs.

Aunt Girlie had a beautiful southern-Louisiana home with a back-yard that dipped down a lush green hill into a pond. The whole extended Carville family was there and, in a way I'd never seen before, James started to flutter over me. Actually fluttered. It appeared to me that they all thought this was pretty natural, that a man should be fluttering around, making me wildly self-conscious, being a little gnat, touching my hair. He kept saying to his mother, "Isn't she just so beautiful?" Meanwhile I'm wringing wet in the Louisiana sun, thinking, "Who am I? What am I doing here? These people all talk funny." They were all, of course, incredibly gracious and wonderful.

James is very conscious of his twenty-one nieces and nephews, although I believe he misunderstands their exposure to the world. Maybe he thinks they have as limited exposure as he did when he was their age, but they have TV and everything. James acted like they'd never seen anybody in a dress before, or anyone who didn't speak Southern.

So he was putting on this whole show for them. He said, "I'm gonna take Miss Mary"—which is another cool Southern thing, they call you Miss Mary—"for a canoe ride." He took my hand and all the nieces and nephews, Pied Piper, followed us down this hill. This was too much. This was *Alice in Wonderland*. But, hey, when in Rome . . . What did I know?

James gets in the canoe. "Come on, sugah, step in."

Of course, James has not balanced the canoe, so I put one foot inside and we instantly turn over into what is not a pond at all but turns out to be quicksand mud. Gook. Muck. Mire.

I emerged with two broken fingernails and pond scum hanging from me like Christmas ornaments. My dress was totally stuck to my body and his white Levi's were full of seaweed.

We were not even out of the water when I started screaming. "I can't believe you don't know how to canoe! You're not supposed to stand up in a canoe!"

He said, "Your center of gravity is off!" A hardly veiled reference to my flawed figure. So within a nanosecond of doing this romantic Pied Piper parade we were screaming at each other.

By the time we got to the top of the hill he was saying, "Listen to her. She's instantly doing damage control. Instantly putting her own spin on it."

We spent the rest of the day snapping and shouting at each other.

When we got back to Washington James would just come around the RNC and dote on me. Total dotery. He'd hang out there and talk to our new chairman, Clayton Yeutter, and flirt with all the girls in the office. Everybody loved him. He'd wander around the building and dote, dote, dote. He would send me huge bowls of fresh flowers, or make his own personal Louisiana tuna fish salad and bring it over and feed me. Of course I really liked it, kind of got used to it, kind of started depending on it.

Then he moved to Philadelphia to run the Wofford campaign.

CHAPTER 5

James

Mary and I had had a fabulous spring and summer. We'd walk in the park, take trips to New Orleans. I had put off moving to Pennsylvania as long as I possibly could, and didn't go until mid-September. The spring and summer of '91 were as good a time as I'd ever had, and I didn't relish the thought of getting caught up in the middle of another political campaign. My one consolation was that it was only an hour and forty minutes by train, and I saw her every weekend.

In early 1991 after the Gulf War, George Bush had a 91 percent favorable and all the press could talk about was the "Republican electoral lock on the presidency," how there probably wouldn't be a Democratic president for another generation. Like losing football coaches giving their beat-up team a couple of days off, on April 20 Paul and I gave a party. Our motto was "This is a party that needs a party." We were seriously in the doldrums. We didn't have a chance. It was a really dismal time to be a Democrat.

Pennsylvania Senator John Heinz, a Republican, had been killed in an air crash, and Governor Casey had to appoint someone to serve his term until a special election could be held. Casey's popularity had taken a pretty big dip since his reelection, and this appointment could either help us or put us even deeper in the hole. Richard Thornburgh, who had been governor of Pennsylvania once and was now Bush's attorney general, was set to resign from the cabinet to run for senator in the special election that fall.

I was part of the governor's screening process. We approached Lee Iacocca, who considered running but decided not to. After a lot of talking, Governor Casey said, "Everyone is coming in here with ideas about a profile of this candidate or that candidate. I am going to appoint someone who has the qualifications to do the job." He named Harris Wofford.

Harris Wofford had been the state party chairman during the 1986 Casey campaign. He had been a founder of the Peace Corps, marched with Martin Luther King, Jr., had been president of Bryn Mawr and of counsel to one of the bigger Philadelphia law firms. There was no question about his ability or the quality of his mind. There was a great deal of question about whether he was in any way electable.

Wofford wanted me to run his campaign. I said, "Whatever I can do for you and the governor, I will."

In the year running Zell Miller's race and Casey's reelection and a couple of others, I had kind of stopped enjoying being a campaign manager. I liked to develop strategy but didn't want to be involved in the nuts and bolts of raising money and developing the budget. I went to Paul, who had been second in command for a lot of campaigns with me now.

I said, "Look, Harris wants me to do this. I really want you to be the team manager. I'll do whatever you want me to do, we'll be a team."

Paul went and talked to his wife, who was probably less than enthusiastic about it; she didn't want him in that frantic campaign tunnel vision. He was working for Dick Gephardt, who said, "I wish you would wait. I'm still thinking about it, I may run for president."

But Paul made his decision and we went to work.

The first poll we did showed Wofford trailing Thornburgh by 47 points. But I thought of the whole campaign as a free kick. What the hell, if we lost no one would blame us.

Paul got fanatical on a whole lot of things, raising money being number one. It was his show and he was going to really put it on. The major problem, being so far behind, was that no one thought we could win. It's circular: If you can't win, you can't raise money; if you can't raise money, you can't win.

The candidate and I were on a fund-raising trip to the West Coast in August. The airline ticket agent took the campaign credit card, ran it through the machine, and the machine spat it back; it was over the limit. I was kind of mortified but Harris was completely unflustered. Here is a United States senator, he is standing at an airline counter with a reservation, and the thing bounces back at him. No problem. We used our own cards and would worry about getting reimbursed later.

In the extremely depressing July poll that showed us 47 points down there had been one ray of light.

Often in our polls we would test people's initial reaction toward the candidates, and then test their reaction again after they had been exposed to other questions, which would provide new information or remind the voter of additional information. And sometimes during the course of a poll, people will change their minds. On question one, "If the election were today how would you vote," they had been 67–20 for Thornburgh. By question fifty it was 43–43. It was a very dramatic turnaround. But we had tried a lot of negatives on Thornburgh and we figured it really wasn't fair; we laid it on him and the numbers moved. We tended to discount it because we had tried to stack the deck and it had worked.

A month later we tried it again. This time, I told our pollster Mike Donilon, "Let's just do the first trial heat regular, and the second question will be message-to-message. Then we'll ask for a revote before it's all tainted by the rest of the questions."

After the normal screening process to see that we were talking to people who could and might vote, we asked, "How do you plan on voting?" By that time it was 65–21. Then we said, "Here are what the candidates are saying:

"Harris Wofford says the rich get too many breaks in America, while working families keep falling farther behind. That's why Wofford supports a plan that would cut taxes on the average middle-income family by more than six hundred dollars and would raise taxes on rich people who make over one hundred and thirty thousand dollars a year. Wofford also supports creating a national health insurance system because he says that's the only way that every working family will get affordable and available health care. Wofford has also introduced a bill that will make it easier for middle-income families to get college loans for their children.

"Dick Thornburgh says we need to fight for traditional American values again in this country. That's why, as governor, he cut taxes, removed thousands of people from the welfare rolls, and left the state a two-hundred-million-dollar budget surplus. And as attorney general he has been fighting alongside George Bush to get the nation's toughest crime law—one that will provide the death penalty for drug kingpins. Thornburgh has also been leading the fight against racial quotas—opposing the 1991 civil rights bill because he says it is a

racial quota bill that forces employers to hire unqualified people
based on the color of their skin.

"Now how would you vote?"

Wofford 45, Thornburgh 42.

Right there we knew that, hey, we could do this thing. People are
talking about dollar issues, not social ones. They needed dollars; now
so did we.

Mary

Cardinal rule 101 of politics is: *Never let the other side define
you.* We let them define us for two years preceding the 1992 presidential campaign. Some of us at the RNC were having ulcers over the
Thornburgh race, even though it's pretty hard to get seriously nervous about a guy who's 47 points up.

The National Republican Senatorial Committee (NRSC) funds
Senate races while the Republican National Committee works with
the state parties. The RNC has a lot of resources and is permitted by
law to do generic get-out-the-vote activities, so it is imperative for the
state parties to work closely with us.

Well, word kept coming back to me that the great thinkers in the
Thornburgh campaign were refusing to give polling data to the Penn-
sylvania state party. Why? Because the state party would give it to the
RNC and Mary Matalin would give it to James Carville.

Which was just absurd. And I was incensed.

In a meeting with RNC chairman Clayton Yeutter, NRSC chairman Senator Phil Gramm also raised the question. Yeutter told me,
"He thinks you're selling your soul for love." Yeutter and I took that
as a joke, and for that matter so did Gramm, but the fact that Gramm
was forced to bring the subject up was evidence that it had become
an issue with the campaign. Yeutter said he'd batted it back ferociously, saying what an honorable person I was, blah, blah, blah.

After that I thought it was over, but the upper echelons of the
Thornburgh campaign discussed holding a press conference to expose
me or discuss the issue of my going out with Carville. Thornburgh
himself had to put a stop to that one. He said I was a professional and
that he was going to treat me as a professional. So, kudos to Thornburgh. But for him, the rest of the campaign—who were friends of
mine—was obsessed with this notion that Carville and I were killing
them. Which is a sign of a ridiculous campaign.

Lee Atwater always used to say that if you, the operative, could get the other campaign focused on you personally, you will always keep them off stride. James had certainly done that. After the Scranton "guru" episode he had the Pennsylvania GOP totally psyched out. I kept telling that to my operatives in Pennsylvania: "Look, tell those guys there's nothing magical about Carville. He's just going to run a good solid race. He's going to keep his eye on the ball, and so is Paul Begala. But he has no magical powers, for Pete's sake."

I didn't get through. They kept waiting, day after day. The watch-word was: What is Carville going to do? They got so distracted think-ing that I was giving him information that they lost sight of their own candidacy and the race.

And they kept talking, whispers getting louder. What was the point? It certainly wasn't going to shake James at all, it only shook me. And it hurt their relationship with the RNC. It was the dumbest thing I ever heard of.

But the rumors caught on, the cumulative effect being that an exag-gerated version of the Yeutter-Gramm meeting appeared in the polit-ical gossip pages. It started in the Washington *Times* and then spread.

I was surprised how thin-skinned I was. It was very intrusive to me and I must concede that I became obsessed. James would just laugh at it but I got frantic.

Atwater's rule on rumors was that the worst thing you can do when there are stories floating around about you is to spread them yourself by calling everybody and talking about it. So of course I instantly vio-lated it. I called everybody. "Who's saying this? I've been working for this party for so long, how could they question my integrity?" Then everybody would proffer an opinion, which was not what I was look-ing for. I talked to Ed Rollins, who used to live with Michelle Davis, Thornburgh's campaign manager. "I know it's her," I said. "Why is she doing this?"

He couldn't answer that, but he didn't deny that she was the likely culprit.

"Look, I want to work on the Bush campaign. If this is a problem on a special election what's going to happen when it's a presidential?"

He said, "It's going to be a problem."

That's when I started getting really crazy. I began figuring ways to redefine the relationship so as not to undermine my chances on the Bush campaign. I didn't know exactly what to do. All the people who were going to decide who got those jobs knew I was going out with Carville. They knew who he was: He was the new Darth Vader.

James

A campaign is in trouble if it doesn't have a rationale. You can plaster your candidate's face and name all over the state, but if he or she's not saying anything, you're not going to make a dent.

Disraeli said, "A good leader knows himself and the times." But over the last forty years we have been conditioned by the elites in this country to believe that a good leader knows only him or herself. There is reverence for the politician who goes out and says, "This is what I care about, this is what's important to me, this is why I want to go to Washington, and the polls be damned."

I mean, if somebody wants to get into politics because they intently and fervently believe in increasing funding for the arts, there are two things that you sort of know about them: They probably care passionately about the arts, and they probably will never serve in the office that they aspire to.

The elite public-opinion makers—newspaper columnists, editorial writers, television commentators and pundits—seem to think that if you go and figure out what is bothering people and then run a race on it, that's somehow a conniving and contemptible thing to do. There is less respect and more suspicion for a politician who says, "I want to go to Washington and help people, and in order to do that it's important to know what people think." If you actually make the effort to go and find what that is, through focus groups or polling or research, you run the grave risk of being called a panderer. The elites may view that as contemptible, but real people view it as responsive to their needs.

Harris Wofford believes in a lot of things, but our researchers came up with three key issues that the people of Pennsylvania cared about deeply: a middle-class tax cut, more affordable education, and health care. Wofford did, too. That's what we ran on.

I had become passionate about the idea of stagnant income growth, where people were constantly feeling like they were working harder but not going anywhere—a relatively new phenomenon in American politics. For the longest time people felt that hard work and diligence would reap big rewards down the road. That's the American way. Or it was. Today there is less faith in that proposition than there has been before. Many people were worried—about their homes, about their families, about their faith in America.

The economic and cultural elites, who are financially and socially secure, aren't particularly disturbed by this, if they're aware of it at all. They are so shortsighted they think they can remain comfortable while other people are not rising. The first time I saw that kind of thing really manifest itself was in this race.

Dick Thornburgh made a colossal mistake almost the moment he entered the race. Here was the former governor of Pennsylvania resigning from his position as attorney general of the United States. At a time when our research showed that Pennsylvanians didn't feel government was paying attention to them, Thornburgh portrayed himself as the ultimate insider.

We were having a media meeting with Doak and Shrum; Mike Donilon was there, so was Paul. As always, we had sent a researcher over to Thornburgh's announcement press conference to get him on tape. The Thornburgh campaign was distributing printed copies of the announcement speech, so we got one. Our staffer faxed it to us immediately. We were sitting around reading it when we came to the perfect gaffe line.

"I have walked the corridors of power," said Thornburgh. "I know Washington inside out."

Everybody went, "Naw, he couldn't have said that!"

It was too perfect. The answer, the whole campaign, was wide open in front of us. We brainstormed for a couple of minutes to get the phrasing just right, then we jumped on it. We couldn't get Harris on camera quick enough.

"I want to clean up the corridors of power," he said, "and turn Washington upside down."

Paul told them, "Running on the Corridors of Power in Pennsylvania is like running on a pro-leprosy ticket in the time of Jesus."

Money was tight and we had the candidate making direct appeals for contributions. Harris Wofford is a fine human being but a terrible fund-raiser. He's too good a guy to ask for money. He had gone to meet with a group of ophthalmologists and when he got back, Paul called him.

"How'd the meeting go?"

"Great!"

"Oh, good. How much money are they giving you?"

"Well, no money, but some great ideas."

Paul started rolling his eyes. "Goddammit, Harris, we can't run this campaign on ideas, we need money!"

"No, but this is a good idea. Dr. Robert Reinecke pulled me aside and said, 'You know, Harris, if the constitution had been written by my intellectual forebears, who were doctors, instead of yours, who were lawyers, we would have a right to see a doctor instead of a lawyer. I think you should go out there and tell people that if a criminal has a constitutional right to see a lawyer then why in God's name doesn't an honest working person have a right to see a doctor?' "

Paul said, "Harris, that *is* a pretty good idea." He quick ran it over to our media firm, and they lit up. "If criminals have the right to a lawyer, I think working Americans should have the right to a doctor." It was *the* line of the year, and it didn't come from the high-priced talent. We immediately put the phrase into a TV ad and got credit for discovering the health care issue.

Health care went to the core of the matter. People were having a hard time taking care of themselves, and the government wasn't doing anything about it. The more we talked about it, the more people responded. It was like, "Finally, somebody in a campaign is talking about something that matters to me." This was not a right-wing flag factory display of empty patriotism—or, on the left, a tangential issue like gays in the military. This was something that was relevant to people's daily lives and you just had a sense that they were excited that somebody was talking about it.

Even though we knew it was a bad idea and could cause some talk, it was inevitable that Mary would get into my office. I hadn't seen her in a while and she came up by train one day. She walked into our headquarters, got me, and we went out for lunch. She wouldn't say it then, but after the campaign she told me she knew we were going to win.

Mary

Every Friday night I'd take the train up to Philadelphia. James would jog to the station, and we'd taxi back together. Before we'd go out we'd stop by the headquarters.

It was the first time I'd seen James Carville campaign. And I did know they were going to win.

There was a buzz to that office. It was nine o'clock Friday night and the place had the energy level of nine Monday morning. There was just too much activity, too much focus in that room to be a losing campaign. There were pizza boxes all over the place, newspapers everywhere, TVs on every different channel, fax machines going, phones ringing, people meeting in all their offices. That doesn't happen on a Friday night unless there's something there. The place was filled with propeller heads—literally: people with propellers on their beanies.

I always felt like an alien in a strange land going in there. People were perfectly civil to me but I was in enemy territory.

They'd be there Saturday morning. We'd stop by before dinner Saturday night, they'd be there. It seemed like it was going seven days a week, practically twenty-four hours a day. I had occasion to call our campaign one Saturday afternoon and there was no answer, which was not a good sign.

Paul Begala was running the show and was clearly a strong and beloved leader. James would come in and throw a football around and do football hollers and get people jazzed up with all this stupid stuff that he does. People would be working and he'd make them come over and watch TV with him and throw them the ball or slap them on the back. I thought, They think he's God. Get me out of here.

James

In October there was a debate between Senator Wofford and Governor Thornburgh. By that time among Pennsylvania Republicans I had a reputation: I was the devil. I was probably not very Thornburghesque in my outlook, in the way I dressed, the way I moved, the way I thought, what I did. I suspect it was because of the Scranton "guru" thing. Every time the former governor saw me he got livid. Of course, when you get a shot like that you've got to take it.

The candidates were in position, seated across a round table and prepared to do battle. They had a 20-point lead but we had already made up 27 points and weren't going away. Right before the debate was to start I just sort of ambled out onstage, leaned over, put my arm around Senator Wofford, and whispered into his ear like I was giving final instructions.

Thornburgh was sitting at the round table and you could see him fuming. He was totally aggravated. It was like Wofford had a conversation going down with Fagin. I saw it, the senator saw it, Fred Friendly saw it, it was clear to everybody.

Except I wasn't saying anything. It was the classic junior high school ploy—"Laugh like I'm telling you a joke"—and it worked.

I couldn't watch the debate. Never can, I get too wound up. I walked in and saw the last five minutes, and Paul gave me a pretty detailed outline of what happened. As soon as it was over Harris came and asked how it went. "Great. It was great." He asked about something specific, and of course I didn't know—I hadn't seen it. I said, "Oh, yeah, that was a definite high point."

Our "favorables" had a 10 advantage, and Bush was down. You could see the movement coming, you could sense it.

One of the things I like to do on the final day of a campaign is a twenty-four-hour-scheduling day. You fill the entire last day with events all over the state. It's a good metaphor. It tells the voters that you really want the job. The people who are already going to vote for you are happy that you're out there; the people who aren't going to vote for you don't care one way or the other; and the important people who are still making their decision see you and think, "This makes me comfortable. This guy wants this job, he wants to do the job."

And it captures all the media reports.

The staff loves it. It's hard to sleep then anyway, and people get to stay up all night in headquarters fielding phone calls and making sure everything is going right. There's a lot of nervous energy and they get to burn it off. Supporters like to see their candidate really putting out. Everybody loves it. It's a good way to seal the deal.

We won by 10 points. A pretty rare upset landslide. Deep down inside I thought we were going to win by a little more.

I probably had a little too much to drink that night. When I woke up I was a public figure.

The New York Times wanted to interview me and Paul. Then we got our picture in *USA Today*. Somebody wanted to talk on National Public Radio. The rush of media attention was on.

I was surprised. Paul and I hadn't really thought about this, we were pretty intent on just winning. In all candor, it felt good. Kind of like your first kiss: "I didn't know that this was going to happen. I didn't know that it was going to feel like this, but hey, this ain't bad."

Mary

It was late afternoon, election day. Thornburgh was losing. It was already dark out. Strategist Charlie Black, Clayton Yeutter, pollsters Fred Steeper and Bob Teeter, and I were meeting in Chief of Staff John Sununu's office at the White House discussing how to spin it. Sununu just kept saying, "It was a terribly run race and it has nothing to do with the Republican party. It was just a badly run race. Okay, that is what we're all going to say. That's the spin. We're all just going to say it was a bad race."

That was the personality of Sununu at work: There is one opinion in the room that counts and it is his. Since arriving at the White House he had packed it with people who couldn't threaten his authority or power. The only guy Sununu listened to was Charlie Black, in my opinion the smartest strategist in the party, but even Charlie wasn't getting through.

So this was how we spun the press: The Thornburgh defeat has no larger significance for the party or for George Bush. The party went into deep denial.

Inside the Beltway, President Bush was getting trashed. He was coming off the Rocky Mountain high of the Gulf War, and the buzz from the press and pundits was that he was spending too much time abroad, that he was a "foreign-policy president," out of touch with the domestic problems of the country. We knew the reporters were going to dig in despite our denials. Their tone was "This defeat is an ominous harbinger for Bush"—and we had to be prepared.

Sununu came armed with numbers. The President had only been out of the country 8 percent of the time he'd been in office. Eighty-one days. We would try not to overly criticize the Thornburgh campaign, at least not on the record. Just dismiss it and get the point out that this was not a foreign-policy presidency and here's what he's accomplished domestically.

We got back to our offices at six o'clock. My assignment was to run these numbers out there. First I called the White House press office, just to make sure I had the right figures. They confirmed them, which meant that the press office was going to be saying the same thing.

My first call was to Ann Devroy at *The Washington Post*. Unfortunately for politicians she has a really astute political mind. I always told Teeter, if we had a strategist on our campaign as smart as Devroy we'd be in good shape.

She knew I was spinning. She let me get through Thornburgh and then I said, "And you know, Ann, this does not augur anything for this presidency. Of course, you all are going to be saying he's a foreign-policy president and that this race shows the level of attention people want paid to domestic problems, but he's only been gone eight percent of the time, only eighty-one days—"

Ann said, "Oh, yeah? Well, why did Sununu just announce you're pulling the Japanese trip?"

"What? No. He did what?"

"He pulled the Japanese trip. Just announced it."

Ann was laughing. I hung up on her. I was stunned. We had just sat through an entire meeting with Sununu telling us to defend the foreign trips and he never told us that within minutes of our departing he was going to spin in the opposite direction. That week, the President had planned to follow a visit to commemorate the fiftieth anniversary of Pearl Harbor with a trip to Japan. Pulling it was a signal that the President was sensitive to the criticism, was implicitly agreeing with the people who said he was too concerned with foreign policy. *They were conceding the attack, and we hadn't even been told!* It was the most insular, damaging, Keystone Kop operation imaginable.

I hadn't had a cigarette for over a year. I lit up and then stayed up all night in my office, smoking, waiting for our formal press conference the next morning.

I could not begin to understand Sununu's motives. If you're trying to get your side of the story out, if you're going to have political spinners, then you've got to have your little legion of people all say the same thing. Did he not trust us? Then why did he have this meeting at all?

The absolute rule of message dissemination and message penetration is consistency and repetition. The principle is the same for political campaigns or companies: Everyone says the same thing, *over* and *over.* What the press used to know about us—in the White House, at the RNC, in primaries, and in the general election—was that we were impenetrable. You would never get anybody inside who would say something different than the party line. It got to the point where reporters were disgusted. They'd roll their eyes and say, "We're not going to talk to you anymore because you all say the same thing." I'd start a sentence and they'd say, "Okay, we already heard that." And they knew that if they went to three people or four or fifteen, they'd get the same drill. And they'd have to print it because they couldn't get anything else.

So I was lying on my couch, smoking, thinking about Ann Devroy. Stunned. Sununu's yanked the Japan trip and we have no comeback for why. The press would obviously take the canceled trip as verification that we were freaked out and as an acknowledgment that our presidency was weak on the domestic front.

It wasn't. We'd passed the Americans with Disabilities Act, the Civil Rights Act, the Clean Air Act, the Surface Transportation Act—and nobody knew about it. Sununu didn't focus the press's attention on them, so the public didn't know. He didn't even return phone calls from one domestic cabinet secretary. He didn't do his job.

Sununu had a history of bullying people and publicly humiliating them. As a result he didn't have the reservoir of goodwill that truly effective leaders have. People feared him, but absent fear there was nothing much to hold his authority together.

When a leader's respect declines, the first thing to go in his organization is discipline. The press loved that. They could and did call anybody and everybody and get their own individual interpretations. Discipline breakdown is manna from heaven for the free press; it's a disaster for a political organization.

While James and Paul were coming from 47 points down, the President had been governing the country. He was in no hurry to get out on the campaign stump, and while his 1988 campaign had begun unofficially in early 1986, two and a half years before the election, by the summer of 1991 there was no 1992 reelection machine in place.

The money people finally forced a meeting in late August. By the time we convened, there were close to forty Bushies involved, way too many for much of substance to get accomplished. All that was determined at Camp David was that Bobby Holt could start thinking about the finance operation. Everyone, at least those of us who hoped we'd be working on the campaign, was disappointed by the resistance to giving the campaign mechanics a kick start.

But we didn't consider the meeting a complete waste. Teeter laid out a strategic road map that could lead us to victory, if we'd just follow it. Presidential elections are about peace and prosperity, and, having achieved peace, we knew there would be even more attention focused on the economy. Our strategy was to make the case that foreign-policy success abroad meant domestic economic prosperity, and the leadership required to attain great success in foreign policy was exactly what was needed to attain economic success at home. Through new democracies, new markets, expanded trade and exports, you would get jobs in America.

This strategy was based on three assumptions: (1) that there was an electorate awareness of our domestic policies and past achievements; (2) that the President would get credit for foreign-policy achievements; (3) that there would be an economic recovery. We thought this was pretty sound.

President Bush's reluctance to go into campaign mode was based on his belief that if he had an officially designated campaign, every trip, every White House event, every policy meeting would be reported by the press in a political context and perceived as having a political motivation. President Bush felt that there were too many issues left before him that needed serious attention without being filtered through a political prism.

He also presumed there were enough experienced politicos around so that, when we did open up shop, we could do it overnight—that we were a turnkey operation.

What he didn't take into account was the strident opposition to Sununu. How was the campaign going to interface with the White House? Our only comparable model was Reagan's 1984 reelection, when Chief of Staff Jim Baker ran the White House *and* called the campaign shots every day. He made the schedule, he decided what was going to come out of Reagan's mouth, he had the big picture. It was transmitted to the campaign by his right-hand woman, Margaret Tutwiler, and then implemented by the campaign.

In 1992, everybody in the Republican interplanetary system knew that was a model doomed to failure were Sununu to remain as chief of staff. So the issue that had been festering below the surface was forced to the top. The double coup de grâce was Sununu's canceling the Japan trip plus not fully understanding the ramifications of the Wofford victory. But his fate was foreshadowed by the ongoing bullying of his colleagues, and his own trials and tribulations—taking government planes to go buy stamps and go to his dentist, which had garnered endless press attacks.

Outside of the finance people, no one was directly confronting George Bush and saying, "We must start the campaign now," because that really meant, "You've got to figure out the Sununu problem." The President is above all a loyal man, and we all knew it would take a lot for him to remove a trusted friend and ally. But finally the anti-Sununu drumbeat was deafening. Out of fairness the President dispatched his eldest son, George Bush, Jr., to quietly canvass the President's other friends and political confidants, to get their generic thoughts on the reelection campaign. There was nothing generic or unequivocal about their responses: Sununu had to go. Junior then went to Sununu and said, very diplomatically, no doubt, "Sorry, old bean, thanks for everything you've done but this just isn't going to work." Or words to that effect; no one ever knew for sure. All we knew was that Sununu submitted his handwritten resignation.

Once that was resolved, the rest of the pieces fell into place.

CHAPTER 6

James

Governor Zell Miller called me in July and said, "I got some-body on the phone, I told him that he ought to hire you."

I said, "Fine. Always good to get work." Governor Bill Clinton was spending the night in Georgia. He got on the phone and said he was coming up to Washington and would like to meet with us.

The governor of Arkansas was coming through Washington; this kind of casual political meeting happens all the time. We sat on the sofa in the bar of a Capitol Hill hotel. He didn't have a big entourage, it was just the governor and Bruce Lindsey, me and Paul. There was sports on the TV; we drank beer and shot the shit about how to run for president. Fact is, I can't remember much about it. Paul does.

Paul had worked on Gephardt's presidential campaign and begged Clinton not to make the mistakes they'd made, to focus not on the organization but on his message: Who you are and why you want to be president.

Clinton had already thought that through. He told us that America wanted aggressive change and that he wanted to bring it. I told the governor the most important thing to us was that the candidate not just be an empty vessel into which consultants could pour meaning, that he have not only ambition but ideas. But that wasn't Clinton's problem. He was full to the brim with ideas. He had a worldview, a vision, a real sense of where he wanted to take the country. He kept leaning forward and talking with energy about how America had to develop its people, had to have skills; about how badly we compared with our European and Asian competitors in terms of investing in our people; about how wrong the eighties had been. But he knew there was a lot of underbrush in there. He kept saying to us, "What I need most of all from you guys is focus, is clarity. I don't know how to bring it down, to condense it."

Paul and I knew we could do that. That's the easy part. I said, "The best thing we can do to help you become president is to help Wofford become senator. We want to go back to Pennsylvania and win this race. If we win this, everything will change. The chances of beating Bush and of you becoming president will go up astronomically."

The meeting lasted about a half hour. Although Clinton hinted at it, he didn't offer us a job and we didn't accept one. We told him, "We're not going to commit to anything until November. After it's over we'll talk again. Be assured we ain't working with anybody else in the interim either." The governor said fine.

I didn't walk away from that meeting with my shoes blown off. You never do. I did know that before I made a decision, this was a guy I wanted to talk to again. After it was over I said to Paul, "Well, that's a nice guy, looks like he has his shit together. How much money did we raise for Wofford today?"

Paul and I had an apartment in Philadelphia together and I remember very clearly sitting there in early October watching Governor Clinton's announcement speech. Even at that time I thought he rambled too much and that the speech was about too many things, but they did a good job. I watched Kerrey's announcement and thought it was sort of botched, hastily put together.

We met with Governor Clinton twice after the election in November. We had breakfast with Senator Kerrey at the Willard and met with Senator Harkin in his office. One of the things we were particularly concerned about was, How would the other people in the campaign take our coming in, how much did people want us there? There were already people in place, people who had seniority on us and some early-bird professional and emotional attachment, and they might feel that we were coming in and taking their spot. Senator Kerrey, for instance, very much wanted us to work for him; I'm not sure his staff did. Senator Harkin didn't have a great big staff to worry about, but he was running as an unapologetic old-line Democrat, and I thought that position had been pretty much consistently rejected by the voters in national elections. I thought that campaign would probably tend toward orthodoxy and there wouldn't be a lot of room for creativity.

Clinton's staff kept calling and saying that they really wanted to work with us. Paul and I decided. Right before Thanksgiving I called Clinton's campaign manager, David Wilhelm, from Mary's apartment, where I was spending most of my nonworking time, and said, "We want to work with you guys."

There was no easy way to tell Mary, but the reality was I probably picked the worst one possible. I knew she'd be upset, and I didn't feel good about having to tell her, so I kind of just didn't say anything until the news got blurted out inadvertently and it was too late.

When we announced our intentions *The Washington Post* ran an article with the headline "Clinton Wins the Carville Primary." Now, on the scale of jealous people I'm probably about average, but I suspect that if I was a consultant on a campaign and someone new was coming in under that headline, it would make me jealous. "Well, look, I've been here . . ." Clinton's campaign had only started hiring about two months before, so we weren't *very* junior people, but I was really scared that the people already there would say, "Oh, yeah, like this guy is coming in to save us from ourselves." I got none of that.

The first time I saw Bill Clinton in an action situation he was prepping for a foreign-policy speech at Georgetown University sometime in early December 1991. There were about fifteen people crowded around a conference table in Frank Greer's office and they were going over a speech the governor was planning to give the next day. I was sitting on the floor in the back against a wall, just taking it all in.

It must be the same as a guy who has spent his entire career in the minor leagues and finally gets the call up to the majors. It was the first time I'd seen major-league pitching.

The guy with the best stuff was him. Clinton. His persona, the questions he was asking, the quality of his speech. I knew I was in with somebody whose skills were beyond those of anybody I had worked with before. I just kind of went, "Wow."

Bill Clinton is one of those very rare people who can walk in and change the chemistry of a room. It's just a fact. The molecules in the room were one way and he would walk in and after he got there the molecules were arranged slightly differently. I have seen a few people in business who have it, I've seen a few people in local politics have it. I've seen people who are governors and powerful senators who don't have it. It's just a way they affect the air.

It was also clear that he knew as much about foreign policy as anybody who was advising him. Or, at worst, he was a pretty quick learner.

In any campaign, but especially in a presidential, there are levels of power and pecking orders. As the campaign goes on the people at the levels switch, your stock goes up and down. Clinton, in a coat and tie, was at the center of the action. Right from the beginning, in orbit number one around Clinton was his top aide and combination policy expert, press secretary, travel aide, and troubleshooter, George Stephanopoulos. Whether it was an economic speech, foreign policy, whatever, George was there to see that the information flow was moving.

It's my style to sit on the floor and watch and listen and say a couple of things if the conversation gets too esoteric or away from the central point. There was nobody there who had any more experience than I did; it wasn't like they'd been there before, either. But I had to get my sea legs before anybody was going to let me get at the helm for any period of time. He gave the speech. I didn't even go to it.

The next time I saw him was at a debate prep before six Democratic candidates were going to go at it on NBC. This was another surprise.

We had run debate preps in statewide races a lot of times. We would just go rent a room with a two-way mirror and the staff would sit behind the glass and there might be three people in with the candidate. If the economic specialist saw something wrong he would pass a note inside. If someone had a good line, pass a note. You didn't blurt something out unless you were what they called a Big Swinging Dick.

Well, there were twenty-five people in that room and they were all shouting. Most of the time you don't want to upset your candidate; hell, people were arguing in front of him. It was pandemonium. Greer and Greenberg and George and the foreign-policy people and the Democratic Leadership Council types and economic-policy people and ex-Mondale staffers—there were twenty-five people, there must have been twelve conversations going at once, everybody was screaming at everybody else. I was used to being a campaign manager and running the show. I wanted to say, *All right, everybody just shut up!* But here I was, just a consultant. I didn't have the standing.

After the first ten minutes I thought, "This guy is going to go ripshit. He's just gonna say, 'What are you people doing? I'm leaving here and I'm coming back in forty-five minutes and I want one person to talk. . . .' "

But Clinton was oblivious to it. Never seemed aggravated. Didn't seem to mind. He kind of reminded me of my daddy. My daddy had eight kids and he had an unbelievable ability to have his life function normally with people falling off him and walking up and punching him in the stomach and scratching his face. He would fix him a plate and sit down at the table and one of the three-year-olds would be climbing on his shoulder and fall on the floor, a baby would poop in his lap.

Clinton was like that at a meeting. It was all going on and he would sample most of the conversations like he was at a tasting. I kept waiting for him to get mad but he didn't. Finally it dawned on me that he was not going to say, "Why don't all of you shut up? I'm trying to run a state, I'm trying to run for president, if anybody has something to say I'll be glad to listen to you but just say it one at a time." It wasn't going to happen. It was just like waiting for my father. They brought some food in and the governor was eating off somebody's plate and somebody was eating off his.

It was at one of these prep meetings that I first met Hillary.

When I was in the Marine Corps there was a way of finding out what was actually the story that didn't appear in any training manual. You're new to the regiment and you know who the colonel is: He's the regimental commander. You know who the executive officer is: He's the old guy who's getting ready to retire. But when you're having a beer at the off-base hangout every troop will tell you, "Old Major Jones over there, you might not see him right up on the chain of command, but if you want something done he's the guy." Well, you walk into Clintonland and you pick up this mythology pretty quick. The campaign scuttlebutt was that Hillary Rodham Clinton was somebody to deal with, a tough woman. A factor.

Now, I'm not real likely to take anyone's word at face value; I like to observe things for myself. You look at somebody's eyes, you listen to the way they talk, you notice the way somebody's child acts around them. I decided the first time I met her that I was going to take five minutes and do nothing but watch Hillary.

You didn't have to be a genius in room dynamics to figure out the drift of her place in the campaign. You got it from her body language, from the deference with which people spoke to her, from the way she was referred to in the conversations that were breaking out around her. She has a way about her.

I should declare myself early: I am a big Hillary fan.

She was just sitting there relatively quietly in the middle of all the planning and screaming, wearing slacks and a sweatshirt, maybe a scarf or something. Greer was having the candidate do cuts into the camera, Greenberg was off talking about a poll, David Wilhelm was talking about one thing, and somebody else in the Arkansas governor's office was saying that we have to do something about a problem in the state. There were about ten conversations going at once, but when Hillary spoke they all sort of toned down a little bit.

It's the E. F. Hutton syndrome. If fifteen people are talking and the candidate is reading a magazine and then she talks and he looks up . . . You probably don't make a note in your diary about it but it becomes part of an ongoing mental process.

I'd been there for about five minutes when she said something that I didn't quite hear. I said, "Excuse me, Mrs. Clinton, but what is it that we are agreeing on right now?"

When Chelsea Clinton walked into the room, Hillary's mood changed a little bit. She whispered something into her daughter's ear and Chelsea said, "I'm going out to play with my friends down the street." It wasn't much of my business but you could just see that this was someone who could be tough if she wanted to, but she wouldn't be gratuitously hard. Some people will run over you just because you are there; other people will run around you, and some will run over you if you're in the way. Hillary won't run you down for fun and she won't run into a ditch to avoid scratching your fender, but if you are blocking something that we need to get accomplished you'll get run over in a hurry.

Where most people made their mistake with Hillary was to think that they couldn't disagree with her for fear of offending her or getting iced out of access to the candidate. That was another straight myth, that whatever Hillary said was law. Hillary didn't by any stretch of the imagination always get her way with her husband.

You could disagree with Mrs. Clinton and that was fine. In fact, sometimes in order to get recognized you had to scream and say some outlandish things. But if you're going to differ with Hillary, be prepared. Go in there with all your reasoning in order, don't just shoot your mouth off and figure it out later. Some people, over a period of time, proved not to have much to offer. They didn't get executed. Worse. They didn't get paid attention to.

But I didn't think the mythology had it all right. Mrs. Clinton was a lot more tender than people give her credit for. I was struck by, I'm not sure "softness" is the right word, but an ability to listen that I think maybe some people might have missed. I felt that this woman was nowhere near as hard-bitten as campaign lore had it. I thought, "This is a tough woman, but this ain't anything close to a mean woman. What I'm going to do is, I'm going to respect her but I'm not going to fear her."

The NBC debate on Sunday, December 15, was the first media event that gathered most of the major Democratic candidates in one place at one time on this campaign. There were Jerry Brown, Bill Clinton, Tom Harkin, Paul Tsongas, Doug Wilder, and the one guy everybody in our camp was most concerned with, Nebraska senator Bob Kerrey.

Bob Kerrey was called a consultant's wet dream. He was a Vietnam War hero, a Medal of Honor winner. He had high-powered consultants Bob Shrum and David Doak, and Harrison Hickman was his pollster. People who knew him said he was a personable guy. He had real credibility in talking about health care; he had actually introduced a bill on it in the Senate.

On top of that he was the same generation as Clinton and was carrying that mantle, and the reporters covering the beginnings of the presidential campaign were really sort of taken with him. He was the glamour guy.

The only thing Bob Kerrey didn't have was a message. He'd picked up some early support, but he hadn't developed a rationale for his candidacy. While that should have given us some comfort, we were more interested in mechanics. We were going after the same campaign workers in New Hampshire.

From early on I was less aware of Paul Tsongas than I should have been. He was a candidate without much money and was running second in a state that was right next door to his. There wasn't anything you could do to pick on him, he was just sort of there.

Tom Harkin was staking out the clear ground as the race's only unabashed old-line liberal Democrat, and he was making a lot of noise. There was always this sense that he could do a lot better in the primaries than in the general because Democratic primary voters are a lot more liberal than the public as a whole.

Jerry Brown was just a nut. There is an optimistic vein that runs through the Democratic party—e.g., Franklin Roosevelt, John Kennedy—and a pessimistic vein. Jerry Brown personified the How Bad Everything Is Democrats: how tough it is and how nothing is ever going to be any good, how everybody is rotten. Maybe he spent too much time with the Jesuits.

Jerry Brown has always struck me as an unhappy guy. You can never know until you've walked in somebody else's shoes, but here's a guy who was twice governor of the most populous state in the union, his daddy was governor of the state, he has a marvelously talented sister who was treasurer of the state—and he never laughed. He was always mad. He had an unhappy message and an unhappy campaign.

Our message wasn't terribly refined at that point. We were talking about a middle-class tax cut, and change, and confidence, but we didn't have a real hard edge, either.

People weren't hanging from the rafters to watch the NBC debate. But what really counts in an early debate is not the ratings but the forty reporters who are there covering it. They would tell you who won the debate; they make the call.

The early media was that Clinton sort of did okay. Then after the polls came out saying that he had done very well, his status as an emerging front-runner was intact. If you think that campaigns pay attention to polls, it affects our judgment by one-tenth the amount it affects the press corps's. They worship the polls. If you want to find a hundred reporters, throw a poll; they'll be out there sniffing at it, writing whatever conventional wisdom they can all find together.

But they've got the pages and the airwaves. If you want to get to the people who you finally need to vote for you, you've got to develop relationships with these people.

The best way to develop a good relationship with a reporter is to call him or her back, fight hard, and don't lie. If you do those three things you'll be all right. The working people, the deadline folks, want to be able to find you when they need something. If they want to check something out, if they want a quote, if somebody makes a charge, they want to be in touch. They don't care if you call them names, they view press-bashing as a part of life the same as we view candidate-bashing as part of our life.

The same day as the televised debate we won the Florida straw vote with 54 percent to 31 for Harkin and 10 for Kerrey. Things were looking pretty good.

Mary

Unlike the rest of my family, I was never a goal-oriented person. My only job objective was to have one that wasn't boring. But once I got into politics all I wanted was a real position on a presidential campaign. Since the 1988 campaign I'd wanted only one job, to be the 1992 reelection political director. In the interim I did everything I could to prepare for that job. If it went to someone better, that was okay. But if I didn't get it because of Carville I'd have to kill him.

The old theory—before the press went crazy in '92 and profiled all the behind-the-scenes politicos—was that anytime you were in the paper for anything other than flacking for your boss or the party, you were out of line. That, more than the substance of our relationship, was what worried me.

Marlin Fitzwater called from the White House at about five-thirty in the afternoon, December 4. "Can you be at the White House tomorrow at eleven-thirty for a briefing and a press conference?"

"Sure. What for?"

"We're going to announce the campaign team." Nobody had called to tell me if I was in or out.

I said, "Am I going to be on the campaign?"

"Yes."

"Well, what's my job?"

"I don't know. Right now you appear in the press release as a blank." He read it to me. Sam Skinner had replaced John Sununu as chief of staff; Bob Teeter would be chief strategist. "Joining the campaign team will be Rich Bond as [blank] and Mary Matalin, who will serve as [blank]."

"What do you think it is?" I asked Marlin.

"I don't know." Of course, even if he did know, it would have been inappropriate for him to break the news to me.

When we arrived at the White House we grouped up around Marlin to read the press release, this time with the blanks filled in: Robert Mosbacher, general chairman; Bob Teeter, campaign chairman; Fred Malek, campaign manager; Bobby Holt, finance chairman; Charlie Black and Rich Bond, senior consultants.

I was named political director.

It was unusual that the political director would be named at the same press conference as the chief of staff, the chairman, and the rest of the bigwigs. But if you look at that picture sans me you had five white boys up there. The reason I was announced in conjunction with the leadership was to have a woman in the picture. I had a very good and important job, but I was there to bring some legs into the photo op.

We were all gathered in Marlin's office. Even Sam Skinner's wife, Honey, was there. Everyone was giddy. It was a promising day. We moved tentatively into the Oval Office. President Bush was in a really good mood, laughing and thanking us and saying how much fun this was going to be. Then we walked to the briefing room to meet the press.

Now, I'm not a shrinking violet, but in this hierarchy mine was the lowest-level job, so I assumed the position of lowest-level guy and walked two steps behind. When we entered the briefing room, which was filled with reporters and photographers and TV cameras, I was standing to the rear of our crowd when I felt about six hands on my back. All the guys were laughing. They were pushing me forward to the front.

I instantly got the picture and started laughing, too. The press didn't miss it, they yucked it up. No one, including me, thought choreographing this photo op was sexist. Every one of these guys had consoled me about James, pushed me, trained me, pulled for me, and helped me get the job. They were all so happy for me.

That picture was all over, including on the front page of *The New York Times*. From then on the press made a standard joke of it: Mary and the White Boys.

There was another famous girl picture. Malek, Teeter, the President, and I were walking from the Oval Office down the colonnades to the residence. Malek and Teeter both pushed me into the picture. President Bush felt this jostling at his elbow, turned around, and gave a look like, "What's going on?" Then he laughed. "Oh, I get it," he said. "A photo op."

When we got back to the campaign office I said, "God, do you think you guys could be more conspicuous?" To which Teeter said, "Look, we hired you for your brains, but while you're here we're going to use the rest of your stuff." Every time we hired a male on the campaign, Teeter's right-hand woman, Mary Lukens, and I would say the same thing.

"Mary and the White Boys" was a headline that stuck. Neither I nor the campaign took offense at it, though we all wished the press would recognize that if you looked around the table at our senior staff there were a ton of women.

Our press secretary was Torie Clarke, who was not hired as a woman but because she was really good; we had to fight to get her. (Torie didn't really want the position, and when she finally accepted it said, "I figured if I didn't take this job I'd wake up and find a horse head in my bed.") Jill Hanson, our regional political director, was the most hard-nosed field operative, responsible for the critical midwestern states. The deputy communications director, who really ran that department, was Leslie Goodman. Finance director Margaret Alexander raised millions of dollars for the campaign, convention, and party. Mimi Dawson coordinated all the voter groups. Kathryn Murray tracked Clinton's every move and bracketed surrogates around his events. Alixe Glen tracked his every word and hounded the press to get our responses in their stories.

Women served as researchers, issue analysts, media buyers, advance men, speechwriters, field directors. This doesn't even scratch the surface. It took three women to manage my division—Pat Giardina, Rhonda Keenum, and Lisa Greenspan. We were in constant contact. The operation would have shut down without them. And the central control was Jim Baker's duo—Margaret Tutwiler and Janet Mullins. Nothing happened if one of those two didn't dream it up or approve it.

Pretty much the first thing I did after I got my dream job was make a really stupid mistake.

Our campaign hierarchy was announced the same week James was named chief strategist. Lois Romano of *The Washington Post* called both of us to get the story. I said to James, "You tell her that we're putting our relationship on hold." All I needed was for the first story on my job to be about me and not the candidate.

James said, "That is very stupid. It's like inviting people to follow us around."

"But we *will* be on hold," I argued, "because that's how presidential races work. And that's why you're a big jerk, and that's why it is stupid for you to take this job after telling me you didn't want to. Because we *are* going to have our relationship on hold, and you don't know what this means. You've worked a bunch of state races. So what? You don't know how terrible a presidential race is." It was a big Miss Know-It-All speech and I was screaming at him.

The people around me were all giving me professional advice: "If anything goes wrong, if anything leaks, you're going to get blamed. It's not fair, it's terrible, that's just how it works."

Their other line of reasoning went, "There will be so much focus and attention on your relationship, so much tension, that you will not be able to do your job."

The personal advice went: "It's too hard. Why do you want to have any relationship now?" (This was before most of them had met James or seen him in action. After they got to know him it was more like, "How *could* you?")

The objections were pretty strident in the beginning. People would say things like, "How could you go out with a Democrat?" Which I always thought was stupid. That's like saying, "I'm a Catholic, how could I go out with a Jew?"

While I was personally devastated by the fact that we were going to be working against each other, I wasn't at all intimidated by Carville's prowess. I knew from watching him in Pennsylvania that James's biggest strength was predicated on his ability to control everything. He is an autocratic campaign manager. He knows how he wants things to go and that's what gets done. That was state race thinking; that's not how presidential campaigns work. In a presidential, the guy who's in charge is the one closest to "the body." From where I was sitting, James was not that close. They had a bunch of Arkansans and other Friends of Bill, and nobody knew Carville. I knew him, and I knew that he was an acquired taste.

But who cared about Carville's problems? We had enough of our own. The White House structure had been demoralized and rendered politically incompetent by three years of John Sununu's dictatorship. When Sam Skinner came in, the first thing he did was bring in an efficiency expert to ferret out the problems. Well, the White House staff was like whipped puppies and the expert was a newspaper; they're Pavlovian, they see rolled-up newsprint and they start wetting the floor. Let's have some sensitivity here. The White House political operation wasn't going to do anybody any good for quite a while.

Because the actual campaign hierarchy was not appointed until December 4, no one had closed down their businesses or made staff support decisions. The election was only eleven months off and no one had done any real reelection work. What we did have was a fifty-state organization book that Clayton Yeutter had taken it upon himself to compile. It was a humongous undertaking that included every political fact that every field rep knew about every state. We sent it to the President and he sent it back, yeaing or naying the choices of state chairmen.

Right after that, to save money, the RNC shut down for the Christmas holidays. Congress went home. So I sat in my dining room in D.C. with my book of George Bush–approved state chairs, and Teeter and I went through the long list and began calling. As campaign chairman, Teeter made the first call. He was sitting in his Ann Arbor office with a one-woman support staff and a college intern. He would call each person on the list, state by state, and say, "George Bush would like you to be his state chairman and Mary Matalin is going to call you and give you the details."

I had one phone with two lines and a fax machine in my co-op—no secretary, no nothing. Teeter would dictate notes on the essence of his conversations with each of his contacts and his assistant would fax them to me. Then I'd call them up. Mind you, this is the reelection campaign of a sitting President.

In addition to setting up the fifty states' leadership, my job included setting up the biggest division inside the campaign, the political division. With Teeter's and Yeutter's sign-off I hired most of the field people out of the RNC, which left them with a huge hole. Their success was critical to our success, so we then had to work with them to fill it. Because of our work at the RNC, Charlie and I had a good historical perspective on the political personalities and their abilities, so Teeter and campaign manager Fred Malek would get our opinions on a lot of their staffing decisions, from research director to press secretary.

I got a vote on the campaign headquarters building and picked one that was across the street from a beauty shop, knowing full well that we'd never be able to ever get our hair cut again if there wasn't ready access. For us campaign women, that was the deciding factor. The salon gave the Bush campaign a discount because everybody stopped in there after they picked up lunch at the deli next door.

So, in December 1991, the functioning Bush campaign was Teeter in Ann Arbor, Malek in his little office, Bobby Holt in Texas, and me. By the time we opened the doors on January 7, 1992, we had the fifty state operations lined up, we had the internal and external field operation in place, we had all the top campaign slots filled, all the offices up, we were filed with the Federal Election Commission and on the ballot in all fifty states, the finance operation was humming, the RNC was back where it was supposed to be. As George Bush predicted, it was a miraculous turnkey operation and we began cooking with oil. Except for the fact that we were suddenly facing a primary.

Pat Buchanan came out of left field.

CHAPTER 7

James

I have a nephew named Jo Jo. He had cancer but he's doing fine now. But before he beat it, you never had a conversation where you didn't talk about Jo Jo. There was no such thing as sitting around the table telling family stories; you might do it for three or four minutes and then you talked about Jo Jo. "How's Jo Jo?" "What do you hear about Jo Jo?" "What's the doctor say about Jo Jo?"

Mario Cuomo was the Jo Jo factor. We didn't know if he was going to get into the race any more than anybody else, but we discussed it a lot. For a while there, each decision depended on what New York's Governor Cuomo was going to do. He was just kind of looming. The specificity of rumors was staggering. Somebody called once and said, "We got the word, it's definite. He's making an announcement at ten o'clock on Monday. He has the plane on the runway."

The thing about reporters to remember is that they like news. Bankers like money, actors like fame, reporters like news. In the late fall of 1991 they wanted Cuomo in the race because he would have been interesting to cover; he was a good story. And the truth of the matter is, we were watching him too.

Cuomo was a commanding presence. He was from New York; he was a great speaker with a built-in national following and a lot of media traveling in his wake. He would have been hell in a Democratic primary.

So much of a campaign is psychology. I had convinced myself that my guy was better. A better candidate. (This was December, I wasn't even thinking of a better president.) We thought Cuomo was getting in, so what you do is you prepare yourself, you convince yourself that this event is going to be good for you. It was like being in a locker room, talking macho, like playing Notre Dame on national TV. "Now people will really know how good we are."

The more intellectual reason for people hoping Cuomo would run was that he would do for us what Jesse Jackson did for Michael Dukakis early on: He would make us look even more conservative. He would be the reference point where we could identify ourselves as the real kind of New Democrat in the race.

I had a conversation with Governor Clinton about it. I said, "If Cuomo gets in, he can penetrate the South. He's going to get a lot of attention right at the beginning but it will fade."

"Do you think he's going to run?"

"Geez, I don't know. He's an unpredictable guy. I talked to somebody today who talked to . . ." We were all feeding off the same rumor tree.

On December 20 Governor Cuomo announced he would not run. I was talking to Georgia governor Zell Miller and he said, "I'll tell you the truth. For our business down here I would rather see Doug Wilder out than Cuomo."

A coherent strategy was beginning to emerge. We recognized that there was no way we could get elected without the Southern black vote. It was pretty clear that we had to win the collection of Southern primaries that constitutes Super Tuesday, and if you start taking out the whites and traditional liberals and other factions that would get spread around our opponents, you were left with the Southern black vote. The black contribution to Super Tuesday was huge. We win that, we win big—and I didn't think we could win with a strong Doug Wilder.

As the first black governor of Virginia, Doug Wilder would have been a formidable candidate in the Southern black community. He would have taken away exactly the voters that could put us over the top in a lot of Southern states. Bill Clinton was from the South; it would have been embarrassing for us to lose these primaries. We'd have gone from an across-the-board winner to a consistent runner-up, and lost the attention, the momentum, the confidence of the front-runner.

On January 8, citing the need to spend time on his duties as governor, Wilder dropped out. That was a big deal. If there was any such thing as a Clinton high command at the time, I think most people in it understood that this was a good day. If someone said, "Tell me five things that got Bill Clinton elected," I'd have to say that Governor Wilder's withdrawal from the race was one of them.

When you're working on a presidential campaign there is nothing else that goes on in the world except working on a presidential campaign. The world just sort of doesn't exist. You read the papers for items you can use *that day*. One of the things that did catch my eye was when President Bush was interviewed by David Frost and said, "I will do what I have to do to be reelected."

We weren't even working against George Bush at the time, our aim was to beat Kerrey and Tsongas and Harkin and Brown. But we were glad he said it. To a political strategist it takes about five seconds to say, "Well, good, why don't you get this economy moving again? Why don't you focus on what's going on? Now you see the real George Bush, this is what's in his mind. Why don't he do something to help the American people? If he worried more about them and less about what he could do to get reelected, then he would be in better shape to *be* reelected."

Here was a guy who was going to get slammed for winning an election in 1988 by not concentrating on the real issues, who was leading a country whose economy was not going well, and who people thought was out of touch. He was the guy who said, "Read my lips: No new taxes," and then raised taxes; who said he would create jobs and hadn't; who'd been the "Education President" and let the schools go all to hell, who'd played to the worst in the American character with the Willie Horton ad, and by his own admission he hadn't changed. Now he says he'll do whatever it takes to get elected. "If he wants to do whatever it takes to get elected, why don't he get this country moving again?"

No Democratic candidate had won a presidential election without winning the New Hampshire primary, and we went right after it. We started our television buys with a sixty-second commercial that Frank Greer conceived and produced. It was his baby and it worked. We wanted people to know that Bill Clinton had a plan for the future. So we developed one and put it on paper. In our spot the candidate said, "I'm Bill Clinton and I believe you deserve more than thirty-second ads or vague promises. That's why I've offered a comprehensive plan to get our economy moving again, to take care of our own people and regain our economic leadership. . . . Take a look at our plan and let me know what you think." On the screen was a phone number where people could call and get a copy. We also made the plan available at public libraries. What this spot said was that we were prepared, we had it on paper, we had substance.

On January 19 *The Boston Globe* published a poll showing us ahead of the field with 29 percent, Paul Tsongas with 17, Kerrey 16. We had moved ahead pretty good. We were all working hard and we were starting to say, "You don't want to think like this, but things could be over pretty quick." If it wasn't euphoria, it was certainly a feeling of strong optimism.

And it was all Clinton. The spot helped, but his performance in the state was making the difference. He was making appearances, heading up rallies, meeting and greeting voters, showing up at shopping malls and coffee klatches. It was a typical campaign and it was moving along quite nicely, impressing people, things were going well.

The truth of the matter is, I was feeling a little unneeded. Kind of like a field-goal kicker on a team that keeps throwing touchdowns. I was definitely a player in the campaign, I was in on all the decisions and had unlimited access to the candidate. If I wanted to go to New Hampshire I went out to the airport, got on a plane, and there was a staff person waiting to pick me up. I would hang out and look at the results from the phone bank and dilly around with a couple of ad scripts, work on some poll questionnaires, or drive over and look at a couple of events. I was kind of a big wheel in a campaign that was doing real well, and I was probably leaving work fifteen minutes earlier than I should have. I just wasn't much needed.

It was a heady time. Our chief media rival had dropped out, the chief strategic impediment to the campaign had dropped out, our poll numbers were right up there, and the other candidates were starting to have a hard time raising money. We had moved into a commanding lead in probably the most important primary state, which was most distinctly and assuredly outside of our region, and we had started to show some perceptible movement in national polls. We were rockin' and rollin'. I was making a contribution, but I don't think Bill Clinton would have been one percentage point worse off if James Carville, or any number of other people on the campaign, had gone to Australia.

There was even a little sense that, "Damn, maybe this thing is not going to be very hard." You would say out loud, "Well, given the

uncertainties of politics . . ." but the thought was there: Maybe for
once the Democratic party would get its act together and produce an
early nominee; maybe we wouldn't spend all our time hammering
each other and we could go out and hammer George Bush and the
Republicans.

The better you do, the more the media is interested in you. They
don't care about digging too deep until they think you have a chance
to be president, then it's Katy bar the door. Suddenly there were
reporters going through Little Rock—the *Los Angeles Times* had set
up a beachhead on a whole floor of a hotel. And there were rumors:
People were passing money around. Republicans. The word was that
if you wanted to get rich you could move to Little Rock and claim
intimate knowledge of the next President of the United States. Take
a number.

I became sort of oblivious to it. I said, "Look, I've been around this
shit. Y'all gonna let this stuff drive you crazy." I had become sort of
this battle-scarred veteran about what I called the strumpet circuit.
Maybe I was breathing just a little too much oxygen, feeling a click
toward being giddy.

Paul Begala and I are believers in the value of opposition research,
finding out everything there is to know about the people you're up
against and using it. What is not widely known is that we are equal
believers in knowing everything about yourself. Here we found a big
gap in the Clinton campaign.

Reports of past affairs between the governor and various women
had come up and been explained away—"Oh, man, this is the same
crap we've been hearing down here in Arkansas for years, it's all been
flushed out before"—and, not to our credit, we accepted it without
looking into the charges much deeper. Everybody operated on the
Smoking Bimbo theory: No one had ever come forward, on fire with
passion, and said, "We did it."

The issue may well have been handled previously, but an accusation in a state race, and the intense press scrutiny during a presidential campaign, are completely different. Illicit sex is a hot topic
everywhere, particularly in political races. Clinton was a relatively
young, good-looking guy with, deserved or not, a reputation. We
should have investigated this line thoroughly and been prepared for
any kind of onslaught, and we weren't.

Cokie Roberts of ABC had brought up the governor's purported
affairs during a televised debate a couple of days earlier, and you could

see she was excited by the story. Later in the week the tabloids were full of reports that the governor had had affairs with five women; a lawsuit from former Arkansas state employee Larry Nichols had named them. That had been an issue in Governor Clinton's 1990 reelection campaign, but the women had all denied it, the suit had been dropped, and the story had long ago been discredited. Cokie grabbed hold of what she could but nothing came of that either, and I was maybe a little cavalier about the whole thing.

I was sitting in the Bat Cave at nine in the morning, January 23, when George Stephanopoulos called. George and I were developing a good relationship. We'd check in with each other a couple of times a day to talk about events or news or plans. George said, "Do you think you can get out here to the airport in twenty, twenty-five minutes or so? The governor thinks it would be a good idea if you came up to New Hampshire with us."

"Sure. What's goin' on?"

"We think that there is some woman who has gotten paid a lot of money who's going to say something."

"Oh shit, George, this is the twentieth phone call. . . ."

"No, I think you better come out here and fly up with us."

I threw some things into a suitcase and got out there.

They faxed us a press release from the *Star*, a supermarket tabloid, and we all took a look at it. In an article being published that day a woman named Gennifer Flowers was proclaiming a long-running affair with Governor Clinton and claimed she had audiotapes of phone conversations to prove it. In fact, Gennifer Flowers had previously denied she'd had an affair with the governor and had threatened to sue an Arkansas radio station for saying that she had. But the *Star* was paying her over $100,000 for her story, and things will change when dollars get involved.

I looked at the press release and said, "Look, this has all been hashed out, it's old news."

What was new was the tapes. If these turned out to be authentic conversations with Bill Clinton, it could cause us a good deal of difficulty; she'd be the Smoking Bimbo. What had he been doing talking to her in the first place? He didn't have to tell me; I knew. She'd been a local newscaster. If you're the governor in a place like Little Rock, Arkansas, it's impossible *not* to know the local news people. I asked the governor about the calls. He said, "I can assure you there's nothing to them. The only thing is, she told me something one time about oral sex and the only thing I can remember is I just laughed, I didn't really know what to say. That may be on there. There was something about Cuomo but I don't think I said anything. . . . The only thing I can remember telling her is, 'Just tell them what happened,' or 'Just keep saying what you've been saying,' or 'Say the same thing,' or whatever." He told me exactly what was going to be on the tape.

Once we reached New Hampshire, George and the candidate flew on to a campaign event and I holed up in the Holiday Inn and started fielding phone calls.

It fell to me to track down Hillary. She was at an event in Georgia and I called a prominent Atlanta Democrat and close friend of mine, Sandy Thurman, and said, "You need to go to Mrs. Clinton and give her this number and ask her to call me. This ain't gonna be a pretty day."

So she called. I was a consultant; I think they probably liked me okay but I didn't have any real kind of relationship with them. I said, "Mrs. Clinton, the governor wanted me to transmit to you, and it's important that you know because you may get asked about it. . . . There's this paper called the *Star* and this woman named Gennifer Flowers . . ."

"Yes," she said, "I know Gennifer."

"She's claiming to have had an affair with the governor and it looks like the media might grab hold of this thing a little bit."

The first thing she said was, "How is Bill?"

I thought that was very illuminating. It wasn't "Dammit" or "I thought this was going to be a big mess." "How is Bill?" Not Governor Clinton the candidate, but Bill Clinton the man.

"As far as I can tell, Mrs. Clinton, he's fine. I know he wants to talk to you."

"How can I call him, what's the best number? I'm going to stay at this number; see if you can track him down."

It was decided by the candidate and Mrs. Clinton that we were going to jump on this thing with both feet. Bill Clinton did not have an affair with Gennifer Flowers. That was a given. I thought about it, and the clear weight of the evidence is that he didn't. First, he denied it—and I believed him. He told me everything that was going to be on that tape before we heard it. Second, Gennifer Flowers was taping him to sucker-punch him, and if they had had an affair, it would have been incredibly easy.

If any woman that I've ever had an affair with called, it would take five seconds to get something inculpatory on tape. Like, "Do you suppose they'll find the American Express card from the night in Dallas?" or "Do you think anybody saw you when you left . . . ?" I would happily engage in that conversation. There is no rational person who has ever done something they didn't want anyone to know about with the opposite sex who wouldn't understand that. It would be very easy, particularly if you were an object of curiosity to the nation, to entice you into being part of it. Try as she might, the tape had none of that.

When Governor Clinton got back to the Manchester airport there were a couple of reporters and a CNN camera crew there to meet him and you could see the story was going to have legs. People and reporters were starting to ask about it. We had to face it head-on. Quickly.

We tried to get the Clintons on ABC's *Nightline*, but it was a logistical nightmare. We wanted them together, sitting next to each other in the studio. They had to be able to touch each other. If this was a real couple they wouldn't be facing accusations of infidelity separated by the entire Eastern Seaboard; they couldn't be separated in any way, it would have sent the completely wrong message. But the weather was bad and Hillary couldn't get out of Atlanta, we couldn't get out of New Hampshire, so Mandy Grunwald went on in their place.

We brainstormed to come up with a coordinated strategy. It was one of those fortunate days when we didn't have the facilities for a conference call, which is probably why we got something done. We decided we were going to run an all-out offensive in the media and make it a referendum on whether people wanted to hear about the real issues of the campaign—jobs, health care, the economy—or just some paid-for tabloid journalism. The governor himself came up with the ideal phrase: "We think this election is about more than Cash for Trash."

Mandy went out and gave one of the better surrogate performances of the campaign. Every time Ted Koppel tried to maneuver the conversation back to the Flowers allegations, Mandy kept focused. "Here we are just a couple weeks before the New Hampshire primary," she said. "People are about to go out there and vote. . . . They have real concerns. And you're choosing with your editorial comment by making the program about some unsubstantiated charges that . . . started with a trashy supermarket tabloid. You're telling people something that you think is important. That's not context. You're setting the agenda and you're letting the *Star* set it for you."

For my part, I'm almost embarrassed to admit it, in between Diet Cokes and a gazillion cups of coffee I kept thinking, "Hey, I have a function now, I'm here, I'm thinking, I'm earning a paycheck." There was action.

It was the most selfish feeling I ever had. It was a very difficult time for the candidate, his wife and family, but I actually felt good. "I have a role." It must be like soldiers who learn to love war. They're sitting there amongst the carnage, looking around, thinking, "I hate to say it, but I *like* this." I knew I was wrong for thinking that but I couldn't deny the thought crossed my mind.

Now there was an enemy. I never liked running against Democrats; I didn't hate Bob Kerrey or Tom Harkin. We were so far ahead, and my candidate was so much more skilled, that you would see the opposition and you were nice to them. That was unsettling. But now there was a sleazeball rag that had paid $100,000 to someone for a story that had no basis in fact and was calculated to do one thing: sell papers. It was the height of yellow journalism, and as far as I was concerned anyone who touched the story was just making the water more yellow.

On Friday the media was talking about the story but they didn't know how to cover it. The networks didn't know what to do with it, the dailies were starting to pick it up. The way the media gets around this is they say, "We're not going to cover the story, we're going to cover the media covering the story." At which point the media evades all responsibility and gets to cover its favorite subject, which is, of course, the media. They're very enamored with themselves.

One problem when you're criticizing the media is that you need them to air your criticism. Otherwise you're shouting into the wind. We were telling the press, "You're overplaying this," and they were saying, "Well, you *are* on TV." Is it true that we kicked the story by agreeing to go on the air? Yes. But we had no other choice.

George was talking to the people at CBS, who had the Super Bowl that Sunday. George suggested that the Clintons appear on *60 Minutes* directly after the game, and CBS accepted. We negotiated terms.

That day Paul and I drafted a memorandum to Governor Clinton outlining talking points for the *60 Minutes* appearance. It's one of about three memos in history that I had my name on that I actually read.

TO: Governor Clinton
FROM: Paul and James
RE: Talking points on *60 Minutes*
DATE: January 24, 1992

A GOOD QUOTE TO USE

The text for your appearance should be taken from Heming-way's *A Farewell to Arms:*

> "The world breaks everyone and afterward many are strong at the broken places."

Make a virtue out of the fact that your relationship has been tested; that you've overcome problems and emerged "stronger at the broken places."

SOME THOUGHTS ON TONE AND DEMEANOR

You are not the victim. Maintain the calm and secure demeanor you've had throughout this. Reporters and voters are like horses and dogs—they can sense when someone is fearful. This is the opportunity you and Hillary have been waiting for all along; the chance to answer this once and for all and put it behind you. Your self-confidence is contagious: The staff and the press and the voters will all take their cues from you. That's what leadership is all about.

Unless you're addicted to blue suits, we'd like you to wear a sweater. (We can't think of anyone who wears a suit on Super Bowl Sunday.)

Don't bitch about the press—that's our job. With the exception of an occasional jab at the tabloids ("They're the folks who say Elvis fathered a child with a nun who gave the child up to a circus family in Yugoslavia"). Beyond that, don't complain about how the press has treated you—you can only look like a whiner.

It's two against one in your favor. We'll get to Hillary's role in a little while. For now let us tell you something you already know: Hillary's the best thing you've got going for you. On camera, it's just you, Hillary, and interviewer Steve Kroft. We like those odds.

60 Minutes *is not out to* "get" *you.* A corollary of the "Don't Be a Victim" rule. What *60 Minutes* wants is good TV. What we want is a chance to state our case to the public, and to put the thing behind us. The ground rules Georgie negotiated for you make it damn near impossible for them to ambush you.

HILLARY

She is our ace in the hole. Like you, she needs to be calm and confident. Unlike you, she can leap to your defense (and, more importantly, to your family's defense) if Steve goes across the line. Her bona fides as an attorney and children's advocate make her far more than some little wounded bride, dutifully sticking by you because she's got nowhere else to go.

She holds the ultimate trump card. At some point she can calmly tell Steve: "The only two people Bill needed to ask for forgiveness are God and me. I believe God has forgiven him; I know I have."

We'll go into this in greater detail in the prep session, but at some point, when y'all feel like Steve is going too far, prying too much, Hillary needs to interrupt and say: "Look, Steve, we've already been more candid, more forthcoming than any political couple in America. We're not perfect. But we *are* a family. It's our relationship; our marriage; our family—and at some point we have to draw a line to protect our family."

THE GROUND RULES

The deal Georgie cut for you is everything we want: The promo says only: "This week on CBS's *60 Minutes*, an exclusive interview with Governor and Mrs. Clinton on their life, their marriage, and his campaign for the presidency." That's half the battle. They are going to promote the hell out of this show— especially since CBS is carrying the Super Bowl and the residual audience will be sizable.

George's other concessions from CBS include: No playing of tapes of any kind; no one appears in the piece except interviewer Steve Kroft, you and Hillary. The segment will run 15 to 18 minutes, but the interview itself will be considerably longer.

The camera is always on you. 60 Minutes is famous for their extremely tight close-up shots, particularly those which come in tight while someone else is speaking. So know that you're "on" even when Steve is asking a question or Hillary is giving an answer. They use a multicamera format, which means less wear and tear on y'all as well as the interviewer.

Finally, we'll get into more details in the prep session. But remember what Confucius said: *"A leader must be a dealer in hope."* Deal in hope. Be confident—you're the luckiest guy in the world . . . and you know it. Show that you're strong at the broken places.

Frankly, I don't know if Governor Clinton (a) ever saw this memo, or (b) ever read it. But it represented Paul's and my best take on what the *60 Minutes* interview was all about.

On Saturday morning I was in Washington at the Madison Hotel to quell a rebellion among our fund-raisers. They thought we were gone. The overwhelming feeling was that there is a predictable pattern to how political sex scandals run and we were in the clutches of a vicious cycle. They were saying, "This thing is going to kill us. Look what it did to Gary Hart. How can you ask us to continue raising money when we are going to be out of the race?"

We weren't thinking we were gone, we were just thinking of how to get through the next hour. We didn't know what the effect of the Gennifer Flowers story was going to be; we didn't know if the polls were going to collapse; all we knew was that the whole thing hinged on the Clintons' appearance on *60 Minutes*.

I was at war. In the strangest way my cylinders were clicking. "We are going to fight back aggressively and we're gonna win this thing!" I told them. "We're not going to let this thing beat us. This is nothing but a trollop and we are going to smash the shit out of her in the news media. We're going to be on *60 Minutes*, the governor and Mrs. Clinton are going to tell the American people the true story. We are not letting this thing go for one minute. We understand this is a serious story. We have it under control and we are going to bounce back; we are going to be strengthened by this. Let the sunshine soldiers and summer patriots go their way. Not only will we survive this but we will be strengthened. We've got them where we want them; we're surrounded, we can shoot in any direction and hit the bastards."

It would be safe to assume that my language was a combination of what you would hear in a Marine Corps barracks and a football locker room. I told the fund-raisers that all this was being driven by money and Republican politics, and that any sense that we would give up at this moment would be capitulating to some of the most cynical forces in American politics. I felt that with a coordinated, well-put-together counterattack, not only could we beat this thing back but we could be successful.

We flew almost immediately to Boston to talk to another group of concerned Democrats and I ran into my first-ever media feeding frenzy. They were screaming at the governor, holding their cameras up above the crowd and snapping away without looking. People with microphones were crawling on people's backs and screaming, *"What about Gennifer Flowers?" "Did you have an affair with her?"*

For about ten seconds I was almost crushed to death. My arms were pinned to my side, I could not move, and I was lifted off the ground by the crowd. I kept shouting, "Stop! Stop!" and some radio guy from Boston yelled at me, *"Shut up. This is a story!"*

We flew from Boston to New Hampshire for an event, and came back that night. *60 Minutes* was going to be taped at the Ritz-Carlton in Boston at noon on Sunday. We prepped for it at the same hotel, on Saturday night and Sunday morning, with the election on the line.

The main concern was what the candidate and Mrs. Clinton wanted, and at every point they said we had to go big and take this on. The governor said, "Look, you know, I'm not going to run for president and have Gennifer Flowers define who I am. I'll answer any question anybody asks. I'm not afraid of this, I'll take it on."

I was struck by his lack of self-pity. I've been in other political crises when politicians have felt and acted like the victim: "Why are they doing this to me?" None of that from Bill Clinton.

By this time the campaign had contracted. There was no screaming horde at the prep session. In a crisis there are no long meetings, no agony. The people in the room were the candidate and Hillary, George, Paul, Frank Greer, Stan Greenberg, Mandy Grunwald, scheduler Susan Thomases, and me.

The governor and Mrs. Clinton knew what they wanted to say. The major personal and political objective of the *60 Minutes* appearance was to show to America that Bill and Hillary Clinton had a real marriage. In my view, if people thought that union was a sham then they wouldn't believe in the candidate's sincerity on any other issue that really mattered. I thought people would accept the idea that marriages go through hard times; they would know it from personal experience, they could relate. But if this wasn't a marriage this wasn't a man.

A lot of times in campaigns, you know something and the people in the campaign know something, and you forget that everybody else out there doesn't know the same things you know. We all knew the Clintons loved each other, but I felt that the average American didn't know much about Hillary and would be suspicious of her. They'd say, "Well, she's just sticking with him because he's a big powerful governor and she wouldn't have much of a life without him. This is sort of a marriage of convenience." I said to her, "They need to know, Hillary, that you are a substantial person. They don't know that you were named one of the hundred most influential lawyers in the country. They don't know that you're a partner in the oldest law firm west of the Mississippi. They don't know that you were the first student to give the commencement address at Wellesley. They don't know that you were a top student at Yale Law School. They don't know that you head up the Children's Defense Fund. For all they know you're some housewife whose whole career is tied to her husband and that you are willing to be some sort of docile wife so you can get your hands on the good china at the White House.

"No one can think that you were forced into this. I mean, millions of women in this country are living in some sort of quasi-slavery here." We were all very simpatico on that.

We posed questions that we knew Steve Kroft would ask. "Did you have an affair with Gennifer Flowers?" You've got to say no. The governor was clear that he had never had sex with Flowers. Clearly he and Mrs. Clinton had decided—and I don't think this was a bone of contention among the people in that room—that, with reference to the larger question, they were just going to say, "We acknowledge that we have had difficulties in our marriage and we don't think that we have to say any more." Governor Clinton said, "People get it." Everybody took their view of what he meant by that. I suspect that I know the view of 95 percent of the American public when he said that, and I think no one thought he was being disingenuous or clever.

I woke up at about four-thirty that morning, January 26, and I could not stop crying. I don't mean tearing up, I mean sobbing for hours, drained, weeping piteously. I was just so scared, mostly for the Clintons; the torture you have to go through to run for president. History was going to judge us; this was going to be in books. I got maybe an hour of sleep—I probably hadn't slept more than an hour on each of the past three nights—and then had to face that day.

My first meeting was with Paul and George and Mandy. We got together, read the Sunday papers, and went over strategy. Everybody was dealing with it in their own way. I was talking and crying, talking and crying. We went through what our goals were. The mechanics of how the show would work; what the political strategy would be; where to draw the line; what language to use on the adultery question. We divided those up for presentation to the governor.

At about ten o'clock we went over it again. Susan Thomases and some family friends were up and everybody was sort of quiet, very respectful, like there was a big game getting ready to be played.

Mandy Grunwald had several important insights. She pointed out that 60 Minutes had Steve Kroft doing this interview, not Mike Wallace or Morley Safer. It was going to be his big moment, they were going to make him a star. First, she said, be ready for him to be more aggressive than you might think, because he wants to prove himself.

Then, the interview would be edited; they were shooting about an hour of tape for a fifteen-minute segment. If you really want something to stay off the cutting-room floor and make it on the air, she said, use his name. In the middle of the interview say, "You know, Steve, the whole point here is . . ." It was a little thing and it was brilliant.

The taping took place at the Ritz-Carlton. The candidate and Hillary and Kroft were in one room with a cameraman and a sound technician, and the rest of us campaign people and CBS producers and technical folk were in another. We were trying to keep the number of people talking to the governor to a minimum.

Clearly the *60 Minutes* strategy was to get the candidate to say he had been unfaithful. Steve Kroft was pulling at him with questions. The stage was set for this revelation, and it would have made big headlines and great TV. But Governor and Mrs. Clinton resisted. There was a line they would not cross. Once CBS saw what was happening they tried to create the news. *60 Minutes* senior producer Don Hewitt knelt down next to the governor and said, "Just say yes or no. Let's get through it and go on to other things."

For every time that a politician lies to the American people, a media person lies to a politician five times. They had told us they didn't want to make this just about Gennifer Flowers, but they had no intention of making it about anything else. I mean, if a network says, "We're going to do an interview, and there's some talk about sex involved, but we don't want to make it just about that," that doesn't count as a lie, because everyone knows they're lying, including them. You don't even believe them when they tell you.

The big advantage in doing *60 Minutes* is that we had a huge audience. The disadvantage was that a lot of what we wanted on the air ended up on the cutting-room floor. There were some powerful scenes that were left out. You can only mention Steve Kroft's name so many times. That was our big mistake. We should have done it live-to-tape, no edits. We negotiated for that but couldn't get it; CBS refused. We should have insisted on it.

I had the usual political thoughts during the taping—"Damn, I wish he'd said it this way," "Good job, I like the way they handled that." Our prep had been good, there were no surprises. But mostly I just watched and thought, "What do they have to go through? All of my life I have dreamed about being in a presidential campaign. Is this what I really wanted?" I was like a dog catching a car; was this the hubcap I was getting ready to eat?

There are times in your life when you choose to be a political professional and times when you choose to be a human being. During this taping I couldn't help but be a human being.

When it was over I ran to Clinton. I couldn't stop crying. I just sobbed and he held me.

Hillary is like me: She really likes room service. I don't know if it's all about rising from humble beginnings, but I think there is something really fun and decadent about room service, and so does she. Before the debate I had said, "Man, whatever you do, tell them to put about three cold Budweisers on ice." And when we got back to the governor's suite I chug-a-lugged them. I know it sounds ridiculous, but that damn ordinary mass-produced Budweiser tasted better than the best glass of Château Margaux anybody ever had. I will never forget how good that beer tasted.

Then I went back to being a political professional.

If campaign professionals have a fault it's that we always like to act, to intervene. We always think there is something we can do to improve our odds. If we were heart surgeons we'd be in there cutting. We didn't know what the thing would look like when *60 Minutes* got through editing it that night, or how people were going to react to it, but we thought it went pretty well. We felt better because maybe we'd got it behind us.

We didn't even do a postmortem. We said, "Let's don't go out and tell the media what happened, we don't know what's going to get edited. Let the event speak for itself." No one wanted to talk about it. In fact, rather than look even a half hour backward, Hillary and Harvard professor and big FOB Bob Reich ran a big policy-wonk discussion about job training, the state of worker skills, education, and income growth in America. The whole thing must have gone on for forty-five minutes, and if you'd just walked into the room and heard the tenor of the conversation, you'd have thought we'd all gone to church together that morning. We did an event on the New Hampshire coast and then flew back to Little Rock so the governor and Mrs. Clinton could watch the show with Chelsea.

The damnedest thing happened, just to show you how I'm wrong about everything. I thought we might be done for. ABC News ran a national telephone poll Sunday night and 80 percent said Clinton should stay in the race. We were in Mississippi and Louisiana for events the next day, and for all my agonizing, when we met the party activists and asked them, "What effect do you think it'll have? What are people saying?" they said, "I don't know, we thought it was pretty good. Nobody's talking about it too much."

They would soon enough. That day Gennifer Flowers held a press conference in New York City and said she and Governor Clinton had been lovers for twelve years. She played the audiotapes of what she said were phone conversations between her and the governor.

So she and the *Star* held this press conference and played the tape. Three hundred and fifty reporters showed up. CNN covered it live.

All three networks led the nightly newscast with the story and reported what was on the tape. Flowers and the *Star* wouldn't give the media a close-up look at the first-generation tape, so the networks had to copy it live from the press conference. She answered few questions, so there was only her accusations and no cross-examination. And they ran with it. It was the worst piece of journalism I have ever seen.

The media were more interested in the story than they were in the truth. They couldn't verify the authenticity of the tape, they knew they were dealing with a suspect organization widely known to give subjects large sums of money for stories, but they were so hot for this story that they just dove in.

The only bright spot of the whole event was Stuttering John. Stuttering John is a radio stringer for Howard Stern and he has a speech impediment. He stammers and takes an age to say what he's got to say, and he is known to ask what can politely be called impertinent questions. He got up at the press conference and called out, "Did he wear a condom?" I mean, even I had to laugh at that.

Do I think that the media and the networks were proud of the fact that they ran unverified tapes as news? No, I don't think so. Everybody makes mistakes. They made a hell of a one. They will admit it to you individually, but they won't do it to the people who watch them because if they admitted to such lowlife activity, they might actually lose their audience.

"Have you lost your minds?" I'd yell at them—reporters, network executives, anybody I could find—and they couldn't justify it. They'd say, "Well, we did it because ABC was doing it and CBS was doing it, so we had to do it."

I said, "Hey, you're like a bunch of school kids." I was mad. I was smoking mad.

Their response was, "Gee, it must be hurting you in the polls."

We decided right away to launch the attack on Gennifer Flowers because we saw an opening: People thought she was a liar or worse. We did a focus group and found that women reacted much more negatively to her than men. One woman took a look at her and said, "She looks like a liar. And she ought to learn to dye her roots."

I was the first surrogate to go after her. By going with the *Star*, taking the money, playing the aggrieved lover, she had put herself in the line of fire, she was fair game. I thought, "Just don't call her a whore—but short of that, let 'er rip."

A lot of the national media felt guilty about the 1988 campaign, where they'd been used by the Bush flag-factory photo-op people and the Willie Horton smokescreen and never got to the issues. They'd always be saying, "That isn't the kind of campaign we want this time." I got on them pretty good. I went to the back of the campaign plane, where they all sat, and really hit them hard.

"You people are like a bunch of drunks. Y'all get drunk in 1988 and then you dry out for four years and then you go up to Columbia, or wherever y'all have your little seminars, and promise yourself that you are not going to do it again. You dry out. And then Gennifer Flowers puts the first goddamn jigger of whiskey on the bar and you are all killing each other to get at it. You get drunk again and now you have a bad hangover.

"In fact, you people are goddamn amazing. You went to college, you got a degree, you are a professional journalist, and you are letting someone like Gennifer Flowers dictate your coverage. What are you doing? This is the crack cocaine of journalism. Y'all are saying, 'I want to get off it, we don't want to cover this story. Gee, we hate this.' But look at your crotch and there's a big wet splotch there."

If there was anything good that could be said about this Gennifer Flowers extravaganza it was that the country and the media was riveted on us. Our name recognition skyrocketed. We were the only game in town. A Southern babe, a Rhodes scholar presidential candidate, a compelling wife, a sleazy tabloid, sex, lies, audiotape—how could you care about another candidate? No offense, but no one was going to cover a Tom Harkin press conference when you had Stuttering John asking Gennifer Flowers if Bill Clinton wore a rubber.

A few days later we got word that Los Angeles TV station KCBS had hired a tape expert, Anthony Pellicano, to examine the Gennifer Flowers tapes. Flowers and the tabloid had refused to let him at the first-generation copy, but even with a duplicate he said the tape had been "selectively edited" and was "suspect at best." He said it was his judgment that some of her conversation might have been dubbed in later, making Governor Clinton seem to be responding to things he'd never actually heard.

I went nuts. What the hell kind of national press corps do we have when no one even thinks to verify these tapes before they pump them all over the airwaves? These people are supposed to have three sources for every fact; where were they when their ethics were being tested? Out looking for ratings.

"Why don't we have the same report that now *we know for a scientific fact*, determined by an expert even from a second-generation tape—the sons of bitches wouldn't give him the original—that these tapes have been edited and distorted! Why don't you lead the goddamn news with that one? I'll tell you why, because you all are more interested in putting some bimbo on the air than in getting at the truth. And the truth is that this is just sleazy tabloid trash and you all should be ashamed of yourselves."

I complained relentlessly and didn't get much satisfaction. I was mad, and I stayed mad. Still, CNN was hitting us pretty good. I was told by people working for CNN at the time that they were livid that we had canceled an exclusive appearance for the governor and Hillary on *Newsmaker Sunday* to go on *60 Minutes;* there is little doubt in my mind that CNN aired the Gennifer Flowers press conference live as nothing more than a payback. Though CNN is one of my favorite networks, I believe they were angry at us and it affected their news coverage.

CNN was shameful on this subject, as was every other media outlet. I think they acted horribly, irresponsibly. It is now more than two years after the fact, we won the election, the people vindicated us, and I'm still mad about it. I mean, 350 reporters showed up at that press conference. Three hundred and fifty reporters wouldn't show up if there was a cancer cure.

Mary

We all sat around and watched the Gennifer Flowers saga and thought it was pretty funny. We made fun of her roots and made fun of the press and said, "God, if that's Clinton's taste in women . . ."

Not that we cared. An Atwater maxim was operative: Never interfere with your enemy when he's in the process of destroying himself. Furthermore, when you're in a primary, the other party's campaign does not even exist. You'll get to them soon enough, but for now you're completely focused on beating the guy on your own ballot. Time is the most critical factor in a campaign, and any amount that

you spend thinking about or acting on something that doesn't affect
your own race in real terms is a total waste. Clinton wasn't even the
candidate yet, so whatever he did to himself, or they did to each other,
didn't affect our candidacy one whit. We had no dog in that fight.

We knew the Democrats were saying we were negative campaigners and had branded us trash-talkers. We did not need to reinforce
their negative image of us, particularly on an issue like philandering,
so we kept out of it. The word went out: Nobody will say anything
about Clinton's personal life. When the press calls for comment: No
comment.

But in our offices all operations ceased and every television was
turned to CNN.

The maximum goal in professional politics is "No surprises." So
when something so unprecedented, so sleazy, so weird was unfolding
before our seen-it-all-before eyes, we were riveted. Here was this
low-rent lounge singer, who was fairly articulate, definitely committed, and *she had tapes*. For campaign operatives, whose whole exis-
tence is dedicated to scripting every minute, foreseeing every
problem, predicting every scenario, we actually felt sorry for the
Clintonistas.

When the campaign opened we had begun a nice ritual: At the end
of every day everybody would come into my office and drink red
wine, watch the news, and just chatter. It had nothing to do with the
campaign, just shop talk. This was shop talk to the max. We weren't
thinking about the effect this episode might have on our campaign,
we were debating, "Oh, my God, what would you do if you were in
a campaign and something like this happened to you?"

The issue of the Clintons' marriage had been around for a while. In
September 1991, Bill and Hillary Clinton had gone in front of the
Sperling Breakfast, a political-insiders group of reporters. They had
come right out and said they'd had problems in their marriage but
that they loved each other and were together now and that's all that
was important. Though they had been whispering about it for weeks,
the reporters were so wimpy when they got the chance to follow up,
they squished. They did not do a Gary Hart.

I theorized that the difference between the Harts and the Clintons
was that Lee Hart looked so pained and pitiful as the "abused" wife.
Women—in fact, most people—can't stand when a guy humiliates
his wife in public. The guy deserves whatever punishment he gets. In
Hart's case it was rabid scrutiny by the press, followed by the public
execution of his presidential ambitions.

In this case, the wife wanted to forget and forgive and stand by her man. They had worked it out, so it's nobody's business. There was nothing pitiful or beleaguered about Hillary. In fact, she was defiant, tough, and sassy. She likely saved the day, and clearly was going to be a force—not background noise—in the campaign.

I presumed that if they'd gotten through the Sperling Breakfast in September, it would not be a campaign issue. More important, we knew that the people in New Hampshire were in such a state of economic anxiety that any issue that did not directly relate to easing their immediate concerns wasn't going to be more than a blip on their political screens.

We all agreed that the best thing the Clinton campaign could do was what's done in court: discredit the witness. Step number two would be to discredit and humiliate the press. Which is exactly what they did. The key to their success was the intensity and consistency with which they went after both Flowers and the media.

We were pretty impressed with the way they jujitsued the Flowers fiasco. In fact, it gave us the heebie-jeebies. Even though we were absorbed in our own primary, the audacity of the Comeback Kid candidacy got our attention.

Of course, I also paid attention to Gennifer Flowers because of James Carville. This was one of the ways we'd keep in touch during the campaign. Reporters who had just met him were calling me and saying, "This guy is a weirdo. He has not shaved in three days. He pads down from his room in the morning with no shoes on, then eats the same thing every day. He's a mess, he talks a mile a minute, you've got to do something."

I was worried about him. The Gennifer Flowers situation was the kind of complete anxiety immersion that can make a campaign's life miserable. So I called him up. "Are you okay? Is everything all right?"

He seemed surprised. "Yeah, sure, what's the matter, what's goin' on?" Like nothing was happening.

"James, you can talk to me."

"I don't know what you're talking about. It's a tough campaign here, we're making headway. Kerrey's commercials really stink."

Earth to James.

That set the pattern for our communications through the entire campaign; there wasn't going to be any communication on what was really going on. He told reporters more than he told me. I was not trying to find out anything about the campaign. What was to find out? It was all there on CNN. I was just reacting to reporters telling me that this guy had lost his mind. Truly, all I cared about was him.

Our campaign got off to a rocky start. We didn't have a made-for-TV economic plan. We were being criticized in the press and by the public for being a foreign-policy presidency. And now we were being challenged in New Hampshire by a Reagan Republican who had the certain ability to derail the President's campaign.

Even though Pat Buchanan announced in December that he was going to run, no one took him that seriously. Most of the people around President Bush considered it a rhetorical candidacy. Buchanan was assuming the mantle of the Ronald Reagan conservatives, evangelicals, and right-to-life wing of the party who believed that President Bush's only mission was to continue President Reagan's policies, and that he'd failed.

Our initial reaction to the Buchanan candidacy was, "Why is he doing this?" Obviously we were aware that the right was sending a message: "Without us, you can't win. And if you don't listen to us, we'll make sure you don't win." They were very concerned about their influence, their whack in the Republican party. But we spent a considerable amount of time speculating as to the psyche of a candidate who was obviously going to lose. There was a lot of inconclusive chatter regarding his motivations—why a good Republican would jeopardize the entire party's future for his own individual agenda— but nobody really went and asked him to get out.

Personally, people liked Buchanan. Those who had worked with him in the Reagan White House said he was a gentle man and an ideologically pure true believer. They knew his wife, Shelley, and his sister Bay, who was running his campaign. He was a gregarious and sweet man in real life. George Bush liked him. There was a ubiquitous sentiment inside the party: "We like Pat Buchanan, he's a good guy. We don't know why he's doing this but we know he's a loyal Republican so let's not start a fight." He was, after all, a Reagan man, and Ronald Reagan's first rule, his eleventh commandment, was "Thou shalt not speak evil of fellow Republicans." We presumed that Buchanan would have his little fun, send his message, and then get out.

Meanwhile, now that we had our campaign machinery in place, we had to focus on the next Herculean task: integrating our operation with the mammoth White House.

The White House is not a campaign vehicle. Although everything an incumbent administration does has political consequences, the whole operation bends over backward to avoid the appearance of politically motivated policy formulation. Sununu had gutted the White House political office to the point that they weren't even equipped to do damage control, which left President Bush vulnerable to exactly the kind of attack Pat Buchanan was best at: anger and resentment.

The administration's job was to set an agenda. The campaign's job was to run on it. My little cog in this big wheel was to make sure the states were holding up their end. I reported to Teeter and Malek. The chain of command in the political division was me and the trusted trio of Pat Giardina, Rhonda Keenum, and Lisa Greenspan, then my deputies Bill Canary and Dave Carney, then the regional field directors, then the state executive directors, who were our links to the individual state chairmen. I wasn't involved in the minute details of each state day to day; I was the problem solver. I'd let everybody do their job until they needed some help. I told them, "Don't come to me unless there's blood on the floor."

You become a campaign state chairman by having whack or respect or a big name, or by bringing a whole team with you. (Of course, the best way to become a chairman is to be a friend of the candidate.) State chairmen are usually sitting governors, if you have them. It was Bob Teeter's theory, and Lee Atwater's as well, that governors know better than anyone how to run state campaigns because, obviously, they've won for themselves. John Sununu had been Bush's state chairman and governor of New Hampshire in 1988. Our first problem was that there was no love lost between Sununu and New Hampshire's sitting governor, Judd Gregg.

The one person who knew anything about running a campaign in our first primary state was David Carney. Carney had been on Governor Sununu's staff in the state, had been planted in the White House political-affairs office when Sununu arrived as chief of staff, and had survived the Skinner takeover. No one at national headquarters really understood the nuances of the internal battle between the Sununu and Gregg operations, not to mention the real "enemies," the Buchanan renegades. Carney knew the terrain inside out and within days wrote an excellent state battle plan. It became increasingly clear that we needed to have our own guy on the ground, and the only guy who could do it was Carney.

I called him at the White House on a Friday and said, "You've got to start by Sunday night." When we were setting up our national operation a lot of people were running around whining, "What's my salary? What's my title? Where's my office going to be?" Carney's only question was "Will my pinball machine fit in the office?"

Dave Carney is a giant teddy bear of a man who sweats in the dead of winter, likes smoking cigars in confined spaces, and dislikes finishing most sentences. His brain works faster than his tongue. He was thirty-two, an extraordinary political strategist and technician, but most important, a wacky and hilarious man. He filled his office with toys from wind-ups to punching bags. Though he doesn't wear it on his sleeve, David is a committed, consistent conservative who knows more about policy than most operatives. I nicknamed him Stud Muffin, which of course he hated.

The only problem with Carney was that Governor Judd Gregg, along with his father, former governor Hugh Gregg, wouldn't let him into the state. The Greggs weren't letting a drop of Sununu-infected blood, no matter how Republican, cross state lines. They threatened to quit. Bob Teeter and I made our first pilgrimage to New Hampshire to try to smooth things over and find out what it was the Greggs needed to quit quibbling and start hustling.

As is often the case in national-state rifts, a lot of it had to do with budget.

There are finite resources and they are controlled by the national campaign. The New Hampshire people had submitted a budget that Teeter and I thought was a joke. They wanted twice what it took to run a primary, and they weren't laughing. They had us by the short hairs.

Campaigns behave just like businesses or the government. Every division—political, communications, research, field operations, advertising, voter outreach, advance, and scheduling—submits a fake, fat budget, and then they fight. We never did that. I told Canary and Carney not to. Just go in there with what you want and don't budge: "This is nonnegotiable." Because it was real and we didn't fake anybody out, Teeter and Malek gave it to us. When we wanted an increase we had good credibility to go back and ask for it.

Of course both parties do their best to circumvent the campaign laws. No sooner does Congress legislate something than operatives figure a way around it. It's a big game. For instance, the state campaign has to pay staff salary and expenses if operatives are in the state for more than four consecutive days; otherwise the national campaign pays. In critical early states, you're always looking for ways to get more money into the state budget. So every four days New

Hampshire operatives would caravan across state lines, sleep in Massachusetts or Vermont or Maine, get up in the morning, turn around, and drive back to work, thereby getting around state limits.

Advertising is also always a bone of contention between the state and national, because so much money is involved. In a New York race, for example, a media buyer's cut could be in the millions; in smaller states the amount is proportional. Obviously the state politicians wanted their vendors to get that dough and themselves to get the chit. The national campaign always wants to have a centralized vendor for bulk discounts, not to mention a consistent message, and usually lays down the hammer on the issue and gets no fight. But this time things were so stressed that it got finessed so more New Hampshire politicos got a piece of the action.

Carney was great and everybody knew he was great. So finally everyone agreed that, in the best interest of George Bush, we'd have conference calls every day between the national campaign, meaning Carney, and the Greggs and all the local leadership wannabes; we'd run this state by remote control.

Meanwhile, on the home front, we were trying to determine the appropriate level of personal campaigning for the President versus Buchanan's gadfly, send-a-message candidacy. We didn't want to overcampaign since it would be perceived as a sign of weakness. On the other hand this guy was making significant headway by virtue of the fact that, having gotten a late start, we had a largely paper campaign and for a while the Buchanan Brigade were the only ones doing retail campaigning.

Buchanan started doing well. He began raising a lot of money from his national direct mail, and he was running a cheap but effective commercial. It showed President Bush saying, "Read my lips: No new taxes" over and over, and it *ran* over and over and over. We didn't need this; Democrats do this. We were all Republicans, and whatever difficulties he had with Bush policies, we thought Buchanan should have been thinking of the greater good of getting a Republican reelected. Maybe he thought we were a shoo-in and he couldn't hurt us. Maybe he'd rather be right than president. No matter. Buchanan got that pit-bull spirit and began snarling.

He made saturation advertising buys, meaning he bought every ounce of time on every television and radio station he could. It was so repetitive that people in our New Hampshire organization would call us and say, "My four-year-old is going, 'Read my lips,' 'Read my lips.' "

The ad and the attitude was slipping into the vernacular, and our numbers were slipping, slipping, slipping.

We were snakebit from the beginning. The worst place in the world to start a reelection campaign was in the state whose economy had fallen the fastest and hardest since 1988. They had been on an economic roll and now they had one of the highest unemployment rates in the country. The recession hit New Hampshire hard and there were no signs of recovery. Here were hardworking people to whom the idea of losing their homes, of food stamps or welfare or any government dependency, was unfathomable, and now it was happening to them. These people were not just scared, not just angry; they were freaked out. George Bush took his campaign to them.

Campaign '92 legend has it that Ross Perot or Bill Clinton brought town hall meetings to the presidential campaign. The fact of the matter is that from 1979 on, George Bush had been doing them. We would put notices in local newspapers, post signs in small-town shops, coordinate them through the local party apparatus, and run these events. We called them Ask George Bushes. The audience would be first-come-first-served; Bush would sit on a stool or stand in the middle of the room and, unscripted, take questions.

In New Hampshire I called them spit-on-your-shoe events, because you never knew who was going to show up and I worried that people were so upset they were more than apt to take it out on the guy who was sitting right in front of them and spit on his shoe.

President Bush began campaigning in New Hampshire on January 15, a little more than a month out from primary day. Carney ran the show from his office in Washington, but for our first day on the road I was assigned to in-state spin control.

In most small states you can go into the major media markets and have local events that have statewide impact. It's called campaigning wholesale. New Hampshire is a retail politicking state. Voters don't want to read about you, they want to touch you. You go into their houses. In New Hampshire and Iowa people are used to having coffee klatches with presidents. Carter and Bush both won Iowa in 1980 by literally visiting with ten people at a time.

We had decided we would physically bring the President into the state no more than three times; we didn't want to encourage the idea that the Buchanan candidacy was significant. Furthermore, the physical act of campaigning in New Hampshire is grueling. Because we didn't want to do it often but still had to cover the entire state, we overbooked him, scheduled multiple stops in multiple cities into his first day, in the dead of winter, with a cranky national press corps in tow.

New Hampshire is too small to navigate by plane, so we had to do long motorcades from one event to another, and in between each event the President sat down with local anchors or print reporters. It was a long, frantic, nonstop day. You don't think of it as a major concern when you're scheduling on paper, but it takes more energy to do a campaign day in a cold climate than it does in a hot one. You're taking your coat off and on and slogging through snow, constantly going back and forth from overheated rooms and auditoriums into the freezing-cold outdoors. You never have the right shoes. It's exhausting.

It was a wet, rotten, cold, slushy-snow day. My feet never dried out. At each stop, getting off and on and off the buses, I kept thinking, "Some hippie lunatic with a ponytail is going to stand up and start screaming at the President, 'George Bush, you don't care!' " Most of the time we were talking to uncommitted voters; we didn't know what was going to be asked and we didn't know how it was going to be answered.

President Bush himself would probably concede that formal speech-giving is not his preferred mode of communication, but he is very good at relating to people one on one and has a breadth and depth of knowledge that allow him to answer every individual question. He can laugh with audiences and tell anecdotes with answers in them. He is comfortable. He liked these events because he could tell he was getting through. In two national campaigns I never saw him go into an Ask George Bush, even with a hostile audience, where they didn't leave loving him. Of course, I was never completely at ease; each time we went into a new one with a potential for upheaval I'd worry.

We walked into a spit-on-your-shoe in the Exeter town hall and people were just standing there. It was stuffy and crowded inside; they still had on their overcoats, their arms were crossed, most of them seemed to be scowling. My stomach didn't feel too good. The President was introduced to polite applause.

We knew our economic message wasn't breaking through. The President's stump speech said, basically, "We have a lot of work to do but the economy is poised to recover. I'm trying to explain why you should have confidence. I've heard your message and I know you're in pain."

But I shouldn't have worried. The audience asked some hard questions and the President hit them out of the park. By the end of the

Ask George Bush, the applause was resounding. President Bush doesn't like to speak from a text; he prefers to work from cards that give him bullet points on various topics. It was our job to make sure the topics got covered, but depending on the environment he often took a tangent. Having won this crowd, he dispensed with his quasi-prepared remarks and just started winging it. In a typical example of presidential verbal shorthand he said, "Message: I care."

On the bus, the White House press corps refused to believe it had been an open, unscripted event. My mission that day was to convince these scribes that the people who had showed up were real voters and not shills. In fact they had registered in a telephone survey as "undecideds" and been invited, over the Bush-favorables, on a first-come-first-served basis. Their questions were their own. But there was evidence, for example, that other campaigns, like Clinton's, were stacking their audiences or pre-scripting their questioners, so the media thought all candidates did it. My job was to disabuse them of that notion. Though the reporters grudgingly agreed that the President had done a good job, they just groaned or laughed at me; they refused to believe that it hadn't been a con job. Their feet were wet, too.

Though President Bush was doing well face-to-face with small audiences, the overall message was lost on the New Hampshire electorate at large. The President had been badgered for saying previously that there was no recession, which is what Sununu, Treasury Secretary Nicholas Brady, and his other economic advisers had been telling him: There is no recession. And technically, by precise economic definitions, they were right. But try telling that to people who were having a hard time. President Bush did, with little success. It was like Dukakis trying to explain disallowing the pledge of allegiance in schools; it was an impossible job. You don't win an emotional argument with a hyper-rational response.

So in an overreactive course correction, the President said to ninety business executives in Portsmouth—and, worse, to a gaggle of national press—"I think I've known, look, this economy is in free fall. I hope I've known it. Maybe I haven't conveyed it as well as I should have, but I do understand it."

Usually at an event, even before it begins, you can tell what you're walking into. You can tell by crowd size, energy level, body language. In a room that loves you, people have brought homemade signs, which are clearly distinguishable from what the advance guys routinely make.

The last event at the end of this very exhausting day was with a group of insurance-office workers in Dover. There was a hum in the room; you could feel people were charged up. People were lined up for autographs and pressing forward to take pictures of the President as he made his way to the stage. Everyone was smashed in, standing on their tiptoes, all abuzz.

Campaign events always unfold in the same sequence: First the Secret Service sweep into the room, looking grim and officious, tiny sound and speaking devices wired in their ears and to their wrists, which they touch constantly. A path clears as everyone goes "Oooooh." Then the support staff, all of us looking dopey and self-conscious, file in like court jesters, and the excitement mounts. Then the press enter—faces the voters recognize from TV—and promenade to their assigned positions on a riser facing the stage. That's the point at which people forget they've been waiting hours and get thoroughly caught up in the "aura." Local politicians, congressmen, governors, senators proceed to the microphone. Buzz, buzz, buzz . . . bang: "Ladies and gentlemen, the President of the United States." Music/applause/flashbulbs . . .

This time, unlike the other events of the day, there wasn't polite applause, there was screeching: "We want Bush! We want Bush!" This didn't feel like a plant tour or a business revitalization event; this felt like a rally.

The President delivered a very invigorated version of his stump speech, and the crowd loved it. He understood that times were bad, he said, particularly in New Hampshire, but he was going to make it better. He was in touch with them, he did care, he did get it. . . .

People were understanding, nodding, agreeing, applauding, smiling. Again, the President decided to wing it.

For a month now Pat Buchanan and the entire Democratic field had been mercilessly and relentlessly bashing him. In an effort to dispense with the partisan and political cat fighting, and to dismiss any perception of self-pity, the President told the crowd, "Remember Lincoln, going to his knees in times of trial during the Civil War and all that stuff? You can't be. And we are blessed. So don't feel sorry for—don't cry for me, Argentina." He was laughing.

The crowd loved it. It got a good laugh. Everyone in the room got it, understood it, received it in the context and with the humor with which it was delivered. I was smashed in with the press and I burst out laughing. So did they. If you had traveled with George Bush for any length of time, which all of these people had, it was a totally normal, endearing example of that form of English which had come to be known as Bushspeak.

Hammering his point home that campaigns were tough, he could cut it, the President quoted a song by the Nitty Gritty Dirt Band. He'd been doing it all day. The line went, "If you want to see a rainbow, you've got to stand a little rain." We all thought that was apropos, and that he was pretty cool for quoting them. Well, this time the President couldn't pronounce the band's name. It was like trying to say "Peter Piper picked a peck of pickled peppers," only country. So it came out "Nitty Ditty Nitty Gritty Great Bird." When he stumbled, everyone thought it was funny; he was undoubtedly not the first person to do so.

So the last event of the day was a gas. Hot crowd, good connect, good substance, lot of laughs. Both the local and national operatives went home thinking we'd seen a fabulous end to a better campaign day than anyone had expected. We could not have been happier with it.

Imagine our surprise, then, to wake up the next morning and find we'd been witness to a disaster.

A besieged Bush, the stories went, who shouldn't be in New Hampshire, a state that he won handily in 1988, is fighting for his political life.

"Come on! This was a great day!"

The press tore into us. Their bottom line was, "Clearly showing his wear and tear and frustration, President George Bush couldn't even get out his name yesterday. . . ." The press corps had decided on its line and wasn't going to be sidetracked by a little thing like what had actually happened. Their analysis was that George Bush shouldn't have had to campaign in New Hampshire in the first place; the reason he was President was because he'd won an upset there in 1988. And here he is on his hands and knees in the state that most represents how out of it he is, a state he won in 1988, a neighbor state to his summer home since childhood, in Maine. He shouldn't even be having a primary, a President should not have to be out campaigning. And his message is "I care. I get it. I understand." What kind of a campaign is that?

The White House press corps sees the President and the Vice President and the cabinet every day. They're cynics; it's a professional prerequisite. The whole outlook of these reporters is, "This guy puts on his pants one leg at a time like everybody else. His job in life is to lie to us, and our job is to catch him—and if he's not lying, his aides are."

Local reporters, who are usually herded onto separate buses, are not quite so jaded. Being in the midst of a presidential cavalcade is not an everyday occurrence for them. Plus, they're always looking for the local angle and trying to get an interview with the President. That's a big deal and they get excited about it.

The White House press corps, sequestered on their own bus, generally could not care less. They are not impressed with campaign events, or for that matter, with seeing the President. I was assigned to their bus. They were freezing, they didn't want to be there, particularly in a primary campaign that shouldn't have been necessary. The only reason they heard the "Argentina" line was because the audience was getting off on it. They had heard the same speech with minor variations seven different times that day, they were bored, milling around, waiting to be able to file their final stories, get a drink, and go home.

There is a pack mentality to the pencil press, and there are leaders of the pack. It's usually the institution, not the reporters: *The New York Times, The Washington Post, The Wall Street Journal*, the *Los Angeles Times*, the wire services, the newsmagazines. The leaders of the pack are unknown to the public at large, but campaign operatives make it their business to know everything about each of them. The names change from campaign to campaign, but in 1992 among them were Andy Rosenthal, Robin Toner, Ann Devroy, Doug Jehl, Jack Nelson, Dan Goodgame, Mike Duffy, John Harwood, Howard Fineman, and assorted columnists.

We called them the big feet. They all hang around together, they're on buses, planes, motorcades; they drink and eat together, they converse, they exchange notes, they draw conclusions that lesser reporters are afraid to disagree with. They determine the "Line of the Day." It's all informal, but everyone gets it.

First the wires file their stories. They service the most newspapers and file continuously, and they keep updating their pieces as the day or event unfolds. Then the other political writers from the dailies file. If these writers vary significantly from what the wires ran as their lead, their editors will go back to them and say, "This is not what's running on the wires. Reconstruct your story."

I'm not making this up. Timothy Crouse's 1972 campaign book, *The Boys on the Bus*, depicted it, and I have asked reporters, "Is this really how it works? If you submitted something totally different from what was on the wires and what was running in other papers, would they ask you to rewrite it?" They all say the same thing: "Yes."

Inside the body of their story they can differ on little things, that's okay. But not on the line. (For the record, editors all deny it.)

I tried to spin Bob Novak on the bus and his outlook was, "Well, what is he doing here anyway?" and "Buchanan is showing surprising strength in the state. He's got a better organization and you guys are a paper tiger."

Now, it's not like the six top daily reporters literally get together and say, "We don't like George Bush and we're going to screw him by really dissembling on this day." But they do all bounce off each other and write stories to fit into a common contextual analysis. Of course, they're not supposed to analyze, they're supposed to report, but that doesn't stop them. They say their job is to offer an "interpretive analysis," because the electronic media covers the actual event. The pack agreed the story that day was that George Bush was floundering, he was rusty, he was a disjointed campaigner, "Don't cry for me, Argentina." If anybody had come back from that day and said, "In a resounding triumph George Bush had an unexpectedly good day on the campaign trail, he won crowds and hit back questions," *that* would have been the big story.

It was at this point that we began to realize that we weren't going to get our message out, that "our" reporters were not going to cut us any slack for a couple of good events, but were going to dwell on a larger context.

President Bush had said the economy was "in free fall." The press glommed onto that one statement and contrasted it with what he'd said before—"There is no recession"—and we had a problem.

Even "Bushspeak" was getting clobbered. Where once it had been endearing, the press now saw it as another sign of the President's ineptness.

Politicians give the same speech over and over. While you may tailor your remarks with a few local specifics, no candidate creates a whole new script each time he or she addresses a crowd. It's near impossible to bring genuine emotion to the same phrases seven times a day, and it's positively impossible for the press to have an emotional reaction to those phrases after the umpteenth hearing. But the danger is, because they're bored and the press is bored, candidates may come to think they're boring their audience. That's the kiss of death to a politician, so the natural tendency is to rush through prepared remarks, no matter how well written or fresh the ideas may actually be to the listening audience. The entire concept becomes so familiar that the candidate starts thinking and expressing himself in verbal shorthand. George Bush does this in spades. The press, who heard him speak almost every day, understood the sentence fragments completely, and earlier in his presidency would insert them in the proper context. The ideas always came through. The meat was what mattered.

But the pack theory of the moment was that Bushspeak, once an enjoyable asset, had all of a sudden become a campaign liability. Bush was supposedly having difficulty communicating with the people. What better metaphor than what the press called his "tortured syntax"?

Pat Buchanan was hammering him for not listening to the people. The Democrats were all saying he "didn't get it." The press took up the cry. In national campaigns, everyone juxtaposes you with your most recent predecessors. And although the media once appreciated Bush's accessibility and informality in comparison to Reagan's limited and controlled appearances, next to the Great Communicator's glib, smooth, canned recitations George Bush seemed even more fragmented. The President went from being amiably if peculiarly communicative to dangerously inarticulate and out-of-touch the moment he said, "Don't cry for me, Argentina."

After they started making fun of Bushspeak, some in the media took a very ugly extra step and raised the question of whether the President was overmedicated, suggesting that perhaps something was wrong with the administration of the supplements he took for his thyroid problem, that he was physically and chemically disoriented and that was why he was speaking in sentence fragments and losing his way.

That really ticked me off. It ticked everybody in the campaign off. The President has Graves' disease, not a common ailment but one very easily controlled by medication. To ascribe to a health or mental deficiency something the President had been doing most of the years they had known him was inexcusable. The subtext of "an ailing President" was introduced into the campaign, as if he was drugged or sicker than anybody knew. That was a real reach and a very revolting intimation.

I became extremely bitter toward the press. I'd watched clips from when George Bush had run for Congress decades earlier, and he made the same hand gestures then. He'd actually said Dana Carvey's tag line, "Wouldn't be prudent." The guy had been like this his entire life. They knew it. I'd call them and say, "You guys, get a grip. What is President Bush saying now that's any different than what he ever said? Why was this cute six months ago and now it's some example of failing leadership or ailing health?"

What complicates things is the rhythm and cycle of a press story. It's trickle-down journalism, and this is why all major stories have an extended shelf life.

The wires and the big feet cover a story first and it appears in the daily national papers. This is the first big bang. The major dailies' editorials follow the first stories, then all the other local papers follow. Then the newsmagazines, which publish weekly, come out several days to a week later, depending on when the story first occurs. By that time big-feet reporters for *The Washington Post*, *The New York Times*, *The Wall Street Journal*, and the *Los Angeles Times* are on to the next cycle of the campaign, or the next cycle of analysis. But the story's not done. As soon as the campaign gets a story under control with the national press corps, it is just trickling out to New Mexico or South Carolina, where people in the field have to handle it.

It's like food poisoning, it takes two weeks to get this stuff out of your system. So two weeks later, in locales across America, they were still harping over "Don't cry for me, Argentina."

During the first stage you'd just be frustrated. It was somebody's job, usually press secretary Torie Clarke's, to call up reporters and blast them if there was anything even remotely inaccurate in their articles. It was pretty rare for the best reporters to have a blatantly wrong fact, but if you found one, you could make the major dailies print a correction or retraction. Of course, it would show up on page A39 in microscopic print rather than in the lead paragraph on page one, where the original story had appeared, but that's a given.

More frequently we'd complain about a distorted or unfair ambience, or if we felt the piece was one-sided. Not that the facts were necessarily wrong, it was more editorial distortion of tone than misrepresentation of fact, and we'd grumble or shout a collective "This is unbelievable."

The grocery scanner story is a legendary example of factual and editorial unfairness.

You've heard of it. This was the scene where President Bush is on a checkout line and seems absolutely incredulous, like he's never seen a grocery scanner before. Like he's completely out of touch with the facts of daily life for most people in this country. Like this wouldn't be the most damaging image imaginable to a candidate who was already being castigated for being upper-class and having no contact with the economic concerns of real people. A cultural stun gun.

The problem is, it never happened. Never. But once it got reported, it was a story that wouldn't die. It lives to this day.

Andy Rosenthal, an otherwise honorable reporter, who wasn't even there, took the story from a pool report and penned a page one story for *The New York Times*, headlined "Bush Encounters the Supermarket, Amazed."

But check the facts. The President was visiting the exhibition hall of the National Grocers Association convention, where all kinds of advanced supermarket gizmos were on display. These weren't everyday grocery scanners; *no one* had seen these, the President and the press included. The President was right to be intrigued and impressed. Everyone in the press knew it. But the story was such a compelling metaphor to make their point, that it took hold in campaign mythology. From then on it was an article of faith with much of the public that Bush was out of touch. We had to fight that through the entire election.

CHAPTER 8

James

They started calling him Slick Willie again. It's a Southern metaphor for someone you can't quite pin down. There was a chain of pool halls in the South by that name, and it was a moniker the governor had been saddled with by political opponents in Arkansas. They didn't like that he had an answer for everything, and that sometimes the answers changed over time.

The fact that the governor had evolving positions over a fourteen-year period was not particularly surprising to me. I would have been shocked—and to some extent disappointed—if every view he had in 1978 remained unchanged in 1992. Bill Clinton had been elected, defeated, then won reelection and served for ten years. You just can't be governor for that long and not have people go back through your record and find changes in your positions. It's called evolution.

I find it appalling that a lot of well-established people don't understand how important political skills are to governing. And the first political skill is to get yourself reelected, because if you don't do that you are never going to get anything done. Another is understanding the art of the practical and the possible. So the appearance of the phrase "Slick Willie" was not particularly noted by me or anyone on our staff. Shows how wrong you can be.

We seemed to be weathering the Gennifer Flowers storm. Our figures showed that support was eroding, but not quickly. We were still talking a pretty good game: "If we win New Hampshire in spite of

Gennifer Flowers, or even if we come in a close second, it'll be a hell of a victory." Clearly Paul Tsongas and his plain talk were starting to make a connection with New Hampshire voters. He was picking up a point or two, but nothing drastic.

Jeff Birnbaum of *The Wall Street Journal* had been asking some questions regarding Governor Clinton and the draft and we knew they were fooling around with some kind of a story. In every election he'd run in, someone would try to call him a draft dodger. There was this legend, the Holy Grail of Arkansas Republicans, of a photograph of Bill Clinton sitting in a tree at an anti-war demonstration at the University of Arkansas burning an American flag. It's a legend, like the alligators in the New York City sewer system—one of those old stories that never were true.

We knew this story was coming, but we didn't do anything about it. There is no other way to put it, our research on ourselves stunk. We didn't know nothing about nothing. Same as on Flowers: "Look, he's been Governor of Arkansas six times, the paper doesn't like him, if there was anything like any of this it would all have been found and discovered. This thing has been looked at and relooked at. It's old news."

Unfortunately, at this point the candidate was far ahead of the campaign. Most of the political skill was with the candidate and we were letting him carry all the weight.

The story came out on a Thursday. The headline read "Clinton, Like Others, Missed the Vietnam Draft; Accounts Now Differ as to What Happened Then." Birnbaum interviewed a secretary at the candidate's old draft board and the former army ROTC recruiter and commander at the University of Arkansas, and questioned whether Bill Clinton, as a twenty-three-year-old Rhodes scholar, might have manipulated the draft process so as not to have to go to Vietnam. "People directly involved with Mr. Clinton's draft status," the paper said, "contradict his version of what happened."

It wasn't the lead story on the networks that night, but I didn't like it.

Governor Clinton was getting exhausted and sick on the trail. The day before the story came out he'd had a high fever, and when he spoke at Concord High School there was so much sweat beaded up on his face he looked like a boxer. He said, "Do you think they'll vote for a dead man?" The road people canceled a speech at Dartmouth and put him to bed.

We had to get into the television news mix at the same time as reports on the original story, so the governor went out and gave his response, which was, Look, I got a high draft lottery number, which is why I didn't go. I went into Arkansas ROTC just like lots of other people but I wound up changing my mind and submitting myself to the draft. I was a Rhodes scholar, I got a deferment. I got a high draft lottery number and I was never called.

Which is essentially what happened. The problem is there are a thousand details between here and there.

Because he was so exhausted the governor wanted to go home for the weekend. He could relax at the governor's mansion like other people kick back at a summer home.

I said, "This is a screw-up. We ought not leave. Why don't we go to the Ritz-Carlton in Boston and don't tell anybody we're there. He likes that, Hillary likes that. But we've got to be in the news mix this weekend." I had learned the hard way that in a really contested race you've got to be out there every day. You lay back for one damn day and it hurts you. "Tsongas is starting to come, if we miss two days out of state . . ."

"This is what he wants to do."

It was one of those gruesome fifteen-people conference calls. Everyone was tired from fighting Flowers. A campaign gets tired sometimes. They need the time off. You argue with the candidate and the people close to the body say, "If he goes up there and he's tired he is going to make a mistake, it is going to be worse." I said, "Aw, the hell with it, okay, but you are going to regret that we did this."

So the campaign went down to Arkansas. The next day I got a call, "Come on down, we gotta get ready. The draft story, man, it's got some currency. They ain't bashful about covering this."

The key to the whole deal was the University of Arkansas ROTC commander, Colonel Eugene Holmes. Whenever this issue had been raised in the past, particularly during gubernatorial elections, Colonel Holmes had been supportive of Bill Clinton. When Paul and I had come on board in December we'd gone through it with the governor. He'd said, "I've been through seventeen elections in seventeen years, boys. In every one of them this has come up; every one, they try to make this issue. And for every one I say the same thing: 'Go to Gene Holmes. Gene Holmes is a Republican, Gene Holmes is a retired colonel, Gene Holmes is the man at the Arkansas ROTC, and he will tell you—I won't even speak to him, but he will tell you that I didn't do anything wrong and I didn't get drafted because I didn't get a low number and I got into the Arkansas ROTC by the normal rules.' "

This time, for whatever reasons, Colonel Holmes told Birnbaum a different story. "Ethically," Holmes said, "I think he should have stayed in ROTC. He'd given his word and was backing out." After he said that he stopped giving interviews. He has rarely spoken to the press since.

This was a big surprise.

Unfortunately, the *Journal* didn't tell its readers that this guy had told a different story for twenty-two years. Colonel Holmes had never once wavered in his support of Bill Clinton, and the governor thought he knew why. He told me that, as a student, he had gone to the colonel and said, "If you think I have an obligation to you I won't go back to Oxford, I'll go to Arkansas." But it was a feather in Arkansas's cap to have a Rhodes scholar and, the governor said, Colonel Holmes had told Clinton that he appreciated the gesture but that he could go back to England and finish up his studies. Governor Clinton felt that he and Colonel Holmes had gotten along pretty well, and that Holmes had supported him because of the honorable nature of his offer. Unfortunately, that line of defense was now unavailable to us. The candidate said, "There is no way I could say that because it would look self-serving and I probably wouldn't get backed up."

In essence, what the campaign was faced with was that Holmes had changed a story that he had given consistently over the last twenty-two years. Anyone—the press, the campaign, the opposition—who tried to reconstruct details was always going to fall somewhat short and be subject to varying memories and interpretations of the events.

To tell you the truth, it is my belief that as a twenty-three-year-old student who was passionately opposed to the war in Vietnam, Bill Clinton probably did what he could legally do to avoid the draft. He hated the war and he didn't want to get his ass shot off. I understand that completely. I was in the Marines at the time and, to a person, the returning veterans would say, "Man, don't go over there. You ain't lost a goddamn thing not being over there." When I found out my orders were not to go, they said, "You lucky son of a bitch. Let me tell you something: You don't want to go."

But in politics you are on record, and often the things you can say are limited by the things you've already said. Bill Clinton ran for Congress in Arkansas in 1974 and for attorney general in 1976. He was first elected governor in 1978. Bill Clinton would not have gotten elected governor of Arkansas in 1978 on a platform of "It was a stupid war, I didn't want to go and get my ass shot off." In 1974 and again in elections since, he had been circumspect about his draft record, saying just enough to satisfy reporters but not enough to inflame voters. It was not an unusual political decision. The draft system was flawed and, within the law, he used whatever means he could to keep from getting drafted.

I think voters pretty much understood that.

It's like if you have a daughter. She's twenty-one years old, she's going to school, and she's home for the holidays. She comes in at seven in the morning. Now, you say, "What were you doing?" She says, "I drank too much and I fell asleep on the sofa." Do you really want her to say, "Well, I got drunk and I got laid"? No. Do you have a pretty good idea as to what happened? Yes. Do you think she's being dishonest with you? No. She just isn't telling you who she fell asleep next to. Now if she says, "I was out feeding the hungry," that's not going to work.

At some level, when you run for public office voters want to draw their own conclusions. It would have been another thing if Clinton had been a hawk on Vietnam, like some of these chicken hawks who talk about how good the war was and how good it was for everybody but themselves to go fight it. As a political consultant I would find Dan Quayle's draft record much more perilous than Bill Clinton's. Clinton's position was totally consistent with his political beliefs at the time; he didn't want to fight that war and he didn't want anybody else to go fight it.

Stan Greenberg, in Washington, polled on Sunday night. Usually you get the raw data late at night and collate it and distribute the results by seven A.M. We said we'd count it ourselves. So I was sitting at the governor's mansion in Little Rock talking about the schedule for the next week while everybody knew we were out in the field waiting on this half-sample. At about one in the morning I called Stan.

"Hey, it's Carville."

"Meltdown. It's worse than you can imagine." Greenberg doesn't sugar-coat his numbers. "We have dropped fifteen to twenty points. Tsongas is way up."

I didn't say anything, just hung up the phone.

There weren't but five or six of us sitting there, including the governor and Hillary. I said, "We all need to get a good night's sleep 'cause we are getting ready to go into the toughest fucking week of our lives. This thing is not good at all."

"Well," they asked, "what are the numbers?"

"We have had a big drop. It's a half-sample, you never know how this thing is going to work out, they've got to check and see if they got the regions right. It might change a few points, but you know with Stan . . ."

"How bad?"

"Well, we don't know for dead certain, but it's a problem."

There is a language, I'm sure, that doctors use to tell you that the tumor is malignant without saying, "You've got two days to live." Consultants say, "It's a problem."

When you drop 15 points in three days you don't need a poll. We knew. Pretty soon ain't anybody asking a whole lot of questions.

"We got trouble in River City," I said. "Negatives skyrocketing. This whole thing is falling apart."

The governor was furious. "We're dropping like a turd in a well," he said. He was sitting there in a baseball cap, sweatshirt and sweatpants, his running clothes, and he started pounding on his thigh, saying, "The campaign isn't on top of things. *It's killing us!* This campaign isn't working. We're losing the educated people because Tsongas is out there on the deficit. Do you know that sixty percent of the people in New Hampshire have college educations and all the educated people are against us now! All the work I've done, all the effort I've put into this—blown away because all you political people think all we have to do is run television spots."

The governor has a temper and he was letting loose. Paul and I tried to tell him that it wasn't TV spots, it was the draft, but he was just pounding his leg and shouting.

Mrs. Clinton, also in sweat clothes, cast all of that aside. It was clearly the draft that had caused this crisis and she knew it. She turned to Paul and said, "Okay, this is what we're going to do. We need to fly up there tomorrow and Bill needs to give a tough, passionate speech. Paul, you and George write it. 'Fight like hell.' You know, 'We're going to fight back.' We need radio commercials."

In the thirty seconds it took Hillary to get our act in gear the governor had finished his tirade and was ready to roll.

"Hershel Gober," he said suddenly. Hershel Gober is a by-God medal-winning Vietnam War hero and one of Bill Clinton's best friends. He is still carrying Vietcong shrapnel in his body. He looks, acts, talks like John Wayne and he was Clinton's veterans secretary in Arkansas. "You call Hershel, day or night, and he'll make a spot." Clinton was into it.

Hillary truly knows her husband. Where Paul and George would try to force the governor to face the issue at hand, she knew he was just letting his anger out. So she let him, and then moved on from there. In a minute we had an agenda of six things to do that kept Paul and George and policy director Bruce Reed and David Wilhelm up all night. They wrote the "fight like hell" speech and made radio spots. They got our fund-raising director, Rahm Emanuel, on the speaker phone and revved him into overdrive until he was cursing and screaming and promising that he was going to squeeze the money as hard as he could, that these people were not going to cut and run on us. What could have been a morose night of licking our wounds and seeing our skeletons in the mirror turned into something pretty exciting and emotional.

We flew back up to New Hampshire the next day. I said to the governor, "Look at it this way. All of your life and all of my life has been training for this week. I mean, everything that we are, we got to have a perfect week. We don't have any room for error. We can survive only with perfection. Our schedule has to be right, we can't stumble."

We got off the plane in Manchester and I walked on ahead with the governor and Mrs. Clinton. George and Paul were about ten yards behind us. It was February 10, George's birthday. ABC producer Mark Halperin walked up to George and slapped him with a piece of paper. "You've got to read this. I've got Jim Wooten and a camera crew here; we want to interview the governor."

The five of us crowded into an airport radio room the size of two toilet stalls and started reading. It was a letter from Bill Clinton to Colonel Holmes, dated December 3, 1969.

The phrase "I want to thank you, not just for saving me from the draft" kind of jumped out. So did "maintain my political viability within the system."

George and Paul, being too young to remember much of importance about 1969 except the lineup of the New York Mets, didn't understand what that letter meant at the time it was written. To them it was an admission by a potential soldier that he wanted to avoid serving his country in time of need—a death sentence to anyone who wanted to run for president.

But when I read the letter I found it wasn't that at all. It was an eloquent statement by a young man with strong convictions, whose friends were conscientious objectors, who opposed the war and didn't want anyone to fight it. In it he wrote: "The draft was justified in World War II because the life of the people collectively was at stake. Individuals had to fight, if the nation was to survive, for the lives of their countrymen and their way of life. Vietnam is no such case."

I admired that young man. "This letter is your best friend, Governor!" I shouted.

Hillary kept saying, "Bill, this is you! This is exactly what you were going through. This sounds like you, I can hear you saying this. This is terrific. This is just what it was like. Now they'll understand!"

The generation gap was about a hundred miles wide.

We bought ads in all the New Hampshire papers and printed the letter in its entirety. Taken piece by piece the letter could have killed us. You had to read the whole thing to understand—and we had to bring the whole thing to the public, we didn't want to look like we were being dug out of a hole squinting.

Nightline wanted the governor, and we wanted him to go on. We weren't hiding, we weren't flinching. We had convictions *and we'd had them for twenty-two years.* We wouldn't let Governor Clinton read the letter on the air—clearly we didn't want the words "thank you . . . for saving me from the draft" coming out of his mouth to be excerpted and made into a sound bite or an attack ad—but we agreed to let Ted Koppel read it in its entirety, which he did.

While we were prepping, Mandy came up with one of the best lines of the campaign. Clinton ultimately used it: "I'm going to try to give this election back to the people, to lift the cloud off of this election. For three weeks, of course, I've had some problems in the polls. All I've been asked about by the press are a woman I didn't sleep with and a draft I didn't dodge."

I thought very early on that Bill Clinton was at his best interacting with people and that the best way for him to influence people was to get to them directly. This was a piece of strategy I was very hot on. I called George and said, "Look, we have got to get him out there at every juncture. We have to do these call-in shows right now because of our credibility. We got to get some college professor to screen and make sure we get ordinary people and tell them they can ask anything they want. We can't taint these people, we can't suggest that they ask something, that they not ask something. The media gets a whiff of that and we're through. And Clinton has to be available to reporters after it is over." George was totally on board, as was TV producer and longtime FOB Harry Thomason.

That's the way it happened. From Wednesday on I have never seen anybody perform at anything near the level of Bill Clinton. He was giving his best speeches, he was reacting with crowds. People were starting to say, "You've stopped the erosion, you might be coming back a little." Our polls showed that we had bottomed out and were, in fact, doing a little better.

Clinton's view was that he didn't want anybody standing between him and the voters, he wanted to meet them all. He actually believed that he could win this thing hand to hand.

Now, New Hampshire is a pretty small state, you could get a lot done hand to hand, but you can't win an election that way. You couldn't overcome the doubts people had about us by shaking every hand in the state, there wasn't enough time. But that's what he believed, therefore (a) That's what he was going to do, and (b) You couldn't stop him even if you wanted. So we hit the road hard and also did the wholesale macro stuff like debates and big TV shows.

But the guy to beat was Paul Tsongas. He was formidable, he had a message, and he was drawing a lot of the cameras as the emerging front-runner, the hot guy. We couldn't go after him because we had too much repair work to do on our own selves. All we could do was tell people what we were about and hope they paid attention.

Friday turned into Saturday, Saturday into Sunday, and maybe we were doing a little better. So finally nobody could stand it anymore. On Monday we said, "Hey, Stan, go out and do five hundred interviews."

The poll came back and it was awful. We had all sorts of reasons for the results, and we found ways to doubt it—two newspaper polls had the race much closer than we did; with such a small sample the plus-or-minus factor is going to be high and the figures might turn out to be wrong; one-night samples are not good indicators because you don't get call-backs, just the people who happen to be home when you call. But hell, we'd always trusted our own polls over anybody else's, they were usually right; and we couldn't take a two-day poll, all we had was one night left. We could tell ourselves lots of things, but the bottom line was that Stan Greenberg was a great pollster and the polls looked like shit.

There was no question in my mind that if we ran third we ran out. We weren't going to quit, we would go South for the Georgia primary and Super Tuesday and try to rescue the situation, but if we ran third in New Hampshire we were probably out of it. The press would say, with some validity, that because of the combination of Gennifer Flowers and the draft story, Clinton had been severely damaged. That would dominate the coverage going down South and we wouldn't survive.

Somebody had to go in and tell Clinton. It wasn't like we drew straws, but I was the guy nominated to go down there and tell him to prepare to lose. I went to his room and said, "Look, there are three polls out there: One is encouraging, one says we could still be in it, and one says that we're in big trouble. Unfortunately, the one that says we're in big trouble is our own."

The governor was not happy. He started going through all the mistakes he thought we had made.

"I cannot believe that we sat here and let Tsongas do this. We knew he was coming up and we just sat and watched. I should have done something. We got too far out there, we didn't come back aggressive enough. It wasn't until the last three or four days that I got out there and campaigned like I like to campaign, voter to voter, hand to hand, person to person. Every time I'd go around there'd be some sort of caravan, there were always people trying to keep me away from things."

As he paused for air I'd say, "I've got to tell you that the Boston *Herald* shows it a little more encouraging."

The governor swung back and forth between criticizing our strategy, criticizing himself, and swearing that we were going to do better. He wasn't totally accepting of the fact that we were going to get our ass whipped.

The mood was awful. Hillary went to bed. She said, "I'm not going to listen to this. We'll know tomorrow. It could be right, it could be wrong. I'm not going to lose any sleep over it."

We were not as steely. Clinton, George, Paul, Mandy, Stanley, Frank Greer, Harry Thomason, and I all sat up in Mickey Kantor's room fretting and worrying and wondering and talking. (Kantor deserves a lot more credit in New Hampshire than he got. He kept the operation focused.) People were kind of bucking themselves up and spouting optimism and talking about the campaign, almost like it was over. Paul thought that was a bad sign.

Clinton was keyed up. It was after eleven and he was ready to go out campaigning. I just wanted to go back to my room, get in bed, call Mary, and figure out how I was going to deal with the next day.

The next morning Governor Clinton got up and got out. There were some hands he hadn't shook, maybe some that needed shaking twice. Down at headquarters things were firing up. They had me talking to phone-bank volunteers at six-thirty with coffee and doughnuts. This was an all-out effort.

There's a huge conspiracy between the campaigns and the news media to keep election night results a surprise. Unless the race is really close, everybody in the business knows who won by early afternoon. Exit polls tell everything. You have the ten o'clock wave, the two o'clock wave, the four o'clock, and the final. The reporters get them and they call you, and you tell them enough about your own polls to get them thinking the way you want.

The first exit poll has a great effect on news coverage. Reporters start writing their stories in advance, in their heads. They don't sit down when the polls close and begin to analyze the results, they've been thinking about it all day and already have a good idea of what they're going to write. It's the nature of the business. When the polls close there is a rush to report, not to find out. A good political consultant works hard to get that first thought spinning your way.

The first exit poll came in.

"Goddamn, we're in here!"

If we played our cards right the story would be Clinton: "Tsongas won and Clinton did better than expected." We had no problem with that story. At that point we got on the phone and tried to encourage it.

The two o'clocks came in and the numbers were holding up.

Then we set about writing a speech for the governor. Bill Clinton had been given up for dead, in the space of a month he'd taken every hit a politician could take. Now he'd made up ground, made a personal connection with the voters, and finished strong. Paul came up with the line about the "Comeback Kid." It was perfect.

One of Clinton's greatest strengths was his ability to take the spotlight that shone on him because of his personal adversity and shine it on the problems of the country and the things he wanted to change. "I've taken some hard knocks in this state but they are nothing compared to the knocks that I've seen people take here in New Hampshire, back home in Arkansas, all across the country."

I went in and said to the governor and Mrs. Clinton, "Look, we're going to run second, we have more aides up here than you can shake a stick at. I'm going to the airport and going to Georgia. I think we have to send a clear signal that we are on to the next fight."

The decision to face the media early and claim New Hampshire as a moral victory was made on the advice of Joe Grandmaison, the former New Hampshire state party chairman who, to his eternal credit, endorsed Bill Clinton the day after the Gennifer Flowers thing hit. Joe said, "You should go down early, go down before Tsongas, and force the story." He took that to Mickey Kantor, who took it to the rest of us and then to the governor and Hillary. Hillary loved it.

Before the returns were complete, shortly after nine o'clock at night, Governor Clinton went before the people at campaign headquarters and the media and said, "While the evening is young and we don't know yet what the final outcome will be, I think we know enough to say with some certainty that New Hampshire tonight has made Bill Clinton the Comeback Kid."

(Several people have wanted to take credit for coining the phrase "Comeback Kid," but there's one person who thought it up, and that person is Paul Begala.)

It was a brilliant tactical move. Because the truth was that the press didn't care that the local boy, Tsongas, won the New Hampshire primary. That's not much of a story, and they're always looking for some sizzle. We gave them a good sound bite, a good moniker for our guy, an uplifting TV moment, and a good bump into the next round. They could follow us to Georgia. I was already there.

Mary

The idiocy of the reporting on election night in New Hampshire was staggering. It started with unprecedentedly erroneous exit polls. We were freaked out by them—stunned. Throughout the day the exit polls showed Pat Buchanan running way up, neck and neck with the leader of the Free World. At one point they showed him actually surpassing George Bush. The supposed fact that this token candidate was going to beat a sitting President lathered the press into a crazy hyperbolic frenzy.

The whole campaign was in a major funk all day. I kept neurotically speed-dialing Carney, begging for some explanation. "What is the turnout? Who's turning out?" We had determined from our own exit polls and from our people on the ground that men were outnumbering women at the polls. So Carney called the phone vendors and said, "Hype it up! Go into overdrive and turn out women! Call back women and turn out women!" Our polls showed that George Bush had solid strength with New Hampshire women.

Throughout the day the media continually tried to suck us into playing the numbers game. "Well, what would you consider a big day for Buchanan?" The Buchanan people were lowering expectations: "If we get twenty to twenty-five percent," they'd say, "we would be very pleased." We were counterspinning: "We wouldn't be surprised if he got over forty percent, given the state of mind of the New Hampshire electorate."

Skip this paragraph if you already know the expectation game: If a campaign can lower expectations, any result above the touted marker is a success. If you can make the media believe that 20 percent is a victory and you come in at 35, you are an overwhelming winner. (See "Comeback Kid," the best expectation game of presidential politics.) Conversely, if they expect you to come in at 40 and you come in at 35, you have failed to measure up, you're a loser. Even if you win! Success is not measured by actual results, but by preconceived expectations.

In primaries, losing the expectation game can be worse than losing the state. Coming in lower than expected, or in the alternative, facing an opponent who comes in higher than expected, not only blows that contest, it sets the tone for ones to follow. It can cost you the next primary down the line. People like to vote for winners, especially surprise winners; they pull away from losers. It's one thing to be an underdog, it's another to be a beaten underdog.

We had scheduled our first nationwide conference call for five o'clock that afternoon. This was to be the national campaign's first point of contact with the state organizations; we'd be talking to our 257 leaders in fifty states simultaneously. This was not "interactive," it was one-way—us to them. We were delivering our message. We needed our fifty states to disseminate to their people and the press exactly what we were saying. No opining or extrapolating or analyzing. We would all literally be on the same page. Just repeat after us: *We won.*

I introduced Bob Teeter in the national headquarters and Charlie Black on the ground in New Hampshire. They gave the entire Republican political universe their talking points, which Teeter et al. had developed during the course of that day.

The essence of our message was that New Hampshire was the "high-water mark" state for Buchanan. "His vote is predicated on frustration and anxiety in the New Hampshire electorate. He will never get more than he does in this state, so do not read more into his figures today. Buchanan is going to lose, and whatever he gets he will never get that high again. So let's just move on and don't panic."

Bob Teeter bravely regaled the troops for about fifteen minutes. He did a great job, but when he hung up he was beside himself. He knew we couldn't stop the press stampede. He said, "That was terrible. It went terribly."

All the media people had filed their preliminary takeout; all the early pundits had gone on the air and said how unprecedented this primary battle was and how Bush was in deep trouble . . . and we won by 16 points. When the votes were counted we took it 53–37.

We won, right? No, we lost. By the time the real returns came in, the press had already written their leads and done their analysis, and they weren't about to change them just to conform to a little thing like the facts. It was the most depressing night I'd ever experienced on a campaign.

Morale is critical to a campaign's forward progress. The one and only reward for working like a dog is victory. Losing is often expected and emotionally acceptable, but to win and be trashed was a universal kick in the gut.

It went like that all spring. Every Tuesday we'd have a primary against Buchanan, and every Tuesday we'd win by increasing margins, and every Tuesday the press would say we lost. It set a heavy pallor on the campaign. No matter how hard we worked, no matter what we did, despite the fact that we were winning and winning significantly, the press kept calling it a loss. It was very demoralizing for the troops out in the field and it was very demoralizing internally.

The media, especially the pencil press, tend to put drama back in their stories by making them horse races. If there's no horse race they have no drama, no story. So they created one. The overarching story of Bush versus Buchanan, as far as they were concerned, was not that we were winning, it was that we were an incumbent having to use up a lot of energy in a primary.

In every campaign in the history of mankind, when you win you win. Not this one.

We sat around and tried to figure out how to get the press to get serious. We were winning every primary and we were getting almost every convention delegate; we were going to be the nominee . . .

Carney and I went to every reporter, we went on TV and radio shows, and said, "Look, it's mathematically impossible for Buchanan to win. He is not going to win any state. You don't need a slide rule, you don't need a degree from MIT. This just doesn't add up for Buchanan. The question you should be asking is, Why is he doing this?"

Meanwhile, from the beginning of time there was battle in our paid-media meetings among Bob Teeter, Charlie Black, myself, Jim Pinkerton (who was special counsel to Teeter), Fred Malek, research director David Tell, David Carney, and the ad team. In our initial discussions, the question on the table was, Do we do *any* negative Buchanan spots? The obvious first response was, "Absolutely not." Even to mention Buchanan would display presidential weakness, showing unwarranted concern about him. However, as the primaries progressed I flipped over to the other side: "This guy is not killing us but he's a gnat, let's just take out the flyswatter and squash him." Some jerk traitor leaked to *The Wall Street Journal* that I said, "Let's cut his balls off." It really embarrassed my dad.

The field division's job mainly involved communicating with the ground troops via telephone and mail. We were conducting phone banks, calling back undecided voters or soft Buchanan supporters and giving them additional information about our opponent. We would say to "undecided" or "soft" women, "If you knew that Pat Buchanan had said women were 'less equipped psychologically for the working world,' would you be more likely to vote for him, less likely, or does it make no difference in your vote?" In fact, our research had dug up that exact quote. Buchanan had done so much writing, had left such a bonfire of a paper trail that the press did not have the capacity to do the kind of research David Tell devoted his operation to. Of course, when soft voters heard his real opinions they flocked away in droves. As we were creating this voter turnabout, we began holding forth in the media meetings: "Let's crush him." No one screamed or stood on a table and kicked. We just said, "Here's an alternate view." We lost.

We agreed to proceed with the positive "Bush Leadership" spots on the theory that (a) you give Buchanan credibility by hitting him; (b) you look weak and panicky by putting yourself on his level; and (c) if it doesn't work you're in deep trouble.

It's a solid strategy, but we should have crushed him.

Though they liked him personally, I never thought the media liked Buchanan's campaign; given their liberal bias they were never particularly interested in promoting his candidacy. What the media liked was the fight.

For weeks then, our strategic position was "Pat Buchanan is a nonfactor." We were not running against him, we were running for reelection. Why should we touch that tar baby? But then, in Georgia, Buchanan started running these outrageous homophobic ads. They showed semi-naked gay black men dancing together in slow motion, clad in chains and leather harnesses, with a superimposed picture of George Bush and a voice-over that droned, "In the last three years the Bush administration has invested our tax dollars in pornographic and blasphemous art too shocking to show. This so-called art has glorified homosexuality, exploited children, and perverted the image of Jesus Christ."

The President was out jogging when reporters first asked him about the ad. "I don't want to talk about all that today," he said. "It's so nice to get out, get a day off." When they asked him if he would go after Buchanan he said, "No, going to be nice."

To the press we were on a "frenetic" campaign swing, which wasn't the least bit frenetic. All the events were orderly and wildly successful. But at one stop, Torie Clarke hurtled off the press plane and hurried over to me. She was hyperventilating. "George Bush has got to say something about these spots at our next event."

You have to understand a presidential press secretary's job to comprehend how exercised Torie was. She had to be accessible to the press twenty-four hours a day. She never went anywhere without a beeper. When we traveled, she was imprisoned with the press horde. If they're all stampeding in the same direction, you just get beat down. You can develop a hostage mentality, like maybe your terrorist captors have a point.

The terrorists today were beating Torie silly with the notion that our not blasting the Buchanan ads was a testament to our own homophobia. I was in my own standard state of hyperactivity and didn't really register how upset Torie was about this. I was barely paying attention to her, and said, "Torie, we're not going to respond. We're not running against him. It doesn't fit our strategy." But Torie was more than a little agitated. She started jabbing me in the chest with her finger, saying with each poke, "We will respond. *We will respond.* We simply must do this!"

That sort of got my attention. "Why should we get off message?"

"Because it's the right thing to do!" By this time she was pounding me.

"No, it isn't," I told her, "because our party *is* a bunch of homophobic bigots!" I turned on my heel and walked away laughing. I thought I'd made kind of a good joke, but she was in no mood for sarcasm.

Torie just about started crying on the tarmac. I think she went back to the press and said we were appalled by this blatant appeal to the worst in human impulses. And, though no one encouraged him, President Bush finally did attack the ads, in response to a reporter's question.

But Buchanan's ads and our response kind of sat with the press until the national convention. In a typical misconstruction, the press perceived our not responding quickly and forcefully to this obvious bigotry as our acceding to it, when really we weren't responding because strategically we didn't want to acknowledge Pat Buchanan's presence.

By the next big primary, Michigan, Pat Buchanan had gone consistently harsh in his rhetoric. Finally, we gleefully agreed: "Let's squash him."

David Tell, our incredibly big-brained research director, had everything on everybody. Tell is the kind of guy, you ask him what time of day it is and he'll build you a clock. He is really skinny, actually bony, wears extremely large eyeglasses, and has a lot of red hair and a huge red beard. His clothes sort of hang on him, and he is given to wearing bow ties. One day he came into my office wringing his hands and chuckling. "*Nyuk, nyuk, nyuk.* You're not going to believe what I've got." He tucked a tape into my VCR.

"Oh, my God!"

It was Pat Buchanan on a TV talk show, saying that he drove a Mercedes-Benz because he "bought three straight Cadillacs. . . . We got three straight lemons." It took less than a nanosecond to recall that Michigan is the auto worker's capital of America. So Tell and I were chortling and cackling, hoping the big guys would go for it.

Tell went to the media meeting and made his case—and they went for it instantly and joyously. We created an ad that would take Pat Buchanan apart. "It's America first in his political speeches," said the voice-over, "but a foreign-made car in his driveway." It was murderous. It was so devastating that Buchanan's campaign-manager sister, Bay, said she advised her brother to hold a press conference, go on camera, and take a sledgehammer to his Mercedes.

The press really liked that ad. They gave us big-time credit for being clever. They didn't know just how clever we actually were. We never blabbed about our phone and mail support, it wasn't sexy enough for them; the press is only ever interested in the ads. But we did a lot of voter canvassing, just to make double-sure people had heard of our ad. Carney had his vendors make up a postcard of a lemon, put Buchanan's quote on the back, and send out thousands to undecideds, Bush-leaners, and soft Buchanans. (If you're running a coherent campaign and you have the money, you always back up your paid-media message with phones and mail. The ground war should match the air war.)

We creamed him.

The press coverage finally shifted from "He's killing Bush" to "What is he, an egomaniac or what?" We won Michigan 67–25. That was pretty much the end of a serious Buchanan opposition.

If we were slow on the uptake about Pat Buchanan, we were no quicker to respond to the whole idea of Ross Perot. He just wasn't a factor in our lives. No one took him seriously. Sure, the day after he showed up on the Larry King show in February and said he would run for president if "grassroots" supporters got his name on the ballot in fifty states, everybody was talking about it. We kind of wondered how he'd go about eliminating the federal budget deficit, as he promised, "without breaking a sweat." But our first reaction, full of conventional thinking, was, This guy is incredibly rich, the people will resent that he is buying the election.

A private citizen financing his own run for president was unprecedented. In state races, when candidates bought and paid for their campaign it always became a negative issue, associated with buying votes. At first we tried to spin it that way. "Buying an election"—it was somehow un-American. We learned very quickly we were wrong. It astonished us, but our early polls showed people didn't care. In fact, they had exactly the opposite reaction, they granted him credibility because he wasn't beholden to any special interests. So we misjudged his appeal from the very beginning.

One of the reasons we misjudged him so badly was that many of the people in the government and on the campaign were from Texas, and knew him, and knew him to be a crackpot. We knew our opponent, and we dismissed him because we knew in real life he was certifiable.

Perot's candidacy was the source of much amusement in Texas political circles. People who had worked with him firsthand were astounded by the gross hypocrisy of his campaign rhetoric. The man running down and against Washington was a consummate insider, a wheeler-dealer; he was a creature of Congress, it was said, a creature of lobbyists. His whole business was spawned of government contracts. He was everything in real life that he was railing against in politics.

He also had a "temperament problem." Many people had seen him blow up in mighty tantrums on numerous occasions and presumed he would blaze out when the klieg lights of the national press were turned on him.

Every Tuesday afternoon we met with the President in the Roosevelt Room at the White House. It was an "expanded" meeting, with about thirty policy and political people, and therefore a fake meeting; any meeting from which leaks are predictable is a fake meeting, so no one really says anything. In our Perot discussions there were two camps: the Perot-is-a-factor-in-the-race camp and the Perot-is-not-a-factor camp. George Bush's opinion was "I'm not worried about him. You guys get paid to worry about him. If you want to worry about him, go ahead, but what are you going to do anyway?"

We were totally split. The Rich Bond/Dick Darman side really wanted to take him out. The other side, including me, wanted to leave him alone on the theory that, one, to acknowledge his presence in the race would elevate his status and credibility; and two, never interfere with your enemy when he's in the process of destroying himself. (Knowing him, we figured he'd destroy his candidacy better and faster than we could.)

Furthermore, no one knew who his candidacy was hurting worse, us or the Democrats. If we shot first, the presumption would be that we feared his strength would come out of our party. In the middle of divisive primary season, we didn't need a whole new round of press stories lamenting the further disintegration of the GOP.

In any event, neither camp knew precisely what to do to take him out.

The Democrats blinked first. Charlie Black and I were speaking at a regional conference of the Southern state leadership in Atlanta, and during my presentation I was making fun of James—always good for a laugh—when Charlie abruptly stood up and said, "Speaking of the opposition, this is hot off the wires and it gives you an indication of how disorganized the Clinton campaign is. Clinton has just personally attacked Ross Perot."

The whole audience gasped in unison. We presumed the attack was strategic, that Clinton's polls were showing Perot cutting into their "change" voters. Of course, there was always the possibility that it was a mistake and Clinton had slipped up, a loose-cannon candidate out of "handler" range. In either event we were delighted.

I called James. "Well, that was really stupid." He didn't disagree, he just pretended like it didn't happen. They pulled Clinton back quickly and it didn't happen again, until shortly thereafter when Democratic National Committee chairman Ron Brown called Perot a "little dictator." We couldn't have been more pleased.

But it wasn't as if we had all our horses in line, either. Over the course of a single weekend, drug czar Bob Martinez, Second Lady Marilyn Quayle, Marlin Fitzwater, and Rich Bond all attacked Perot. Marlin called him a monster. As it was unusual for Mrs. Quayle to be openly partisan, her remarks got a lot of play: "I think it's pretty sad when somebody captures the imagination of the country with money and no policy. He doesn't stand for anything, and that is worrisome to me, that you can in essence buy an election without ever standing for anything."

This is a perfect piece of evidence that we did not have a strategy on Perot. The campaign had decided to remain silent, and here top Republicans appeared to go out of their way to slam him.

We knew from our internal polls that Perot's using his own money was the most positive aspect of his campaign. The Second Lady was out there thinking she was attacking Perot while in fact she was say-ing the single most positive thing she could about him. Out of loyalty to the President—whom Perot was bashing daily—and utter frustra-tion over another impediment to getting our positive message out, everybody started freelancing. Unfortunately, the attacks looked orchestrated.

The press went crazy. They shifted off Clinton and onto the pre-sumption that *we* were scared of Perot. In fact, our polls showed he *was* taking Clinton's "change" voters. Why should we care?

James

Perot didn't loom heavy in my mind that early. We were in a hell of a dogfight to secure the nomination, which was our number one priority. Hillary and Susan Thomases were the ones who thought Perot was hitting a sore nerve and was going to be a major factor in the race. They said, "You guys better watch it."

But we had a lot more than Ross Perot to worry about. We came out of New Hampshire on the defensive. We were headed south, where we were supposed to win. We had a Southern candidate, a Southern campaign strategist, we were on our own turf. We felt like we could survive anything—but we could not survive a close race in Georgia. If Tsongas came out of Georgia with 40 percent, or if our vote total was under 50, it would have been devastating.

The week after New Hampshire we came in third in Maine and third in South Dakota. We hadn't won anything. We were still a vir-gin. If you couple that with the fact that we weren't going to win in Colorado or Maryland, you could begin to hear the refrain: "Can this guy win one?" which the media would have blown into a full-fledged catcall, "Can anybody here play this game?" We had to win in Geor-gia. Governor Zell Miller had endorsed Clinton.

If you play *Family Feud* and ask a hundred people to name a South-ern state, I believe Georgia would come up more than any other. Georgians don't like being lumped in with everybody else; they feel they have a mystique: "We're Georgia." In politics many states are important, but winning the Georgia primary establishes the candi-date that's doing well in the South. There was a move afoot to sepa-rate the state and increase its influence even further. The Georgia primary, originally part of the Southern bloc on Super Tuesday, was moved forward a week.

There wasn't much of an argument that somebody outside of Georgia could muster against it, and inside the state the bases had been covered. The governor and the speaker simply wanted the Georgia primary to stand out and be influential among Southern primaries . . . and to help Bill Clinton.

Mary

James delivering the Georgia primary panicked me early. In 1988, Lee Atwater got his home-state political pals to move the South Carolina primary up before Super Tuesday because we knew we would win there and it would catapult us into that cluster of primaries which he termed a firewall, which is what we needed to win the nomination. I knew Zell Miller was Carville's client and when I saw him move up his primary *before the campaign started* I presumed it was Carville's doing. Clinton could use it as the same launching pad into Super Tuesday that we had used South Carolina for. Manipulating the primary system so a specific candidate can get an advantage is a smart thing to do, and not often easy. Carville was better than I thought.

James

I ran the primary out of Atlanta. I was away from the New Hampshire cold, the weather was nice down south in late February, I knew everybody down there, I was sort of comfortable. Then it sort of dawned on me that the Georgia primary was mine. If we didn't do it here we weren't gonna do it.

Tsongas had a hot hand. He had won New Hampshire and Maine, had a good-sized lead in Maryland, which had a lot of college-educated voters, and looked strong in Colorado. And no one had taken him on. He was Saint Paul. I'm sure that he is a good person, and the guy had waged a heroic struggle against cancer, but his worldview was substantially different for the Democratic party than the worldview I thought was the way to win.

Tsongas had the cultural agenda of Boston and the economic agenda of Wall Street. He would rather take a dollar and invest it in a company than take a dollar and invest it in a human being. His whole message was "I'm not Santa Claus. I can't do anything for you. It's up to the middle class to do something about the budget deficit." At the same time he was one thousand percent for abortion and one thousand percent for the whole conventional liberal social agenda.

He was coming out of New Hampshire a winner and he had the national media. About 85 percent of the national media believed in more pain for the middle class and shared his agendas. That doesn't mean they are bad people, it's just the way they think. We had to do something about that. We were down to politics now.

When I'm running a campaign I always say I want the people I'm running against to catch the clap and die. There is a time in politics when it's all or nothing, and this was all or nothing. Tsongas was getting unbelievable press. There was no scrutiny; we were getting all the scrutiny and we were smarting. We decided that the best way to handle this guy was to tag him straight on. We started hand-to-hand combat.

The real secret of the Southern primaries is that, increasingly, the most influential people who participate in them are black. White participation has fallen off considerably; therefore, the black vote has become increasingly important. This is particularly true in an all-white field, where, in a state like Georgia, 22 percent of the registered voters may be black but 30 to 35 percent of the Democratic primary voters may be black. If one candidate is able to amass 80 percent of the black vote and a decent share of a fragmented white vote, you have a big winner. A professional political strategist would know this, a *Southern* political strategist would know this by instinct.

The way to work the Southern black vote is person-to-person testimonial campaigning. Almost door-to-door. Black people believe black leaders; they distrust white ones. To a lot of black folks a national campaign is just a bunch of white guys running for something, which is why you go out of your way to win the approval of the notable figures in the local community. I'd run campaigns in Georgia and Kentucky and Louisiana; I knew who the neighborhood activists were and I understood their importance. We knew which preachers to call, what churches to show up at; we knew who was the guy to see and which women actually ran the communities.

When I first started in politics there was a black political leader down in Baton Rouge who said, "I'll tell you a secret in dealing with the black vote: The wife can be more effective than the man. And never come to a black event without your wife, people will automatically assume that you don't take your woman around." In Georgia and throughout the South, Hillary made huge early contributions. We scheduled her hard and she was a good campaigner with a real rapport with the black crowds. I don't have any doubt that if you told Hillary, "You can do one of two things: speak at a Wednesday night social in a black church in northwest Georgia or go to a social function in northwest Washington," she'd go to the church. She likes it, it's not pretentious, it's kind of fun. Diversity matters to her. And statistics tell you there are a lot of old people in black churches who tend to vote, so it's a very influential place to campaign. The standing joke was that people would call in from the states and say, "If Hillary can't make it, can you send Bill?"

There was no way Tsongas, coming from up north without her kind of intimate introduction, could understand exactly what she meant for us.

We worked hard for personal testimony. We got out black legislators, political leaders, and clergy to come out and endorse Clinton and talk about law enforcement. Atlanta mayor Maynard Jackson, Andrew Young, Congressman John Lewis—a lot of them were for us already, but the governor of Georgia is a man with some sort of say down there. If you have a sitting governor, there are a lot of black legislators and elected officials who don't want to displease him. They are friends, they do official business together, they have been knowing each other. This was kind of key. The governor would call the legislatures and say, "Look, I'm with Clinton, and Hillary is coming through." Two days after New Hampshire, Governor Clinton came down to Georgia and held a rally at the CNN Center and we had so many public officials and people on that stand that the damn thing fell down.

Considering the importance of Georgia in both the primaries and the general election, I would be hard pressed to get an argument to say there was a more influential political supporter in the Clinton campaign than Zell Miller.

And, of course, there is Jesse Jackson. I was sitting next to Paul West of the Baltimore *Sun* on a plane from Washington, D.C., to Atlanta sometime between the New Hampshire and Georgia primaries when Reverend Jackson, who was also on board, passed me a note saying he wanted to talk to me. I was happy to.

Jesse Jackson is a very engaging and charismatic man. I hear people talk about him and I don't think they understand what a powerful personality he is. My sense of him is that he is a pretty tough guy. He understands that politics is a rough business and he understands that sometimes you may have to screw him, but you've got to understand that he may screw you back. I also think he has a good understanding of the amount of power he has. He has a lot of power.

In 1984 Jesse Jackson produced one of the phenomenal feats in American politics, and you've just got to give him credit for it. From 1984 to 1988, through sheer raw political appeal—the ability to get votes—he got the black political establishment behind him. Although I think he has an entirely different view, I think he did some things in 1988 that hurt the Democratic ticket. I don't think the black political establishment was particularly enamored of his candidacy—he was not going to win, and he prevented them from making the standard beneficial political deals with the candidates who could—but he just became *that* popular and they had no other choice. He forced them to endorse him in 1988, not through the threat of him winning but by his appeal to black voters. He didn't have a lot of them in 1984; at that time he had charisma, a fresh face, and a lot of white liberals. He had a lot more four years and a whole lot of political work later.

We drove from the airport together and he told me, "Clinton is going to win this nomination."

I wasn't giving anything away. "This thing is very dicey," I said. "Tsongas is—"

"Look, don't bullshit me. I know Clinton is going to win. These people are not going to beat him. We need to open up a dialogue." I agreed.

You can get caught up in the Jackson mystique. In the next few hours I went with Jesse on one of his visits to a school in Atlanta. From there we had stopped by Reverend Cameron Alexander's church, a huge deal in Atlanta. I had work to do and was about to go back to the campaign but Jesse said he was going to lunch at Paschal's. Paschal's is the black Southern establishment's legendary restaurant of choice. I called the office. "Look, I'm going to be late but I have got to walk into Paschal's with Jesse Jackson." I mean, walking into Paschal's with Jesse Jackson would be akin to having Ring Lardner and A. J. Liebling come back to life and walk with you into the Algonquin.

Jesse had made no commitment to any Democratic candidate. He had promised us that he would tell us before he made any announcement. Jackson was playing it close to the vest, hoping to pick up an ace. He had said publicly that he would campaign with anyone who asked him, which was fair enough, and when Tom Harkin had requested his presence in South Carolina Jesse went with him. Six days before the Georgia primary I got a call from George.

"There's a problem."

The governor had been doing back-to-back interviews via satellite, and during down time between them, when he thought the microphone was off and the tape stopped, he had been told, erroneously, that Reverend Jackson had come out for Harkin. Clinton had gone ballistic, on mike, with tape rolling.

My first thought was, "God, I hope he didn't say something racial."

I don't think of myself as a prejudiced person, but given my age and where I come from I do from time to time stereotype people. If some high-speed hot-rod moron cuts me off on the highway I am very likely to say in a moment of anger, "Get your redneck ass out of the road," or "your Cajun ass," or "your Yankee ass," depending on what I see of them and their license plate.

Bill Clinton, on the other hand, is more free of prejudice than any human being I know. Furious as he was, he didn't say one of those things. Not even close. In a moment of real anger and stress, when the stain of bigotry will appear, Bill Clinton came up clean.

"It's an outrage," he said. "It's a dirty, double-crossing, back-stabbing thing to do. . . . For me to hear this on this television program is an act of absolute dishonor. . . . He has gushed to me about trust and trust and trust . . ."

It caused a flap, which was predictable, and other campaigns—notably Harkin's—picked up the tape and the story and started running black radio ads saying that Clinton was attacking the Reverend Jackson. We couldn't control the other campaigns, but we had to make sure Jackson didn't fan these flames.

First we had to make contact with Jesse.

Bert Lance and Jackson are very close but Lance and Clinton never got along very well. However, Governor Miller's secretary, Mrs. Mary Beazley, had worked for Lance and was also a great lady and a good friend of mine. (Mrs. Beazley was the only one I ever met who told me she never really liked me going out with Mary. She said, "James, I can't believe that you are going out with no damn Republican. I'm sorry, I just ain't for this." But she was for just about everything else.) This was so familial; I don't think Tsongas really knew the depth of the old-boy network he was up against. Mrs. Beazley put me through to Mr. Lance.

I said, "Look, you gotta help me here."

Lance said, "I'm going to call Jesse and find out where he is, 'cause you need to talk to him."

Mrs. Beazley buzzed me and said, "Reverend Jackson is at this number and he's waiting on your call."

I'm not good at soothing politicians, it's not what I do well. I don't have the patience for it. I read somewhere that Bob Beckel, who was

Mondale's manager, had something like seventy-three meetings with Jackson in 1984. I wasn't sure I was up to it.

Before you pick up the phone and call someone, you try to figure out what's at work here. One question was, Is Jackson hurt? Maybe he was, though I don't know how he could stay hurt once he was made aware that Clinton was acting on erroneous information. The larger question in my mind was, Is Jackson going balls-to-the-wall on this thing? Is he going to put his prestige on the line and say, "Don't vote for Clinton"?

I called him Senator.

Jesse Jackson is the shadow senator from Washington, D.C. I lived in the district so that's what I called him. He's never objected to it.

"Senator," I said, "I know we have had a little setback and I know that the governor is going to want to speak to you."

He hit me pretty good. He said, "I am very hurt. We opened this line of communication, and for Governor Clinton to do this to me is not conducive to the things that we talked about."

"Well, I understand how you feel, Senator, and I hope that you understand that the governor was given incorrect information, he was under a mistaken impression."

"This is very serious," Jesse said. "The media has been calling me to say something and I think I have been extremely restrained and extremely mature in the way I have handled this."

"Oh, you certainly have."

It was a conversation that I imagine diplomats have with each other. Very couched, stilted, careful language. I didn't say, "Hey, Jesse, how's your hammer hangin'?" the way I might have with people I knew better.

I told him, "I know that the governor would like to speak with you and he will call you tonight."

"This is a setback in our relationship," he told me. "If the party is going to stay together we can't have these kind of setbacks. It is very harmful."

Jackson didn't want to talk to me. I was the one calling because he and I had established the beginnings of a relationship, but clearly the step had to be on what he felt were parallel levels of power, Clinton to Jackson. Later they did make contact. As it was described to me, the governor explained to Jackson the circumstances under which these remarks were made and that he had obviously been supplied with erroneous information. Jackson listened and didn't comment. The conversation was described to me as cool and correct.

Jesse Jackson is a talented man with a great deal of charm and personal magnetism, and I think he believes what he says. I like the idea of the Rainbow Coalition, that you can get people from all strata to share a common economic goal and all come up together. It has never been achieved in this country and it's a pretty tough thing to achieve. However, his view is not as expansive as it needs to be for the party to be successful in a general election.

I suspect Jesse's dream has always been to break out and have major influence beyond his core constituents, which he has not been able to do and which I suspect is going to be very difficult for him to do. Within the parameters of his constituency, however, he is a person of considerable power. Watching him at work is a pretty impressive sight. He is a pretty impressive guy.

Georgia, Colorado, and Maryland all held their primaries on the same Tuesday. There was a debate in Georgia the preceding Sunday, and we were going to fly up to a scheduled event in Prince Georges County, Maryland, before a debate later that evening. The Atlanta *Constitution* said they wanted to have a Sunday afternoon meeting with Governor Clinton. They went so far as to call Governor Miller and ask him to persuade us. We told them, "Look, if your endorsement is already decided then there's no point in us talking to you. If we have a chance to get your endorsement we'll do it." They said the paper's endorsement was still an open question.

We were just done doing a big event down there, we had done Georgia churches all morning, we had two other primaries to run in less than forty-eight hours, and I held up the whole schedule after the Atlanta debate so Governor Clinton could eat lunch with the editorial board of the Atlanta *Constitution*. They knew that if they kept us tied up for a couple of hours we were going to miss the scheduling opportunity in Maryland, and they sat there with us.

The next morning they endorsed Tsongas.

I was told by ten people with one hundred percent confidence in their accuracy that the editorial endorsing Tsongas was being written as we were meeting with the editorial board. If they had said, "James, look, we have this thing written, we are going to endorse Tsongas, but we would love to sit there and lollygag around and bullshit with Bill Clinton," I would have said, "To hell with that." Instead they wasted our most precious commodity, time. We got to the debate in Maryland, not the event. It was a prime example of a newspaper not just trying to influence an election through an editorial but through deceit. We ended up losing Maryland by 7 percentage points, and with a better effort and a stop in Prince Georges County we could have come a hell of a lot closer, if not won it. That sham meeting was one of the great chickenshit maneuvers of American journalism.

The Atlanta *Constitution* poll showed us up 40 to 20 over Tsongas, with 24 percent undecided. But it was published on Sunday and had been taken over a five-day period, so nobody really knew where we were. At about ten in the morning on primary day Gwen Ifill of *The New York Times* told me, "The Tsongas people are saying that they are going to win Colorado, they are going to win Maryland by a lot, and they are going to come closer than people think in Georgia." I don't know if it was rational or not, but I became convinced that that was what was going to happen.

Governor Miller likes to go to a restaurant on Peachtree Street called Houston's, so we went there and were nervous beyond belief. I said, "Man, these yuppies are going to be voting like crazy in suburban Atlanta." He said, "I know. This thing with Jesse, I'm telling you, I think it's hurting us out there."

We convinced ourselves. I said, "I think we're bleeding out there." He said, "No, we're hemorrhaging, man . . . everywhere." Our crazed, depressing expectations reached the point where we thought we were going to lose. I didn't even think it was gonna be close.

We went back to headquarters and the first exit polls came in with us running at about 60 percent. I went into the governor's office and said, "Look, this thing is a little . . . a lot better than we thought." His face looked like I'd told him, "It's not malignant." Between the support of the Georgia political establishment, regional bias, knowledge of the South, and a strong black turnout, we won 57–24. Jerry Brown won Colorado with 29 percent, we had 27, Tsongas ran third with 26. Bob Kerrey dropped out on Thursday and Tom Harkin dropped out the next Monday.

Super Tuesday shaped up as a battle over Florida, where Tsongas had decided to make a stand. The other states had basically been conceded, the Northern ones to him, the Southern ones to us.

Florida's voting electorate has a lot of transplanted Northerners, but a bunch of them don't vote in the Democratic primary. You have a pretty heavy Jewish vote, but most of the Northern non-Jewish retirees are casting Republican ballots. Most of these retired ophthalmologists ain't hanging around the Democratic primaries.

Tsongas was never comfortable in the South. He held up a stuffed animal, said it was a "pander bear," and accused Governor Clinton of pandering to voters. Everybody started making fun of him because of his accent. In the South, *panda* and *pander* don't rhyme. He was accentuating the fact that he was different from the voters.

And he didn't look strong in making the charge. Southerners are used to powerhouse politicians. Big men, if not in size then in stature. Men who cut a large wake when they pass. Tsongas was already frail, in comparison to Clinton, and though the health issue wasn't being talked about, it was there, and when he held up that panda, well . . . a Southern male would not hold up something that looks like a teddy bear. My mother, Miss Nippy, said, "Y'all really scared of that poor little man? He can barely talk."

In an election year that was shaping up as one of substance not photo ops, Tsongas was known as a man with a plan. People knew that he had a strategy, on paper, that he was going to use to get this country going again. I told Mandy Grunwald, "We ought to run a spot telling people what's in the plan. They don't know what's in there, they just know he's got one."

Mandy worked up a spot called "Page." It was excellent. "Page 22—he proposes another capital-gains tax cut for the rich. Page 21—cuts in cost-of-living increases for older Americans. . . . And page 50—a fifty-cent increase in the gas tax over ten years." It took the plan from some imagined financial fix to the disappointing facts of life as Tsongas saw them. He did call for cuts in Medicare, and that ain't popular among retirees in Florida. In Florida people drive distances—this is not Massachusetts or New Hampshire—a fifty-cent increase in the gas tax will hurt them directly. These were not popular concepts, but they were Tsongas's concepts, and they were concepts we accentuated through our ads. Hell, yes, let's tell them what's in his plan.

The first time we hit him with those spots it really hurt him. It didn't take long for them to take effect. Our polls told us that. You can tell when somebody has a glass jaw, and after three days of TV his jaw was shattered. He had nothing to come back with; we'd smacked him with his own bad news.

We won Florida 51–35, a decisive win on a turf that Tsongas had chosen. Super Tuesday turned us into the front-runner. We won big in Florida, Hawaii, Louisiana, Mississippi, Missouri, Oklahoma, Tennessee, and Texas, and ran second in two of the other three.

Illinois and Michigan came next. David Wilhelm had been involved in Illinois politics for a long time and had almost all the state's political people lined up wall-to-wall with us.

You've got to understand the nature of the Democratic party. It's been this way for a long time. The elite wing is made up of Volvo drivers, people in Montgomery County, Maryland, or suburban Boston, well-educated cultural liberals who abhor politics and think it's something that will dirty their hands. That was Paul Tsongas's core constituency, and there are a few of those on the north side of Chicago.

I asked the cab driver on the way in from the airport, "What do you think of this guy Tsongas?" It's just typical campaign-guy chatter, you always try to talk to the cab driver on the way in, a rolling focus group. He said, "Man, he can't deal with nobody, he ain't got nobody for him, he can't deal with these people." It struck me that in Chicago, and in many other places, politicos were a fact of life and a candidate's inability to deal with them was a sign of weakness.

I think a mistake we often make in politics is to assume that because everybody hates the legislature or hates Congress, you can attack them. It turns out that's not always so; people don't like the institutions but they view them as a fact of life. If your candidate can't deal with the institution, he is thought to be a weak person.

I brought this informal one-man focus group finding up at a meeting, and a lot of our Illinois people said, "Yeah, these people don't like the organization, but they understand that it's been here forever and if you're ever going to get anything done you gotta be able to deal with it." There's a lot of this "throw the bastards out" talk, term limits and the like, but the bottom line is that most people want the system to work for them and want somebody representing them who knows how to work it.

We won Illinois 52–26 and Michigan 51–17 over Tsongas, with Jerry Brown getting 26 percent. I was in my office two days later when John Shakow, a campaign worker who had come to work for me, said, "Look at this. Tsongas is getting out of the race."

I said, "Get out of here."

Sure enough, there he was saying he had suspended his campaign. He kind of lingered around for a while and threatened to get back in, but my sense is that he was really devastated after Michigan and Illinois.

Of course, what happened then is that we got cocky again.

CHAPTER 9

Mary

It is widely held by political operatives that the advantages of incumbency are highly overrated.

On the plus side you have the reliability and predictability of always getting news coverage, the certainty of name recognition, and the ability to grab "leadership" headlines by acting decisively on the hot issues. Big deal. The White House press corps's attitude and daily *modus operandi* is to challenge everything a president says. As Torie used to say, "If we could prove George Bush walks on water, they'd say he can't swim." The primary opposition winner gets instant I.D. and reliable press coverage because he's tailoring his events to get on the news every night. The Clinton press corps, assigned to an insurgent campaign, had a different job and a different attitude; they simply covered Clinton.

On the minus side, the mechanics of incumbency are a nightmare.

It costs a great deal more money when you're in office to drag the campaign and White House entourage from one place to another. Not only is security much tighter for a president than for his opponent, which inhibits "movement," you've got Secret Service agents in a constant state of high freak, preventing normal people, the ones who are going to vote you back in, from getting up close.

Also, it's more difficult to be an incumbent because you've still got to govern. One of President Bush's biggest, endless complaints was that, when we kept him on the road for three days at a time, he felt he was neglecting the reams of work on his desk. I don't know what the President does besides the things we see him doing, but I suspect it's a full-time job. Challengers can fly from place to place taking pot-shots at incumbents; presidents have to keep governing.

But the most frustrating, miserable, teeth-gnashing problem for a reelection campaign is weaving into the existing governmental structure. It wasn't personal, we pretty much all liked each other, and everybody, of course, loved George Bush—but the people at the White House thought the campaign people were dopes, Nean-derthals, and thugs. White House people, as a personality type, are staid, bureaucratic control freaks; campaign people fly by the seat of their pants. They didn't like that we were horning in on their jobs, and they really didn't like that, in a campaign setting, we were equipped to do them better than they were.

We couldn't *order* the White House staff to do anything. Before George Bush got into campaign mode, all we could do was suggest. So we'd say, "We think the President needs to go to the following states . . ."—assuming we were all speaking the same language, we fig-ured the White House would set up the right kind of event, one which would serve the President's dual objectives of governing and *getting reelected.*

Well, they wouldn't. They just didn't get it. Their advance team was government-, not campaign-oriented. For instance, the White House staff sent President Bush to a televised political event at an environ-mental cleanup enterprise in California. Now, it was bad enough that at the very moment the President was extolling its virtues, the com-pany was being sued by the federal government. But White House advance, in a campaign advance nightmare, sat the President in front of a giant sign with an 800 number clearly visible to all the cameras. When viewers called the number prominently displayed over the President's shoulder, thinking it was a presidential call-in line, they got Evergreen Environmental Management. They began hysterically speed-dialing CNN in Atlanta. "What's the deal?" Watching this unfold in my hot, smelly headquarters office, I screamed out loud when the CNN anchor broke in to tell his viewers the 800 number was *not* a Bush or CNN call-in. *"What lamebrain vetted this trip?"*

The White House would consistently screw things up that to us were second nature. Little foul-ups, from bad camera angles to empty chairs in an audience being visible on a newscast, would happen every day. But annoying as they were, they were only symptomatic of a larger, more dangerous problem to a reelection campaign: Campaign people and government people just have different MOs.

It's almost genetic. On a campaign, everything is constantly changing. Entire states sometimes get blown off the schedule at a moment's
notice. You've got to be adaptable. On one trip when we were finally
in full campaign mode, Teeter sent me data on the Air Force One fax
that suggested our numbers had improved and we did not have to go
to a scheduled trip to Louisiana. The campaign, which has to pay for
political trips, agreed that we didn't want to waste the money. So,
while Air Force One was in the air, I yanked the trip. You don't do
things like that to the White House; they went absolutely nuts. If
they'd had a parachute, I swear they would have ejected me.

Even the incumbent's advantage of getting first crack at the headlines can be a debilitating distraction. Before we could get our campaign sea legs we had three serious headline-grabbing events in rapid
succession: the primary, which wouldn't end because Buchanan
wouldn't get out; the entrance of Ross Perot, which compelled the
press to react to Perot and not to us; and, out of nowhere, the Los
Angeles riots.

The riots began on April 29 and ran for four days. Because they
were the epitome of an official government problem, the partisan
campaign could not have anything to do with them. We could not
afford to be accused of playing politics with the major issue of the day.

This is not in the government handbook, it's just an unequivocal
political rule, spawned, as most of them are, by the press. The media
ascribes political motivation to all official activities. The campaign tries
mightily not to feed into their suspicions, lest the candidate appear pro-
pelled by political, as opposed to good-government, impulses.

Our regularly scheduled political meetings at the White House
were canceled. We could not traipse over there even for administra-
tive meetings because any footage of campaign operatives filing into
the White House while a riot was going on would look like an effort
to "politicize" a national crisis. We were forbidden to speak to anybody about the problem, or have any public input whatsoever. Where
a challenger's political advisers could craft what he should say, where
he should go, who he should see, the President's election team had to
be kept as far outside as possible. The press was poised to accuse us of
trying to manipulate a national crisis for partisan political gain. The
reality was, of course, that it would have been a real reach for us to
discern *any* political gain from a domestic crisis (which the libs were
quick to blame on us).

The White House staff never really recovered their political instincts
after John Sununu's reign of terror. Sununu's successor as chief of staff,

Sam Skinner, was by his own admission in over his head at the dual job. Skinner was a very good administrator, and in a noncampaign environment he would have been a successful chief of staff. But his first reaction was always governmental, not political. Obviously the President had to respond to the L.A. riots, but to avoid having them become a political albatross called for political, not programmatic, skill.

Bob Teeter and California governor Pete Wilson were good friends, so we at headquarters were in contact and keeping abreast of developments. But we could not directly weigh into the President's response; specifically, could not collude on his impending visit to the riot scene. Good people—but not *our* people—were putting his trip together on the ground. Despite the inherent political ramifications of the visit, there was no political thinking in its planning. The thrust of the event was governmental. No political speeches on heinous criminal behavior; lots of walking tours and gray-suit meetings.

We were in an uproar. With or without campaign input, everything a president does is political. If he handles a crisis well, his favorables increase; if he screws up, they fall. There are ways to do the right thing domestically and internationally while scoring political points at the same time. On any other "official" trip during the campaign, at least one "political" person went along. If there was any trouble, any need for spinning, the political guys were there to put it into context. Not this time. And predictably, the press spun out the Democrats' version of another problem caused by twelve years of Republican urban neglect.

Although "official" on the outside, the White House was plenty political internally. The inside squabbling revolved around Jack Kemp. It was a constant fight. The press was aware that Kemp irked Sununu and the White House boys; he was disregarded in cabinet meetings and cut out of the loop. But he was the one guy with authority and expertise in the area of urban problems.

The President's protectors in the administration were afraid Jack Kemp was going to get out in front of George Bush. Nobody outside saw this, but it took up a lot of energy inside the White House. The last thing anybody needed, when the President had a domestic crisis on his plate, was for him to be invisible and for Jack Kemp to be out front.

President Bush didn't care, he just wanted to fix the problem. And this was the conflict for George Bush: He liked being President, he liked dealing with problems. The press deemed him an "in box" President, but that was his very real skill. He was obsessively concerned and totally absorbed in trying to solve the issue in front of him. He called meetings, he brought in minority leaders and big-city mayors. "What should we do? How should we fix this?" Bush knew and appreciated Kemp's experience with minority communities and urban initiatives. He was calling on Kemp, and the White House staff were tripping over each other to make sure Kemp didn't get in any photo op.

These were dog days for the campaign. For several days, if not weeks, we were stalled, off message, and getting pummeled by the Democrats for creating the L.A. problems in the first place. The Democrats were in spin overdrive. All the big media analysis pieces focused on how this crisis could occur, and they largely concluded it was the Republicans' fault. The Republicans were blamed for urban blight.

These demagogic attacks demanded a concerted political response. But the directive came down, "Do not comment. Do not give any political analysis of the riots." It was a lose-lose situation. We lost campaign momentum, not that we had any, and it re-raised the Democrats' best issue. The White House was not equipped or inclined to do political damage control and, our worst fears confirmed, the political damage mounted steadily.

The response to the L.A. crisis was a prime example of the big difference between government workers and campaign people. What is second nature to people like Bob Teeter and Charlie Black and Rich Bond and White House political director Ron Kaufman and me did not even get processed by Sam Skinner and his crew. They were administrators first; we were partisans; we spoke a different language.

At first they threw the fear of government into us. White House counsel C. Boyden Gray said nobody but Skinner and Teeter and Fred Malek could communicate with each other unless they got specific permission from the White House counsel's office. If we wanted to plan with the White House political director or intergovernmental-affairs director or communications director, we had to go through a lawyer. A lot of my daily work was, "Look, our guy in Georgia says we need to get the vets' issue into the speech." To speak to the speech-writer or anyone at the White House, in every single instance I'd have to write a memo, go to Teeter, explain what we needed and why we needed to speak directly. Teeter would have to go to Skinner, Skinner would have to go to Boyden. Boyden would have to consider it, give the permission, get back to Skinner, who'd get back to Teeter or Malek, who would get back to me. By that time we'd given the speech, minus the local input.

In the beginning everybody complied. No one wanted to create an ethical problem for President Bush by violating these rules, so we remained hamstrung. We couldn't interact during the day, so I'd call people at home, secretively, at night. Well, that's not how campaigns work; they've got to be instantly responsive. It didn't take us campaign maniacs more than a week to start operating under the principle of "Commit the sin and ask forgiveness if you get caught." Boyden's rules were violated on an hourly basis, though we intermittently spat out a memo to throw him off our trail. We didn't do anything illegal, or even unethical, just insubordinate. We figured the free world would survive our insubordination.

But goofy rules aside, we still could not *order* the White House to do the things we needed to reelect George Bush. We obsessed over our electoral maps, media markets, issues national and local. We plotted out detailed presidential events and utterances. Though we spun in separate orbits through the critical pre-convention weeks, we presumed the campaign and the White House were on the same wavelength. Most days we weren't on the same *planet*.

James

With Tsongas out and only Jerry Brown to beat, we were cocky and we got sloppy.

For instance, Governor Clinton created a story when he played nine holes of golf at an all-white country club.

It shouldn't matter. Clinton's a progressive from Little Rock, he's got a 100 percent record on civil rights, everybody knows what side he's on. It was clearly not an intentional racist gesture or even a case of willfully looking the other way. I hardly think it goes to the soul and character of the man.

I mean, I understand how it could happen. When you're in the middle of a campaign looking for a quick bit of relaxation, you find the nearest spot and you're glad when you find it. Yes, with some overview and a knowledge of the history of country clubs in general, you would think someone close to the body would check it out before the governor stepped on the course. But nobody asked, "Is that an integrated club?" It was a mistake, a lapse in concentration. You wish it wouldn't happen, but it's hardly the S & L crisis.

My first reaction? "How could he do something so damn stupid?" He gave Jerry Brown something to do and it kept us from talking about our issues in the news mix. Because of Clinton's outstanding record on civil rights, the thing kind of petered out after two days, but it was avoidable.

We made another mistake that week. We didn't have a clear chain of command and it was catching up with us. I was the Georgia guy, David Wilhelm was the Illinois guy, in Connecticut the baton passed to Stan Greenberg. Stanley was our pollster and the acknowledged expert in the field. Connecticut senator Chris Dodd was his client, and Stan's wife was a congresswoman from the state; he ought to know. Stanley said we were going to have problems in Connecticut.

I don't know how that decision got made. Harold Ickes, a lawyer and influential friend of Clinton's whose father had been in FDR's cabinet; New Jersey politician Dick Leone; and Susan Thomases all said we could win Connecticut and we'd have a lot more problems winning the New York primary two weeks later. There were a lot of Friends of Bill in New York, FOBs who had a personal stake. We went there.

We had come out of Super Tuesday, we'd rolled in the South, we'd rolled in the industrial heartland; we came to Connecticut and got beat by Jerry Brown. It was a bad defeat, no question about it.

We got some bad stories. I think it was legitimate for people to say, "He's getting a little more than one in three Connecticut Democrats to vote for him, he couldn't beat Brown, can he win the general? There is real doubt."

So Brown rolled into New York. We were in the field polling and Greenberg called me and said, "We've got trouble." We were behind Brown. Then there was the little problem with marijuana.

The subject had never come up in debate prep but this wasn't a confrontation, this was a local Sunday morning interview show. When the governor got asked if he had ever smoked marijuana he said he had tried it when he was a student in England but that he hadn't liked it. As a nervous afterthought he said, "I didn't inhale."

I was in the control room looking at the monitor when I heard him say it. I said, "Well, there goes another two days."

Aside from giving fodder to every stand-up comedian in America, the governor cost us time. Instead of talking about how to get drugs off the streets of New York we were talking about Bill Clinton smoking pot at Oxford.

First of all, I believe him when he says he didn't inhale. Let me say: I have smoked marijuana, I have inhaled. For somebody who had never smoked marijuana before, the first time you take it, if you did a survey I guarantee you that for half the people not inhaling would be sort of a normal reaction. But the press immediately decided that saying he didn't inhale was a metaphor for someone who wouldn't take responsibility.

If he was going to lie, why didn't he just do it in the first place: "I never tried it"? If somebody from Oxford existed who had seen him Bogarting a joint, they would get dragged out of the woodwork to say, "What are you talking about, the guy was a pothead." No one ever came forward.

In politics today, if you ask an officeholder who is forty-six, forty-seven years old whether they have ever smoked pot and they say, "Yeah, I tried it when I was in college. Never much cared for it, didn't do much for me, but I did try it," it really doesn't matter. Governor Bruce Babbitt and Senator Al Gore admitted as much and weren't automatically disqualified from pursuing higher office. But when Bill Clinton was running for Congress in 1974 as a former McGovern campaigner, it did matter. He was twenty-eight years old and the question got asked: "Did you ever smoke pot?" His answer was, I never broke the law here in this country.

That was a good and truthful answer then. If, in 1974, he had said, "Well, I tried it once when I was in England but I didn't inhale," the local voting public would have been outraged. "What were you doing in the same room with these drugs?" This is Arkansas, 1974, the tail end of the counterculture; here's a college student, a *McGovern* worker, appealing to the good folks to put him in office. He could have kissed his political career good-bye.

You are able to be more candid about pot smoking in 1992 than you were in 1974, but it's the 1974 answer that you have to build off. If you lied in the past, then you are open to the accusation that your entire career is built on lies, and that can be fatal. That's what we were trying to head off.

Bill Clinton hadn't lied. He had given an adept political answer at the time.

Of course once the press got a whiff of this they got a good buzz.

There is one school of thought that says that anyone who went to college in the late sixties and didn't smoke pot wasn't paying attention. It holds that people of that age and culture vote together, therefore pot smoking is some sort of cultural bellwether. It holds further that Clinton's candidacy was a transition greater than the one between Eisenhower and Kennedy's "new generation of Americans born in this century."

I don't buy that. I do not believe in generational politics. Not all World War II veterans vote alike, not all Vietnam veterans vote alike, not all Vietnam teach-in veterans vote alike. It's widely held that young people are liberal and that they get more conservative as they grow older. But in the modern day, the most popular politician with younger voters was Ronald Reagan. I do not think that people vote generationally.

(ABC News's Jeff Greenfield is of the Vietnam generation. He and I used to discuss all these TV infomercials, which I get a kick out of. His idea was to have Zamfir, Master of the Pan Flute, play at the Democratic convention; more people would know him than knew Al Gore.)

So this pot-smoking thing wasn't going to do us any good. All it was going to do was sic the New York media on us louder and stronger.

The New York media had this idea—I don't know where they get it—that they are smarter and bigger and tougher than anybody else. Reporters would come up to you and say, "How are you holding up with us?" They would actually go around looking for quotes about how tough and mean they were. Maybe it was a New York way of making conversation.

No one in our campaign felt intimidated by New York and its media. Mandy Grunwald understood it. We were on her turf; her dad had been editor in chief of *Time* magazine. She knew more people in New York media than anybody else. She gave us the scoop. "Look," she said, "it's just a giant monster that has several deadlines a day and has to be continually fed. Either you feed it or it feeds on you."

Two days after the inhaling firestorm the *L.A. Times* came out with a poll that said that 39 percent of Americans thought Bill Clinton had the honesty and integrity to serve as president, and 38 didn't. We were on the respirator again.

One of the major elements that saved us in New York was the fact that we were running against Jerry Brown. He was not ready for prime time.

Our huffing and puffing in Connecticut had put some wind in Brown's sails. But a little success is a dangerous thing. One of the lessons that presidential politics teaches us—it taught Tsongas and it taught Brown—is that when you get thrust into the spotlight, if you don't have a very good campaign you get confused. If you don't have it thought out beforehand you're in a lot of trouble.

If I was going to run a long shot in a presidential race I would spend the time and money to have a contingency plan in place in case I got a hot hand. One day you have to deal with four reporters and fifty checks coming in; the next day you have forty reporters and five thousand checks. And you better be able to deal with it.

Jerry couldn't. He couldn't get a schedule out. His social life and friends were suddenly fair game. In a devastating blow that advanced our cause tremendously, Senator Pat Moynihan pointed out that Brown's flat-tax idea discriminated against lower-income people.

Then, Dennis Rivera, head of the Local 1199 hospital workers' union and a very powerful guy in New York City, switched his allegiance from us to Brown. He and Jesse Jackson were close and we were told that Jackson convinced him to make the change. Shortly thereafter, Jerry Brown announced that, if nominated, he would select Jesse Jackson to be his vice-presidential nominee. Jackson, for his part, didn't endorse Brown but said he was moved by the gesture. Their picture together appeared on the front page of *The New York Times*.

Well, Brown just plummeted. That photo did it. I mean, his Jewish vote about disappeared.

I know, after all the anger and repercussions about Jackson's referring to New York City with the slur "Hymietown," that Jesse has tried to repair his reputation with the Jewish community. As of April 1992 it hadn't worked. If there is a more politically sensitive vote in this country than the Jewish vote, I ain't run across it yet. Jerry Brown made *the* major mistake. At that point the party was over for Jerry. He knew it, but he kept running.

Jerry's campaign was a distraction we didn't need. Our organization, which had been tight in New Hampshire, was starting to grow, and the internal workings weren't smooth. It was kind of like a floating crap game with different players getting their hands on the dice. Harold Ickes was the New York campaign manager, Mickey Kantor ran the meetings in the staff room; Mandy, because she was from New York, was sort of the consultant with portfolio; Susan Thomases had a lot of say-so. There was nobody in charge.

As a result there was no focus. If we were not saying who we were and what we stood for, it was left to the media to do it for us—and they were not our allies. They were sniffing around after loose women and loose joints.

Finally we said, "Look, let's do what we did in New Hampshire. Let's get out there and let people see us. The tabloids are defining us. No, let's *us* define us. Screw them."

The New York primary, with its huge media coverage, affords you a lot of ways to communicate directly with the voters. The Sunday morning interview was one way; the *Donahue* show, which taped in Manhattan, was another.

All Donahue wanted to talk about was Gennifer Flowers. We went on the show and figured we'd put the story to rest, but on the air Donahue kept raising her wildest allegations and going right after Clinton. When the audience took up for Clinton—one person got up and said, "Given the pathetic state of most of the United States at this point . . . I can't believe you spent half an hour of airtime attacking this man's character. I'm not even a Bill Clinton supporter, but I think this is ridiculous"—the press coverage began to turn. We were not going to be a punching bag anymore, we were going to go out and be a hell of a lot more aggressive.

But this was just another example of our campaign moving in fits and starts. We would roll, get cocky, get sloppy, get beat back, get rolling again, get cocky, get sloppy, get beat back . . . And what happens when you do that is you get tired. You just get whupped.

A state race normally doesn't start in earnest until Labor Day. Then you run for two months, end up winning or losing on the first Tuesday in November, get drunk on election night, have a hangover, and then take the whole rest of November off, do Thanksgiving, see your family, get through Christmas, and start thinking about the next election cycle. In a presidential, particularly in primary season, you run one race and in another week you've got the next one, then the next. You have your victory glass of champagne and, boom, something else is going on. You train for it, you don't go full speed the whole way, but every now and then you just don't get up off the floor as fast as you can. It's a real stamina test. I was always amazed at Clinton's stamina. Amazed. Plenty of times I had to take myself out of the game. I'd just go back to Washington and lie down for a day, answer the mail, go to dinner with Mary. Anything, anything you can imagine except deal with a campaign decision.

We won New York with 41 percent of the vote. The Brown/Jackson pairing turned it around. Brown got 26 percent. Tsongas, who was already out of the race, beat him by 3 points. On the same day we won primaries in Kansas, Minnesota, and Wisconsin.

You'd think we'd be satisfied; our man was going to be the Democratic party candidate for president of the United States. We'd beaten all comers, we'd convinced Democratic voters that we were their man, we had come from nowhere and engineered a nice victory.

I was miserable.

What did we really have? We were about to catch the fish, but the fish was going to be dead. We had high negatives, a fairly fractured party, and a campaign structure that changed from state to state and shook like Jell-O when we stood still. We were winning battles and losing the war. A *New York Times* poll showed we had only 15 percent favorable. Bush's support was eroding, but we didn't look strong enough to take it over. On top of that, we were not the insurgent candidate in an insurgent year. With Perot in the race it was going to be hard to convince people that we were the ones with new ideas. From New Hampshire on I got more and more depressed. It all came together in New York; if we didn't do something fast we were going to get killed in November.

Mandy, Stan, and I met in Mickey Kantor's room at the Sheraton New York Hotel on Seventh Avenue and Fifty-first Street. Our expertise was polling, media, and getting the job done. With the nomination basically in hand, we said, the campaign wouldn't be needing us day-to-day for a while. We had the luxury of time; we wanted to split off and find out how to build a general election campaign. Mickey said fine. We called it the Manhattan Project, and if we weren't building a weapon to revolutionize political warfare, we were at least looking for a way to drop the big one.

There were two basic things we didn't know and had to find out: One, had people given up on us? Was Bill Clinton a damaged candidate? There was a lot of stuff out there—Gennifer Flowers, the draft, Slick Willie—and we didn't know if general election voters had said, "To hell with this guy." And, two, we didn't understand the exact nature of our problem.

It was my feeling that people didn't think Bill Clinton was disreputable, they just didn't know where he stood or how long he would stand there. "We don't have a draft problem," I told Stan and Mandy, "we don't have a Gennifer Flowers problem. We have a 'Slick Willie' problem."

We ran focus groups in Kansas City, Ohio, California. We'd eat lunch and bounce it off ourselves and the waiters. This went on for two and a half months.

We didn't come close to an answer for a long while. In mid-May a national CNN/*Time* poll had Perot ahead with 33 percent of the vote, Bush second with 28, and Clinton last with 24. People were talking about, if you didn't get 25 percent of the national vote, the Democratic party wouldn't qualify for federal matching funds in the next election. We were facing oblivion.

Ultimately what we found was that people didn't know who Bill Clinton was, and what they thought they knew they didn't much like. We did a focus group in Allentown, Pennsylvania, and one woman told us, "Look, if you asked Bill Clinton what his favorite color is, he'd tell you, 'Plaid.' " We used to refer to it as the "plaid problem."

That's what not having a message does to you. A political campaign is a constant quest to define yourself. An inability to define yourself lets others define you. The other difficulty, when you're without a central theme, is that you tend to define yourself on that given day. Days change, and with the press with you at all times to chronicle your campaign they are professionally interested in those changes. They like nothing better than for you to make microscopic alterations in the fabric of your candidacy; they're there to unravel you.

What we needed was a harder rationale, a well-stated reason why Bill Clinton was running for president. What saved us was that we knew it was there. When we would get behind, as in New Hampshire and New York, we would force ourselves into a rationale; when we'd get ahead we'd lapse out of it. We needed to refine our plan, pinpoint the elements of our economic vision and our political vision, and contrast it against George Bush.

We became a lot more definitive about things. We changed the way that we talked, we accentuated the times in Bill Clinton's record when he had taken on tough fights.

Part of what we began to change was the way we answered a question. We needed an internal discipline against going on and on and on and on.

Let's say somebody asks, "What's your position on the balanced-budget amendment?" You can answer by saying, "Well, there are certainly some good elements to it, but you have to weigh those against the bad. And I think when you look at it in its totality it is probably not the best public policy as constructed. But it is something that we need to continue to look at and monitor because if we are unable to get the budget deficit under control, we may have to look to some pretty bold measures to do that. So while I have an open mind on it right now, I would oppose it."

That was not the answer to give.

The answer to give was, "I'm against it. Now let me tell you why."

For all his political skills and formidable intellect, Bill Clinton had one blind spot: Hillary. He was aware of her intelligence, her ability, her importance to the campaign. I don't think he knew how unpopular she was at the time.

We were at a Holiday Inn in Charleston, West Virginia, and had the results of a dial group that we had just done. In a dial group you've got a group of people watching a video with their hands on a dial; they turn the dial up if they see or hear something they like, down if they don't. The video can include the candidate's speeches, interviews, ads, anything. Once we had tabulated the results, we superimposed them as a line on the screen and ran the tape for Clinton. He had never seen the technique and was pretty fascinated. It gave him an immediate reading on what he was saying and how he was saying it.

Hillary was not particularly popular at this moment in the campaign, and when she appeared on the screen the dials just plunged. All of them. I mean they dropped into a trench. Clinton looked at the chasm line and said, "You know, they just don't like her hair."

I dove under a coffee table. If I caught somebody out of the corner of my eye I was gonna die laughing. No one could talk, no one could even make eye contact. There was this stifled silence. I stayed under that table, pretending to tie my shoe. No way I was standing up. Finally Clinton left the room.

You know how you laugh so hard you're scared you're not going to catch your breath? People were collapsing.

"They don't like her hair!"

This was a man who desperately loved his wife. He could not deal with the fact that, at the time, Hillary was unpopular. Couldn't deal with it? He couldn't see it! If someone asked me one moment to remember from the campaign, it would have been "They don't like her hair."

These were hardly our salad days. The campaign had very serious structural problems, and we started having meetings to try and create a functioning organization. First off, we needed a communications director. The first name we came up with was Paul Begala. The governor discussed it with him, but Paul didn't feel he could accept. Paul's wife, Diane, was due to have a baby that July, and he'd promised he would be home. The only other person who could do it was George.

Then we tried to formulate our general election strategy.

Ross Perot made our strategic problems even tougher than they already were. His presence complicated our message. He had already staked his claim to being what we wanted to be, the anti-Washington candidate. Perot had something I think every politician wants: He was heading a popular movement. We were heading a political party. Most politicians would rather be in his shoes. Clinton felt that Clinton himself was the legitimate source for a lot of what Perot was say-ing. "What are you talking about?" he'd say, "I *am* him. He's doing the things I did. We were doing the town hall meeting before he did."

The candidate wanted to be the ultimate change agent in the race. The strategy people, on the other hand, would say, "Don't try to out-Perot Perot, try to out-Clinton Perot." We wanted to take it more on our turf, which was investment in people. We struggled for slogans and positioning.

It took almost three months, but finally our thinking began to crys-tallize. Clearly where we were was "Putting People First." Asking who came up with the phrase is kind of like asking "Who came up with the idea of the off-tackle play?" Ask five people who came up with it, they'll all say they did. I believe it was me, but I could be wrong. Putting *something* first was an old political saw: "Put New Jersey First," "Put Virginia First." It just sort of expanded to the most uni-versal of all universes, "Put People First."

Perot wanted to be an outsider and shake the government up. Bush was saying the government shouldn't do anything. We were different. We said the government ought to invest in job training and health care for its people, and not engage in the procedural or stylistic tech-nicalities like lobby reform and congressional pay raises that Perot was promoting.

In any campaign, everybody wants to accomplish everything. The real hard part is to get to where people let you accomplish anything at all. Governor Clinton didn't want to cede any issues to Perot. He said, "I've been talking about these things for two years, why should I stop talking about them now because Perot is in?" Our response, and it was not easy to confront the governor with this, was, "There has to be message triage. If you say three things, you don't say anything. You've got to decide what's important."

So many people believe the job of a political strategist is to take an empty vessel and fill it up. That happens periodically. But usually you already have a full vessel, or an overflowing vessel. One of my favorite expressions is "It is okay for a political candidate to have an opinion on everything under the sun, it's just not okay to render said opinion." Campaigns get into trouble for saying too much; when you say a lit-tle, you say a lot. Repetition is your friend. Our job is more often tak-ing a full vessel and emptying it.

CHAPTER 10

Mary

Someone in the media has an original thought. One. Then the entire national press corps is done for the day, or week, sometimes longer. Once the press line has been established, you can work for hours, days, even an entire campaign and not budge it. This is pretty infuriating when they're not seeing things your way. Which is pretty much all the time. The only thing to do is get out there when the story line is being created and demand they hear your side.

My reporter friends insist that they don't advocate or condemn a candidacy. What they say they do is follow the polls. If a candidate is on a downward slide, they pile on. If a candidacy is in an ascending trajectory, they pump it up. At least in the beginning, I suppose that's true; they generally don't pick a candidate and go out and support him. In the end, they like the fight.

Campaign operatives learn quickly there are rules for dealing with the press, and there are rules for them dealing with you. I got taught by one of the American originals, the syndicated columnist Jules Witcover, who has covered every presidential campaign since Eisenhower versus Stevenson. I love the guys (and they were mostly guys) who literally hung out with John F. Kennedy in one of the last races where you could hang out with the candidates. They have endless great war stories and are less knee-jerk in their coverage than the younger reporters. Jules in particular has a perspective. He doesn't get exercised over the day-to-day events of the campaign so much as he considers "What did this whole week add up to?" or "How does this event fit into the bigger scheme of things?" The older guys always come at it with a wider view.

Witcover is especially fastidious about "the rules." When I first got into national politics and was learning the ropes he told me, "Look, let me explain something to you. If you don't want your name attached to a story, you say 'I'm on background.' If you only want your thoughts used and not your words or your name, say you're on 'deep background.' If you don't want me to use anything, you go 'off the record.' In all other cases, you're on the record. I'm going to print what you say. That's just how it works."

It sounded easy. But when you're first talking to the press you feel like a jerk saying, "This is on background." Some time later, Jules and I were talking about the abortion issue. I was spouting off about how I thought the debate and dialogue had matured on both sides. To substantiate my point, I referenced the absence of screaming rhetoric with an unfortunate choice of words: "You don't see 'fetuses,' you don't see 'hangers' dominating the debate." It's an easy topic to get graphic about. He printed it.

My riff became the "Quote of the Day" in *Hotline*, the political junkie's bible. When I saw it I called Jules immediately.

"How could you do this to me?"

"You know the rules. You should have said, 'I'm on background.' "

It was a lesson I learned on the spot. He showed me not only how the system worked, but by cutting me no slack whatsoever, he taught me in practical terms that no one is going to give you anything. You can't call people back after something has come out of your mouth and say, "I meant that on background" and *expect* them to let you off the hook. It's a judgment call on their part. I have on more than one occasion really screwed up and had to go back and ask a reporter not to print something I'd said. I meant to say it on background or I didn't mean to say it at all. My usual line is "I'll give you my firstborn male child if you don't use it." If you're really in a lot of pain sometimes they'll let you slide. Of course, as the world works, that means next time you've got to give them some real juicy tidbits. You owe them.

You talk at your own peril. In the press it breaks out in the same way it does with all human beings: Some people have a strict code of honor which they adhere to under all circumstances, and some do not. You only learn who's honorable and who isn't through experience. There are blatant violations of the code, and spiritual violations. A blatant violation is obvious: A reporter quotes you after you've specified you're on background or off the record. You get really wary with that guy then; nothing is off the record, even when you specifically stipulate it's off the record.

Spiritual violations are trickier. Because of the way I talk, my rhetoric is identifiable. In the 1992 campaign if they used one of my "Maryspeak" lines unattributed (as in "a source close to the campaign"), they burned me. If a reporter quotes a background source in a way that's clearly identifiable, and they know it, that's a spiritual violation.

My gender also caused problems. Reporters could never say "she" when referring to their source because Torie and I were basically the only "she"s on background from the campaign. So they had to resort to tortuous sentence construction, which pretty much gave us up anyway. They couldn't say "he said," because that would be a lie, and they couldn't say, "she said," because that would reveal us, but an ungendered quote implied they were covering up for a woman.

The relationship between operative and reporter is a precarious détente based on mutually assured destruction. Operatives use their power as the source of information to control the agenda; reporters use their power as disseminators of the operatives' information to expand the agenda. But a source's power is very tenuous because there's only one way to enforce it and that is to state your position and nothing else. However, since no reporter wants to be your shill, they'll always try to drag something, usually something stupid, out of you. If they get it, you've become a leak.

Negative leaks—information or perspective that works against your candidate's best interests—are obviously bad. But not *all* leaks are bad. If you want to get a behind-the-scenes story out about your guy that shows him clearly in command in a quasi-crisis, or moved to tears over some American tragedy—whatever—you can leak a reporter an *exclusive* peek at your guy's private moment, and chances are he'll print it just because no one else has it. Reporters aren't in the business of making your guy look good, but that's a good leak.

Another one is the floating of an idea in the press without attribution, just to gauge the reaction. If it gets shot down by pundits and colleagues, you deny your campaign said it; if it's embraced, you put it out formally with your guy's name attached.

A problem with incumbents is they hate bad leaks so much that they start clamping down on *all* leaks, and you lose a very useful tool. Eliminating leaks is near to impossible, but John Sununu had a Gestapo method that infuriated everyone. First of all, we Bush loyalists never, ever leaked anything negative about the President. That stuff came from detractors around town, all attributed to "a source close to the White House" or "a GOP activist." Well, that could be anyone in D.C. *who wasn't a Democrat*! But Sununu had his assistant come in every morning at four-thirty or five o'clock and yellow-highlight all the unnamed quotes; then they'd speculate as to the identity of the source, and with no other evidence than their suspicions, report "leakers" to President Bush.

For reasons I've never figured out, I was on Sununu's hit list early. It started getting back to me that Bush was unhappy with my "leaks" to *Washington Post* reporter Ann Devroy.

If I'd had a harpoon, I'd have speared Sununu. I never leaked to Devroy. Sununu couldn't control his own traitorous troops at the White House, so he told Bush the leaks were coming from the outside. Sununu was executing his political enemies by falsely accusing them of committing Bush's worst peeve. The upshot was that the circle of Bush supporters outside the White House quit working the press out of fear that we'd get blamed for negative leaks. In the critical months leading up to the campaign, our press relations had degenerated significantly; no one could return political calls except Sununu, and he had the political acumen of a doorknob.

When we worked the media we stuck to our story. When it comes to *policy* issues, sticking to your story, while boring for the media, is good for America. The leadership of this country should be focused, should be able to tell the American people where we're going. A united voice from the administration gives the public a clear view of its direction; clarity gives the public confidence. That's why unified "talking points" are so important. Sure, they limit the scope of an issue, and sticking to them leaves you open to charges of media manipulation, but when you're working off talking points you have a better chance of projecting coordinated policy, which is what the public expects and deserves from the leadership of the nation. Sticking to your story on *political* issues is a lot tougher.

A perfect example of how the lack of talking points can kill you is the media hubbub around the 1988 nomination of Dan Quayle for vice president.

At the GOP convention in New Orleans, no one knew who the VP nominee would be. Every morning at seven we had a logistical meeting detailing the events of the day. We'd receive our talking points and then spend the rest of the day disseminating them to the delegates and the press. Right before we would go on the convention floor we would regroup and be told, "Here's the theme for the night. Here's your talking points." Campaign media "bookers" spent their whole day scheduling GOP spokesmen, and from four in the afternoon until the convention's evening session was gaveled to order around seven-thirty that night, nonstop, we'd each do sixty or seventy stand-up interviews with local and national radio and TV. You go from one microphone to another, perpetually disoriented and exhausted. You're just a piece of meat and you say the same thing over and over again.

Vice President Bush revealed his selection to no one until the last conceivable minute, the afternoon he arrived in New Orleans. Everyone was caught off guard and unprepared. Surprises at conventions are the last thing you want; everything is scripted and planned for down to the minute. Once you're there, you're on autopilot. A surprise is like losing an engine in midflight. The lack of preparation for Quayle's selection was more like a midair collision.

The press was even crazier than we were. They hate secrets and live in mortal fear of getting scooped. They were hyperventilating by the time they got the word, and they pounced on Quayle.

We were clueless. We'd been given briefing books on every conceivable selection, from Kemp to Dole: their backgrounds, what we should say about them, why they were the perfect selection. . . . We'd gotten nothing on Quayle.

No one knew who Dan Quayle was. Obviously, we knew he was the junior senator from Indiana, but the surprise of the selection extended even to the research gurus. The big-cheese briefers slunk into the pre-convention organization room and handed us a single photocopied page from the *Almanac of American Politics.*

Now, that's a great resource tool if you already know the basic philosophy of the politician you're looking up. It tells you what committees they serve on, their margin of victory, Ronald Reagan's vote history in their district, their congressional voting record. It's an invaluable reference book, but that's all.

And that's all we got. Nothing about Dan Quayle's politics, his personality, his character. Worse, no written points detailing a political or philosophical explanation for his surprise selection. We went into battle unarmed. Amongst ourselves we bunched up and whispered, "Wasn't he involved in that Paula Parkinson thing?" We were given no political information whatsoever. Not even any backgrounder on "Who *is* this guy?" Nobody even knew what he looked like. Most deadly, we had no damage-control points on his heaviest political baggage, his service in the National Guard.

When the frenzy around Dan Quayle erupted, nobody could beat it back because nobody had any talking points. If we'd known his strengths we could have spotlighted them. We were unprepared and it cost him his public image. I will always contend that his unfortunate and undeserved reputation as a dim bulb can be laid directly at the feet of the people who didn't give us any damn talking points. He took all these hits and we didn't know how to defend him.

The press makes talking points seem like thought control. They're not; they're just all the good things you can say about a subject rolled into one. It's disorienting for the public, subject to intense information bombardment, to receive inconsistent blather from their government and their candidates.

If political operatives were the media's only source of information, the power would be all ours—which is why running a tight ship was so successful in the Reagan White House. But we rarely control the agenda, because reporters always have the option, which they exercise with regularity, of calling around us. Once they find another way in, we are forced to talk to them on their terms.

The best hope for any success once you're in their web is to abide by a few cardinal rules for dealing with the media.

Cardinal rule #1: *No matter what, don't lie to the press.* You can say "I don't know." (Some politicos simply cannot form their lips to say "I don't know," which I think is stupid. If I'm not in possession of the facts it's always safest to own up to it.) You can say "I can't tell you," or my favorite, "With bamboo shoots under my freshly manicured fingernails I would never tell you," or the ever popular "That's my story and I'm sticking to it." But you cannot lie. Not on background, not off the record, never. Forget that lying is unethical. If a source ever lies to a reporter and gets caught, you will forever after be tormented by that reporter. They will play with you like a kid pulling the wings off a fly.

The flip side of lying to a reporter is being misquoted by one, or being taken out of context in a malicious way. When a journalist betrays you, you have only one defense weapon: You don't return their phone calls. They have burned a source.

Cardinal rule #2: *Never let them get hungry.* Rule #2A: *Feed them as well as you are being fed.* They're riding around in buses all day, they're bored, they're hot, they're cold, they're hungry. On one trip the campaign got hot food, the press got stale sandwiches. Very bad idea. These people are, as Jules Witcover said, captives to convenience. If they're starving, if they can't get to a phone, if you don't get them a text of a speech and they have to recall it all themselves or go back and listen to their tape recorders, they get cranky. It's not like they're going to write better stories if you take care of them, but if they're feeling cranky they're going to write cranky.

Cardinal rule #3: *Remember their deadline needs.* Forget road events after four P.M. Reporters have to (a) hook up their laptop computers; (b) retrieve their notes and recordings; (c) construct a coherent story; (d) feed it to their home base; (e) explain it to their editors; (f) backtrack on their editors' questions. The crunch time for most dailies is five to seven P.M. Unless there's some extraordinary event, first editions are put to bed by eight P.M., so beat stories have to be in by seven. Anything you say or do after that time is a tree falling in the forest. Electronic press has an even earlier cutoff point. They generally like to use footage from afternoon events for the nightly news.

Cardinal rule #4: *Don't tire them out.* Even if the candidate can do six events in a day, and a lot of times he has to, that translates to nine events in reporters' body time. If we're leaving the White House at six in the morning, they're leaving home at four-thirty. If we get home at ten at night, they get home at one. The press don't get chauffeured motorcades to their homes.

You can't take these guys out on the road for ten days and wear them out. They get overtired and they miss the story. After two days all they want to do is write out their notes and go to sleep. You can't get a good spin on the story because they've lost it.

Cardinal rule #5: *Remember, they may be liberal scum but they're still human beings.* Since I'm a conservative, my first reaction to the press, in toto, is that they're a scurrilous bunch. But as a Midwesterner, I always react to people in general by liking them. Some people are wary when they first meet strangers; my first reaction to anyone I don't know is to like them. I always consider individuals first. And I've always liked reporters as individuals. They're smart, they're informed, they're hardworking. They're kind of creative, they're ambitious, they have interesting lives. In the soul of every good reporter is really a novelist or historian. They're the kind of people I'm attracted to.

Some of them, I know, aren't going to like me on general principles. They just have preconceived notions about conservatives, like they're looking for a pulsating 666 on my forehead. Nothing I can do about those people. For instance, I think in real life I would like liberal columnist Michael Kinsley, if I ever got to know him. But he's one of those guys who I just know is going to hate me no matter what comes up. If you know somebody's going to hate you then your first reaction is, at a minimum, to be wary. And probably not to like them before they don't like you, so you don't feel rejected. So I basically always stayed away from predictable libs.

But most of the regulars who reported on and traveled with the campaign were really good people. One time in Michigan I was blabbing with my old pals and missed Air Force One. I got stuck on the press plane, or the animal plane, as we called it, which is when I really developed an understanding of the physical demands of their job. Air Force One was "wheels up" two hours earlier; the press were still on the ground filing their stories. Their plane was crowded and disorganized and buzzing. No stewards, individual phones, copy machines, or hot food. This was flying steerage.

It was alien territory. When I got on I flopped down in the front and stated, "I'm having a glass of wine and I don't want to hear anything from any of you guys, okay? I don't want any questions, I don't want any badgering, I don't want anything. Let's just have a couple of drinks here and chill out."

So we had, like, half a drink and they started asking questions.

I begged, "I'm not doing this. I'm not doing this. I'm going up with the pilot if you guys don't shut up."

Susan Spencer of CBS and Ann Compton of ABC were sitting behind me. I love those two. Separate from all of this is a kind of camaraderie among women. Not an "I am woman, I am strong, we're all oppressed and we're in this together" kind of bond. It's more, "Oh, thank God we can talk about PMS" kind of thing. Women are always subliminally conscious of the extra burdens that fall on women who do these kinds of jobs. As in, no one takes out our dry cleaning, no one cleans our house, no one gets the groceries . . . None of the women have wives.

So we were bonding and some man, who hadn't heard my self-proclaimed set of rules for that leg of the trip, trolled up from the back of the plane and started being a reporter.

"Don't ask her questions!" Susan Spencer snapped. "Leave her alone."

Okay, this is sexist, but I have a special affection for women reporters. They generally work their stories harder than the guys do, they always get multiple sources for their information, they usually keep an open mind. It is a rare instance when a woman would not let me give my side, or didn't try to confirm it once I'd given it. I can't remember one Sunday afternoon the entire campaign when I wasn't bothered, even at home, by Robin Toner of *The New York Times*. The girl just never quit working.

Ann Devroy of *The Washington Post* is a very special case. She understands politics. Politics is not a science, it's an art form. Some reporters don't get that. Some politicians don't get it. Ann does. I love talking to reporters who understand politics, and I love talking to Ann . . . even when she was blasting us, which was about every day.

I first met Devroy in 1988 when she was the *Post*'s political editor, which meant that all the political reporters would funnel their stories back to her desk and she would decide what got in and what needed more digging. She was always fair. She would call up and say, "So-and-so has filed a story from Michigan. Are these all the facts? Are we going in the right direction?" She was very precise about her work. Before and after her editorial assignment she was on the White House beat. She knew it better than we did.

Devroy had covered George Bush from the beginning of time. She knew him inside out, which of course worked to our detriment. She has a photographic memory and didn't even need to look at her files. If the President said something that did not in every aspect and detail reflect what he had said in the past, she knew it and had no qualms about calling it to the world's attention.

She has a galaxy of sources, from secretaries to janitors to Hill insiders. The whine of her competitors was that everyone leaked to her because she was *The Washington Post*, but the fact was she dug like crazy. She'd have her facts all lined up and her story down cold and then she'd call and put you in the position of confirming or denying. She broke a lot of big stories but she was always fair.

Nobody lied to Ann. If you lied to Ann she'd haunt you for the rest of your life. She would specifically keep calling you so she could put you in her story and trash you. You just don't lie to Devroy.

The White House hated her guts. Called her the Bitch Queen. They never said Ann Devroy's name over there, they always said "the bitch" and everybody knew who it was.

She is a good reporter and my good friend. We used to laugh on the campaign that my biggest sin was not being Carville's girlfriend, it was being Devroy's girlfriend.

Right now I am breaking another cardinal rule: *Never thank a reporter for doing a good job.* It's the worst thing you can do to a reporter. Michael Wines of *The New York Times* wrote a piece during the general election campaign that just stuck out as totally and completely fair. Because it was almost a once-in-a-campaign occurrence, I remember reading his piece, putting down the paper, and saying out loud, "Oh my God, I can't believe somebody actually wrote what was happening." Torie Clarke and some others of us who were on the trail at the time went to Michael that day and said, "Thank you for a fair piece." He looked at us like we had the plague.

There are very few secrets on a campaign. The next thing we heard, a bunch of other reporters were grousing about Wines and accusing him of being a shill for Bush, of being "in the tank." By paying him a compliment we had compromised him. Reporters will always warn you, "Just don't say anything good about me, it'll ruin my career."

James

The other side of that is when a reporter pulls you aside and says, "I want you to know, I'm voting for you guys."

I don't want to hear about it. "No, man, don't tell me that." That guy, he's going to go out of his way to screw you. It's almost like some affirmative-action program. Because they like you they figure they've got to be really tough on you to be "fair" to the other side.

Mary

Campaign coverage swings like a pendulum. I think the grossly generous press treatment of Clinton in the general election, for example, was an overreaction to their overkill in the primaries. Their excuse for being so tough on Bush in '92 was that they felt they had gone easy on him in '88. They also conceded they were punishing us for not running as tight an operation this time as we did then. They gave us grudging respect for '88, they gave us no latitude for the looseness of the '92 operation.

James

No one understands the power of the media in this country. I went into this campaign believing they were powerful. I didn't know. The power they have is staggering. And they really do guard it.

They like to think of themselves as learned and insightful and thoughtful and considered. They claim the mantle of truth. Hell, truth is they make instant snap judgments and after that all of their time, all of their energy, all of their creativity is spent on nothing but validating their original judgment. Something happens and three minutes after the event they all talk to each other and decide "This is the story," and the story must remain thus in perpetuity. They claim the moral high ground; their job is to report facts and tell people the truth. But information is secondary to them, self-justification is primary. Once the collective media mind is made up, it will not change.

Until you understand that, you can never understand the media. *Their original take is the one that's going to last.* Knowing this, as a political strategist, it is your imperative to get out there right away and make sure your side of the story is the one they see and hear and write and say. That is why you have to be in the first news cycle, not the follow-up; that is why we try everything to get our story out first and best. It's why we went down first in New Hampshire and claimed victory. History gets created in about three minutes. Don't miss it. If you get there a moment too late, you're dead.

Once they've got their story they stick to it. At some point they stop thinking about an issue and just pursue it. There's no one who has dealt with the national media who has not gotten any number of phone calls saying, "I'm writing a story and I want to say this. Can you say it for me?" Reporters try to get you to say what they want you to say, not what you've got to say. If you say what *you* want to say, they keep coming back to try and get you to say what *they* want you to say. I tell them, "Look, we're going to be on this phone an awful long time. Now, do you want me to tell you what I think? Because I'm not going to tell you what you *want* me to think."

They made up this phrase, "spin doctors." The word "spin," I think, means what political strategists do when we go out and put our candidate in the most favorable light. That's what spin is. Well, la-di-da, guess what? They're right. What do you want me to say? Of course. That's my job. Why don't the media just admit the truth about themselves, that they're way more into self-justification than information? Then we could go on from there.

Take, for example, Bill Clinton. Here was a guy who was my age, who grew up in the South, who cut his teeth on his passion for civil rights and his opposition to the war in Vietnam. And a bunch of Yankee yuppie reporters decided that he was Slick Willie. It's an article of faith among the national media that Bill Clinton was an ambitious politician who tailored his positions to get elected since the doctor slapped him on his butt when he was born.

I kept saying, "What are you guys talking about? Do you really think that a guy who was an utterly, totally ambitious political animal would have as his two defining moments entering politics his opposition to the Vietnam war and his passion for civil rights? Look, I'm the same age as him. Do you think that a political consultant, if he was conniving to get his guy governor of Arkansas, would have said, 'What you've got to do is go to Texas and be George McGovern's campaign manager. And you have to take a really strong civil rights stand'? Are you guys nuts?"

They would listen to me but they would never accept any evidence to the contrary. They couldn't say, "This is a complex man who has beliefs, and who, like a lot of politicians, is ambitious." If an undeniable fact runs counter to the story they want to write, they will ignore the fact.

They try to be honest people. A lot of them I like. But they're so into self-justification that they have turned journalism into the one institution in America with the least capacity for self-examination and self-criticism. If a political professional criticizes them they say it's the government that's doing it and hide behind the First Amendment. These people think the First Amendment belongs to them. It doesn't; it belongs to the American people. The ultimate arrogance is that they view any criticism as some sort of censorship or media-bashing. Democrats have Republicans to criticize us; Republicans have Democrats to criticize them. Ford's got GM, GM's got Ford. But the media, they never criticize each other. Thou shalt speak no evil of another reporter.

There is a natural conflict between reporters and campaign strategists. Reporters, from the day they walk into journalism school, news is defined to them as "something different." Every day the media get up, they're looking for something new and different to report. What campaign strategists are about is focus, repetition, consistency. Every day we get up, we're trying to get them to report the same thing over and over.

So how do we get them to do it?

If you want schoolchildren to eat spinach, you cannot serve them hamburger. If you give them a choice, they ain't going to eat spinach. Now, you can trick them a little bit. You can put some Parmesan cheese on the spinach, you can put on some olive oil, some garlic, you can sauté it, you can add some mushrooms, some hot bacon drippings. But you've got to have spinach. Kids don't like spinach every day. They want cheeseburgers and ice cream, so it's an ongoing struggle.

The media's dietary habits are not particularly healthful. They kind of like their high-fat foods, like cheese fries and patty melts: Gennifer Flowers, Hillary's hairdo. They're not too big on the garden vegetables of the campaign, like job creation and health care costs. And usually, the further down the food chain you go, the worse the dietary habits get. New York tabloids, they like really greasy cheeseburgers, like whether you inhale or not.

Candidates are always asking, "Was the media happy?" Our job is not to make them happy; their job is not to make us happy. Our job is to get them to report what we think the campaign message is. Their job is to report what they think is news and controversy. So we have to make our ideas look controversial. We have to make them look appetizing. We've got to cook this spinach at the right temperature.

I can show you poll after poll that says that people don't vote based solely on the abortion issue. But I guarantee you that for every story out of Washington on education funding there are twenty on abortion funding. Why? Everybody's for education; there's no inherent conflict there. On abortion you've got interest groups on each side, you've got fire, you've got rhetoric. It's a point of conflict. It's cheeseburgers.

I think there are very few dishonest people in the media. Do I think they are out of touch? Yes. Do I think that they love to cover themselves more than they do the candidates? Yes. Do I think that they like to create news where sometimes it doesn't exist? Yes. And do I think that they feed off each other and look at stories in a pack? Yes, I do. But do I think they're bad people? Quite clearly, the answer in almost all instances is no.

One of the shabbiest journalistic techniques that I know of is the man-in-the-street interview. Reporters go out and interview ten people. Do they report back that nine out of ten were for Clinton or for health care or pro-choice? No. They put one person on the air saying one thing and one saying the exact opposite, so they can give equal weight to the positions. In the guise of equal time they have badly skewed what people really think. We call it "equivalency journalism" and it's a very bad trait.

There seems to be more tolerance for sloppiness now than there has been before. If a reporter gets a fact wrong, more often than not he's not even upset. A journalist ought to be outraged by a factual error; it calls into question the profession's entire credibility. At the very least they should say, "I can't believe I did that. I feel terrible." But I've never seen a reporter kick a trash can over the fact that he made an error. Mostly it's "Oh, well, okay, what do you want me to do about it? I'm on deadline. You gonna call my editor and get me in trouble?" I'm not likely to do that, I've got to work with these people. Maybe you get a retraction. But an original error in a page one story isn't properly corrected by a retraction on page A20. Other reporters pick up the incorrect story and it just keeps getting spread over and over again.

The real change in media coverage is the emerging power of CNN. CNN has become a very, very important player in presidential campaigns. *Headline News* as much as anything, but certainly CNN news more than regular network news.

It used to be that the Associated Press had the real effect on campaign coverage. *The New York Times, The Washington Post*, and the other majors are all morning papers, while the AP serviced afternoon papers with the first take on breaking campaign events. They were the first story that other people in the media could see.

But there are fewer and fewer afternoon papers in the country, and CNN is on all day, every day. The way the news cycle now works is that you have an event in the morning, the reporters go up to their hotel rooms and are working on their stories from one to two in the afternoon, and they're looking at *Headline News*. It's now becoming an article of faith that television is more important than print, so the first television coverage they see is CNN. If you want to find out what's going on, it's the only game in town during the day. That has an effect. A reporter says, "Well, look, this is what they took out of it. I might have taken something else, but I don't want to be wrong."

According to surveys, CNN does quite well in terms of credibility factor. They don't have a lot of viewers but, hell, as long as you have a hundred reporters looking at you and they are filing stories, you don't need to have numbers to have influence. That influences us. I would say I pay more attention to the CNN people covering us than the amount of viewers would indicate. CNN's influence is definitely growing.

CHAPTER 11

Mary: A Day in the Life, Washington

James would wake me up from wherever he was. Most mornings he was my alarm clock. It was the one phone call all day guaranteed not to be a problem.

We didn't say anything very deep. Neither of us was about to reveal any campaign secrets, so the natural impulse to share your workaday difficulties or successes with the person you loved had to be completely suppressed. Mostly I asked, "What are you doing?"

"I'm going to work. I've got to meet Stan for breakfast."

"What are you going to have?"

"Same thing."

"What do you have on today?"

Hardly Romeo and Juliet. It was a daily ritual to maintain some semblance of continuity. It was just a point of contact. If we'd ever said, "This sucks, I can't stand it, I miss you so much," I think both of us would have broken down.

Immediately after I'd hang up with James I'd start getting a stomachache and grinding my teeth. Then I'd go make this terrible instant coffee; I didn't have the extra three minutes to make the real stuff.

I was always tired. At night I couldn't fall asleep. I never didn't dream about the campaign, and when I woke up it was like pulling out of a coma. I'd shower, wash my hair, and run out the door.

We had a senior staff meeting at the White House at seven-thirty every morning so I sped over there. I'd pull my hair back in a wet ponytail and put my makeup on in the Jeep.

White House security is serious business, you don't just pull in and ace somebody out of a parking spot, you've got to be expected and "cleared." Now, we had these morning meetings every single day, and every single day, without fail, they didn't clear me into the White House parking lot. Some days my car was cleared but not me. I had to sit there, always late, while the clearance was tracked down. The guards at the door, this got to be a big joke for them. Everybody recognized my red Jeep and they just knew I wasn't going to be cleared in.

So I'd be late, my hair would be wet, I'd have smeared mascara all over myself, and I'd run in last to the staff meeting.

It was always held in the Roosevelt Room of the West Wing of the White House. A very quiet four walls. Navy waiters glided around with little silver coffeepots. The place was filled with stately furniture, Remington bronzes, one of those tick-tick-tick loud old clocks over our shoulder. The lights were dimmed, the fireplace dark. It was like being in an old library, your whole behavior changed by virtue of the atmosphere. Every whisper echoed.

There would be about thirty people seated around a huge polished conference table, with another dozen or so in couches and wing-backs at the perimeter of the room. Sam Skinner would preside, and try as he might, nothing of consequence would ever be said. Even though Sununu was no longer there, his practice of humiliating White House staff in public had left them in a state of constant intimidation. It was a habit now to say only what was absolutely necessary—which, of course, did not spur many creative discussions.

We'd go around the table and everybody would make innocuous announcements. "Today the President is going to be in South Carolina." Big surprise, we've known that for three weeks. "From there he's going to Atlanta." The only time anyone said anything of relevance was if there were economic or unemployment figures that hadn't been released; that was an important piece of data. For the rest of it, people were keeping quiet for fear of humiliating themselves.

There was an unspoken but free-floating attitude at the White House that the campaign were monkeys, and at the campaign we thought the White House couldn't walk and chew gum.

For the longest time we just couldn't get the campaign out of first gear. The succession of destabilizing events—the endless primaries, the falling poll numbers, Ross Perot, the L.A. riots—increased the friction. Everybody was feeling demoralized. No one was pointing fingers, but we all knew we'd never get any traction until we could solve our fundamental problem: coordination between the White House and the campaign. The senior staff meetings were designed to improve communications, but from our perspective the meetings became pointless. First, the White House staff usually had a negative reaction to anything we suggested. Second, even if a decision did get made, about 70 percent of the people at the morning meeting didn't have any authority to execute.

There was also the endless concern about leaks. No real decisions were made at the seven-thirty meetings because, from a group that size, the press would get them by eight. Sam, who was perpetually upbeat and always quoting Knute Rockne or some other sports guy none of the women had ever heard of, would usually use them as opportunities to give us locker-room lectures about "We're all in this together." Nobody needed to hear that stuff. Maybe it's a male-bonding thing or something I just didn't get, but it always felt like such a waste of time. There was not a moment of effective planning accomplished at any one of these morning meetings.

Nonetheless, we repeated the ritual every morning from seven-thirty till eight. Then Torie and Teeter and Fred Malek and I would drive back the several blocks to campaign headquarters and sit down for our own senior staff meeting and finally get down to business.

We were on the twelfth floor. Teeter had one corner office, Malek another, Mosbacher the third one, and I had the fourth. The conference room was located between Malek and Teeter and they would sit at opposite ends of a long table in it and the rest of us would drag in our own folding chairs and gather around.

Every campaign component was represented: press, communications, field, research, outreach, legal, treasury, scheduling, advance, issues, and the Vice President's office. We would spend the first few minutes trashing the White House meeting, until Teeter and Malek sat down; they forbade us to bad-mouth the White House in their presence. We'd tell jokes and read the papers and gossip. Teeter or Fred would tell their own jokes, which shut us up, and then work started.

Our meetings were informal, congenial, and very real. Teeter had a daily agenda, which was partly reactive to the day's papers or new data. Dave "Stud Muffin" Carney would tell what was going on in the field and review the ground or local event of the day. Torie would give a rundown on what the press was thinking, doing, and saying; Charlie would add his own press report and give spin guidance. Since my job was mostly reactive, I would chime in with analysis—"Here's another undercurrent." Meanwhile I'd be drying my hair.

The last item on Teeter's agenda was the day's proactive assignments. For instance, when President Bush announced his economic program, the Agenda for American Renewal, each division on the campaign got an assignment to support the message. Communications assembled talking points, political relayed the data to all the state chairmen and helped them with local activities, like press conferences and rallies. With this overall day's plan in place, the rest of the day was spent in smaller groups working out the details. The whole meeting took a half hour. Then I'd beeline through the kitchen for my sixth cup of coffee, pass Torie's office and joke some more before I'd settle into my office and get to work.

Unlike the White House offices, mine was the size of a kid's bedroom and felt like a dorm. Campaign headquarters sprawled over several floors in a modern office building that was all windows but you couldn't open one of them. We were on the twelfth floor, they turned the air-conditioning off after six at night, at noon on Saturdays; they didn't turn it on at all on Sundays. There was no ventilation. Not only am I a smoker, but everyone else who smoked came to my office to puff up. I had three smokeless ashtrays and two fans going at all times. Between the constant traffic, the fans, phones, TV, radio (tuned each day to my pal Rush Limbaugh), I was working in Grand Central Station.

The floor of my office was industrial blue, ugly, crumb-filled, cigarette-burned carpeting that never got cleaned and always did stink. (I know because frequent screw-ups caused me to lie flat on it, my best thinking position.) My desk was one of those old wooden schoolroom numbers with drawers that wouldn't open or close, which was all right because I didn't use them anyway, except for one that was filled with makeup, junk jewelry, hair rollers, pantyhose, running clothes, and gym shoes. On weekends I would run the forty-five minutes to work, take a shower, and dump my stinky clothes and sticky towel into the drawer. About once a month someone from my staff would get brave, go in and clean up all this stuff, and send it out to the laundry.

I'm not an "in box" kind of person; stuff just kind of piles up. My desk was filled with polls and maps and memos and calendars and schedules and mail pieces and radio scripts and phone data. Mary Lukens would come in for a smoke and hide all the confidential material. She said, "You can't leave this stuff lying around."

The old credenza behind my desk was no better. That was where I put everything that ostensibly had to be read, material that just stacked up and I never got at. It was a nuclear-waste zone, position papers interspersed with hair spray, old bagels, grapefruit-juice bottles, ashtrays, cartons of cigarettes. Papers I really didn't want to get lost, or needed to look at, I would tack onto the wall.

Two giant maps hung behind me, one that Lisa, Rhonda, and Pat put pins in to designate where the President, Vice President, and surrogates had campaigned. Next to that was a congressional district map that showed the presidential vote percentages in 1988, a targeting map. A smaller map outlined the Areas of Dominant Influence, ADIs, or national media markets. In the midst of all the critical data hung a bulletin board that ended up being comedy central: the lemon postcard from the Michigan primary; the woman postcard with Buchanan saying that women are not psychologically equipped to serve in the workplace. One of my favorites was a photograph of Hillary Rodham Clinton making these curly, witchy hands. It was inscribed: "I'll get you, my pretty. And your little dog Toto too!" James saw this in some magazine profile of me and got really ticked off. Another relic I dragged from campaign to campaign sat on the credenza: a poster of a very distraught woman saying, "Oh, my God, I forgot to have kids!"

I had a couch, two chairs, and three phones. I brought in a small icebox that I'd had since my first campaign, and people rolled in and out all day bumming Cokes and cigs.

My only personal decorative touch was an almost life-sized photograph that the White House made up for Lee Atwater. I took it from behind his desk at the RNC and hung it right in front of my face. Every time I looked up I would see Lee, in better days and fine health, jogging with President Bush. It was my little secret hourly inspiration.

Tucked among my rising tide of paperwork was a tiny framed photo, about the size of a quarter, of James standing with his arms out, straddling some boulder in Big Sur in jogging shorts, black socks, and loafers. It was the nerdiest thing. Nobody saw it—and if they had, I would have denied it was him.

One of my telephones had a number only James knew. When it rang, it was James. This was supposed to be a big secret, but, of course, everybody was on to me. "Must be Sparky," which was my "secret" code name for him. It became known as the Sparkyphone.

But you're not at the campaign to be pleasantly inspired by your workday surroundings; all I cared about or needed was a phone and a pencil and a pad. By eight-thirty I'd already have two phone sheets full of calls to return. Everybody wanted to know what we were doing, when, why. And those who didn't want to know, I also had to talk to. I'd sit at my desk, punch up the phone, start setting my hair, fixing my makeup, have my ritual dry bagel and Diet Coke, and go about my business. I stayed on the phone all day.

I blabbed with state chairmen, schedulers at the White House, advance guys on the ground in various states, my field guys on the ground. I must have had a hundred conversations a day with Stud Muffin Carney, who was one floor below, about the details of every operation we had running. I checked in constantly with Charlie Black to make sure we were on simultaneous spin. The day flashed by— orchestrating, juggling balls, passing information back and forth, translating, making sure what was supposed to happen was actually getting done. All of it interspersed with an endless river of calls from nosy reporters.

One of the first things I taught my assistant, Lisa Greenspan, was to ask, "What is the nature of your story and what is your *honest-to-God* deadline?" That way I could give her an exact answer and she could call some of them back. Time is the most critical element in a campaign. There's never enough and you can't make more.

She tried to organize reporter calls in order of importance and deadline. First, the networks—ABC, NBC, CBS, CNN—obviously, because they have the greatest reach and therefore the greatest influence. A good photo op on CNN was worth more than half a page of exposition in *The Washington Post*. The nets were generally easy because they pretty much already had their analysis in place when they called; they never wanted to pick your brain, they just wanted to get some atmospheric from the campaign.

Next, the print guys, the majors: *The Washington Post*, *The New York Times*, *The Wall Street Journal*, the *L.A. Times*. I almost always called the Washington *Times* pretty early because they were the least likely to attack President Bush.

Returning press calls can be painful, especially when you're losing, so a high priority was self-indulgence. I'd call women reporters back first; you could do a little chick-chat while you worked. Next, reporter friends: Jules Witcover of the Baltimore *Sun* was always acting curmudgeonly, but was a real sweetheart. At the time, he was trying to adopt an orphan baby from Romania, and the nightmare stories of holdups and near misses really helped me keep my perspective. Next, reporters who make you laugh: John Mashek of *The Boston Globe* prided himself on his dumb jokes. Columnist Bob Novak prided himself on writing every dumb thing we did. He was so bad, you had to laugh. Next, reporters who weren't uptight or were just plain smart: *The Wall Street Journal*'s Jerry Seib, the Baltimore *Sun*'s Paul West, *Time*'s Dan Goodgame.

The rule is you had to return all your press calls, but the guys who had burned you in the past or who were just badgering jerks, you put them off until their absolute deadline.

So the day clichéd by with no time for long-range plans; it was all problem solving or reacting. Lisa would rotate priority calls, interrupt me with meltdown emergencies, and handle the rest herself.

It was crisis management by the hour.

For example:

At the beginning of the campaign, during the primaries that nobody expected we would have, we had one window in the Georgia primary, right before Super Tuesday, where we thought we could wipe Pat Buchanan out. There was a pretty big conservative Christian Coalition element in Georgia that had grown in the Republican party from 1988 to 1992, and he was going down there to take advantage of that available faction and make his stand. We wanted to win Georgia big and take him out with one clean shot.

Stud Muffin collected all the available data on the ground, and then he and I suggested to Bob Teeter the most likely successful battlegrounds for events. There are always advance guys and logistics guys, but Carney was the political overseer, making sure everything was happening right on the ground politically. I was the problem fixer.

And don't think these problems were brain surgery. Here's a typical crisis: One day, without total approval from the campaign, the Georgia state chairman scheduled President Bush, an Episcopalian, to attend the local Episcopalian church. It was a logical enough decision, if you're not in politics. It leaked to the press.

Congressman Newt Gingrich went crazy. "We've got to go to a Baptist church!" he screamed at me. "Twenty-four point four percent of the vote is Baptist!"

I switched the church.

I didn't tell Teeter; there was no time for that, and the decision was too obvious to discuss. I just said, "Switch the church," and told Carney to make the necessary arrangements.

Well, the next thing I knew it's in the papers down there that Bush is not going to worship with the Episcopalians, he's going down the road with the Baptists. This is a half day on the phone. The state chairman is freaking out, so I've got to call him and explain why we need to go to a Baptist church. Then I have to tell Teeter, who snarls at me because the President hates having his religion politicized. Meanwhile, Carney's taking a lot more grief than I am, so we have to keep each other updated. Then I have to call Newt back and calmly tell him he's right about the Baptist church and that we're going to try and go there.

It's already in the papers that we're switching, so the whole point of going to the church is undermined because it looks like a political event and not what it was, George Bush doing what he does every Sunday, practicing his faith.

This was only one event out of a two-day excursion. And the easiest one, at that. We hadn't even begun to deal with the guts of the trip.

Georgia has a strong military constituency. The administration was fighting with the veterans at the time and we needed to do a veterans' event to get back in their good graces. We wanted a picture of George Bush, a genuine war hero, with real veterans in a typical veterans' situation.

To save the campaign's limited resources, the trip was designated "official White House business," not political. So, under White House counsel C. Boyden Gray's rules, a crazy telephone tag ensued. I was not permitted to coordinate or even talk to veteran leaders on the ground. I had to call the veterans liaison at the White House; he would call the Georgia vets, translate back to me, then me to Carney, Carney to the Georgia political group, they'd revise the event and the word would go back to Carney—to me—to the White House—to the Georgia vets. Meanwhile, the Georgia vets and political guys lived together!

The White House called back and said, "We're right in the middle of this V.A. hospital funding fight. You can't go to any V.A. hospital."

I'm sure that was a life-and-death matter for someone, but not for me. All I knew was that politically, we had to get with these vets. By now, our political guys on the ground in Georgia had committed to the veterans that they would see George Bush. The White House was saying, "No can do."

We were determined to get our veterans event in; we just had to figure out how. What we decided to do was have him drop by a bingo hall and the attached bar where veterans hung out.

It was a "spontaneous event," but in presidential politics there's no such thing as a spontaneous event. A "spontaneous event" is a prearranged stop that the advance guys just don't tell the press about. A challenger can be driving down the road and say, "Hey, pull over at that McDonald's." It's very different when you're maneuvering a President around.

I hoped the advance guy on the ground knew what he was doing. I was anxious because this was our first campaign trip since New Hampshire, we hadn't seen the joint, and we were on the line.

The White House crew on the plane was extremely dubious. They were always trying to knock things off the schedule and we were always trying to add things on. They already didn't want to deal with the vets, they are always uncomfortable with anything spontaneous, and they had to do all the staff work. The campaign just said, "Go there," and they got stuck doing all the briefings, security, and advance work attendant to a presidential visit.

Plus they were confronted with Bush himself, who doesn't want to do seventeen events.

So it was a Saturday afternoon and I was at home, paralyzed with anxiety. This didn't happen to me very often but I hadn't been able to *touch* this trip, to *feel* it. I wasn't there, didn't see it, hadn't talked directly to the people on the ground myself. The phone rang, it was the White House Georgia political man on Air Force One, Andy Foster. Technically, he shouldn't even have notified me, but we were friends. He said, "Skinner wants to bag the bingo event."

"No!"

"That's what he says."

I went nuts. I was curled up in my bed, freaking out. I had to get hold of Teeter; only he had the juice to put something back on the schedule. If I couldn't locate him, the most important element of my whole trip would be lost. I tracked him down at home in Ann Arbor.

"Air Force One is trying to bag my bingo event!"

Bob Teeter isn't involved in this level of minutiae.

"The bingo event?"

I went through the whole story, the vets, the V.A., the spontaneous drop-by, the photo op.

"What do you mean?" he asked. "You scheduled the President to meet the vets in a bar? Are they going to be drinking? Is he supposed to have a beer with them? Is it going to take a lot of time? Who else is in the bingo hall? Where is it? Is it a racially mixed audience?"

I couldn't answer his questions because I hadn't seen it. I was giving Teeter information I had gotten from an advance guy who shouldn't have told me in the first place. This was not good.

Teeter called the plane. There was no one on Air Force One to argue my side. I didn't know what the White House staff on the plane was telling Bush about the event, and there was nobody there I trusted to tell him what he's supposed to do there.

"What am I doing next?" he would ask. It's the candidate's constant question.

"Well, you've got to go to this bingo event."

"Bingo event? Why am I going to a bingo event?"

No one would say, "You're going to meet with a group of veterans so we can get a picture and use it to influence voters across the state of Georgia." More likely, "Because the campaign is brain-dead."

But no one would blow off Bob Teeter. He phoned the plane and both explained the event and talked them into putting it back on the schedule.

The next thing I heard, Skinner's guy was calling from the motorcade, screaming. Something like, *"Where the hell is this place? How far is it? We're out here looking for your bingo hall. What the hell are you doing to us?"*

A "spontaneous event" is supposed to be on the way to wherever you're going, a drop-by, not more than a few minutes out of the day. The motorcade was lost.

Meanwhile, at the bingo hall, the vets were getting ticked off. The ranking officers were all in full dress, standing around in the back room, Lord knows how many beers into the wait, having been jerked around seven ways to Sunday by reports that he's coming, he's not coming, he's coming. Other veterans not so high on the chain of command had been told to show up in full dress but hadn't been told why. They were being kept at the bar—"Sorry, can't leave yet"—standing around saying, "What the hell's going on?"

The motorcade had been driving around in circles. The presidential limousine, flying the seal of the United States, followed by a fleet of immaculately polished follow cars full of dignitaries, with an armada of press buses in tow, making rights and lefts in small-town Georgia. Finally, forty-five minutes later, they found the place.

This was a "spontaneous event," and for obvious security reasons the advance men weren't allowed to say the President was coming until only a few minutes before he arrived. So when George Bush showed up the reaction among the nonvet locals was, "Hey, you're breaking up our bingo game." There was mildly scattered applause but it was more like, "What the hell is *he* doing here?"

But when the President met the veterans, the photo op went perfectly. To the people in the immediate vicinity, the event was less than overwhelming. To the larger viewing and voting audience, it had the desired positive impact. Whatever the logistics screw-up, we got what we wanted: a picture of President Bush surrounded by a large and smiling group of Georgia veterans at their favorite local watering hole. It was worth every agonizing moment.

In early summer, when it was clear that our White House–campaign coordination wasn't improving, we instituted yet another group grope: evening senior staff meetings, a matching pair of political bookends for our day. We would go to the White House and sit in Sam Skinner's office until ten P.M. and go over the same stuff that we went over that morning, that we'd gone over the day before. Effectively ending the day at six, which is what that meeting did, just meant I couldn't get my job done. I needed more than nine hours to get through the day, I needed thirteen, fourteen, fifteen. So I wasn't getting my job done and we weren't getting anything done sitting around talking to ourselves. The short and the long of it was that the campaign chairman, the campaign manager, and the political director spent the top of their day and the end of their day—and hours on the phone in the middle of the day—with the White House. None of us could do our own jobs. I got so frustrated I would leave those meetings sputtering, kicking my tires.

Teeter was perpetually patient, he never lost his cool. At worst, he'd hang up the White House hot-line phone behind his desk and mutter, "Christ." Mostly he cleaned and recleaned his eyeglasses . . . his frustration indicator. Malek, who had made millions of dollars running gigantic corporations and was never without his trademark checklist of things that never got done, tried to keep himself and us upbeat. Veterans like Marlin Fitzwater just quit coming to meetings. Dick Darman would pace up and down, exasperated, yelling. The ever-optimistic Charlie Black would say every morning, "Damn, we're snakebit."

We all had our coping mechanisms. But we all knew George Bush's reelection was sinking into quicksand. If we managed for one minute to forget it, the entire outside world, from the press to our own guys across the country, called hourly to remind us. The only thing going for our campaign was Bill Clinton's baggage. But a bad opponent is not a good strategy. We were barely hanging on.

I never got home before eleven. When James called and said, "I'm in," I went down for the count.

CHAPTER 12

Mary

Sam Skinner's deputy, Henson Moore, a former Louisiana congressman and gubernatorial candidate, was strolling genially back and forth on Air Force One. The speech President Bush was supposed to deliver when we landed wasn't done; we didn't have a cohesive message for the day, we were definitely off our original strategy. Henson said something like, "Hey, how about something like this—'Jobs, Family, Peace.' Nice sound bite." This is the way policy got made.

It was a good enough phrase, it got into the speech, and out of nowhere the media went crazy. They kept badgering us, "What do you mean by 'Family'?" The press all thought it was a not-so-subtle cut against Clinton, who had been talking about his rocky married life. They, not we, made "Family" the centerpiece of our campaign. It wasn't intended to be. This was never any kind of strategic decision. Our central strategy was to position George Bush as a leader with proven international skills who could bring export jobs home to America.

In fact, we would rather have focused on "Jobs" and "Peace." "Jobs" was our soft spot and "Peace" was our legacy. We automatically presumed the Bush electorate was pro-family. Our vulnerability was that people didn't think we could continue the massive job creation of the Reagan years, or get through the recession. We needed to focus our message on economic job stability. The standard presidential campaign rule is, You don't focus on cultural issues unless peace *and* prosperity are assured.

But it wasn't only the press that reacted. For totally different reasons, the diehard conservatives, who were always suspicious of Bush, glommed onto "Family." To them, that was *the* issue. They were always fighting about it; I called it the chicken-or-the-egg argument. "Is it the bad economy that causes families to decompose or is it the decomposing family that creates a bad economy?" They were obsessed with the government's complicity—the fallout from the Great Society programs—in contributing to the disintegration of the family. I agreed with them, but the public perceived *us* as the government, not the forty-year-controlled Democratic Congress.

A subtext of the "Family" issue was how television, movies, and the Left Coast libs were glorifying nontraditional values. So on my way to the White House morning meeting, wondering whether I or my car would be cleared in that day, my daily crankiness was stunned out of me by a radio news blurb reporting Dan Quayle's assertion that the lack of family values caused the Los Angeles riots. "It doesn't help matters," he said, "when prime-time TV has Murphy Brown—a character who supposedly epitomizes today's intelligent, highly paid professional woman—mocking the importance of fathers by bearing a child alone and calling it just another 'lifestyle choice.' "

No one said anything at the White House senior staff meeting. Back at our campaign meeting, I said, "Right message, wrong vehicle. Murphy Brown is the second most popular woman in America, next to Barbara Bush." (Which some lying, traitorous lowlife scum ran out and told the press, because it subsequently appeared in one of the newsweeklies and instantly got back to Quayle's chief of staff, Bill Kristol.) Everybody looked at me. They said, "Who's Murphy Brown?"

I loved *Murphy Brown*. I couldn't tell you what night it was on but I always managed to be home for it. It was the only program, besides the news and the "talking heads" shows, I watched. I never thought of the show as liberal, I just liked the strong, annoying, pigheaded, big-mouthed woman.

"Furthermore," I said, "are we inconsistent or what? She did not have an abortion. They could have done a whole show on how she got an abortion. But she chose to have the baby, she wanted to have a baby, she was going to take care of the baby." I was trying to explain why we were being potentially intellectually inconsistent, and nobody knew who Murphy Brown was. They only knew it was a problem because the press was crying, "*Murphy Brown, Murphy Brown!*"

Dan Quayle and Kristol were still on the road. We all agreed, without knowing what we wanted him to say exactly, that we had to get to Marlin and get him to shut the press down.

I didn't know if Marlin Fitzwater knew who Murphy Brown was, but our gist was, "You can't back off Quayle. Don't let the press misread what he said. Contrary to their mindset, the 'Family' issue has nothing to do with Clinton's character. This is about the factors that have contributed to the breakdown of the family—like infantilizing government programs, and trashy TV." As an aside, I *thought*, we threw in the choice-not-to-abort angle.

Marlin tried to calm the clamoring press. "The fact is," he said, Murphy Brown "is demonstrating pro-life values, which we think are good. She is having the baby, so we're not very comfortable getting involved in criticism of her show."

Oops, wrong emphasis.

Another ongoing problem was the fact that the press was always looking for some evidence of our trashing Quayle. And Quayle's staff, in turn, was paranoid. Bill Kristol was a pragmatic politician and a conservative true believer, but when push came to shove he'd go conservative before he went pragmatic. So he was hysterical calling from the West Coast. "You are back there bad-mouthing me, you can't walk backward on this, you've got to defend us."

I tried to calm him down: "We're not abandoning you, we *are not* abandoning you."

Marlin had said, and many Republicans were saying, that the Vice President had delivered the speech on his own, without consultation with the White House; we hadn't seen the speech before he gave it. Normally, that was code language in the press for distancing yourself from the damage.

In fact, the campaign had gotten the speech the night before, as we routinely received copies of such speeches. If anybody looked at it, they probably thumbed through the first few pages, assumed it was okay, and didn't pay much attention.

We didn't disapprove of the speech, we just couldn't translate it into political terms. People who had heard the entire speech said it was solid and thoughtful, but the D.C. crowd who heard only the Murphy Brown sound bite came to other conclusions. So there were Quayle and Kristol hanging out there in San Francisco and us back in Washington, ostensibly cutting the limb off behind them.

I like to think we were loyal, but it's hard to defend something you haven't seen, didn't know was coming, and wasn't central to the message we endlessly and fruitlessly kept trying to get out, especially in the face of a crazed press.

Our old discipline would have dictated: Everybody knows at any given time where any spokesman for the President is and what he is going to say—especially one as high up as the Vice President. Presumably, all "movements" and statements are part of a campaign strategy. But no one in Washington had the facts; we had to respond to the press version of facts. That's what kicked the story. That's what always kicks stories, when the press can divide and conquer.

We had two options. The easy one was to concede incompetence because we didn't know where the Vice President was or what he was talking about. The preferred option was not to look like idiots and to pretend we knew what he was saying and profess it was part of our strategy to emphasize family values.

Buchanan had the far right wing on the warpath; Perot had some appeal to anti-government GOPers. We needed to consolidate our fractured base, and a values appeal was always good for that. However, the problems with this speech at this time far outweighed the benefits.

Because we did not coordinate, it spun out of control, which threw the campaign off for a couple of days. The flap blew Quayle's speech out of proportion and left the impression that family values was *the* message of the campaign.

The fact is, we kinda lost track of where he was and what he was saying. No one believes this, but *there never was a strategy to place family values at the center of our message.* Family values is always part of the conservative philosophy, but *it was never pulled out to be the central campaign message.* We were desperately trying to develop an *economic* centerpiece.

The *Murphy Brown* flap created another problem: It re-raised the always-just-below-the-surface Dump Quayle issue.

Now, there are always internal problems at the White House between the Vice President's office and the President's. It was really bad in the Reagan years, because the Reaganites hated the Bushies; they were outright rude and ostracized the Bush staff. I never heard President Bush say so directly, but it was in the vapors: Because his staff had been treated so badly, Bush was very good to Quayle. He also truly liked and respected the Vice President, and took his counsel. The rest of the President's staff was not always as generous.

Dump Quayle rumors popped up at the drop of a hat. My standard joke with the press was, we couldn't bump him because all the bumper stickers and stationery were printed BUSH/QUAYLE '92. This little piece of sarcasm was based in reality. When we were getting ready to formally file our reelection papers with the Federal Election Committee and had to list a name, Charlie told Bush if we called the reelect "Bush/Quayle '92" it would shut down all the Dump Quayle rumors. Bush jumped on it. We all knew Bush's loyalty quotient precluded any discussion of adjusting the ticket. Plus, we all liked Quayle. (Ironically, we were more loyal to Quayle than Quayle's staff was to Bush. His office was a veritable leaking sieve, and, worse, much of the Bush- and campaign-bashing emanated from there, though Quayle himself was always loyal.)

In the middle of our defense of our Veep, the campaign received a bombshell. All previous data had shown that the vice-presidential candidate had no statistical impact on an election, one way or another. Now, for the first time in modern polling, data indicated that a vice president—Quayle—was a drag on the ticket. The memo read:

"There is a potential 4–6 percentage point net gain for the President by replacing Dan Quayle on the ticket with someone of neutral stature. . . . Over one half (55 percent) of the non-Bush voters report they would be 'more likely' to vote for the President if he replaced Dan Quayle on the ticket. . . . Even a 40 percent plurality of the Bush voters say replacing the Vice President would reinforce their intentions to vote for the President."

Though this secret memo included several modifying caveats (e.g., press and party reaction, which might mitigate the positive effects of removing him), its findings were so unique and unsettling that they reopened the debate among Bush's closest friends. It took several forms: Move Quayle to Defense, Defense Secretary Dick Cheney to State, Secretary of State Jim Baker to chief of staff; or, Get Quayle off, put Colin Powell on. Whatever the scenario, an absolute prerequisite was that Quayle himself step down voluntarily.

The deliberations were cut off and put to rest by a stroke of Kristol Machiavellian genius.

Though the press had no idea actual data existed—and, in fact, we continued to insist vehemently that "Quayle was a neutral in our polls"—Dump Quayle rumor reports started appearing. Bush had lunch with Quayle every week, and though no one except those two knows precisely what was said, they couldn't have avoided what was now in the press's mind an open question.

Following their luncheon, Kristol put word out that Bush had affirmed Quayle's position on the ticket. This caused the press to put the question directly. "Mr. President," Charles Bierbauer asked, "is the

Vice President's chair a little uncertain these days?" At that point, with no plan in place, the President had no choice but to reply, "No, it's very certain."

Bush likely would not have entertained any Dump Quayle scenarios, no matter how bad the data was, but now he was on record.

Dan Quayle is an honorable guy. I believe if he had known empirically he was hurting Bush, and if a face-saving plan had been worked out, he would have pulled himself off the ticket. He said so that night on *Larry King Live*. He was never called upon to do so.

I thought that, by doing this maneuvering, his staff was not only selfish vis-à-vis Bush, but short-sighted vis-à-vis Quayle. You can make a pretty good argument that Quayle's pulling himself off the ticket and moving to become secretary of defense would have been such a dramatic and courageous act it might have repaired all the damage of four years of unrelenting press attacks.

Of course, this snafu played right into the Democrats' hands. No way they wanted us to get a foothold on an economic message. They were dying to define us as right-wing Cro-Magnons. They smartly overplayed the schism between the Bush moderates and the Buchanan message-senders.

James

My feeling was, they had just gotten through this bruising thing with Buchanan; they were obsessed with the Republican right, and this was a way to speak to them. Quayle was their designated hit man.

I didn't think it was particularly smart strategy. In fact I think they really hurt themselves by being consumed with shoring up the Republican right wing. They fell sucker to the "38 percent" strategy, which held that in this race, a three-man race, whoever could keep their core constituency and grab a little at the corners could win the election with 38 percent of the vote. As far as I was concerned, that was a losing proposition.

In the Bush camp and in the Clinton camp there were people who wanted to push the party further to the extremes. There was a faction in our party—Harkin, Jackson, labor, feminists—that wanted to run on a typical, unapologetic liberal Democratic agenda. The fact that Perot was in the race gave credibility to this strategy. Jesse Jackson and some others were saying that we could run a 38, 39, 40 percent strategy and that would be enough to win. Look at all the votes Perot is getting, they'd say. If we moved more toward the center we would not energize our own voters.

Whenever I hear a campaign talk about a need to energize its base, that's a campaign that's going down the toilet. It's a pretty good indication that they're not eating up any territory, they can't get anybody in the center to support them, they're getting shelled back into their own bunker. We resisted the idea of running a 38 percent strategy and tried to stay in the New Democrat mold. The person who resisted most firmly was the candidate. He didn't even talk about it; the idea was summarily dismissed. I think it's a prime reason we won.

But we had our own problems. We won the California primary, and the senatorial candidates didn't know if they even wanted to be seen with us. We had won more than the required delegates, we had the nomination, but we stunk. I kept saying, "What will we tell the people?" We didn't have the clarity, the crispness, the rationale that we needed to win the general election. It was going to be a bruising, competitive campaign. It was going to be negative. It was going to require a certain skill. I mean, we weren't running against Jerry Brown anymore.

The day after we won California, Perot hired Ed Rollins and Hamilton Jordan as his campaign managers.

Hamilton Jordan had run Jimmy Carter's campaign in 1976 and won. Ed Rollins was senior adviser to Ronald Reagan's campaign in 1980 and campaign manager in '84 and won. These guys could obviously do the job. On the other hand, I wondered, Why are they doing this? It seemed like they both were risking a lot. My guess is that they were in it to be in it. Both of them had played in the big game before and they wanted to play again.

A political campaign, when it's going right, is very sexual. It's very gratifying, it's very intense. It builds up to a climax, if you will. And once you get that feeling, there's nothing that can match it.

I'd had it in small doses, in gubernatorial and senatorial races. It's so definitive. Outside of athletes, most people don't have that sort of definitive resolution in their lives. When you win on election night, for twenty or thirty seconds you get to breathe the most rarefied air. You go through it with people, you go through it with your candidate and your staff. And people watch you breathe it.

It's fun playing the game, it's fun being in the battle. Everyone in the country is watching this one event, say a presidential debate, and, hey, man, you're playing in it. Ninety-three million people worldwide watching, reporters from all over the world sitting there covering it, and you know what the guys onstage are getting ready to say. Sometimes I'd just sit there and say, "Damn. Here's James Carville of Carville, Louisiana; Ascension Catholic High School; ex-Marine corporal; schoolteacher in Back Vacherie, Louisiana; LSU. And here I am in the middle of the biggest goddamn event on the planet earth . . . and I know everything. Ain't this fun." There's something to that. You can't deny it.

You always want to think you're detached from the job, but I never could be. I believed in what we were doing. I'd find myself saying, "I have to look at things in an analytical, calculating way and not let my own emotions get in there."

I say that, I always try, but it never works. I end up hating the opposition, I hate the media, I hate everybody who is not completely swept up in getting my candidate elected. If you're not in a campaign, if you're not living it every day, if you're not working eighteen hours a day, you're not part of this.

You have to be really intense, you have to be really mean, you have to play really hard. Because everybody is playing hard. You're not engaged in a civics lesson here, you're engaged in an American presidential campaign with the leadership of the world at stake.

And, it almost never fails, I always fall in love with my candidate.

I thought the country was headed in the wrong direction, that too few people had too much money. I felt wholeheartedly that if Bill Clinton got elected more people would get an education and be able to realize their potential. I thought, and still think, that Bill Clinton is a great man.

For that reason alone I didn't want to lose.

I don't know how much of that brought Rollins and Jordan into the race. They had played and won. It's the high-water mark of the political business. To have done it, as they both did, and then come back and do it for a third-party candidate would have been legendary.

But would Perot listen to them? You can go to the best doctor in the world, the best lawyer in the world, hire the best consultant in the world, but if you don't listen to what they tell you it doesn't matter. People who knew Perot said it was going to be pretty rough for them going down there.

In a strange way, hiring those two gave Perot what he didn't need—and what we needed for him to get: even more media coverage, more stress, more intensity. It got him on the front page of *The New York Times*, which was newsworthy for an insurgent candidate, but it remained to be seen how they would handle him, and how he would handle them.

Mary

It was much more of a kick in the gut to the Republican community than to the Democrats because Ed Rollins was a bigger deal to us than Hamilton Jordan was to them.

People in the business had heard that something was in the wind. Ed Rollins's wife, Sherrie, had left flacking for ABC News to join the White House in the public liaison office. Sherrie and I were hourly communicants because so many of her events had potential political pitfalls, and she actually took our advice on how to get around them.

Ed Rollins had had bad relations with President Bush going back to the days when Lee Atwater squeezed him out of the '88 campaign. Rollins, when he was running the National Republican Congressional Committee, also let a memo slip to the press saying that members should "not hesitate to oppose . . . the president" on the tax issue. That was grounds for unequivocal ostracism from the White House. His boss, Congressman Guy Vander Jagt, had to go apologize to President Bush, but the damage was irreversible. When Sherrie was hired, the press speculated that she was given the job to keep her husband muzzled.

So I was talking to Sherrie every day. One spring day Ed called to alert me that there was a house near his that was for sale. James, who owned nothing but a Schwinn three-speed, had been talking about buying a house, so we went and took a look; it happened to be one of the only times during the campaign that he was in Washington. On the way back we stopped by the Rollinses', and Ed, rarely at a loss for conversation, hinted that he had been talking to the Perot people. He also said that a Democrat was considering joining.

We weren't out of his house two minutes when Carville was on the car phone blabbing his brains out to Stephanopoulos. The next day Bob Novak called Rollins and asked him about the Perot campaign. Rollins denied having anything to do with it, then called and yelled at me for blabbing. I hadn't said anything to anybody, but couldn't account for my no-account boyfriend. Of course then I called Sherrie. "What's going on with Ed? He just spent the last five minutes ripping my face off."

Sherrie broke into tears. "Oh, no, he's considering going with Perot."

"You're kidding. He can't do that. You're absolutely kidding."

This conversation, or variations thereof, went on for two weeks. Every time I'd mention it, or even if I didn't, she would bust out crying. She was (a) just getting in the swing of her job; and (b) knew what this would do to her social life. Ed was sure to get trashed, ostracized, mutilated by their entire circle of friends.

Rollins was up in his mountain house considering his options. Jim Lake, who had worked with him back on the first Reagan campaign, was calling and saying, "What are you going to do?" "You know," Rollins told Lake, "this guy can really make a difference."

That was enough for Lake to get dispatched for a personal talk-it-out, day-long Republican pilgrimage up this mountain. Ed hadn't even said he was going to take this job, but his best friend, Lake, was packed off to talk him out of it, for his sake and ours.

Lake came down off the mountain convinced he had won back his old friend. But no one, including Jim, was really surprised when Ed jumped ship.

The trashing of Rollins commenced full throttle. We didn't really believe Ed would have any impact on the Perot candidacy, because he and Perot were both notoriously strong-willed and we figured they would clash in short order.

Bashing Ed was painful for the people who liked him, but it was nothing personal. The point was to undermine or minimize his defection. Rollins going to Perot ostensibly did reflect worse on our candidacy than on Clinton's. Here was a guy who had been an integral part of the Reagan White House and thought so little of Bush that he bolted for a third-party nut. *That* was a news story.

Hiring Rollins lent Perot an air of credibility at a time when word was starting to spin out about what a dictator and crazy person the millionaire was. And they played it very well. But it did not shake us up. The concern inside the campaign was not commensurate with the level of good spin they got. We figured they wouldn't last long.

James

The same day that Perot announced he was hiring Ed Rollins and Hamilton Jordan, Governor Clinton was scheduled to make an appearance on the Arsenio Hall show.

We were winning primaries—New Jersey, New Mexico, Ohio— and we were being ignored. From the L.A. riots on, the governor was speaking brilliantly—he even threw away his prepared text at a stop in New Orleans and spoke from the heart for a full hour about race in our lives and in our cities—and was totally ignored. Worse, A. M.

Rosenthal used his column in *The New York Times* to wonder why Clinton wasn't saying anything about all this. It was the worst thing he could have said, broke the governor's heart. Race is an issue that is at Bill Clinton's core; he was speaking about it passionately, and no one in the media was noticing.

For months Mandy had been saying we should do pop culture media, that there was something going on there that the rest of us in the campaign didn't know about. It wasn't just generational. George got it and Dee Dee Myers got it, but though Paul is as young as they are, he isn't plugged into pop culture and he didn't get it. I didn't much know who Arsenio Hall was. But when no one else would cover us, Mandy finally prevailed.

She chose Arsenio because he was somewhat more political than the other talk-show hosts and he had done a very good job during the riots. His studio was close to the riot zone and he did a show the first night with just him and Mayor Tom Bradley answering questions from the audience. No band, no jokes, no nothing. Mandy sent the road team a tape of that show.

The governor thought the Arsenio Hall show was kind of entertainment with a social conscience, and he knew it appealed to young people, who he really did want to speak to. Clinton is pretty young at heart. He's a lot more culturally hip than I am. He's got a Mustang convertible that he likes to drive; he knows the words to pretty much every Elvis Presley song. When someone suggested he play the saxophone with Arsenio's band, he was all for it.

The day of the show, Hillary, the governor, Paul, and I watched the tape to get a sense of what we were getting into. Then we went to the studio. Three women in our traveling entourage—Dee Dee; David Wilhelm's wife, DeGee Wilhelm, who worked as the candidate's travel aide; and the trip director, Wendy Smith—all looked at Clinton and decided he was way too stiff. They made friends with the show's wardrobe people and got them to pull out a bunch of Arsenio's ties and picked the loudest one for the governor to wear.

Clinton loves loud ties, had a nice collection of them, but Frank Greer had literally taken them all away because they weren't "presidential." (Clinton saved one and gave it to Paul. It had hot-air balloons all over it. He said, "Begala, I can't throw this away. It's one of my lucky ties. And this is you, it's all hot air.") Paul swears you can track Bill Clinton's mood by the ties he wears. If Clinton is wearing a straight conservative tie, it means his confidence level is down. If he's wearing some weirdo neckpiece it's a real good sign.

This may seem like frivolous image-crafting but in fact they were helping him in ways that people don't see. It wasn't only that they wanted him to look more hip; they knew him well enough that this was going to symbolize their message to him: "Don't listen to the old stiff guys who are telling you to act like you've got a corncob up your ass. Be yourself."

They gave him this tie and he loved it. He put it on right away. Then they took the cool-looking sunglasses with black frames that Paul was wearing. There was the moment's hesitation—"You tell him," "No, you tell him." Finally Paul said, "You know, Governor, I think you ought to wear these." The candidate was hesitant; he didn't want to make a fool of himself. He put them on for rehearsal and it worked. Then he put them in his pocket.

The road people were on the set with the governor; I was in the holding room. Right before the show Governor Clinton came in and said, "James, they want me to wear these sunglasses. What do you think?" I said, "Governor, I'm pre-Beatles. Paul is post-Beatles. This is definitely a post-Beatles call."

Mary

Everybody on our side thought that wearing sunglasses and playing the saxophone on the Arsenio Hall show was kind of stupid and silly, but mostly unpresidential, and we said so. Nobody thought it was a very good idea. It certainly wasn't an option for our candidate.

My idea of a president is not somebody I can go hang out with. I don't think I am in the minority on this one. Most people, if they don't want their president to be like royalty, want him to be something bigger than themselves.

But in the context of this campaign, with that candidate, I have to give the Clintonistas credit for understanding they could get away with it. Our saying "It's not presidential" made us look arrogant, elitist, and out of touch. It was one of those things that, when it was coming out of your mouth, you knew it was right on one level but wrong on another. We were right in saying that Bush couldn't, shouldn't, wouldn't do it; we were wrong in saying that it was bad for Clinton.

The lesson here—again—is there is a different standard of campaign behavior for incumbents than there is for challengers. I don't think even the Clinton people would recommend that kind of a scene

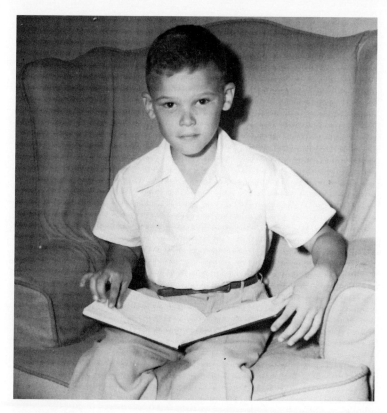

The Carville family's Christmas card in 1952 had this photo of eight-year-old James.

Season's greetings, 1963. Back row, from left: James, Steve, Miss Nippy, Chester, Bill. Front row: Bonnie, Gail, Pat, Angela, Mary Anne.

James lined up as an end on his high school football team in 1961. He was seventeen.

After temporarily quitting college, James joined the Marines for two years. Here he is in 1967, the year before he returned to Louisiana State University.

In 1958, the Matalins lived in South Chicago, an ethnic enclave of Croatians (like the Matalins), Italians, Poles, and Serbs. Clockwise, from top left: Mary, Renie, Steve, Stevie, Eileen.

In her first coalition-building experience, Mary was elected homecoming queen in 1970.

Mary and younger sister Renie at Renie's college graduation in 1978.

Harris Wofford's 1991 landslide
upset victory in the Pennsylvania
Senate race, directed by James,
laid the groundwork for
the 1992 elections.
(AP/Wide World Photos)

Robert Casey, a three-time loser in races for Pennsylvania governor, finally won in 1990
with the guidance of an aggressive Carville strategy. *(AP/Wide World Photos)*

Lee Atwater, the victorious chairman of the Republican National Committee, dancing with Mary at President Bush's 1989 inaugural party; Mary became Atwater's chief of staff. *(© 1989 Rebecca Hammel)*

December 4, 1991: The White House announces Bush's reelection campaign team. From left: Robert Mosbacher, Charlie Black (partly obscured), Bob Teeter, Rich Bond, Fred Malek, Bobby Holt, and Mary Matalin. *(© Jean Louis Atlan/Sygma)*

Pat Buchanan, the conservative commentator. The Bush camp was unprepared for his tough primary rhetoric and his refusal to back down. *(AP/Wide World Photos)*

Strategist Charlie Black and Mary meet with Dan Quayle at the White House. *(Courtesy of the White House)*

Dave "Stud Muffin" Carney,
national field director;
Mary Lukens, chief aide to
Bob Teeter; and Mary taking
a dinner break in Matalin's office.

Rich Bond (seated), the
chairman of the Republican
National Committee; and
(standing, from left) two staff
workers; Bob Teeter, campaign
chairman; and Fred Malek,
campaign manager, at
the post-election political-
division party.

Deputy campaign manager Jim Lake
and research director David Tell
strategize at Bush campaign
headquarters.

Steve Provost, a top Bush speechwriter, wolfs down some brain food on Air Force One.

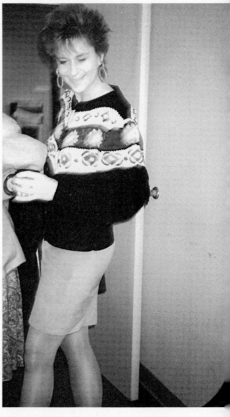

Torie Clarke: the genius communications strategist—not your mother's Republican.

Talk-show powerhouse Rush Limbaugh, left, and the President's son (and adviser) George Bush, Jr., at a New Jersey rally the day before the election.

Margaret Tutwiler, the assistant to the President for communications, does some spinning a week before the election.

Janet Mullins, the assistant to the President for political affairs, is about to board the Bush campaign train three days before the election. James Baker III is giving an interview, lower right.

Torie and Mary on the campaign trail.

When Bill and Hillary Clinton were interviewed by *60 Minutes* about the state of their marriage, James counseled that the couple take an aggressive stance. *(AP/Wide World Photos)*

Bill Clinton got the solid electoral showing he desperately needed in the New Hampshire Democratic primary. Here, he's debating with opponents (from left) Senator Tom Harkin, Senator John Kerrey, Paul Tsongas, and Jerry Brown. *(AP/Wide World Photos)*

James in rapid-response mode. *(AP/Wide World Photos)*

Bill Clinton with Hillary Rodham Clinton and Chelsea after accepting the Democratic nomination at the convention in New York City. *(AP/Wide World Photos)*

Bill Clinton with Al Gore shortly after Clinton chose the Tennesseean as his running mate. *(AP/Wide World Photos)*

James with Paul Begala, his partner in the consulting firm of Carville & Begala, shown here at a political roast of Carville after the election. *(© 1992 Dennis Brack/Black Star)*

James faces off with Ed Rollins, right, Republican campaign consultant, on *Face the Nation* with Bob Schieffer. *(RENI)*

Mary spinning two days before the Republican convention in Houston. *(AP/Wide World Photos)*

On the tarmac, just off Air Force One, Bush campaign team members (from left) Ron Kaufman, political director at the White House; Mary; White House press secretary Marlin Fitzwater; and presidential assistant Phil Brady. *(Larry Downing/Sygma)*

In the "War Room" in Little Rock (seated, from left): speechwriter Michael Waldman; George Stephanopoulos, director of communications; James; and Diane Blair, campaign researcher; (rear) Roger Martin, researcher; and Heidi Chapman, press assistant. (© 1992 David Burnett)

Mary gives her campaign's view of Governor Clinton.

Mary and Ron Kaufman on Air Force One three weeks before the election, discussing what was becoming a very tight race.

Home-made campaign posters on Air Force One: "family values" (at left) and a reference to the dance craze that swept the plane in the campaign's waning days.

If Bill Clinton could go after Generation X, so could George Bush; here Mary is interviewed by MTV correspondent Tabitha Soren.

Mary and President Bush on the campaign train late in October. *(David Kennerly)*

October 15, 1994. The second debate took place in Richmond, Virginia. *(AP/Wide World Photos)*

At a Washington function after the election, Mary interviewed James for her new job.
(Dennis Brack/Black Star)

At their Thanksgiving Day, 1993, wedding, Mary, James, and Mary's father, Steve, march with a Dixieland band through the streets of New Orleans.

ALL PHOTOGRAPHS ARE COURTESY OF JAMES CARVILLE OR MARY MATALIN UNLESS OTHERWISE INDICATED.

for their guy in the future. Can you visualize Bill Clinton putting on sunglasses and a hot tie and playing the saxophone on late-night television now, as President of the United States? It's not presidential if you're President.

James

There are two issues that are central to Bill Clinton's entire political life. One is the importance of self-empowerment through worker skills and education; the idea that we don't have a single life to waste. The other is the need for people to come together and get along. He is highly uncomfortable, both in public and in private, with any kind of sharply divisive racial, ethnic, or religious message. Both he and Mrs. Clinton believe that diversity is a goal in itself.

Speaking against intolerance is a staple in Bill Clinton's political repertoire. He is not shy about telling white audiences that bigotry and racial prejudice are unacceptable. But until he spoke to the Rainbow Coalition in June, he had never addressed the issue to blacks.

In March, during the Illinois primary, we were presented with Gus Savage. Savage was a Chicago congressman prone to making bigoted and anti-Semitic statements. He has said that the Jews are out to get him, he called Ron Brown "Ron Beige"; every time he had a problem he would blame it on the white media. I said, "What we ought to do is go to Chicago and endorse Gus Savage's opponent. We ought to just say, 'Look, I can't in good conscience say that someone who has these attitudes and has made these comments about Jewish people, or white people in general, ought to be in Congress.' "

We kicked around this idea pretty hard inside the campaign for a day and a half, two days. I said, "It will show some political courage, it will lick the 'Slick Willie' problem, and in the end it ain't gonna matter."

Mandy, Stan, Paul, and I were for it. But the political people on the ground in Illinois said, "We don't have time to put it on the schedule, it will break into a big story, we will peel off some of the black vote, some of our supporters are for Gus Savage and it will hurt us, it will suppress turnout; Savage has stayed out of our business, we ought to stay out of his; it ain't worth it, we are getting away from our main objective, which is to win these primaries; we are going to win this thing, why fool with it?" It was a persuasive argument. We were going to win the nomination. Monarchs don't like revolutions. The idea never got to Clinton. And Gus Savage got beat.

It seemed to me like a blown opportunity. Whatever we might have lost in Illinois we would have gained somewhere else.

In May, in an interview published in *The Washington Post* two weeks after the L.A. riots, a rap singer called Sister Souljah had made some truly intolerable, racist remarks about white people. It wasn't a song, it wasn't art, it was a political statement in the aftermath of a riot, telling people to kill other people. "If black people kill black people every day," she said, "why not have a week and kill white people? You understand what I'm saying? . . . So if you're a gang member and you would normally be killing somebody, why not kill a white person?"

Paul was on the road with the candidate when the story was published, and they were horrified. Clinton felt very deeply that Sister Souljah had gone way outside the lines. He was going to Los Angeles to speak to a group of Hollywood people called the SHOW Coalition and the night before, Paul wrote a speech that included a section about Sister Souljah: "The media, too, has to examine who they're putting forth as role models. You have to think of the message you are communicating when a rap singer like Sister Souljah can call for the killing of white people and no one in a position of responsibility challenges her. This is my challenge to you: to continue to be vigilant, vocal, and visible in your opposition to bigotry, stereotyping, and discrimination—but also to have the courage to condemn *all* racism, no matter what the color of the person espousing it."

The SHOW Coalition turned out to be a charitable group, not an entertainment-industry forum, and when Governor Clinton got there he felt it would be inappropriate to lecture these people when they were already there to give money to charity. So the speech got put on the shelf.

A month later the governor was scheduled to address Jesse Jackson's Rainbow Coalition in New York. Mandy Grunwald brought it to our attention that Sister Souljah was scheduled to speak the day before we arrived. So we were confronted with a moral dilemma and a strategic choice: Do we say what we believe about this woman, which Governor Clinton has already thought through and we have written up and know is in his head and in his heart? Or do we just gloss it over for the sake of political peace?

I thought we were vulnerable. We went to the candidate and said, "Look, if I was the media, if I was the Republicans, *if I was Dan Quayle,* I would say, 'You're a big man. You go to Macomb County, Michigan, and take some blue-collar white folks and give them a big lecture. And you go out to your friends in Hollywood and tell them about the need to come together. But here's a woman who has taken a very cavalier attitude over the murder of white people, and you freeze. You talk of moral leadership but you give us none. What kind of man are you?' " It would have been a pretty devastating attack.

We decided to go with the speech.

People thought Clinton was looking for a way to stick a thumb in Jesse Jackson's eye and that he found it by embarrassing Jackson in front of his own organization and criticizing him for the moral failure of having invited Sister Souljah to speak. But that's not true. No, Clinton did not go the extra mile to tell Jesse what he was going to say before the event, but our view was, Tough. Jesse didn't come to us and say he was going to get Dennis Rivera to switch the hospital workers' union endorsement to Jerry Brown in the New York primary. He didn't clear it with us when he went to the Democratic Leadership Committee and attacked Clinton and the moderate wing of the party. We had no obligation to clear our remarks with him or anyone.

I stayed away from the event. I didn't need reporters saying the whole thing was a political move orchestrated by the Cajun Svengali. This wasn't political posturing. Clinton said, "Reverend Jackson was right to criticize H. Ross Perot for making intolerant statements about gay people. But he was wrong in not condemning such hateful comments from Sister Souljah—and the Rainbow Coalition is doubly wrong for giving her a national platform."

Paul tells me that Jesse was only mildly upset while Clinton was speaking. Afterward he stood up and gave a wonderful benediction, literally calling God's blessing upon this man. Then afterward, they went into a private meeting and things got a lot worse.

Reverend Jackson presented Governor Clinton with a ten-page, single-spaced memo stating how and why he could help the ticket if he, Jesse Jackson, was the Democratic nominee for Vice President. Clinton wouldn't even look at it. He said, essentially, "I'm not going to even consider you. We're too incompatible. I'm not going to do the traditional political thing, I'm not going to insult you the way that Mondale and Dukakis did and pretend that you're being seriously considered. Those guys never seriously considered you."

The Sister Souljah story blew up in the press. Five days after the fact, Jackson told Johnny Apple in an interview in *The New York Times* that Governor Clinton had "again exposed a character flaw" by not taking the matter up with him privately. It was a "Machiavellian maneuver," he said, intended "purely to appeal to conservative whites by containing Jackson and isolating Jackson."

The truth of the matter is, if Jackson had never mentioned it, the Sister Souljah reference would have been pretty much of a nonevent. It might have made paragraph eight of a news story, if that. We had achieved one of our strategic aims, which was to inoculate ourselves from criticism that we just spoke out against white racism and not black racism. But when Jesse jumped out there it became a big story, and I don't think there's much doubt that the story helped us. Clearly there wasn't going to be a picture of Bill Clinton and Jesse Jackson arm in arm on the front page of *The New York Times*. But the distancing from Jackson wasn't calculated; we were going to appear at the event, Sister Souljah had preceded us, we felt we had to speak out. In doing so, were we disappointed that we got favorable political fallout from it? No. But we weren't out there pushing the story.

Mary

Clinton spoke from the heart? It was fortuitous serendipity that they had an opportunity to disparage Sister Souljah? They never intended to distance themselves from Jesse Jackson? Trust me, you *never* get that lucky in politics. Everyone in politics understood their continuing need to assuage Jesse, still a phenomenal force in their party, while simultaneously backing away from him, so this profession of utter innocence just makes me laugh out loud.

We thought it was a stroke of genius. Clinton was running as a so-called New Democrat when the Democratic party had previously been captive to minority extremists, mostly identified with the leadership of Jesse Jackson. It wasn't a black thing, it was a liberal thing; all across the board Jackson is liberal, and proud of it. I admire his perseverance, even if it is wrongheaded. Any Republican who talked about issues like welfare reform would get accused of race-baiting or bigotry, and any Democrat who didn't talk about them (and therefore against the African-American leadership) wasn't going to get the middle-class Reagan Democrats—the key to winning any election.

We wondered from the beginning how they were going to deal with the Jesse Jackson factor, and they did it in one fell swoop.

Not only did they not kowtow to him, they publicly humiliated him. I don't know how far that traveled in the electorate, but in political circles the Clintonistas got a lot of points for courage and for staying in the mainstream. It was a particularly creative coup because they never frontally assaulted Jesse; they picked the vehicle of this clearly radical-looking, radical-sounding crackpot, the total antithesis of the middle-class Reagan Democrat they were trying to win back. The fact that Jackson was so angry not about Sister Souljah but about getting rejected out of hand for vice-presidential consideration was news I didn't hear until after the election, and then not even from James.

Of course, I wasn't hearing much of anything, since our troubles blocked out the whole rest of the world.

Okay, so Dan Quayle encouraged a Trenton, New Jersey, schoolboy to misspell "potato." Good spelling is not a necessary prerequisite for service in high office. All this said to us was what we already knew: Dan Quayle had been eternally Quayle-ized. He could do twenty good things for twenty consecutive weeks and then do one stupid thing and the press would revert to their original opinion of him. Our reaction was, "Oh, well."

We prepared for press speculation that President Bush would dump him, but we hardly thought a spelling error constituted sufficient grounds for being dropped from the ticket. We had been through the anatomically correct doll, *Murphy Brown*—there was a whole list. We knew the real day-to-day Quayle, and he was really smart. Of course there was no way, when something like this happened, that we could convince the press of our version and avoid a media brouhaha. Even the Vice President's staff made jokes. But it didn't affect our lives. Contrary to even the Veep's staff's conjecture, we never pulled back from him or whispered that he was a potatoe head.

The more important story at the time was in *The Wall Street Journal.* They reported that Ross Perot had regularly engaged private detectives to gather information about his employees and competitors, frequently focusing on marital infidelity. Perot wouldn't talk to them about it.

We'd been waiting for this one. Those of us in the leave-him-alone-he'll-self-destruct camp of the how-to-deal-with-Perot debate breathed a collective sigh of relief. All along we'd been saying, "If he's that wacky, the press will start hitting him." The press had resisted for a very long time. Now, we figured, once that floodgate had opened the media would fall all over itself going after him because there's such a wealth of material.

It also gave us a legitimate and clear opening to take shots at him.

It's sort of an unwritten rule of politics: Once the press has gone after a candidate, the opposition can open fire too. If you go on the offensive too early—as we did when Marilyn Quayle and Marlin Fitzwater, et al., zeroed in on him—then the presumption in the press is that you're attacking him because he's scaring you, he's cutting into your support. At that point you become the story, not your opposition. Once the press started breaking stories suggesting Perot was autocratic and paranoid, then the candidates were free to jump in with barrels blazing.

Dan Quayle didn't waste any time. That same day he said in a Washington speech, "It would be a serious mistake to replace a genuine statesman with a temperamental tycoon who has contempt for the Constitution of the United States." The Vice President's office came up with that speech, we didn't ask him to make it, but they ran it by us and we did not disapprove.

A couple of days later, the *Los Angeles Times* reported that in 1986, during a power struggle with General Motors chairman Roger Smith, Perot had told some of his aides that they might have to nuke GM by turning off the company's computer system. A couple of days after that, *The Washington Post* reported that Perot had a falling-out with George Bush in 1986 over the MIAs. "The world is full of lions and tigers and rabbits," Perot was quoted as saying. "And you're a rabbit." Then, said the *Post*, Perot sent his people to find Bush's dirty laundry. Three days after the *Post* story, Perot accused *our* campaign of "dirty tricks."

"There has been a ninety-day effort to redefine my personality by a group called opposition research of the Republican party," he said. "They're generally known as the dirty-tricks crowd."

We weren't above leaking damaging opposition info, but this wasn't our stuff. GM board executives had repeatedly called us with Perot stories; we'd had this one, but the press found it all by themselves. All this flurry of Perot-bashing did was convince us we didn't have to do anything, the press was going to do it for us. They would call and say, "Did you know this, do you know that?" and we would say, "Yeah, man, but go get it yourself."

You usually don't want to be attached to a negative story about your opposition. The media give more weight to stories they dig up independently; they're more likely to be suspicious of the ones you direct them to. They had come down on us like a ton of bricks when we were calling Perot a snake-oil salesman, so we made the tactical decision not to lay it all out for them. We figured the Perot stories were sitting in Texas as big as a rock; once the press went looking they couldn't miss them.

What the "Perot investigates Bush" story did was give us a hook, it gave us Perot's motive: Perot hates Bush. The media instantly ascribed this motive to his candidacy, which undermined some of his attacks on us. "He hates Bush," we would tell them, "so of course he's going to trash Bush. How can you believe anything the man says? It has nothing to do with reality; it has everything to do with this guy's own parochial, vindictive, paranoid interests."

This was manna from heaven. We still didn't know what strategy to take in a three-man race, but anything we would normally have done—leak stuff, put out his negatives, attack him—the press was doing for us. We were all high-fiving each other, happy and relieved we could now just put him on the back burner, secure in the knowledge that a free press would free us of Ross Perot.

Even better news was the fact that the Clinton campaign had released their "Putting People First" plan. It was good for both of us. It was good for Clinton more for the fact of having a plan than for what was in it. This was the Year of the Plan, and he had one and George Bush didn't. In fact, when we finally did put our plan together the goal was to make it one page longer than Clinton's and to put a cover on it that was clearly visible to a camera. The reason the Clinton plan was good for us was that it finally gave us real substance to campaign on—or, more precisely, against.

There are always three generic components to a campaign strategy: record, qualifications, and character. Go after his; promote your own. In this election, the Clinton opposition offered slim pickings. You couldn't get any traction from Clinton's record. We had stark and damning Arkansas statistics but no one cared one whit about them. The best you could say about the Arkansas Clinton created was that, of the fifty states, at least they weren't dead last. Although the statistics amounted to a devastating exposé of his liberal record, no one could absorb them all. Rather than whip through the numbers, the only shorthand coherent for a thirty-second ad was that after a decade of doubling spending in every quality-of-life measurement from education to crime control to the environment, the standard of living had gone down. A failed governor from a small state. However, disparaging his abysmal record as a stand-alone strategy was not enough.

We couldn't lean on character because the press refused to believe that what we were calling "the character issue" was *not* the womanizing, the pot-smoking, the draft-dodging. To us, the character issue was about poor judgment, flip-flops, evasiveness, saying whatever the electorate wanted. Which left only qualifications. His qualifications were his ideas. What were his ideas? We were thrilled he finally told us.

"Putting People First" was replete with inconsistencies. Rule number one in analyzing the opposition's data: If you can find anything in their plan that is demonstrably erroneous, it discredits the whole plan. Well, David Tell crunched Clinton's numbers and they didn't add up. For example, they said they were going to raise $45 billion in revenues by taxing foreign companies doing business in the United States. The highest number coming out of congressional committees that had considered the same revenue-raising proposal—*committees controlled by Democrats*—was $1 billion. It wasn't like he was diddling over a couple of bills, he was $44 billion off!

They said they were going to get $150 billion from taxes on the top 2 percent of American taxpayers. We had IRS computations that said there was no way you could get anything close. So we pounded them for a good long while, and when they "corrected" their numbers we pounded them some more.

Best of all, "Putting People First" added up to typical old-fashioned tax-and-spend liberalism. The upshot of crunching through the numbers was that Clinton was proposing to double the spending of Dukakis and Mondale combined, and triple the tax increases.

We had been flopping around like a fish on the beach all campaign long. Now we really had something to work with. Inside campaign headquarters the atmosphere changed. Outside, too. Clinton's economic plan was ostensibly complicated, but we all understood its failings and could state them clearly in a thirty-second sound bite. We looked smart, we felt smart. Even though our polling numbers were terrible, we were beginning to feel pretty good for the first time.

CHAPTER 13

James

President Bush's reneging on "Read my lips: No new taxes" was the most famous broken promise in the history of American politics.

Mary

In fact, he apologized but no one heard him.

I first heard the idea from Fred Cooper, our Georgia chairman, in early January 1992, before the campaign doors were even opened. It made a lot of sense, but in politics, logic doesn't always rule. Before we understood the magnitude of the problem, "flip-flopping" sounded more akin to burning down the village to save it.

So we dismissed any mea culpa plans until the drumbeat became deafening—probably not coincidentally, in the Georgia primary. Cooper laid out the concept to the President at a Camp David weekend.

So during the Georgia primary the people at the national campaign began having discussions in earnest about how to neutralize this killer issue. We had tentatively arrived at the conclusion that the President had to say the budget deal had been a mistake. But this was a major statement of policy that demanded precision wording and we had not come up with the exact phraseology that would serve the President's needs. It was extremely important that this public apology not be lost in screaming accusations of flip-flopping, a vulnerability we had suffered from since our 1980 "choice" to "life" switch.

The discussions elevated to the presidential level, but the whole idea was still in the talking stages. Then the President went out and, on his own, laid out this mea culpa to a local Georgia newspaper. He just did it. We didn't know he was going to do it and we weren't as prepared as we should have been to take advantage of it.

My first knowledge of the statement was when Teeter called me late one night on my private line, which he never did, requesting, without elaboration, that I get my hands on an early edition of the Atlanta *Constitution*. Carney, the Wonder Boy, somehow got a fax, which we read with mixed emotions. Again: right message, wrong vehicle. The national press was not gonna take kindly to a major strategic shift being dribbled out to what it considered a local outlet. We certainly didn't get the clean slate that we needed out of it.

Part of my job and David Carney's job was to talk to our people in the field, gather a consensus of what they were saying, and bring it to the high command. They all had their gripes about how the campaign was being run, but there were two universals. One was, "We've got to start fighting. It looks like we got no fight." The other was that everyone, like Fred Cooper, hated the damn budget deal and they wanted the President to apologize for it.

As early as the primaries, everywhere our operatives went, all the real voters they talked to said, "He broke his promise." That's all people would ever say about President Bush. They were deaf to anything else he had to say. They tuned him out. It was more than just raising people's taxes; by breaking his most famous promise the President had lost his credibility. The Georgia primary mea culpa had gone nowhere, so when we had the opportunity to once again apologize— this time in the larger and more visible forum of a Barbara Walters interview on ABC—we pounced on it. The President wanted to make certain that this time the country recognized he had learned his lesson when he told her, "That was a mistake, because it undermined to some degree my credibility with the American people."

Though the political press pummeled us for what it perceived as a piece of political expediency, it was very good news for the several concentric circles of the campaign.

The campaign operates on three levels: what's happening on the home front, what's happening with the electorate, and what's happening with the press and the pundits. Our team loved it. The President's mea culpa restored credibility to a man with a deep sense of honor, it showed that he was big enough to admit a mistake, and it reasserted the universal Republican philosophy that *any* tax increase is bad policy. The leadership in the states was ecstatic; they could look their workers and voters in the eye and tell them the President understood.

For opinion makers, it reaffirmed the Republican principle that raising taxes in a recession stunts growth and is destructive to a recovery and the economy in general. The *Wall Street Journal* types, who had pummeled the President for taking the counsel of economic advisers Dick Darman and Nicholas Brady, began touting, with relief, that Bush did indeed recognize the workings of the economy.

James

He could apologize all he wanted; we were not going to let the American people forget that he had gotten elected on a promise that he didn't keep.

Mary

Stud Muffin took it upon himself to do a Bush '88 promises analysis. We kept, by his count, 279 promises and broke only 1. But, man, it was a whopper.

So, we had put a major problem behind us (as best we could) and Clinton had created a major problem we could ride on. We were feeling okay. Then, on June 30, *The Washington Post* came out with their poll: Clinton 33, Perot 31, Bush 28. On April 9 we'd been at 36.

If we'd woken up one morning and dropped 8 points, people's hair would have been on fire. But the shift had been gradual, maybe just a point a week, like a death march. Starting from the day we opened our doors, we marched ever onward and downward. At each downtick, Teeter would say, "That's absolutely rock bottom. We can't go any lower—we're at our base." Well, our base must have been in quicksand.

When in doubt, spin. We spun like dervishes.

We trashed Slick Willie, who had taken the lead for the first time. We minimized the Perot vote: It was not a vote at all, only a symbol of the American voter's anger and frustration, and a continuation of the earlier primary urge to send the President and Washington a message. We berated the press: "These polls are meaningless. The first reliable poll won't come until after the conventions and into the general election."

I'm telling you flat out, it was all spin. We didn't know what to make of the quicksand numbers. We were freaking out. When we walked into the staff meeting that morning, there, in Teeter's chair, sat a five-foot-high inflatable version of Edvard Munch's *The Scream*. It looked the way we felt.

We didn't have a vehicle to move our numbers positively because we weren't in campaign mode. We were operating on defense, and as Atwater said, "Any day you're not moving the ball forward, it's moving backward." It was pretty damn scary.

Scarier yet, we believed our own spin.

It was around this time that the press started smelling blood. They had never thought it remotely conceivable that George Bush could lose, but when the negative data remained consistent for about a month, reporters started hypothesizing about the possibility of an incumbent upset. They liked that; it made for a season of good stories.

This changed our job in a hurry. Instead of sitting around thinking up ways to improve our numbers, we had to ward off ever-escalating accounts of our death. It wasn't yet damage control—the dikes hadn't broken—it was staving off erosion. The tide of public opinion and stepped-up press attacks was eating away our fortifications and we had to find a way to shore them up.

We were clueless.

We continued our bookend meetings at the White House. I'd be having nicotine fits and we would be agonizing, "What do we do?" We had to define the President, while still defining the other two candidates. We had always shared the theory that people were attracted to Perot because he was voicing their frustrations, but we now came to the consensus that when push came to shove no one would waste their vote in a presidential campaign.

The Democrats had no time to kick around theories; their train was moving, they were rolling into their convention. Ours wasn't until August, so we had some choices to make as to how to spend our advertising dollars and position our President in the interim. We sat in Skinner's office one night, picking over stale sandwiches he had brought up from the White House mess. Finally, two hours into the meeting, we got serious.

"Let's go back to basics. If Perot wasn't in this, what would we do? Would we go positive on us or go negative on Clinton?"

The standard rule of thumb is that when you've got high negatives you can't go negative on the opposition because the ensuing backlash from the public—who always profess to hate negative campaigning—accrues to you. To withstand the backlash, you've got to get your positives up before you go negative. That's the book. But at one of our meetings someone said, "Well, what if we went negative on Clinton?"

Everyone gasped. "Unthinkable."

"Well," I said, "our objective is not to increase Clinton's negatives in a vacuum, it's to appeal to Perot voters, to define Clinton in such a way as to make Perot voters peel off in our direction, not his, when they get around to focusing on the choice." We began a discussion of what it was the Perot people actually cared about, and how could we craft a negative Clinton message that we could run between the conventions.

Teeter got excited. "Bingo," he said, "we actually have an option." Bob Teeter is, under normal circumstances, consistently professorial, intellectual, contemplative, and lengthy in his explanations. Kind of a monotone guy. But when he gets excited he talks faster, smiles like a mischievous boy, and wrings his hands diabolically. People started to laugh.

No one had really been happy with the option of just doing positive Bush because we didn't think we'd break through. And besides, going negative puts everybody in a mischievously productive and creative mood. For campaign junkies, it's a much more psychically rewarding challenge to slash the opposition than to cobble together another round of gushy, flag-waving, isn't-our-guy-great ads.

We spent the next three hours coming up with ideas. I don't remember another time on the whole campaign when Teeter, Charlie, Darman, and I were happier. Perot people, we knew, were obsessed with the deficit and frivolous government spending, which opened up the Arkansas record as a strategic attack point. We had massive data on Clinton clearly showing that after ten years of him as governor of Arkansas, state spending had doubled and there had been absolutely no improvement in any of the standard-of-living measurements—not education, not crime, not teenage pregnancy. We could say with conviction and authority, critical in negative ads, that he was a big spender and the programs he spent lavishly on *didn't work*. Yahoo. What could the voters expect from a combination of a tax-and-spend Democrat in the White House and free-spending Democrats controlling the Hill?

The umbrella issue that subsumed the Perotista concerns of deficit control and frivolous spending was "responsive government." How responsive would government be if both Congress and the White House were controlled by one party? Yahoo, again.

Teeter took a bunch of good ideas back to the ad guys, who came up with a series of excellent storyboards. Everybody was pumped.

The Madison Avenue guys were cool and accomplished. They had created the "Heartbeat of America" Chevrolet ads. We were expecting great things.

I wasn't a regular at the media strategy sessions so I missed what happened in between the hot storyboards and what was ultimately produced. When they finally cut the ads, the New Yorkers gave a big presentation and showed about eighteen rough cuts. George Bush talking right at you. George Bush on crime. George Bush on education. George Bush on domestic issues. The ad guys seemed very pleased with themselves.

It was a very strange set of spots. They had President Bush speak directly into the camera. The only visual for both the thirty-second and sixty-second ads was Bush's head, and it was cropped at the top! Instead of a fluid speech they chopped one sentence into another, and through abrupt cinematography and edgy editing put together a package they thought was kind of avant-garde and cool.

President Bush isn't avant-garde and cool, he's the President of the United States. I was stunned.

When the lights came up all I could say was, "What's the message?" We weren't selling cars here. There was only one ad with a comprehensive overall theme as to why people should vote for George Bush, and that, it turned out, had been written by Charlie Black.

But I was the only one who spoke up, and I didn't do it very loudly. No one confronted them. The protocol of our ad meetings was very polite, and I was not a regular participant. Afterward, I beelined to Carney for a reality check. "They're awful! They stink! The data says people have stopped listening to George Bush, so what are we doing with George Bush talking heads?" It just didn't make any sense. "This is what everyone's complaining about. It's sentence fragments. It's Bushspeak! If we think people aren't hearing us, and all we're doing is talking in the same way we always do, this is five million dollars' worth of trees falling in a forest. I don't get it. The visual is wrong, the concept is wrong. And furthermore, there's not even a good positive message."

I truly do not know how we went from heady yahoos to yo-yo talking heads. Obviously, we chickened out. The consensus moved to conventional wisdom. To slash or not to slash was a recurring discussion; it went on in New Hampshire, it happened again here. We were beaten back by our original fear that the press would kill us. They'd jump on us for being negative campaigners.

The Democrats had laid that groundwork and now it was paying off in spades. Even before the '92 campaign they began to box us in. From the time he got to be DNC chairman, Ron Brown carefully laid on the media the definition that we were the most despicable, negative, lowlife, cretinous, slimehead campaigners God ever created. He never let up. Any time he found the slightest inkling in a local campaign, state campaign, an RNC statement, anything—he would blow it wildly out of proportion until it became an article of faith in the press, and therefore the country, that Republicans were negative campaigners. We couldn't begin to lay out Clinton's negatives without Ron Brown and the press jumping all over us for sins we had never committed. The argument went that the press would go crazy over negative Clinton spots and we'd never get another shot at getting our own positive message out.

In the end the campaign ended up running $5 million worth of George Bush positive talking heads. You don't get many windows of opportunity in a campaign. You don't even always know when you're in one. We threw $5 million out of ours.

James

Every poll, public and private, indicated that people had serious problems with our candidacy. At the beginning of the Manhattan Project we weren't sure we could find the problem, and if we did, we weren't sure there was an answer to it. There was a real fear that we were in mildew, that there wasn't a way out of this, that maybe the voters had just given up.

We did focus groups, dial groups, polling—and the results gave us a lot of hope.

The two most significant and encouraging findings of the Manhattan Project were that the public in no way had given up on Bill Clinton and that they actually wanted to hear more information about him. That told us pretty conclusively that we had a good case to make; we just had to get out and make it. They wanted to know who he was, and to make a connection between where he came from and where he was going.

Our problem, we found, was that people viewed the candidate as too political. Every time we used any kind of political language in a dial group, people didn't like it. The worst words were, "I promise, if I'm elected . . ." "I can get this many electoral votes . . ." People were turned off by any sort of political rhetoric. But they had not made a final judgment.

They had a nice sense of Bill Clinton as a person. "Suppose he lived next door to you, what do you think he'd be like?"

"Probably would be great, the kind of guy that if you ran out of sugar you could always go over and get some."

"Would you let your children stay over?"

"Of course, yes."

What was troubling to people, we found, was there was a lack of consistency coming out of him. It's not surprising; I don't think our campaign at the time was giving them much consistency. I said, "I think our problem is that people think we are just about whatever the day is, as opposed to something over a consistent period of time." We were going from primary to primary, we had a state-by-state message and no overall plan.

We had been out there since January, really visible, moving around the country, traveling. The staff was tired, the candidate was tired, we were getting bad polls, we were in the doldrums. We had to fight our way out. In May and June we were a campaign without a rationale; we were at the tail end of the primaries; our enemy was out of ammunition and was starving to death. We had a couple of clubs so we could go in there and finish them off, but there was another enemy over the hill. Jerry Brown had nothing, but on the other side of the hill there were George Bush and Ross Perot armed with howitzers and bazookas.

We had to develop our own weapons system.

A campaign is driven by its rationale. (Some people call it a message; I like "rationale" better.) It can be a good rationale, a bad rationale, or no rationale at all. David Duke certainly had a rationale for his candidacy—it was very easy to know why he was running—so the idea is not just to have a rationale but to have the right one.

People will look back on some races and say, "So-and-so didn't have a rationale and he won." Well, he ran against someone who didn't have one either. If a child molester beats a child molester, does it follow that the way to get elected is to be a child molester? No, it's just two people running, somebody's got to win.

We went back and talked about how we'd worked in the beginning, with crispness and clarity. We had lost our clarity and we had to recapture it. We had strayed so far from our roots that some people began coming up with new political positions for the general election. The strategic team was saying, "We don't need new positions, we don't need different positions. We just need fewer of them and articulated better. We have too much out there. There's too many things that we're saying that are sort of off the central point. Let's go back to the central point. We've got to talk about fewer things more often."

Where campaigns get into trouble is (a) when they try to make a candidate into someone he's not—it can't work in a presidential race, the scrutiny is too intense and you'll get caught; and (b) when they try to do too many things. The constant friction point between a strategist and a candidate is "Just stay on one point." We want them to make one winning point over and over again.

It's understandable; if a candidate is any good he or she has got lots of ideas, a vision, and wants to share them. They want to present themselves as people of greater depth than some one-trick pony. But if that one trick is a winner, a strategist will call for it every chance he gets. Let the candidates display their range once they're in office— they'll have to. What we care about is getting them there.

We had to make decisions about our strategy. Bill Clinton was a founder of the Democratic Leadership Council, which had as its goal to reinvent government. Do you run as a New Democrat—a reinvent-government, DLC, centrist Democrat? Your message there would be, "The government needs to think in new and different ways. We need to do things like move away from welfare toward work." You can run as a "People First" Democrat and say, "We have to invest in people; the real wealth of this country springs from our people, that's why we need more job-training programs and student loans made available to people, so they can be empowered." You can run as a health-care-cost Democrat. You can run as a deficit-cutting Democrat. We talked about all of those things, but to run successfully and win *you can't be all four of them*. Voters will say, "He's out there talking one game one day, another game the next." They're not inconsistent with each other, but nothing gets through.

We were trying to take this whole mass of positions—all of which Bill Clinton believed in, all of which showed who he was—and condense it and distill it into something really hard and clear. What we ultimately came to was to present ourselves as a "different kind of Democrat," with a strong emphasis on the economy. There, we could draw our basic distinctions. That was what Clinton was most comfortable with, what he had talked about most consistently, what he most believed, and what was best for us.

It began to work. Between June 7 and 28 the *Washington Post* poll had us picking up 7 points. It looked as though we had bottomed out and were coming back. Maybe we would get over 25 percent and qualify for federal matching money.

Once we began to get a handle on the rationale, the consultants got together one night and said, "Look, we've got to do something structurally." This was the end of a month-long conversation. "We have a direction, but there's no implementation, we have no research, no method to respond. We have nothing."

We needed a central command headquarters and we needed someone to run it. There were some names thrown around, people from outside the campaign who had worked on the Mondale race, or with Carter or Dukakis. That didn't go on long; everybody felt it had to be somebody internal, someone the Clintons and the campaign people would accept. George, Stan, Mandy, and Paul said, "It's got to be James." It was a conspiracy by about ten or twelve people to create a power center. You couldn't call it anything less than a naked power grab.

I went over to the governor's mansion to bring the idea to Hillary. We sat outside on some wire-mesh patio furniture and I told her, "We just can't take it no more. We're not remotely prepared to run the general election now. It's going to be horribly tough. We've got to be very nimble, very aggressive, and we don't think we're there—not just in the decision-making process but in terms of research and preparation for battle. We have a pretty short window, and we have the convention coming up, and the vice-presidential selection. . . . We all feel like we need to put together a command control, somewhere all the parts of the campaign can come together. The pollsters, the media people, everybody's got to have a desk right there. It's got to be the focus of everything, the place to get stuff out, a place that runs on speed. We've got to put one person in charge of running it. And, frankly, we all feel that it's a role that's particularly suited to me."

She said, "It sounds good to me. I'm going to talk to Bill tonight. He's expressed some frustration, too, and I think this would be something he would find appealing. We'll let you know tomorrow."

I went over to the mansion the next morning and got called up to the residence. Governor Clinton was in his underwear, looking in his closet for a shirt. He said, "Look, you've got to do this thing. Get it done, but I don't want to start a big internal struggle. I don't want you to run over anybody."

▪

There was only one place to put our headquarters: Little Rock. There was a considerable move afoot among some of the campaign operatives, consultants, workers, for whatever reason—some of them sound, some of them selfish—to move the campaign headquarters to somewhere more accessible. Chicago had some currency. Washington. I kind of liked Atlanta—somewhere there were a lot of good restaurants, somewhere people could get in and out.

Basically, I think the decision started and stopped with Chelsea's softball season. To the Clintons, Little Rock was home. Neither Mrs. Clinton nor the governor ever really considered having the campaign headquarters anywhere else.

George said it first, and it became our code: "Unless you're here, you're not here."

One of the great advantages of Little Rock was that there were no direct flights from Washington, D.C. It took some doing to get there. I didn't want the media coming into town on a stopover and dropping by all day and night. I didn't want them sniffing around the city, I didn't want our people having to deal with them all the time. The city was ours.

There was some lack of enthusiasm about the command center at first. No one actively got in our way, but somehow the phones didn't get installed on time, the carpenters didn't come in and get the place together. Some people in positions of authority weren't all that excited about letting something go from their purview. It was definitely a power shift and it took some getting used to.

Meanwhile, there was a vice-presidential candidate to choose.

The strategists were encouraged to foster ideas, but the integrity of the selection committee—Warren Christopher, Vernon Jordan, Madeleine Kunin—was pretty well maintained.

I thought we should send an unconventional signal. Picking General Colin Powell would have done it, definitely. He's a guy who people are going to discuss. There was as much talk about Bush picking him as there was us. Word was received that he wasn't interested.

My favorite was Senator Bill Bradley. He was a different-thinking Democrat. Represented New Jersey, grew up in Missouri, not a typical politico but very, very solid on race relations, and a thoughtful guy. I kept calling his senior counselor, Anita Dunn, and saying, "I really would like to push this thing." She called me back and authorized me to tell no one but the governor that both the senator's wife and his personal assistant (who was also my good friend), Marina Gentilini, had been diagnosed with cancer, and he didn't feel, given those circumstances, that he could run.

Clinton decided on Al Gore pretty much from their first meeting. I think they hit it off real well; there was a great deal of comfort between the two. Gore had been around the track once, he'd run for president. I think Clinton also felt that picking Gore was different and unexpected. The drawback was that it was two guys from the same region, but nobody viewed that as a big problem. I had the sense fairly early on in the process that the governor had made up his mind; he'd have to be talked out of choosing Al Gore, as opposed to talked into it. Absent some clear and compelling reason to discard the senator, this was a done deal.

Of the consultants, Stan Greenberg was the first one to be staunchly pro-Gore. The more people thought about it, Al Gore seemed like a pretty good choice: good on the environment, strong senatorial record, Vietnam War veteran, a moderate who would fit in with Bill Clinton's New Democrat agenda. A good choice.

When George and I were called over to the governor's mansion to discuss the range of possibilities, it was more to inform us of Clinton's opinion than it was to solicit ours. The governor said, "Do you know of any good reason why I shouldn't do this?" I looked at it like when you go to a wedding and they say, "If anybody knows why these people should not be united in holy matrimony, speak now or forever hold your peace." There was about as much chance of me blurting something out.

Governor Clinton called Senator Gore at eleven-fifteen that evening to inform him of his decision, and Senator Gore accepted. Reporters were called around three in the morning with the selection so it would get into the morning papers.

The announcement ceremony that day was one of the single most remarkable events of the campaign.

There is a huge backyard at the governor's mansion in Arkansas, with a balcony to walk out on. The Gores had flown in for the official announcement. It was a nice summer Thursday, bright, kind of warm. We were all happy that the choice was behind us and we could move on toward the convention and the general election. It kind of felt good to be out of doors for a change.

The minute you saw the two families on that balcony you knew it was a masterpiece.

They had a vibrancy, the families clicked, there was more there than we had known. They didn't look like politicos, they didn't look like traditional Democrats. They looked like challenging politicians.

After the families had come back in off the balcony and gone downstairs to the basement, I walked up to Mrs. Clinton and said, "Hillary, I know we're not supposed to say this in the modern world, but I got to tell you, you looked pretty cute out there today in that dress." She busted out laughing.

Mary

We all watched that scene on the balcony. The reaction was, "Oh, my God." The Clintons, the Gores, all those beautiful kids in front of that quintessentially American red brick mansion, looking youthful and cheery . . . it was Nirvana, the pinnacle of political introductions. You couldn't have made up a better visual. Plus, their timing was impeccable. They had a perfect picture for their timely message: change, youth, dynamism. We were looking at the mother-lode of nomination coverage. We were all awestruck. We were all clutching our stomachs.

The Clinton people spun Gore out precisely the right way. Only one screw-up: They said he had intellectual heft. But that heft was based largely on his having actually written one book on the environment, *Earth in the Balance*. To anticipate our attack, and therefore be prepared with responses, some DNC staffer went through it page by page and wrote a memo that detailed how moronic it was. The memo was accidentally faxed to a Republican office on the Hill and we had a field day with the lefty gobblydegook like, "We now know that [the automobile's] cumulative impact on the global environment is posing a moral threat to the security of every nation that is more deadly than that of any military enemy we are ever again likely to confront." But, to their credit, the Clintonistas got him out of the box in a very positive way.

James

The Democratic National Convention was in New York City. On a good day in New York it takes time to get around. During a convention you can't get anywhere. The wait for the elevators was excruciating. You've got a gazillion places to be, all at one time, and the Secret Service has commandeered one elevator for the candidate and is continually checking and rechecking it. So you're late, you're supposed to have a meeting in the Cabinet Suite, the adrenaline's going pretty good, and you're standing there cursing for ten minutes, kicking the damn doors, waiting for the elevator. Of course, that doesn't matter because Clinton is going to be late anyway.

And everywhere you go you've got to be your best. You know your message, you've got it prepared like a great meal before you step into this media feast, the trick is to keep it fresh under the hot lights. You've got some new lines—the media likes piquant verbal spices in its political gumbo—but this is the one time and place when the message has to be presented perfectly.

The further west you go, the better conventions are. You finish earlier because of television. In California you can go to the hall, give your acceptance speech at six o'clock, do your business, go by some cocktail parties, and be asleep at eleven. In New York the sessions didn't finish before eleven-thirty, then you'd go do TV and media interviews for an hour and then hit the circuit.

Those media interviews are on the convention floor. You stand there and do one after another. At first you think, "Oh, boy, look at all these people paying attention to me." It's great. But after a while it's just work. It must be like the first time you have your at bat in the big leagues: "God, I can't believe I'm here." After two thousand at bats, it's like, "All right, let's go, let's get this thing on." And you have good at bats and bad ones, some times are better than others.

There are convention cocktail parties and dinners all over Manhattan every night. Fund-raisers want you to come by so their people, who are giving a lot of money, are able to say, "I was with the Clinton people earlier, and . . ." Reporters who you know want interviews, people who you don't know are looking for jobs, friends want to have a drink. It's New York. Everybody you ever knew in your professional life is all in one city, people you worked in campaigns with, cried with, bled with. You'd like to see them. And everyone's calling you saying, "I need to talk to you." Talking is the last thing I want to do, it's what I've been doing since the moment I woke up. This is New York, I want to go to a fine restaurant, shut up, and have a master chef serve me one of the world's great meals.

Finally I couldn't take it. I moved out of the Inter-Continental, where the campaign was staying, and took a hotel room some blocks away just to escape.

■

Day one of the Democratic National Convention was made for me by the emergence of Governor Zell Miller as a national political figure. You know Ann Richards is going to give a good speech, she's a great speaker and a real crowd-pleaser. No one was surprised when Mario Cuomo gave a good speech at the convention; both of them came through with what I would call expected high performances. But Governor Miller and Paul worked very hard on Zell's speech and it was acknowledged by most people as the best one of the night. It was good, sharp, funny, acerbic, a real high point of the convention for me personally.

The main speakers on day two were Jesse Jackson and Jimmy Carter, but the major issue had to do with the adoption of the platform. Tsongas's people presented a bunch of proposals, all of which were defeated. My good friend Governor Bob Casey wanted to address the convention on the issue of abortion. He was not granted that opportunity.

A political convention is not some kind of lyceum movement, it's there to promote the candidate. The truth of the matter is, the question of abortion is decided in the Democratic party. American Democrats, as opposed to American Republicans, have decided that it's a pro-choice party. It's a pro-choice party that has pro-life people in it, always has, always will. It's hard to argue with that.

Pro-lifers Ray Flynn, John Breaux, and Wendell Ford *all* spoke; they had endorsed Clinton. Governor Casey had not. He had been, in fact, highly critical of us and was a thorn in our side in the Pennsylvania primary. I was mad at him. But I am convinced that he believed and meant what he said. I also believe that a political party has a right, an obligation, to say that if you don't endorse the candidate, you can't speak at the convention.

Mary

This was the most flagrant, revolting hypocrisy of all time . . . *and they got away with it.* If we had not allowed one of our pro-choice governors to speak at our convention, the press would have pulverized us. I've never seen the press cut any campaign so much slack—ever. Here's this key governor from a pivotal swing state they needed; he's an original, total bleeding-heart liberal who goes for every goo-goo spending program known to mankind; a colleague of Clinton's, not to mention a truly loyal Democrat and a sweetheart of a guy, and they muzzled him. It was unprecedented, and they didn't get *any* crap for it.

James

Look, we don't fashion ourselves as being part of some free-speech movement. We were there because we wanted to win, which was very unusual for this party.

In my experience there are two kinds of Democrats: There's the optimistic "we can" Democrats, and there's the pessimistic "Everybody is stupid but us and we have to remain true-blue; if these dumb people don't want to follow us, to hell with them; it is better to lose nobly than to win crassly" Democrats. The problem is, they lost consistently and they didn't lose very nobly.

Many people in the elite wing of the Democratic party would rather lose what they consider "on principle" than win by appealing to the popular masses. "Federal funding of abortion is a principle; making student loans available to everybody is pandering." Go figure that. Somehow the right to a government-funded abortion is a greater principle than the right to an education. That has never resonated very strongly with me.

But this year was different. We had been out of power for twelve years and even the wackos were on board this time. If you've been in a twelve-year drought, so what if it ain't Evian water, you drink it, it's wet.

Mary

Meanwhile, all during the Democratic convention I kept getting really odd media calls about President Bush's health, as well as the physical condition of Mrs. Bush and Mrs. Quayle. Reporters were asking all of us whether Marilyn Quayle had ovarian cancer and was that the reason we would use to get Dan Quayle off the ticket. I was incredulous. "I find it highly suspect that all these rumors have just exploded. There's a big mushroom cloud over Madison Square Garden. You deny they're coming from the Democratic scum when the calls are all coming from you and you all are there, wallowing in the pond? All the evil people in the world are congregating in Madison Square Garden and all of a sudden all these ridiculous rumors are running rampant."

James

I was sitting in a room at the Inter-Continental the last day of the convention when John King from the Associated Press called. "Hey," he said, "what do you think about Perot dropping out?"

"What are you talking about?"

"Perot's having a press conference in fifteen minutes. He's going to drop out."

"You've got to be kidding."

"That's what our people in Dallas tell me."

"Let me call you back."

I ran down the hall to where they were prepping for the governor's acceptance speech. "Somebody turn the TV on. John King said that Perot's dropping out."

So we turned the TV on and there came Perot. Clinton's in the room, senior staff, the whole team. Damned if Perot isn't doing it. When he got to the part about the "revitalization of the Democratic party," we all started clapping.

I had one of those campaign necessity lunches at the Yale Club, but before I left we went over the strategy we were going to use in dealing with the media around this turn of events. "It's 'We want to continue to run this race. Our message is . . .' and roll out our message. 'Mr. Perot's decision is his.' Just say that and not much else."

Fine. George went down and gave a fairly vanilla statement to the press and I went to this luncheon and felt pretty good about things. I didn't know why, but it all felt pretty good to me.

I walked back to the hotel and wasn't in the lobby five seconds when Paul pulled me aside. "Look, man, we got to get straight signals here. We've got to spin this thing as being good for us politically, because the Bush people are out-spinning us. They took the tack that it helps them and the stories could come out that this is a good thing for Bush."

All right. You couldn't turn around in that hotel without bumping into the national press corps, so I took two steps and held a press conference. "There is now one change candidate in the race instead of two," I told the reporters. "There was one status quo candidate before and there is still one status quo candidate. This is not just good for us, this is good for America. It will allow people to see that all-important contrast between old ideas and new ones. This is a big plus for Bill Clinton."

Mary

Ed Rollins had either quit or been fired the day before, depending on whose version you believed. When word came down that Perot was getting ready to hold a news conference we all piled into Teeter's office and bet a buck apiece on whether or not he would stay in the race. No one believed Perot would actually drop out. We just stood riveted to the television, laughing like crazy. Then we kicked into high gear.

The name of the game that day was who could call Perot's people the fastest. We were actually prepared. Carney's field troops had already developed a state-by-state list of all Perot's leadership, their addresses and phone numbers, and knew who was worth getting and who wasn't. All our operatives were on alert, and the minute Perot was out Carney got on the phone to them. They, in turn, got to our state campaigns, including governors and chairmen, who by that night had all managed to hook up with the Perot leadership. By the next morning we had identified those who were going to switch to us, and followed up with press conferences in several states to show off the Perot heavyweights who came out for Bush. By the end of the week we had fleshed it out pretty well and had hired a very key Perot worker, one of the lawyers who had originally helped him get on the ballot in fifty states. I was quite proud of our effort.

I was in absolute glee because I had this picture in my mind of the communications nightmare that James, George, Paul, and Stan had to be going through in New York. The most difficult thing to get working right at a convention is your communications system. It's critical that you have the ability to be in constant contact with everybody at any given moment, and even with beepers, walkie-talkies, cellular phones, and designated "hot lines" installed everywhere, it's next to impossible to find people. I'd been hearing from my press friends how hard it was to get around, you waited forever, nobody knew where anybody was. I figured, Here's all these Clinton guys spread all over town the day of Clinton's acceptance speech and Perot drops out; they had to be in a frenzy, it would be just nuts, and we'd have the advantage of getting to Perot because we were all centralized and had our operation and support staff around us.

For weeks we had been keeping up a brave front without actually knowing what to do about Perot. Republicans didn't know, Democrats didn't know, the pundits and opinion-makers didn't know what his impact was actually going to be. During the time when we should have been thinking about how to win a general election vis-à-vis a Democrat, we were playing Rubik's Cube trying to devise a three-way strategy with no recent precedent, no fallback, one with which we had absolutely no experience. It was a real emotionally draining brain-waster. Perot never opened his mouth without trashing Bush; he reinforced our negatives, he did a lot of Clinton's dirty work for him. Now that he was gone we could do what we all were trained to do, run a two-man race, Republicans versus Democrats, and quit futzing around with this other stuff.

My first reaction was "We have the advantage here," which is a perfect example of how stupid one woman can be. Once we rounded up the Perot organization we realized how hollow our advantage was. It didn't matter that we were getting all these Perot people; the vaunted Perot juggernaut was a paper organization, it was meaningless. Initially we got some good inside scoop out of it, but these guys didn't have any whack. Signing up Perot's organization was a joke compared to what was actually happening for Clinton. He was getting Perot's vote. In addition to the normal bump Clinton was going to get from his convention, that giant sucking sound we heard was all those Perot change votes moving en masse to Clinton.

James

We knew we were having a pretty good convention. We felt encouraged. What we wanted to do was top it off with a great, defining acceptance speech. It turned out that the acceptance speech was the last event of the old regime.

There were too many chefs in the kitchen cooking it up. Paul worked on it; Roy Spence, a friend of the Clintons and a prominent Texas advertising executive out of Austin; speechwriter David Kusnet, George, me, Frank Greer, Stan, Mandy. The governor writes most of his speeches in his own hand; very seldom does he just take something and give it. Of course Hillary was involved. The writers were working in one room, there was a podium set up in another where the governor could practice. Roy Spence kept telling the governor to go slow.

Bill Clinton is known for speaking at length, and it was my feeling that the speech itself could have been more focused and shorter. The *Man from Hope* film that Harry Thomason and Linda Bloodworth-Thomason produced made all the necessary connections between who he was and where he came from; it was successful to the extent that it gave the national audience a good sense of why Bill Clinton was Bill

Clinton. But he spoke for fifty-four minutes and twenty seconds. Too long. I give the speech a B-minus. I wouldn't count it as a disaster, but I felt with a sharper focus and less duration we could have brought it up to an A-minus. But all in all I thought we had a good convention.

Mary

In the history of political conventions, Democrats are notorious for bad ones. They don't run on time, they're fractious, they're brokered, the delegates fight and have demonstrations, and the worst of their kooks misbehave on national TV. Everybody knows that. But as far as reporters are concerned—which is equally, if not more, significant—they hate Democratic conventions because the facilities are no good, they can't find anybody, everything is discoordinated. Again, the key to the press is accounting for its need for convenience, and Democrats had always screwed it up.

This one had none of that. There wasn't anything particularly special the Democrats did this time except that it was done right: It ran on time and they stuck to their message. It was a classic case of political expectations. Because the Democrats had never run anything but Keystone Kop conventions in the past, the press gave them triple bonus points for simply, one time, getting through a convention as smoothly as the Republicans do every time.

Although you had to hand it to them on a couple of scores: Clinton didn't fold to Jesse Jackson, he ignored Jerry Brown, and the campaign contained their hypocritical muzzling of Governor Casey. All during the primaries, literally right up to the convention, there had been a cacophonous chorus of congressmen in deep denial over Clinton's inevitable nomination—"We've got to run Gephardt," "We've got to run Bentsen." Pundits tracked down historians, and everybody spouted their own brokered-convention theory. Somehow, once they were in New York, the Clintonistas shut all the claptrap down. Clinton went in there on his knees and sprinted out as America's panacea. It was the most stunning 180 I'd ever seen in politics.

James

The addition of Al Gore, the subtraction of Ross Perot—it was a different presidential race than it had been a week before. ABC had us in the lead 54–31. We had a head of steam. But you also knew that all of this was going to dissipate pretty quickly. Jimmy Carter had a 33-point lead after the convention in 1976 and ended up winning by a point, so we weren't taking anything for granted.

We had accomplished a lot, but we knew we had outrun our supply lines; we didn't have anything sustaining us. The general research was woefully behind, the scheduling operation wasn't set up yet, the opposition research on Bush was just plugging into the DNC and not generating any information on its own. Betsey Wright's Arkansas record was the strongest section we had. Senior economic adviser Gene Sperling, a real workaholic and one of the heroes of the campaign, was getting his people together, and the foreign-policy people were moving in, but we were still not a very coherent group.

The last day of the convention we went to the candidate and said, "People have to be a lot clearer on what this campaign structure is about. Somehow, things aren't getting done as fast as they could. We've got to get this thing up and going."

The morning after the acceptance speech, his first day as the Democratic nominee for President of the United States, Bill Clinton gathered all the senior people in the campaign to his suite at the Inter-Continental and laid down the word. He said, "This thing has been presented to me and I want to do it. We're going to have a headquarters; James is going to be in charge of it. I want all the strategic decisions to flow through him."

Just to show you what a genius I am, the first major advice I gave the candidate was not to do the bus tour.

Campaign manager David Wilhelm had come to us with the idea prior to the convention. David ran races in Chicago, he's a traditional Democrat with close ties to labor and a very good relationship with the African-American community, particularly Jesse Jackson. He was always the person in the campaign who looked out for the traditional Democratic constituency. He suggested it to George, who came in and said, "David's got a pretty good idea here. I think it can work after the convention. We stop at these places, we have the press along. . . ."

I thought it was a symbol of the old Democratic party. People traveling in buses was a throwback, I figured, it would not send out the message that we are a new, modern campaign. I told him, "I think a train would be a better symbol. It's not so much a connotation of going from bus stop to bus stop, or this kind of *Midnight Cowboy* thing. And I think we're going to find that it's expensive." It turned out that train trips cost a whole lot more. Then I said, "Can't we get RVs or something, as opposed to buses? Something that has a suburban connotation?" They told me, "Look, it's not a bus like you think of a bus." I don't know, I was thinking of some kind of chrome Silver Eagle like country bands use; they had in mind a more modern vehicle.

The more we looked at it, the more sense it made. Dukakis had disappeared after the '88 convention and had never recovered. Now that we had a big bump, a good lead and some momentum, we wanted to stay in front of people, keep in the news cycle every day. A caravan could do it.

The bus tour had the right touch, a personal approach to the country as Clinton and Gore saw it firsthand. Originally the bus tour had a northern route, through Michigan and Illinois, but we switched it a little more south, through New Jersey, Pennsylvania, West Virginia, Ohio, Kentucky, paralleling the Ohio River.

Al Gore, it turned out, was the single most disciplined candidate for national office since Ronald Reagan. He adhered to message structure and he was very seldom caught what I call "playing Moses," wandering in the desert, going all over the place.

As the bus was speeding south and then west, I was flying to Little Rock.

Mary

We probably would have seriously panicked after the undeniable success of their bus tour if we hadn't been so preoccupied with the machinations of preparing for our own convention. But what really saved us from melting down was the ever-increasing confidence that James A. Baker III, despite his consistent private protestations, would move from the State Department to the White House for the general election.

It was no longer even remotely debatable that the lack of a strong political team in the White House was hindering our ability to get anything done. We at the campaign spent all our time trying to coordinate with or clean up after them. It was our fervent belief that Baker would not only fix those problems, but his considerable political skills would pump up the overall effort. Just thinking about his coming over kept us on an even keel.

CHAPTER 14

James: The War Room

Hillary named the War Room.

"We need a focal point," I told her. "It's gotta look like a military campaign. I want some maps up there, some signs, anything to project a sense of urgency. I almost wish we could get some big electronic color-coded map. I want . . . you know . . ."

"Yeah," she said, "a war room."

Information is the major weapon in a political campaign, and the new headquarters in Little Rock had to be a place where someone knew everything there was to know. We had the technology, we had the information, and we could bring it out and use it whenever and wherever we wanted. So much of what happens in a campaign is that you have information, but unless it's instantly retrievable it doesn't do you any good. You're always fighting deadlines. Time is your enemy, and I had to come up with a way that we could really get people wired up.

The last time a Democrat ran for president it seemed like he never responded, or if he did it was weeks too late. Part of our strategy was to say, "These are not the wimpy Democrats that you knew before. These are New Democrats."

You create a campaign culture, and ours was based on speed. We were open all night, a round-the-clock operation—that was a key psychological fact. "When people come in here I want it to feel like a place of action, something's happening, something's going on here.

We run, we don't walk." You saved two seconds running to the copy machine but it was psychology, it was establishing a culture. The first rapid response was inside the headquarters itself. I had a T-shirt that read, "Speed Kills . . . Bush." There was always a hum going through the War Room, a buzz. I wanted to create an atmosphere where every second counts.

The sign went up early, within the first couple of days, as soon as somebody could go to the store and get the dry-erase board to write it on.

I wanted to say something concise that people would remember. I wrote:

> *Change vs. more of the same*
> *The economy, stupid*
> *Don't forget health care*

I hung it on a post near my desk. It was not any big deal, just a reminder of what we were about. It had two essential elements: It was simple and it was self-effacing. I was trying to say, "Let's don't be too clever here, don't come down here thinking we're too smart. Let's just remember the basics."

In addition, we had to get up to speed on our research, and fast. The tenor and quality of our research changed dramatically when Eric Berman came to Little Rock.

I also wanted to make the War Room home. At forty-eight, I was probably the oldest guy around. A lot of the War Room was twenty-somethings, and the campaign was their life. I had been a Marine, and I'd found that while you can make a lot of friends in a lifetime you never really make friends that are of the depth you make in the military. If you know somebody at work or in school you might spend all day with them or see them in class, but at the end of the day you go home and they go home. When you're in the military, at the end of the day you all go home together.

Well, in a campaign you make a lot of army buddies. For a lot of these people the day ran eighteen hours. They had no life. It was not unusual that people would leave, go take a shower, and come back for the seven A.M. meeting.

The War Room was up all night. Nocturnal information coordinator Ken Segal and his assistant, Matt Smith, would come in at ten P.M. and tape *Nightline*, the news, and anything else that was on. The big function of the War Room was to be the nerve center and instantly assess news as it came up. We had somebody on the dock in Washington every morning to get the early *New York Times* and *Washington Post* and fax them to us. The fax machine was running all night with press clips from all over the country, small papers and all of the major dailies, especially from the battleground states. The field people would fax in intelligence reports, what was going on, Bush was coming there, whatever they'd learned since the last fax of the evening, and these guys would work all night and put together a briefing for the morning meeting.

Every morning I would get my wake-up call at six-fifteen at the Capital Hotel, brush my teeth, throw on some jeans and a shirt, and call Mary on the phone wherever she was. She liked me to call her, and I liked to call. We weren't going to talk all day and it was nice just to make contact. We couldn't talk about work, and there was nothing else going on in either of our lives except our work, so mostly it was, "What time are you going in today? Are you going to be back in Washington?" She'd ask me what I was wearing. From the time I put that phone down until I called her late that night, my life was going to be nothing but conflict; this was a little peace we could enjoy before the bombardment started.

I missed her. But how I felt about her would also depend on what day it was. If we were going good, I felt sorry for her. If they were going good, I didn't feel sorry for her, I was kind of pissed off at her. Mostly I felt, "Wouldn't it be great if we could do this together?" I had way more confidence that we would work out than she did.

But I had to go to work. A guy's storming the beach at Iwo Jima, he's not thinking about his wife, he's thinking is he gonna get his ass shot off.

I am a creature of habit. I would go downstairs for breakfast, have my orange juice, bowl of cereal with skim milk and bananas, and cup of coffee. Stan Greenberg would come down at about twenty to seven and sit and tell me the night's polling. He had his people up all night getting him sometimes half-samples, sometimes full ones, and he'd tell me the national number and key states. Then I'd walk the couple of blocks to headquarters and go straight into George's office. He'd tell me what the papers had going on and I'd tell him the polling. Then, at 7:00 sharp, not 6:59, not 7:01, we'd start the day with the morning War Room meeting.

At the beginning the concept was that there would only be one representative from each division and they would report back to the rest of their group what their particular responsibility was for the day.

Scheduling people, advance people, field people, political people, communications, the press, research. But I didn't want the War Room to become an elite team within the campaign, some sort of badge of honor. I didn't want to build up resentment from other parts of the campaign; I wanted to include them. It was important that the War Room be reflective of the campaign as a whole, therefore War Room meetings were open.

It turned out that people just wanted to come. Paid staffers, volunteers. Sometimes there were seventy-five or eighty people in the room at seven o'clock in the morning. We would discuss very sensitive and strategic issues, we would show TV spots before they came on the air. My theory of leaks is, the more you worry, the more there are. I didn't worry. People in campaigns are a lot more trustworthy than they are when they get to government. Nothing ever got leaked.

We'd start off with Ken Segal's press briefing. Everybody in the campaign was given the clips to work with. He would go on for about ten minutes. Then we'd have what we called the GOPWatch, where Bush and Quayle were going to be that day. This wasn't any big secret. It was posted in the press room and the whole White House press corps knew where they were going. You could call up our headquarters and ask "Where's Clinton going to be tomorrow?" and whoever answered the phone would tell you.

When Perot was in the race we changed from GOPWatch to Opposition Watch, OPWatch, which was more problematic because you never knew where Perot was going. He'd just kind of get up in the morning and take off.

We had the ClintonWatch, our candidate's schedule, and the GoreWatch.

Then the field reports would tell you what was going on out there. "In Louisiana our people say that Bush is running a spot saying that Clinton is going to destroy the oil industry and that Al Gore's environmental policies would cause a complete shutdown of offshore drilling and cost two hundred thousand Louisiana jobs." Then someone else would report, "In Colorado they're saying that Clinton's military budget will cause two Colorado bases to close. We just picked up the endorsement of the Rocky Mountain News, and this talk show that everybody listens to had a straw vote and Bush beat us fifty-five to forty-five, but that's really pretty good because he beat Dukakis sixty-two to thirty-eight." Then somebody would give a briefing on what's happening with the campaign and the ecology issue in Oregon.

Generally in there somewhere we'd stop for a minute and watch someone from the campaign on the *Today* show or *Good Morning America* or *CBS Morning News*. If it was me or George we'd have taped it, gotten over to the studios at about six A.M., and then gotten back to watch it at the meeting.

Then we'd have what we called assignments. "Okay. We start today in Toledo, then after that we go to Ypsilanti. From there we're going to Chicago and then we're going downstate to Carbondale. What's the big event? The media event today is going to be in Ypsilanti and we're going to talk about whether all utility vehicles are classified as a truck or a car, and how the Bush administration changed its mind."

Somebody points out that an adviser to Bush's campaign represented Japanese auto dealers to get an exemption through and we ought to tie this to "business as usual." "Business as usual means that a lot of people in Michigan go out of business, they insist on having business as usual. . . . That's a good line. Let's be sure somebody jots that down before I forget it.

"What are the figures, what are they likely to say? Do we get in the news cycle? How can we make this bigger than a Michigan story, into a national story? How do we contrast ourselves? What are they going to say? Is this protectionism?"

This was cleaning up because we had worked out the answers and were getting ready for our regular morning talk with the candidate on the road. "Is there anything that happened recently that we're liable to get a question on out there? Where is Bush? How will he respond? Will he be hitting us? What do you think they're going to be doing to us?"

"Bush is going to be in Nashville. We figure they'll attack Gore, that's why they're going there."

"Well, maybe they won't. Maybe it's a Clinton attack."

"They're going to do the country music thing, it's going to be a culture day for them."

"Quayle's in Pueblo, Colorado. Gore's in Bangor, Maine. Just local press there. Don't think Quayle's going to do much 'cause he doesn't want to step on Bush's Nashville story. Reporters tell us there's a sense on the Bush plane that he's really going to hit us hard tomorrow. The Bush people are sort of putting it out."

George would say, "There's a story brewing out there that Clinton doubled the state budget in five years and is really a free-spending Democrat. We've had a couple of calls on it, the Bush people are putting it out, and *The Wall Street Journal* is going to say . . ."

"Well, Betsey," I'd say, "what's the deal?"

And Betsey Wright, Queen of the Arkansas Record, would say, "I'll have Diane Blair get back and see what it is. When we get that we'll see what our answer is going to be."

Then Mandy Grunwald would show the spot we've got up now and we'd have color-coded maps of where we're running TV and where they're not.

Notes were taken at every morning meeting. Sometimes there were words of wisdom. In the August 26 notes is this exchange:

> The ERA:
> It is about a socialist, anti-family political movement that encourages women to leave their husbands, kill their children, practice witchcraft, destroy capitalism, and become lesbians.
>
> —Pat Robertson

> These are not nice people.
>
> —J.C.

From October 23:

> Remember: Do not have substantive phone conversations on cellular phones.

We tried to move these meetings along; we had work to do. "All right, let's break it up and get out of here."

It's seven-thirty.

After the morning meeting George, Stan, Mandy, and I would go into George's office and call the road. We were the War Room, they were the Road Warriors. Conference call. We'd be all draped over chairs or leaning into the speakerphone. If the Road Warriors were out in the West we'd have to wait a little bit, but depending on the time zone, if they were in the East or Midwest we'd wake up Paul or Dee Dee Myers and say, "Well, what's going on?"

There was no such thing as a good night's sleep. If everybody wasn't dreaming about the campaign they were at the very least grinding their teeth. You woke up and hit the ground running.

Paul was one of two or three Road Warriors responsible for being in constant contact with the War Room. He was combination strategist, chief writer, press flack, shock absorber, you name it. He was a very talented guy who performed a multitude of functions. Clearly one of the more capable people ever to work in a presidential campaign. He would say, "Elvis is really tired." In road terminology, Clinton was Elvis. "He thinks we're not responding to Bush, that we're getting too patsy and it's absolutely insane that we're going to Ypsilanti. Every time we go to Michigan, Governor Blanchard calls him and says, 'We can't get out of the Detroit area, it's sending the wrong signal to downstate. Why is it that every time we go to Michigan we go nowhere but within fifteen minutes of the Detroit airport?' "

The answer, we say—and Paul knows this, of course, but we say it out loud anyway—is that there are a lot of registered voters in that media market and it speaks beyond that.

"Well," he says, "you just need to know he's going to be hopping-ass mad about this being the fourth trip in a row to a Detroit media market, and has anybody in their life ever heard of Kalamazoo?"

Next:

"We're gonna have to make a decision on this NAFTA thing in a week," Paul says, "and he's complained that he has no time to look at it, no time to think about it."

So now at least we're forewarned. We call the candidate.

"Good morning, Governor. It's George and me and Mandy and Stan Greenberg in the room here. And also we've got Sylvia Mathews from our economic team, who's another Rhodes scholar, but we'll forgive her for that. She's going to give you a briefing on exactly the ramifications of these import quotas. . . ."

Most days he came out swinging. "James," he'd say, "I'm just telling you and George right now, y'all are trying to kill me. I'm tired! You're trying to kill me. If somebody doesn't get in there and do something about this schedule I'm going to make a mistake." The guy's not fuming, he's boiling over and it isn't quarter past eight yet. The first time I heard it I thought, "Whew, this guy really is mad. I'm gonna get fired."

Every candidate hates his schedule. Susan Thomases was our scheduler and there is not a scheduler in the Democratic party that I have not had knock-down, drag-out fights with. Scheduler is the worst job in the world. I have never seen or heard anyone say, "Boy, I'm really happy with this schedule. This schedule really makes sense to me, it's the right mix of where we ought to be and the right amount of down time and the right amount of time out there." No. A schedule is like medication, you're always sick and you're constantly adjusting the dose.

So we've got the candidate in a lather.

"All right, yes sir, I know, sir, but this is where we've gotta be because it's one of our most important states and we haven't been there in three weeks. Honestly, Governor, we've got these little green states, which means we've been there too much; and we've got white states, which say that we've been there about right; and we've got blue states that say we've never been there enough. This is a dark blue state, Governor, that's why we've got to be there."

Bill Clinton is nothing if not reasonable. "Well," he says, "why didn't somebody tell me that?"

"It's in your briefing book, Governor."

"Who in the hell's got time to read the briefing book?"

"Okay, fine."

"And yesterday I saw Dan Blue in North Carolina and he said, 'I'm telling you, Bush is killing us—he's killing us with that ad on guns out in rural North Carolina.' Y'all are sitting there but I'm telling you, I'm out here, I'm not back there, and these people are telling me. . . . I saw Governor Hunt and he's an old friend of mine and he said, 'Bill, you've got to do something about it.' "

"Sir, three days ago we put a spot up that says you've been a hunter all your life and that Arkansas has more sportsmen and outdoorsmen per capita than most any other state, and you're committed to hunting and fishing. . . . Remember, we told you about that."

"Well, who in the hell can remember all this?"

Which was Mandy's cue to jump in with the radio scripts and TV traffic decisions: Are we going positive? Are we going negative? Are we doing a spot that hits Bush for "No new taxes"? Are we going to do one about the Arkansas record and job growth in Arkansas? Are we going to do a health care spot or not? Which spot have we had up? Do we change the mix in the state? Should we continue with a welfare spot in Georgia?

At the same time Greenberg chimes in with a thirty-state analysis coming in on the polls, plus the national analysis.

"Look." Mandy is getting impatient. "We've got to make a decision by noon on a traffic change. We've already hit eight hundred points"—which means that the average TV household will see a spot roughly eight times a week—"and if we don't do it today they're not going to be able to change it for the weekend and the spot is going to be stale. Somebody has *got* to approve these scripts." Now's the time. That day we're getting out radio scripts for thirty states. You could fax them to the candidate but he'd never read them.

Now, Clinton can't approve thirty radio scripts in thirty states, but he has to hear the highlights. He's got to be notified. You don't do a major media campaign without telling the candidate. Not this candidate, anyway.

In ten minutes he has absorbed the radio information, the TV traffic, and the polling data, and made his choices. "All right," he says. "Now, we're going back to Michigan again. If that's what you all say we've got to do, I guess so. But I'm just telling you, Jim Blanchard says we got to get out of this Detroit thing. . . ."

Sometimes we'd forget and have a staff person in the room, or a local representative would be there for a briefing with George, and the call would be on the speakerphone and you could see them turning absolutely white. Like, "Geez, man, he gets on Carville and Stephanopoulos pretty good. They get blasted." But the governor didn't stay mad for long. He'd always end up the calls by saying something like, "Well, y'all are good guys." The governor would hang up and we'd say, "Not bad. It was a decent one this morning." We'd call it the SMO, the Standard Morning Outburst.

It's part of Bill Clinton's personality that he would never be short with a medium-level aide. He would only rip into people he thought could take it. He's not the only person in power who ever raised his voice. I thought it was healthy that at least there was someone he could yell at. I did it all the time.

But the truth of the matter is that he was all smoke and no fire. Campaigns are like that. You have a burst and then it goes away, then you have another burst and it goes away. George and I knew that we were two of the very few people Bill Clinton could fuss at. There was Bruce Lindsey, Paul, maybe Dee Dee on the plane. But on the phone it was only me and George. There was no other outlet to hear his complaints. And candidates will have complaints.

Remember, this ain't no easy work out there. A candidate can't ever say anything outside of what he's supposed to say, he can't snap at anybody, he can't express any of the normal frustrations that people get to express in their everyday life. One emotional outburst and it shows up on CNN as "an unseemly display which calls into question Governor Clinton's very ability to lead the government and the country." "He's treating the people who work for him like dirt. He doesn't understand the problems of the selfsame people he claims to represent."

After the SMO it's about nine o'clock and the War Room is cooking.

As the radio scripts are coming in—and I don't read them either, they get talked the way they're going to be heard by the voters over the air—David Wilhelm's having a meeting about what states to stay in and target, what to run in different places. People are shouting that we've got to have a specific spot in Illinois. Then a call comes in from one of our operatives in the field: Bush is now attacking us for spending growth.

It didn't take a scientist to figure that this was coming, and we already had the answer. Everybody used to tease me that the James Carville intercom is a scream. "Where's the stuff out of Betsey's shop?" Somebody hands me the figures: The inflation rate over five years was such and such, and actually according to the National Council of State Governments, Arkansas state spending ranked so and so.

"Okay. Will somebody get that out to the press? *Please* find out what did spending go up when Bush was President. Somebody get that to me *right now*. Goddammit, am I the fuck gonna sit here all fucking day waiting for you fucking assholes to do something? I want that sheet of paper *now*! Get somebody that's on the ground where Bush is and get him the fuck out there and hand it to the press, and I want them to get it before—you understand me?—*before* Bush steps up to the microphone because I want him to get asked about this. Now, if you can't do this, go do something else for a living. You understand? There's plenty of work, we can send you right up to fucking Montana, they need plenty of field people there. You can knock on the goddamn doors all day if that's what you want to do. Now get out there and somebody get something done and quit whining me with this shit." People are backing away and scurrying.

Then five minutes later another hell is breaking loose and I'm screaming, "Why didn't somebody tell me about this?"

"Well, we just tried to tell you and you said—"

"Well then, just tell me if I've got to know it, now goddammit . . ."

Somebody else runs in and says that Louisiana senator John Breaux is livid because we were supposed to go to Lake Charles and then to Lafayette, but the governor is tired and we want to try and get him out of it. He wants to spend the night at the Arkansas governor's mansion and we'd have to leave Little Rock at six A.M. to get to the morning event in order to get to Lafayette at nine-thirty, which we have to do because that's already scheduled, invitations already went out. So we'd called Breaux and said that we're not going to do the Lake Charles thing and he's really mad. So the phone is ringing and it's Senator Breaux on one line and Governor Clinton on the other.

"Hey, Senator. Can you hold?"

Clinton is screaming into the receiver: *"Why did somebody call John Breaux and cancel that thing in Lake Charles? He called me on the phone."*

"Governor, we're trying to sort of pare back, you know. Mrs. Clinton called me and read the riot act to me because—"

"Well, don't do that. I got to do this event. You can't just go ahead and cancel something like that."

I get back on the phone with Senator Breaux, and he's not happy. "I've had it with these amateurs in Little Rock, James. I keep trying to do something here. I'm trying to help this ticket out."

"Yes sir. Well, I just talked to the governor and we are going to go to Lake Charles. That's correct."

The next thing you know, scheduler Susan Thomases is coming in shouting, "Somebody is undermining me! Hillary told me to change this. *You're* going to have to call Hillary and tell her why you did it. No one will stand up. And that's why we're always in trouble. Because the white boys in the War Room won't stand up to anybody. As soon as some politician calls in you're all caving in to him."

It's not too long before somebody tells me, "It's Mrs. Clinton on the other line." I pick it up immediately.

"James," she says, low volume, high intensity, "I really want to tell you, I'm going to be very assertive about this. Bill is *exhausted*. I asked you a week ago to do something about getting the schedule under control, and now I find out that we're leaving at six o'clock to go to Lake Charles. Why did this happen?"

Now, you don't want to say that the governor called me from the road and demanded it.

"Yes, ma'am. Well, Senator Breaux had already sent the sort of invitations out, and he's really been a good supporter, and I'm from Louisiana and if we don't do something in that southwest Louisiana media market . . ."

Mrs. Clinton knows how to lose a skirmish and win a war. She says, "We're just going to have to get better control over this. I'm going to be back in Little Rock, and I think what we need to do is you and George and Susan need to come over and I'm going to have to look into this thing myself."

"Yes, ma'am, yes, ma'am."

"I am very, very firm on this. Chelsea has a volleyball game and Bill has not been able to see one. He's aggravated, he wants to and I want to see if we can do something about that." The volleyball game is at six o'clock Thursday night.

"Ma'am, there's a fund-raiser scheduled." I can hear Ron Brown before he has to call: *"How can you cancel a fund-raiser for a volleyball game? This is all of our top people!"*

That conversation isn't over a minute when George is at my desk. "James, I've got to talk to you really bad, right now. You've got to come in." So I go into his office.

"We've got to talk to Betsey. The *L.A. Times,* man, whew, I just got off the phone. They have a story that Clinton's uncle contacted somebody at naval ROTC. I'm supposed to call the guy back in forty-five minutes. We've got to find out what was said."

George and I sit around for a couple of minutes trying to decide what we say. We call in Betsey Wright, and she says, "I've been talking to him for four days and I can't get you guys to concentrate on anything. I've told you all that this was coming up."

Mandy busts back into the office. "If somebody doesn't authorize these spots we're not going to be able to get them out!"

Somebody else is beating down the door, saying, "They're having a state meeting down there and they're trying to make decisions and you guys are not in there, somebody is going to have to do something!"

Then it's Senator Bob Graham on the phone. He's got to talk to us right away about a trip to Florida.

That's every day. And every day at about eleven-thirty I said adios and went down to Your Mama's, a country cooking place. Usually by myself. George would always eat at his desk. Sometimes Stan would join me, sometimes Mandy, Mike Donilon, if he was in town. Just somebody who I knew and who knew I didn't want to be bothered. Lots of people ate in the War Room. I would always try to go out. I just had to.

I'd come back at noon, lie on the couch. "Okay, where are the scripts?"

People would call in with information and we had to be on top of it. Democratic pollster Geoff Garin would call and say, "I'm doing a poll for Feingold in Wisconsin. What are you showing?"

"Last night we had it up by eight."

"That's not what I'm showing. I'm showing you guys only up by three."

"Somebody!" I'd shout over the couch. "Stan, call Geoff to see if our sample is the same. He's got things a little more pessimistic than we do, see if we can reconcile this."

But mostly I'd work the phones, returning calls. The phone slips stacked up like unpaid bills and you were always calculating which to get to first—where do you spend your political capital and get the most return? I like to return calls at noon because most people are eating at their desks and you can get to them immediately. So I've got my feet up, lying on this rented couch that got more and more broken in as the campaign went along, and I'm either putting out fires or fanning the flames.

New York Times Washington bureau chief Howell Raines is on the line saying he's been trying for two weeks and his people can't get an interview with Clinton. They've spent all this money, they've got an obligation to cover the campaign, they're a major American newspaper.

"Okay, Howell." I shout over my shoulder, "Somebody find Dee Dee and find out why Gwen Ifill or Robin Toner don't have this interview."

There would be reporters wanting stories, there'd be local politicians with places for the campaign to go, there'd be requests for interviews. And then a staffer would come tell me there were people downstairs who wanted to see me. "You've scheduled this thing with the BBC at two-thirty."

"How in the hell did I put the goddamn BBC . . . I can't . . . Nobody votes over there! . . . Who scheduled . . . Who'd be so goddamn stupid as to put the BBC . . . ?"

"Well, you did."

"When did I do that?"

"You told the guy a week ago. He flew in from London just to talk to you. Remember he called?"

"Well, who let me do that?" I've got no time to return calls to people who can do our campaign some real good, and now I've got to talk to a film crew broadcasting back to an entire nation that doesn't cast the first vote in our election. "How could I be so stupid?"

So the BBC comes up and I'm talking to them and answering calls and drinking Diet Coke and keeping all the balls in the air.

Sometime around three o'clock George comes in. He's been talking to the network people most of the day, and George says, "Man, we're *really* going to get hammered tonight. Andrea Mitchell on NBC is doing a thing, they found somebody to say that our budget numbers are inaccurate." He tells me what's on *Headline News*, and that he thinks we're going to be on ABC, and what CBS is up to.

At the same time, the daily polls are coming in. The ABC/*Washington Post* is going to have it at this tomorrow, CNN is going to have it at that. The *L.A. Times* just did one and found something else.

Meanwhile the road has called maybe four or five times, each from a different location. Paul is completely pissed.

"The Beast is all lathered up about the *L.A. Times* thing, man, that's all they want to talk about." The Road Warriors called the media the Beast; it lumbered and foraged and demanded to be fed. "Elvis goes up there . . . you just wouldn't have . . . God, it was just sickening. He hit the message hard, we had a good statement, and then right out the chute he takes a question and it makes news. Says, 'Bush is attacking my character.' "

George, who is on the extension in his office, comes in and says, "Well, that's it, we blew it. We're going to have another character story tonight. We just missed a whole day."

Then you start throwing stuff. It's tirade time.

"I can't believe that we have sat here all day trying to get this thing focused on one issue and we've gotta take a question and that's it, we've blown the whole news. So now we're gonna have a story—instead of talking about how we can make the economy better, we're back into whether we can remember something that happened twenty-five years ago. I just wish one time in this campaign we could get it twenty-five minutes from now instead of twenty-five years ago!"

I'm on a roll.

"These goddamn reporters, all they care about is making trouble. They don't care about making any news, they don't care about covering what you are, all they want to do is cause little eruptions out there!" Boom, boom, boom, boom, boom, boom.

There must have been a hundred TV sets in the headquarters. If there was one thing you always heard in the War Room it was James Earl Jones's deep bass voice going "This . . . is CNN." TV was where you could see the fruits of your labors. Was the story that we wanted getting on? Was what we were trying to accomplish getting up there? People had TVs at their desks, in the pressroom, you had taping sets where they would splice everything together, viewing sets. There were three big ones high up on the wall opposite my desk, and at five-thirty Little Rock time everything stopped for the network news.

George was the maestro, with all the knobs and remotes, and everyone would stand around and look at the networks and make comments. Right when that was over the road would call, because like as not they weren't anywhere near a TV set at five-thirty, they were in transit, and they'd say, "What happened?" We'd fill them in and they would go back and try and spin the reporters for the next day.

At seven we had the night meeting. Big meeting, full room. I would compare how many people went to the seven-in-the-morning meeting with the seven-at-night one. Night meetings generally tended to be a little bigger, which caused another tirade. "I'm going to start passing out tickets at the morning meeting to let you into the night meetings." We never did, but sometimes I would notice someone who hadn't made it there that morning and I would single them out. Called it getting put in the box. "Yeah, you're in the box tonight. What do you think, you can just wander in here any old time you please?"

Every Friday we named the Employee of the Week, who would get a gold star and a jar of barbecue sauce. When I was in the first grade, if you did something real good, the teacher would put a gold star on your forehead. Same thing here, and everybody would clap.

What did you have to do to be named Employee of the Week? You got four Chicken Georges to show up in North Carolina, or you highlighted a point in the briefing book and saved us from eating a bad story. Somebody in research had stayed up all night to get something out, or someone in media had serviced radio tapes to every station in California. People liked to be noticed, and we liked to notice them.

War Room chief of staff Ricki Seidman and creative ramrod Bob Boorstin would usually decide who it was, and the honor was passed around generously. "Oh, God, it's Friday. Hey, Ricki, come over here, who's the Employee of the Week?"

She'd quick pick someone and tell me.

"Who's that?"

"You know, she's the person that . . ."

"Oh, yeah, sure, she's great."

As soon as the seven o'clock meeting was over I was out of there. I probably worked the least amount of hours of anybody there, and that was twelve and a half. The place was still in full roar when I left. The big slack-cutter was that the Sunday morning meeting started at nine. Saturdays at eight. I heard people say, "Wow, man, we don't have to get in until nine!"

But those were the War Room twentysomethings. I was forty-eight years old that October, and forty-eight-year-olds ain't gonna work no seventeen, eighteen hours a day, seven days a week, and be effective. For some people in Washington the number of hours you put into a workday is a badge of honor. They work forever and they brag about it. I think that's ridiculous; they ought to work a lot less. Campaigns work too much and don't think enough. It is my firm belief that the single biggest commodity that a campaign strategist has to trade in is judgment. I needed to be clearheaded for this marathon.

I would walk back to the hotel and put my running shoes and shorts on. I ran for thirty minutes every night. My route never varied.

I'd go to dinner two or three nights a week at Doe's steakhouse. Nine o'clock. As soon as I walked in there they knew: Bombay Sapphire martini, straight up. I didn't have to say a word. Fried shrimp, boiled shrimp, tamales, or steak. And french fries. That's it. No menu, no nothing. Some days we'd go to the Blue Mesa Grill, which was a very good Southwestern restaurant, and there was an Italian restaurant where we went every Saturday night. We were very, very routine-conscious. Every time we tried to go somewhere else, we didn't like it. But Doe's was the ritual. It was a place where you could eat red meat without guilt.

I would say I ate with George six nights a week. Usually with Mandy, Stanley, Mike Donilon. Once in a while a reporter, if we knew them and they'd been covering us a long time, would come with us. The conversation would sometimes be the day's postmortem, sometimes plans for tomorrow. A lot of it was, "I just can't think about it no more, man."

I'd be back in my room every night at ten-fifteen and I'd call Mary. "I'm in. I'm going to bed. I talked to Mama today. I'll be glad when this is over. I'll call you in the morning."

It was a struggle to stay up for the ten-thirty news.

And every day at six-fifteen the phone rang.

CHAPTER 15

Mary

So we were waiting for Baker and trying to come up with other sanity-saving devices. We theorized, after observing the Clintonistas in the primaries, that they had a disorganized campaign and a potentially undisciplined and hot-tempered candidate. There appeared to be no clear line of authority. In rare instances, like when Carville beat back the Gennifer Flowers and draft-dodging explosions, it was controlled chaos; but left to their own devices, without the pinpoint demands of a crisis-management situation, it looked pretty much like free-floating confusion. We had confidence. Even though they had the easier message ("change") and we had the harder job (defend), we were the better team. In the end, we figured, experience would win because we weren't going to choke when we hit the bad spots.

I strongly promoted this theory. Some of our people had worked in state races against Carville and they were psyched out by him. I said, "So what? He's never worked on a presidential campaign, he's never even been close to one; most of those guys haven't. It's a different animal. They're not ready for prime time, they're not going to know how to do it. There's no chain of command and they're trying to bring all these warring factions into one campaign. Carville won't deal with those crazy lefties. Nobody will be in charge and they'll just implode."

We chalked their trouble-free convention up to Ron Brown, who had been through it countless times. We gave him credit for all the things that went right. All the things that went wrong—like cutting out Governor Casey, which we thought was gross and potentially exploitable—we laid at the ham hands of the campaign.

We tried to get Casey to convert. This was Sununu's idea, or at least he was the designated contact to Casey, whom he knew from their days as governors and their kindred right-to-life positions. Casey remained loyal in public, but Sununu professed to know that he was fuming mad. Sununu made a valiant effort, but we weren't too surprised when Casey decided to stick with his party. Apparently, the Clintonistas dispatched Gore to make peace and blame his insulting treatment at the convention on Brown. Everybody but Casey knew that was a bald-faced lie, but the governor was too good a Catholic to believe anyone would flat-out lie to his face.

To keep our hopes up, we prophesied that they were going to be as disorganized in the general as they'd been in the primaries. It was pretty tough to keep hoping the bus tour was a fluke. But while we gave them grudging respect, we were slow to understand how really good they were. We thought it was a unique event, a piece of good luck spawned from the dynamics of the race, the momentum of Clinton going from third to first. We thought the press was contrasting it to the poor performance in the primary and giving them more credit than they deserved. We were pretty confident they wouldn't be able to sustain that level of expertise for the rest of the campaign.

Republican campaigns put a big focus on who's got what titles. It's not an ego thing, you want to have clear lines of authority and accountability. We could never see that on their campaign; we never knew who had what title or how they fit in. We'd see George Stephanopoulos doing communications work, policy work, he was all over the place. We knew there had to be internal philosophical struggles because there were practical politicians like Carville and ideologues like Susan Thomases and Betsey Wright, apparently with equal access to Clinton. I figured there was a battle for the soul of the candidate going on over there . . . with Carville temporarily winning.

I knew James; he had been able to succeed by virtue of having absolute control of everything. And I knew that presidential campaigns are never like that. Knowing, also, that he didn't have any patience (at least, with me) I figured that sometime around mid-campaign he'd just blow.

The rest of our team thought he was gonzo. They thought he was a hothead, particularly too hot for television. They'd seen him out there spinning, and he did have this demonic, hot persona on TV. We all extrapolated from that that he was hot in his decision-making. Too hot.

But we underestimated his effectiveness. He did, indeed, look like a crazed person, but James came off on TV as a fighter. His eccentricities, which would normally distract attention from his candidate and create a negative for the campaign, served as a positive.

The press dug him. They thought he was this really unusual cat. They applauded his idiosyncrasies.

And James knew how to work the press. Before the '92 campaign, he had studied the '88 campaign and understood the Dukakis mistakes, the most notorious of which was *no* response team. From that understanding came his *rapid*-response team, which he bragged about shamelessly. He would sell the process as much as substance. The Clintonistas got a whole spate of stories on how cool they were because they were responding quickly. Big deal, it was nothing more than what should normally be done in a campaign. But because the Democrats had been so poor at it four years earlier, now they were geniuses for getting it right. We really underestimated his multilevel shamelessness.

The campaign transition from thinking Carville was certifiable to giving him bemused respect began when he and Charlie Black were teamed up on the news shows. James still looked demonic, but now he was punching through. Charlie would come back from mud-wrestling with Carville and say, "You know, he's smart. And he's really a good guy." Off camera, before they would go on the air, James would just jabber and send messages to me. "Hey, Charlie, where's Mary today? You gotta go and tell her hello. What's goin' on? We got to get a Coke when this is over." If I knew Charlie was going on with him I'd send messages back: "Tell him I said hi. Tell him his mother called." Charlie would come back and say, "James says hello. And he got a few good licks in today." Or, "I kicked his butt."

James

One time during the campaign, Bob Teeter and I did a corporate roundtable in front of the heads of all these major companies and he got up and said, "We got Carville just where we want him: Perot's got his voters and I've got his girlfriend." Up till then I didn't even know the guy had a sense of humor.

Mary

So after the bus tour it dawned on us that these guys were going to be more worthy adversaries than we had expected. That didn't scare us. What freaked us out was their hunger level. What these guys lacked in experience or organization they made up for in energy and ruthlessness. We had the desire, and more energy than our critics gave us credit for, but we weren't obsessive twenty-four hours a day like the Little Rock crew. Just being in Little Rock fed their obsessive work habits. There wasn't anything else to do. Most of us had been living and working in D.C. for a decade; we had rounder, fuller lives and a familiar environment, which was distracting. A real D.C. distraction is the fact that everyone who lives there, from Hill aides to department bureaucrats, fancies himself a strategist. No one thought anything of showing up on your doorstep and telling you how the campaign should be run.

But their around-the-clock work environment produced some valuable campaign accoutrements. One day we got hold of a copy of their morning briefing book. (I'd be more than happy to take credit for putting a mole in their operation—that would be a substantial coup and I would certainly brag about it if it were true—but this was nothing so sophisticated. Someone left the document on a plane and it made its way, as all things eventually did, to Carney.) In these papers was a compilation of local print and TV coverage, editorials, cartoons, what was running on the wires overnight. It ran about fifteen pages and told you who was saying what, state by state. It was phenomenal. Clearly, someone had stayed up all night gathering and processing this information. We subsequently learned that this wasn't some special package, it was standard operating procedure. We, on the other hand, had no central information repository. We had separate state political field and press reports, but the national campaign had no such user-friendly compendium of how things were playing out there in the real world.

I don't mean to leave the impression that we were obsessed about the Democrats. I may have obsessed about Carville, but any time we spent analyzing them was in keeping with another Atwater rule: Know thine enemy. In the same way campaigns search out their opponents' weaknesses, they also look for staff vulnerabilities. It's just as important to know how to rattle the staff as the candidate. So it wasn't idle professional curiosity that compelled us to study James or

George or Betsey or Hillary. It was imperative to study their work habits to be able to predict their next move.

The worst time on a campaign for the field operation is when there isn't something hard-charging to do, and that is always the summer period after the primaries, preceding the conventions. It's dead-air time, the headquarters staff is working on the convention, and operatives on the ground hate it.

The thing that makes campaigns work is constant motion. The state organizations and your team in the field, who literally, physically get out the vote, are only excellent when they're running on four hours' sleep and are focused on some mission. You can't have people running, running, running, and then stop. It's like hitting a brick wall, and it takes that much more energy to get them running, running, running again for the general. So you have to keep them working in the dull days, and in fact it is the only time you can get the boring and nitpicky but necessary tasks out of the way, like state lists of Democrats for Bush, or referenda and ballot initiatives, volunteers to monitor and call radio talk shows.

Teeter kept asking me for these lists, I kept delegating to Carney. Carney's guys took the assignments like castor oil—field guys are fighters, not list-makers.

Further frustrating the fighter mode, Stan Huckaby, our national treasurer, who knew where every single penny of the $40 million primary budget was, started reclaiming unspent funds for our national media blitz. For our political division this meant closing down all the state offices. So Carney and I got daily harangues from the field: "How can we do anything with no headquarters?" A logical question.

But they were more than bored and homeless. They were thoroughly frustrated. All these hyper guys were hamstrung: "There's no campaign out here. You guys aren't giving us anything. There's no reason to vote for George Bush. Clinton's on us every day, and we don't know anything about him. It's worse than shadow boxing. We're not fighting, we look like wimps, this is the worst campaign in history."

President Bush wasn't in campaign mode. The press, our field force, the public at large were all looking for some complicated reason. But it's very simple. President Bush liked to govern. The longer he delayed the beginning of his campaign, the longer he delayed being viewed—and having to view everything—through a political prism. He had a job to do and he liked doing it. He was President; he wanted to *be* President.

We knew Bush's internal campaign clock was not going to start ticking until the convention. We had to keep our troops pumped up till then. Dave Carney, Torie Clarke, and I sat in my office one Friday night drinking red wine and plotting. Every day, Bill Clinton, who was campaigning full throttle, said something that did not jibe with his own previous statements, or he was lying about us. Slick Willie was big-time getting on our nerves, not to mention getting all the headlines. This week he pushed us over the edge. He went to Houston—George Bush's hometown—did a police event, and spewed out this egregious lie about George Bush wanting to cut federal funding for local law enforcement.

The Clinton people were thumbing their noses at us. No way they were going to win Texas, but that wasn't their point. To go into George Bush's hometown and do a cop event was really an in-your-face move. (It was not lost on us that this was an exact copy of our going into Dukakis's home base of Boston in 1988 and doing an environmental event.) Everyone was ticked off about it. Rich Bond called and yelled at me. "If I was over there this never would have happened. This is a thumb in the eye! How could we let him go into Houston, George Bush's backyard? That would be like us doing an event in Little Rock!"

Bond's honor was insulted. There wasn't anything we could do to stop their event—it's not like we could have called out the National Guard—but he was right. This was beyond campaigning—it was a personal insult.

In every campaign there's a time when you shift from pushing through every day to full battle alert. From that point on, you're totally myopically fixated on destroying the enemy. The whining and hand-wringing stop; obliterating the enemy is the operative obsession. This was that time for me. My brain just snapped.

Torie was also on the verge of entering the kamikaze zone. She was one of a kind. Had these lime-green and hot-pink suede miniskirts, which she wore with matching tights. She had a blond-red spiked hairdo. This was not your mother's Republican. She was smart and quick. She was also a genius at communications plans, and had been trying to devise one that would be ongoing, would build each day on the day before, and would get our side into the Clinton stories. The Houston event inspired her. Sitting right there, she came up with the idea for a daily, red-meat press release, starting one hundred days out from the election. Carney came up with the Clinton "Lie-a-Day." I loved it.

We brought in our issues director, Jim Cicconi, and research director David Tell, two big brains, to flesh out the concept and give data daily to a team of "writers." We were always coming up with these wacky projects and trying to pass them off on other people. They liked this one.

Since it was a somewhat negative, not to mention juvenile concept—"The One Hundred Lies of Bill Clinton"—we decided to release it under my name, rather than the campaign chairman's or manager's. We had been in dormant mode for so long this looked like the first whack coming out of the box, so the press started calling immediately.

I wanted Bob Teeter and the other big guys to have deniability. You couldn't write these things in the sarcastic, tongue-in-cheek, on-the-edge style necessary to get attention and have Teeter or Fred Malek's name attached to them. So I didn't run the actual releases past them at all . . . and only sometimes the concept. They trusted us to comply with the number one rule: *Source every word*. Which I always did.

The fax attacks had two prime targets: our field force and the media. The press rightfully glommed onto it as an *event* in the Bush campaign. The field troops were frothing at the mouth.

From the kickoff, they loved these faxes. They loved the style, they loved the material. It gave them a whole new piece of ammunition that they had been dying for. We had been sending them reams of Clinton information, but it was not user-friendly. Field folks don't need things they have to wade through; they want to say it in two sentences, they want to say it the way normal people say it.

The first fax accused Clinton of raising Arkansas taxes and fees 128 times. Attached to it was David Tell's excellent research.

Michael Kinsley and all these guys went absolutely crazy. They called the tax fax a lie and negative campaigning. Carville was calling him and everybody else, dancing on the head of a pin, claiming that fee increases weren't taxes, that we were jimmying the figures. He got Kinsley to write this column about what a bunch of liars we were. We didn't really care what Michael Kinsley was saying, because every time he or the Democrats said the charges weren't true, they had to repeat them. Plus, they were true. They were all documented by the government of Arkansas. Go argue with Arkansas, we said. The headlines would always be "Clinton's Tax and Fee Increases." Go ahead, Clintonistas, keep pushing it out there.

James

Democrats are taught from an early age that you can't talk about taxes. Republicans are taught from an early age that you can't talk about health care. So the tendency of both is just to leave them on the table.

But this time a very important part of our early strategy was not just to neutralize the tax issue but to try and win on it. Arkansas under Bill Clinton had a very low rate of taxation. For all his campaign promises about "Read my lips: No new taxes," George Bush had reneged and raised them. How could he criticize Bill Clinton as a tax-and-spend Democrat when, in 1982, Ronald Reagan had presided over the largest tax increase in American history and, as President, Bush had raised taxes himself. That was a big, big deal in this race.

When this fax came out it caused us concern. They kept repeating "128 tax increases" and they were starting to break through.

We were in Texas when the list was published. I said, "We have to bring Clinton out on this and attack the list. We have to do this." If we could take the tax issue away from the Republicans, we could win this thing.

We worked this 128 taxes hard. We pushed it. We researched this list, we ridiculed it. We put out a list of our own saying that Reagan and Bush had raised taxes 611 times. We told everyone who would listen, and some who wouldn't, that their list was bogus. They were calling the extension of dog-racing season a tax hike. Increased fines for drunk driving were a tax hike.

It took a while but we started to win. Our polling showed that people thought the "128 taxes" charge was unfair. We beat it back. We were the first Democratic presidential campaign in my memory that was in a fight with the Republicans on taxes and was coming out ahead.

On the Saturday before Labor Day I was sitting at my desk in the War Room when Betsey Wright came in and said, "We've compiled this list and NBC wants it."

Betsey had done some research and found that Bill Clinton had not raised taxes 128 times, he had raised taxes 34 times and increased fees 93 times. Sarah, the thirteen-year-old daughter of one of my former girlfriends, was sitting there. She did the arithmetic in her head, looked up and said, "James, if you do that, they're going to say that's a hundred and twenty-seven."

"Betsey," I said, "don't give that list to anybody."

"Well, it doesn't count because—"

"They're going to say that we verified their number. We know how many times that's come up. It's going to be a verification. Don't."

"All right." And she walked away.

That night I took Sarah and Vicki Radd, a lawyer who has worked on lots of Democratic campaigns, to the nicest restaurant in Little Rock. We had a good meal, came back, and were sitting in the bar of the Capital Hotel. God knows what I'm doing at quarter to twelve at night with a thirteen-year-old in a hotel bar. So we were sitting there and I saw Gene Sperling. He looked like somebody had died. He was shaking.

"You're not going to believe this."

He showed me a front-page story from the next day's *Washington Post* saying we had put out a list showing that Clinton had raised taxes 127 times.

"I think we ought to call George," he said.

"No, I ain't gonna sleep tonight. Let him go ahead and sleep because he'll have to think tomorrow. It'll take me two days of bouncing off walls to get over this."

Even the reporters were stunned. They said, "What do you mean?" I talked to David Maraniss, who had written the piece. He told me, "Betsey Wright just handed me this list and it was right there. I was sort of dumbfounded myself."

She just handed it to him. I'll never know why. We asked her and she said, "Well, a lot of what Bill had done was being misinterpreted and I wanted to set the record straight."

That's all well and good. It's just that in the macro presidential political game, if you tell the media and Republicans ninety-five good things about somebody and five bad things, guess what's going to get reported.

Given the tightness of the news cycle, the press can't absorb all the information out there. And people sure can't absorb all of that information. So you're trying to put out what information you can, and one little number becomes a big number. It becomes a symbol. The damage wasn't in the 127 taxes, it was that we could no longer contest it. We could no longer say, "Just like you said you wouldn't raise taxes and you did." Or, "Just like you said that I raised taxes a hundred and twenty-eight times. Every independent person has looked at this and said it's just not true."

Our inability to keep hammering that home did affect the bottom line of the campaign. We could still defend pretty well, we could still do the "No new taxes," but we lost the ability to hit back and front.

It was gone. Sometimes I would be driving down the road and just start beating my head against the steering wheel of the car. Just go into a tirade.

Mary

Ann Devroy called me at home and said, "You're not going to believe this. Maraniss has a piece for tomorrow's paper. The Democrats say it's not a hundred and twenty-eight, it's a hundred and twenty-seven."

"That can't be true."

She was doing a fact-check. Did we have something to do with this?

"No, we didn't. And I can't believe it, it must be wrong. Verify our numbers? They'd never be that stupid. James would never let that happen."

The next day when the story ran the entire political community on both sides was aghast. We didn't even want to respond to it at first, nobody could believe it, we thought it was a press mistake. Slowly, it dawned on us: *They screwed up big-time!* Then everybody went into total guffaw.

James

When you lay out a presidential strategy in a paragraph, there are probably five or six elements to it. Betsey knocked out one of the major strategic underpinnings of the campaign. It took me mentally two days to get back in the game.

Mary

The Fax Attacks, as we called our Clinton Lie-a-Day releases, got really good play. We were actually getting in the stories. Being so successful, it kind of got people psyched. I got into it and so did the research people. At the morning meetings everybody would chime in, "What should we fax today?" The communications people had joke writers and other wise guys down there who would take the first crack; then, because I had a very distinctive, sarcastic writing style and they were put out under my name, I'd Mary-ize them. Once the press got on it, everybody wanted a piece of the action. Tell would dig up great issues and had all the background to refute every Clinton lie, flip-flop, and evasion. Because they were both substantive and funny, everyone wanted to work on them and read them. It became a pet project.

The Fax Attacks took a lot of time, which no one really had, and getting them out was a logistical fire drill. The first week I was on a trip. It's hell getting faxes on Air Force One. They are all sent from a central, secure room in the basement of the White House. Some official down there determines the order in which they're sent, based on importance for the President. My faxes always got aced out by National Security memos, so I'd get them faxed to me on the ground between events. Usually, we were bolting from one event to the next, and by the time I located the staff fax we were moving on. Many a fax got done via beeper, cell phone, walkie-talkie, or word of mouth. A prescription for disaster.

But it was worth it.

Clinton had made two diametrically opposed statements to the Arkansas *Democrat-Gazette* about Desert Storm. It was classic Clinton and deserved the name I gave him: "Silver-tongued Straddle Pander." At a news conference that day, some reporter read to him from the fax and asked him what he really meant. His campaign had not prepared him for this and were shocked. Clinton got mad and huffy and stormed out.

I was in California with Bush; headquarters kept faxing me all these articles about the play of that one, and I was in hog heaven. I couldn't stop laughing. To get Clinton flustered was to make the press see that everything we said about this guy was true: He had a character problem, and it was a Slick Willie problem, a waffle problem.

We knew from our data that we couldn't attack him on *personal* character, it wouldn't play. Also, Bush himself was adamant about staying off Clinton's personal problems. But "character," if defined as having no core of beliefs and being all over the place, was in bounds. So Dan Quayle started repeating the name Clinton had earned in Arkansas, calling him slick. The press theory then became, "The President's not going to attack Clinton, you're going to have Quayle be the pit bull."

By the time we got back from California, the press was into it. A reporter from *The New York Times* was trying to get me to say that (a) Dan Quayle was going to be the pit bull; and (b) we were going to attack Clinton on his personal problems. I told him, "He is not going to be a pit bull and we are not going to attack Clinton. It is not our strategy or his job to attack Clinton on these issues." The reporter kept badgering me about Why is he out there attacking him, you're exploiting the womanizing and marijuana issues. I tried to explain to him that, no, we weren't. We're not going to do that. We are going to point out how his character works: We're going to show the slick side, the waffle side, the all-things-to-all-people, the chameleon-on-plaid side of Bill Clinton. I said, "The larger issue is that he's evasive and slick. We've never said to the press that he's a philandering, pot-smoking draft dodger."

"The way you just did?" the reporter asked.

"The way I just did. But that's the first time I've done that. There is nothing nefarious or subliminal going on."

He was badgering me, I was jet-lagged, but that was no excuse. It was a full-battle, but undisciplined, response. That night I was talking to Carville and I said, "I don't know if this is going to go anywhere, but I think I called your guy a philandering, pot-smoking draft dodger."

"You did not."

"He probably won't write it."

"He's going to write it. You shouldn't have done that. I can't believe it."

"Well, I didn't say it."

James

Of course *The New York Times* was going to run it. Everybody was waiting for somebody to say something. The media was going to jump on it: It was a good story, and they were kind of bored and wanted some action. I said, "I've got to recuse myself on this one because anything I say, people are going to say it's because of Mary." My personal opinion was "Don't overplay the thing." Bush had said he didn't want his campaign to engage in "sleaze," and Dee Dee Myers said Mary had crossed the sleaze line and ought to resign. I thought we looked foolish saying somebody ought to resign over something like that. Our thinking was "Hey, look, it's politics. People say things, they get out of hand. Let's get back to the issues. They can't get the economy going so they're trying these false issues. It's sort of typical politics that people are going to reject."

Mary

The story broke real fast. Within hours of its publication, Charlie started taking incoming. He didn't know what I had said, let alone why, but he and I were always in sync. He went right into Charlie mode: "Clearly what she meant was . . ." and without clipping me for shooting from the hip, explained the character issue and why it goes to the heart of who Bill Clinton is, why an evasive, indecisive, and slick character would result in a weak President. He struggled to get that story under control without saying "Mary's got a hair trigger; you know Mary." Charlie was a true pal.

Nevertheless, the Democrats went into high hype. Ron Brown and his cronies held a press conference and called the Bush campaign "state-of-the-art sleaze," and laid out all these nonsense non sequiturs of negativism that supposedly emanated from the Bush campaign.

I was plenty sick and tired of these charges of negative campaigning. Research had given me a three-inch binder of truly gross negative attacks the Democrats had made on George Bush: Congresswoman Maxine Waters called him a racist, Bill Clinton called him a personal tax evader, Tom Harkin disparaged his "family jewels." I sat down to write a fax about Clinton's flip-flop on health care, but I got distracted reading the coverage of Brown's press conference and was getting madder and madder thinking about the Democrats and this hypocritical attack on us. They'd been doing nothing but all-out trashing George Bush from the beginning of the year. Of the 169 days they'd been on the road, they had never missed a day trashing him. President Bush had been complaining about the constant attacks and the fact that no one was getting into Clinton's stories and defending him.

So I set the health care fax aside. It was midnight and I couldn't sleep. I got up and opened a bottle of red wine. Still couldn't sleep. I was lying there in bed drinking red wine at two in the morning. I couldn't relax; too much adrenaline. Beyond tired. I got up and began going through the volumes of Democrat attacks and started writing.

I read everything the research team had compiled—good, bad, indifferent, it didn't matter. I knew this guy inside out. This was not good. I knew much too much about Bill Clinton.

For instance, I knew he'd sit on airplanes and do crossword puzzles. Why that seemed relevant at two in the morning, I don't know. The next day was Sunday, big puzzle day. I figured I'd write one for him.

At his press conference Ron Brown had cited categories of our alleged attacks. I used the same categories. And just like in a crossword, the answers, all impeccably sourced, were written upside down at the end.

That same week President Bush had uncharacteristically told hecklers at a rally, "Sit down and shut up!" I started with that.

Sniveling Hypocritical Democrats: Stand up and be counted—On second thought, shut up and sit down!—

Today, the Bush/Quayle campaign provides Slick Willie with a little "Holier Than Thou" Sunday puzzle. Do this one before your crossword puzzle, Bill. . . .

Category 1: "IT IS CLEAR THAT THIS IS PART OF A PATTERN"
1. Which candidate "dogged by criticisms that he shades the truth for political benefit . . . admitted there was a deliberate 'pattern of omission' in his answers on marijuana use"?

. . . . . .

Category 6: "THEIR TACTICS ARE STATE-OF-THE-ART SLEAZY"
22. Which campaign had to spend thousands of taxpayer dollars on private investigators to fend off "bimbo eruptions"?

1. Bill Clinton, Los Angeles Times, 7/21/92. . . . 22. The Clinton campaign. Official campaign "Bimbo Patroler," Betsey Wright, in response to 19 bimbo allegations since the Democratic Convention and 7 earlier bimbo sightings, Washington Post 7/16/92 and 7/26/92.

This was a masterpiece, if I must say so myself. Twenty-two questions in all. I stayed up all night, got the draft to Leslie Goodman—our Deputy Dawg fax attacker and smart, hardworking fool who was the only one in the office, the sweatbox, on a Sunday—who formatted the thing on her computer. We went back and forth about a dozen times to make sure everything was right. It never occurred to me to send it to Teeter.

During the day I got a call from Andy Rosenthal of *The New York Times,* who was on the road with Bush. We started yacking about nothing in particular and I was in sleep delirium and laughing so hard telling him about the puzzle and the final couple of paragraphs, which made a big to-do about Clinton's eating too many jelly doughnuts, and we were guffawing together when he said, "Don't you think that's a little harsh, to attack his eating habits?"

Nah.

We faxed it out at the normal time. Leslie checked the wires Sunday night, and they played it exactly as we wanted. We got a good story about "Bush campaign attacks Democrat hypocrisy." They used the example of Maxine Waters calling Bush a racist. We were triple excited. Our faxes were now getting covered every day, we were getting things out there on the Democrats and Bill Clinton.

I got up the next day, *USA Today* played it the same way. *The Washington Post* played it the same way. They were tracking our faxes. We had become regulars. Couldn't be better. The only paper I didn't have at home was *The New York Times*.

The phone rang.

It was six in the morning. James didn't usually call until six-forty-five. Any time your phone rings at six A.M. during the campaign, it's not good news. I didn't pick it up. The answering machine clicked on: "This is the White House operator. Sam Skinner is looking for Mary Matalin."

Then Carville called. "Something must be wrong and I don't know what it is," I told him. "Do you have the papers?"

"No."

"Well, what could it be? Do you think it's the 'philandering, pot-smoking draft dodger'?"

"Nah, you would have already heard that."

"Anything happen in the news? Do you hear anything?"

"No."

I was feeling a little queasy and didn't want to call Skinner back until I could call around and find out what the topic was and have an answer. I called Carney.

"Anything wrong with the event?"

"No."

I could spot a road problem if someone told me what was going on. I called the usual suspects on the ground. Nobody had anything.

I got a call from Mary Lukens in Bob Teeter's office. "Teeter wants a copy of your fax from yesterday," she said. "Skinner's looking for it. Did anybody sign off on this? Did the White House see it?"

"The White House never signs off on anything. And no, I didn't give it to Teeter or Malek."

She was very calm. Too calm. I directed her to Leslie Goodman, then asked, "What's the problem?"

"I don't know. We just got a call from the plane and they want a copy. I can't tell you any more because that's all I know."

I called my office and made them go through all the papers. "Get to *The New York Times* and see if they covered the story." When they came back to the phone there was dead silence.

"You sure you want to hear this?"

"Read it to me."

Under a headline that read "Bush Campaign Issues Stinging Attack," my pal Andy Rosenthal had led with what he called my "sharply vituperative" fax. He reminded his readers that President Bush had restrained us from "sleaze," and said I "ridiculed everything from [Clinton's] eating habits to his family life." His major focus was "bimbo eruptions." Rosenthal also said the fax "threatened to drown out the President's own message" that day in Chicago. Stephanopoulos was in the story, calling the fax "sleazemongering."

My little support staff was being incredibly loyal. "Mary Lukens just came down here for a copy of the fax. Should we give it to her?"

"Yes, give it to her! Make sure they get it to Bush *immediately*. And read me the story again, slowly."

Teeter was on his way back from Ann Arbor but managed to track me down. "I don't know what the problem is, just get me a copy of the fax." I went into full-fledged anxiety attack.

Now I had to go to the seven-thirty White House meeting. Women are not even supposed to wear pants suits in the White House, but I knew I was in store for a tough day, so I threw on jeans and boots and a nice blouse and a tie. This was not a day to be sitting around having the blood flow to my brain constricted by pantyhose.

The military guy who opens the gate to the West Wing Complex usually stands there like a Buckingham Palace guard; if you're a wiseacre like me, a stupid daily game is to try and make him look at or talk to you. I'd always say, "Good morning. How are you doing?" and they weren't allowed to say anything. This time I ran up the stairs and said nothing, and for the first time, the guy's neck moved. Uh-oh, this is not cool. As I passed through the metal detector and the outer chambers, all the guards blanched. It's E. F. Hutton time.

I hated these White House meetings and I was late again. As I walked in, thirty heads turned toward me. When they saw I had jeans on, there was an audible gasp.

"Excuse me, excuse me for being late."

We went around the room in another game of show-and-tell. When it came to be my turn I figured I'd start with a wisecrack.

"Well, the President is in Florida today and I promise not to say anything lest I step on another good story."

The larger picture was that on the very day I was making headlines about "bimbo eruptions," George Bush was having his first and best day of the campaign. I had committed the all-time, number one, maximum campaign sin: I had stepped on it.

Not a crack. Not a smile. I was a leper with open sores.

Unlike campaign meetings, where people get right in your face, no one at these sessions would ever directly say, "What a screw-up." As they went around the table it was "We had a very good day yesterday. But, of course, there was another story which superseded the campaign event." Everybody got his chance to say it. "In George Bush's speech yesterday, he did point out . . . But, of course, that didn't get into the story." They did not deign to say the phrase "bimbo eruption."

"Do we have a copy of the fax?" someone asked.

I said, "Yes, we're getting it to Air Force One and we're getting it on the road."

Teeter and Malek were not at that meeting. I was the only one from the campaign. I tried to explain what the fax was about, but clearly that was inappropriate. There was nobody in the room with the faintest possibility of understanding what I'd been up to.

I went back to campaign headquarters in utter shame. I had stepped on Bush's story and I knew this was going to grow into something bigger. The President was still on the road, which meant that instead of covering day two of his trip, the media would be asking him about me. The story was not going to die by this evening's news; it was definitely now a two-day story. I was sick to my stomach.

I was also panicked because I was not on the road to explain and spin this myself. I did not think the White House people on the plane would react well to this kind of thing. Marlin would have been able to beat it back, but he wasn't in charge that day. His deputy, Judy Smith, was on the trip, and she hadn't been through any campaign firestorms with us. I knew she was going to get gnawed at by the piranhas, and, unlike Torie and me, wasn't into the daily nuance of campaign spin. She was a government spinner. So I was thinking, Poor her and poor me, this is one of those stories that without dogged diligence can get totally out of control.

What we needed from the President's entourage was, "We are not negative campaigners, the Democrats are. Here are twenty-two perfect examples. That's our story and we're sticking to it." Their tendency, given the ongoing friction between the White House and us, was to say, "The campaign got out of control, and against the President's explicit directive, raised the woman issue and crossed over the line." We had to prevent that at all costs.

I ran the entire six blocks from the White House to campaign headquarters. Everybody at the eight o'clock meeting was deathly quiet, which was very rare; people are usually throwing things at each other and spilling coffee and hanging out the window at these meetings. I walked in to stony silence.

I couldn't look anyone in the eye. "I apologize to this entire campaign for screwing up the President's day. There is no more egregious offense than stepping on your own story, and I apologize." Then I looked up. "But I say to you now, let's make a decision. Either fire me or defend me. One thing we can't do is go down the middle on this. I deserve to be fired, but just do it or go the other way; let's not be half-pregnant here."

There was a burst of applause.

"Fire you? We love you!" They all knew the vehicle had been ham-handed but the substance was accurate. Everybody was slapping me on the back and talking about the fax and laughing at Clinton. Then I started crying. "Thank you, everybody." I was with my family again. I told them about the White House meeting and they said, "What a bunch of weenies."

Of course. The campaign sorted through the fax and got what I'd been up to immediately. Betsey Wright had invented the phrase "bimbo eruptions." I had quoted *her*.

Now, I usually have pretty good political judgment, but it never occurred to me that "bimbo eruptions" would set off any bells and whistles. Wright hadn't said it in some private, off-the-record, secret meeting; I got it right out of *The Washington Post*. She had bragged to delegations at the Democratic convention that she had paid a first installment of $28,000 to private investigators who had to sniff out what she called "bimbo eruptions." To me, the story was the $28,000. That is a budget for three Rocky Mountain states. My mind went immediately to "How can they afford this campaign? There must be some money going under the table. If it's not, they're spending tax-payer dollars—matching funds—on a bimbo patrol." I, of course, thought this was hilarious . . . and tactically significant. That's three fewer states they can do, that's money they're not spending on campaign tactics. I thought it was an absolutely unprofessional, irresponsible allocation of resources.

So I crafted the question, sourced it, and if anything, thought I had a money story, not a personal one.

Try saying that in a sound bite.

"Nevertheless," Lukens reminded us, "Skinner's calling from Air Force One. I don't know what they want, but we've got a problem here."

We all sat down to figure out what to do about it. I said, "Maybe I ought to apologize. I should apologize to the President."

Charlie and Lake were adamant. "No, don't make a public apology. The Democrats *are* hypocrites."

"I won't apologize for attacking the Democrats, I will apologize to the President for screwing up his day."

Charlie Black said, "Say what you need to to the President, but *never* say the word."

Teeter mandated, "Never shall the word 'apologize' appear in anything. Yes, we have to put out a statement, because those guys on the road will not be able to handle this story. But we are not apologizing for anything."

"But I feel so bad about the President. He finally had a good day and I want to apologize to him."

They all agreed, "Not even in person. Not even personally do you apologize for anything. Whatever you say to him, if you talk to him, is between you two—but don't ever say you apologized."

I tracked down Torie on the road with the "animals," who were waiting for Air Force One to arrive. I explained the situation to her in shorthand. She didn't even need an explanation, she just wanted to see the fax. "You got it, girl?" I asked.

"I got it." She went back into the pressroom and faced the mob, who by this time had talked to their offices and were foaming at the mouth. After the usual back and forth, she finally yelled, "It's the truth, pal, write it!"

Then I slammed into my office, slammed the door shut, slammed down a Coke, and slammed out my statement. I was still sick to my stomach, but I had a good steam going.

It ran three pages. I showed it to Teeter, who threw it back at me. "Go back there and write two paragraphs." I went back and wrote that I apologized to the President for ruining his day. Brought it back in. Mild-mannered communications director Will Feltus screeched, "Go back and rewrite this and take out 'apology.' " He followed me back. Okay, okay, get out of here, I get it.

I wrote:

"With respect to our project to expose daily the negative campaign against the President and the hypocrisy of our opponents, it would appear to some that I might have violated, at least in spirit, the President's dictate to the campaign that we avoid references to Governor Clinton's personal life. I regret if the tone of my statement left the wrong impression in that regard. I stand by my criticism of the Clinton campaign and the Democratic Party for their unprecedented hypocrisy and for daily disparaging, in the most egregious and personal terms, the President of the United States."

I brought it back to Lake, Black, and Teeter, who all smiled. "This is it." I typed it up and we got it out on the wires.

Finally, Sam Skinner got hold of me. I was respectful, deferential, apologetic, without saying the word "apology."

"Sam, I feel terrible. You guys worked so hard. It was a good event. I stepped on the story, I'm really sorry, but here's the facts."

He said, "The President is really upset."

"The President's upset?"

"He wants you to put out a statement."

"What kind of statement?"

"He wants you to apologize."

"Sam, are you telling me, without reading it"—they had not gotten the fax yet—"that the President is upset and wants me to apologize? That does not sound like the President to me."

"Well . . ."

"Did he say 'apologize'?"

"Well, he didn't actually say 'apologize.' "

"Good, because I've put out a statement, and it's a nonapology. So you guys cannot be running around out there saying that I've apologized."

"What did you say?"

I told him. "What do you want? I'll put something else out."

"No, no, no, we can't put out another one. This will do."

"Look," I said, "it is out. These are the facts. I will tell you, man-to-man, I am sick about screwing up the day. But we cannot let these guys divide and conquer us. Only the weenie *New York Times* attacked us. Everybody else played it right: The Democrats are negative, hypocritical scum. I did not 'cross the line.' You cannot, in any way, give ground that I crossed the line."

"Yeah, yeah, yeah, I've got it."

The "Sparky" line behind my desk had been ringing all morning and I hadn't had a second to answer it. Then a huge bouquet of fresh-cut flowers arrived, the likes of which you never see except at a Mafia funeral. They were from James. The card read: "Some days I like diamonds, some days I like stone. I love you every day."

Oh, man, I must really be in trouble if he's sending me flowers.

My assistant came in. "Air Force One is on the phone. It's the President." I caught my breath, shut the door, and picked up the receiver.

"Mary? Pit bull?"

It was a really bad connection and I just started weeping.

"Mr. President, I'm so sorry. I wasn't being trashy. I didn't cross over the line. I can't believe I screwed up your day." He couldn't get a word in edgewise.

He tried. "Listen, I don't want to—" I was sobbing and snorting. "Thatagirl. I don't want to dampen your enthusiasm. Just be careful. Don't cross over the line. I don't want to dampen your enthusiasm. The Democrats have been attacking us. And you're right to fight back. Just be careful. Don't cross over the line. And don't let your enthusiasm wane. Thatagirl."

"Oh, thank you, Mr. President. I love you, Mr. President." I could hear in his voice he was sort of chuckling. "Have you seen it?"

"No, I haven't seen it yet."

"I promise you I didn't cross over the line. . . ."

"I appreciate your defending me, I really do. Thatagirl. And keep it up. Keep that enthusiasm. Don't cross over the line."

Torie had the frothing press on the ground under control. The campaign was behind me, and big support was coming in from the field: flowers and fruit baskets and wine and hundreds of calls. I was beginning to feel a little more stable. Then Judy Smith went to the press pool on Air Force One and said, "She spoke to the President and apologized."

Someone in the media told her, "Her statement doesn't sound like an apology." So then I got another fifteen sheets of phone calls, "Did you apologize or didn't you apologize? Did Bush ask for an apology?"

Big deal. Torie was getting whiplashed on the road. Pandemonium had broken out among her animals. We went back and forth on the phones all day. When you're on the road you're in a cocoon, you don't know what's playing out there, what's on CNN, what the home base reporters are up to; you're dead center in the action and you don't know what's going on in the world.

I said, "CNN is running Judy saying I apologized. They have Dee Dee Myers saying I should be fired."

Torie never gave ground. She spent the whole day beating back the animals and the White House, who had managed to make the story worse.

Unless you've been there, you cannot imagine how the press can twist whatever you say. I knew that I—the victim or the perpetrator, whichever way you want to look at it—could spin out of this. Torie could do it, Charlie could do it. Judy Smith and the rest of the White House staff couldn't. It's not a talent they have. (I couldn't run a government, okay?) But what we had been trying to tell them was that if they didn't chop the press back with a machete they were going to get pushed into a Twisted Sister version of what happened, which would create a third-day story and further disarray in the campaign. Which is exactly what happened.

I got Torie on Air Force One and cussed out the White House weenies something fierce. Torie cussed them out just as bad. We were really going at it, inventing new and improved insults we'd never say to anybody's face. It's a campaign form of deep-breathing exercise.

This was the day from hell that wouldn't end. Driving back from Andrews Air Force Base that evening, Torie received a message from some reporter, who read her back a verbatim transcript of our cussing conversation. The lines on Air Force One are "insecure," and, as they were flying back to D.C., some reporter picked us up on a police scanner. He said, in essence, "I have a colorful conversation between you and Mary Matalin. Can you verify this?" He gave her enough of it that she knew it was real.

We were wiped out, but managed a fresh panic attack. We couldn't remember exactly what we had said. We'd been so furious we could have slammed anybody, from Judy Smith to the White House, to Clinton, to anyone in between. This tape could contain details from my meetings or hers and compromise our operation. Replete with wash-your-mouth-out-with-soap words. It was a very raunchy conversation, guaranteed to be most unpleasant in print.

Without a court order you can't use tapes of private conversations when the participants don't know they're being taped, it's illegal. Our crack lawyer, Bobby Burchfield, couldn't get the newspaper's publisher on the line; we had him call their lawyer and threatened to sue their butts off if they printed one word. Torie was off the wall, cursing out the reporter, the receptionist, anyone she could get on the line. We didn't know until the next day that Bobby'd beat them back.

James

It was a Friday morning in July, and the truth was, George and I were both tired and sick of Little Rock. We had been there every day since the convention and we really just wanted a weekend away. We made up an excuse that we were going to go meet with the ad people in Washington, and hopped a flight.

Right before we landed, George showed me *The New York Times* and said, "James, look at this."

There it was: "bimbo eruptions."

"What are we going to do about this?" he asked. He was starting to wonder, Was I going to attack Mary?

The plane landed but got stuck on the tarmac. Ground traffic. It wouldn't move, it was just sitting there.

George's beeper started going crazy. It was registering 911. That hadn't happened before. He said, "911, what could be 911?" His first thought was that we had dropped out of the race.

When we finally got off the plane we rushed to a phone.

The news was awful. One of our top fund-raisers, Vic Raiser, and his son had died in a plane crash. We rushed over to the Bat Cave to see Paul and find out about Vic's funeral. But while we were there we planned a counterattack on Mary.

We put out statements. Paul and George worked on them while I tossed around ideas. Even though it was the woman I loved, I had to do my job. I told George, "Hey, she said it, she's gotta be held accountable for it. We gotta do it." But right after our statement went out, I sent Mary four dozen roses.

We'd landed at around eleven in the morning. At one o'clock that afternoon, totally frantic because all this shit was going on, we looked at each other and vowed never to leave Little Rock together again. We thought it was just bad luck.

I knew Mary was having a hard time because reporters were calling and telling me. I knew what it was like when something like that happens to you on a campaign. You've got all these phone calls going back and forth, and it's the road, and people keep shooting at you; the press is hounding you, wanting answers to this and answers to that; they won't let you breathe; people in the campaign are saying, "Well, that's it, she ran her big mouth." You've got no control. You're trying to explain, "Well, what I meant was this and what I said was that, I was just quoting what somebody else said . . ." and you're not getting through. For twenty-four or forty-eight hours it's gut-wrenching, your life's flashing in front of you and you don't know how it's going to end up.

Then George came in and said, "Bush is making Mary apologize." That's the final humiliation, when your own people don't back you up. I kind of teared up on that one, tried not to cry in public.

I used to think about Mary constantly during the course of the day. Most of the time it was at a constant low level, but every now and then I'd get a question from a reporter that would spark it, and it would always take me forty-five minutes or an hour to get myself back to the normal state that you should be in in a campaign. I knew that I loved her. Sometimes I would get kind of freaky and think that she didn't love me.

Mary was almost a cult figure in the War Room. During the campaign, whenever she was on TV people would come and tell me. She'd be up there going, "Tax-and-spend Bill Clinton with his disastrous Arkansas record, who could never tell the truth . . ." and people would say, "Hey, there's Mary. She's cute." In the entire campaign, neither Bill Clinton nor Hillary Clinton ever said one thing to me about dating her. No one except Betsey Wright ever mentioned it. Betsey was very disturbed that Mary was plagiarizing her on "bimbo eruptions"; she was not amused that somebody was exploiting her lines.

But of course, this "sleaze factor" was a campaign issue and the whole story did feed into an existing perception that people had that the Republicans were dirty campaigners. We walked out and got surrounded by all these reporters, who had to ask me about it. "How does it feel to have your girlfriend being rebuffed and humiliated by the President? Does it hurt?"

"It hurts a pretty good bit," I told them. In the middle of this crush of people and cameras I started to get emotional. Then I came up with an old religious line. "Well, you could . . ." I said, "you can hate the sin and love the sinner. She's an A-plus operative who pulled a C-minus stunt."

Mary

When I heard about that one I went nuts.

"Somebody get me a tape of that! Call CNN and have them send a tape over, I can't believe he said that!"

I knew this Romeo-and-Juliet thing was a big attraction for the press and they were dying for a reason to report about us. CNN was running it every hour, it was on the wires, it was never going to go away. I was furious with Carville because he knew good and well that his getting in the story would make it not a three-day story, we're talking about a four-day deal. How dare he! He got to look like a good guy, saying nice things about me, but it was really a backhanded way to keep the story alive and keep the campaign off our game and off our message. Plus, it was a way to reinforce their charge that we were cheesy sleazeheads.

That night it was the lead story on all three network newscasts, the teaser, even before they got to the report. "Our top stories tonight . . ." and there I was, name and picture, "Bush campaign aide" and this hideous mug shot of me.

That was it. I refused to speak to Carville. I ripped the Sparky-phone out of the wall and didn't talk to him for a week.

James

I thought it was a good line. I didn't want to hurt Mary, I just wanted to keep a hand in Bush's face. Anything you can do to apply a little pressure over there is fun. You want to know that there's some pain going on. Every campaign likes to say, "Man, they're really hurtin' over there."

What I like to do is, on Friday afternoon at four-thirty, five o'clock, launch a barrage. All they're thinking about is getting out of the head-quarters early for the weekend and we just lay in a savage attack. You always speculate about, "There must be a little pain over there now. They're having to scurry around." I always like to hit the guy on his day off. The idea that there's suffering going on on the other side is appealing.

Mary

I'm glad I didn't talk to you for a week. If I had known what a sadist you were, I wouldn't have talked to you for a month.

James

You didn't like my "A-plus operative but a C-minus stunt"?

Mary

 No. And the "sinner/sin" thing stunk. And what was that fake crying bit?

James

 That wasn't fake.

Mary

 I've seen you fake it before.

James

 I was upset for you, honey.

Mary

 I couldn't get out from under. I couldn't return reporter phone calls on any issue because if I did they would ask me about the faxes and I'd get in the stories again. I couldn't get any work done.

Smack dab in the middle of all this, Rhonda stood white-faced and ramrod-stiff at my office door.

"Now what?" Always ready to shoot the messenger.

"Phone call," she whispered.

"I'm not taking any calls!"

"It's, it's, it's . . ."

"What?"

"Rush Limbaugh."

"Rhonda, I hate you, get out of my face." Rhonda is one of those perpetually chipper Southern women. She was always trying to cheer up her caustic Yankee boss.

"I'm not kidding. Rush Limbaugh himself is on the line."

To the political-division guys whose job was to be the link with real voters, Rush was truly "the man, the legend, the way of life."

I picked up the phone and heard the unmistakable voice. Honest to God, my mouth went dry and my palms got sweaty. Everyone grouped up outside my office, peering in through the glass door. No one, myself included, could believe it was actually him. I figured it was Carney messing with me again.

He was incredibly deferential and respectful. Didn't want to bother me, but was wondering, if it wasn't too much trouble, could he get a copy of the "hypocritical Democrats" fax.

I was worried he was going to jump on me for distracting from the President's message, but Rush sounded so kind on the phone I just launched into a defensive explanation of the whole mess. I was amazed when he agreed with me. He understood the hypocrisy immediately.

To my even greater amazement and pleasure, he did a whole monologue to my notorious fax:

"Now it's finally happened that the Bush/Quayle team is fighting back. Finally, they're pointing out the hypocrisy. Finally, they are telling the truth about the Democratic ticket. And at the first sign of trouble, somebody caved in and demanded that Mary Matalin apologize. I hope this is nothing more than the lawyer in court who knows he asked a question that's going to be objected to, but he asks it anyway so the jury can hear it. I hope that's what Mary Matalin is doing, and I would encourage the Bush/Quayle '92 ticket to keep this up. The liberal Democrats have been lying about Reagan and Bush in a low-ball, sleazy way for years. It's about time that stopped and fire was fought with fire."

I had Rhonda make about a thousand copies and I handed them out like cigars after a birth. I always carried one with me, and when things got to be too much I'd plug in my Walkman and let Rush unplug me.

He had a sixth sense about the rhythm of the campaign. When I was feeling despondent or out of it, wherever we were, without fail, the White House operator would find me with a call from Rush. It was always a rush to hear from him.

The story spun on and on. Rick Berke, in *The New York Times*, got some unnamed senior Bush aide to say the fax was "like the sarcasm of a thirteen-year-old." "Some suggested," Berke wrote, that I was tough on Clinton to "compensate" for dating Carville.

Now this really was a sin: I was becoming a campaign issue. Another Bush day was ruined; there were all these "Did she apologize or didn't she apologize?" stories—and, worse, personal-feature sidebar stories of "She's overcompensating because she's a woman." Imbecilic, not to mention sexist. The story was totally out of control.

Bob Novak wrote a scathing column about Sam Skinner weaseling out of my defense. He said the fax was a sign of the campaign finally coming to life, and that the lack of a defense was another example of the White House screwing up. The press had been dying to write about the campaign/White House subtext, now they had a hook. But while it felt good to be defended, it didn't do the body of the George Bush election team any good to have one arm protected by getting the other ripped off. In public I blamed nobody. Novak called me and tried to lay the mess on Skinner, and worse, said Bush was a squish. I told him, "That's absolutely not true. How dare you blame Bush! The President could not have been more supportive. You're wrong that he didn't defend me, you're wrong that he pulled back."

"You have your choice," Novak told me. "Come on *The Capital Gang* or *Evans & Novak* and tell your side of the story."

"I'll take *Evans & Novak*, because I'll be the only guest and maybe I can explain it all in a half hour." I went on on Friday. By then it was a five-day story.

"The coup de grâce that made me snap," I said on the show, "was the Boy Wonder ticket launching their campaign calling us a negative campaign. . . . I dressed it up, you know, like wearing a little hot red dress to a state dinner. You get noticed. . . . I don't apologize for it. . . . I did not think I was getting into the sleaze business by repeating what their campaign had said and had twice been reported in *The Washington Post*."

Regarding me and Carville, I said, "I think the media does not know how to cover what is an unprecedented relationship, but it is very sexist. . . . Does anyone say to James when he makes one of his blunderous mistakes that it's because he's thinking about me, or that when I hit the mark on the Clinton campaign that he must have told me? Of course not. How can I think this is anything but sexist?"

Appearing on the show was another bad call. I had the reverse Midas touch; everything I touched turned to dirt. The next morning George Bush was at Kennebunkport with some National Security people, working on Bosnia. I was in Washington, trying to pack and get down to Houston for the pre-convention activities. CNN was running the press conference from Maine and I had it on as background noise. Bush made his opening remarks about conflict in the Balkans and then John Mashek of *The Boston Globe*, because of my

Evans & Novak appearance the day before, gets up and asks the President of the United States, the commander in chief, the leader of the free world, had he asked Mary Matalin to apologize.

I about died. It was the sixth day; George Bush was in the middle of dealing with a real live war and he's getting asked about *me*. President Bush said, "For nine months, the other side has been hammering me. We put one toe in the water to fight back and they start yelling, 'Negative campaigning.' . . . We've got a very good bulldog in Mary Matalin, and she's going to keep doing it." ABC called moments later and wanted to rehash the week's events. I spent the rest of the day on the phone with them, begging them not to, but sure enough, on Monday morning ABC and CBS ran the damn thing again. That night on *McLaughlin*, Jack Germond lambasted me for pulling "a sophomoric stunt," while Eleanor Clift said I was "trying to out-Carville Carville." I sat in my office, mortified. "I can't believe I am the Issue of the Night." It had been an entire week that we'd been off message.

Not that he was in any way a decent support system, but when push came to shove I could at least know that James would be there. This time I was too infuriated to speak to him, and hadn't all week. I was leaving for Houston the next morning, and I knew he didn't know where I was going to be, and in the madhouse of a convention setup there'd be no way for him to get hold of me.

I wasn't returning any reporter calls—not that the story was dying, but if I had gotten in the stories, that for sure would have kept it alive. Ann Devroy said to my assistant, Lisa, "I'm not calling as a reporter, I'm calling as a friend. I need to talk to her."

I got on the phone. I thought something was wrong. "What's the matter?"

She didn't say, "Hi," or "How're you doing?" She said, "I cannot stand to hear a grown man cry. He is sobbing. He is sobbing into the phone. You've got to call him."

"He is not sobbing."

"Mary, he's been calling me every hour, every day. I can't talk to him anymore. As a friend, you've got to get him off my back. And as a human being, I can't take this. I can't stand when men cry."

"You are making this up."

"I swear I'm not. He won't stop crying and I'm really afraid he's gone off the deep end."

"Ann, he's just manipulating you. This is all theatrics. He's crying so you'll call me up and say he's crying so I won't be mad at him and *I'll* feel sorry for *him*." By this time I was screaming at her. "I don't feel sorry for him one whit. He kept these stories alive!"

"I can't stand this!" she shouted. "You're screaming at me. He's screaming at me. I don't even know him, I'm not covering the Clinton campaign, I don't have time for this. You're my friend and you're being a slob of a human being. I'm telling you, this guy is cracking up!"

So, to get him off her back—and because she did convince me that he really was upset—I called him.

He was calm as the bayou. "Hey, what's goin' on?"

"Excuse me?"

"What's been happening?"

"James, this has been the worst week of my life. Do you know what's been happening this week?"

"Oh yeah, you know, the fax or something."

"I don't believe you."

"Well," he said, "why haven't you called?"

"Why? I've been busy!"

"Yeah, I've been busy too."

Man, this guy could really get under my skin. I hammered him. "I just think that was a really pathetic, low-life thing for you to do, to get in those stories. You kept those stories alive."

He maintained deniability. "I wasn't the commentator on it. I specifically stayed out of it. George and Dee Dee were the commentators."

"What do you mean, you stayed out of it!"

"They caught me. I was walking into the governor's mansion."

This was nonsense. "You cannot go to the bathroom without starting a press feeding frenzy. You know darn well what you did."

"I did not. I don't know how you could be mad at me. I was saying how much I loved you. I was saying how good you were." That's James. He always goes on offense, especially when his actions are indefensible.

"Well, you are wrong and you know you are wrong. And furthermore, you put Dee Dee out there to call for my firing."

"They shouldn't have done that," he admitted.

"*Yeah*, they shouldn't have done that." I only had one opening. "You made me a hero in the field."

"Yeah, I know. That's why they shouldn't have done that. That just martyred you. It was a really stupid thing for us to do."

CHAPTER 16

James

Mary and I didn't do a lot of serious talking from January to November. It was mostly "What are you wearing?" in the morning and "How was your day?" at night. I had to be careful about seeming like I was probing. If I said, "Were you out in Montana?" maybe it'd seem like I was trying to determine her campaign's scheduling secrets. Of course, there were 150 reporters traveling with George Bush, so those secrets weren't hard to find out.

Mary

It was weird, though. We'd be very purposeful in not trying to pull information from the other guy, but I would always sit there during our conversations and try to read his mood and see if I could make some sort of diagnosis about the campaign for the day.

James

I'd do the same thing. When she didn't sound too good, I'd figure, "They're in pain over there, I can tell." And, of course, everybody loves that. The way they'd answer the phone at Republican headquarters when I'd call, I'd make into a matter of great significance.

You're in the middle of a presidential campaign and you're trying to read something into the way that Rhonda Keenum answers the phone. That is campaigns. That is politics.

Mary

Rhonda Keenum, the best backup in the continental U.S.A. and a real sassy Mississippian, would have PMS and James would translate it into, "Oh, it's a bad campaign day."

What I recognized as emotionally bizarre was to be loving James one second and hang up and tell Carney, "Something really bad is going on over there" the next—and be happy about it. This instantaneous emotional shift was really kind of sick.

One of the actual serious campaign conversations we had was the night before the Florida primary, when James was about to go on television against Jeb Bush, the President's son and our Florida chairman. I told him, "Say anything you want about the issues, but stay off the Bush family. Please."

James

I did the Jeb Bush slobber for Mary. They expected me to be very aggressive and I came on and said, "Jeb, you run a good campaign down there. Let me congratulate you. The problem is, you know, you don't have a very good candidate." Which got a laugh.

The truth of the matter is, President Bush would much rather have me attack him than attack one of his children. Most any candidate would. In almost every instance, people in politics feel that their decision to run for public office has caused their children some harm. They have been away too much, they figure; there are things they could have done that they didn't do; their children have suffered because of their ambition. A different career choice would have meant more time with their kids and more money. George Bush made a million and a half dollars in public office. Given all the things that he's done, he could have been a Houston wheeler-dealer and made that in a year.

The media loves to make it personal. They asked Quayle what he would do if his thirteen-year-old daughter grew up and got pregnant and came to him for advice. Would he counsel her to have an abortion? I found the whole line of questioning offensive. If some reporter asked that question and the candidate reached across and slapped the crap out of him, I'd say he had it coming. I don't think it is fair to a thirteen-year-old child to discuss her private sexual decisions publicly. I don't think it's necessary to make a point. You can get at the same thing without using people's own minor children as an example. I don't mind talking about adults, however. If you've got an adult child who's on the board of an S & L, that's very, very fair game. Just leave the little kids out of it.

I never mentioned Chelsea's name to anybody outside the campaign. You might say to the Clintons, "How's Chelsea?" or "Does she like the new school?" "How's her softball team doing?" If anyone ever said more, he was just stupid.

We felt the Republicans had made a big error during our convention by letting us have our week in the sun. George Bush made a big show of going fishing. We weren't going to let them off the hook, we were going to use the Republican convention in Houston as a shakedown cruise for our rapid-response team. We even kicked around the idea of sending the candidate down there to respond in person, but ended up giving him a couple of days off.

All candidates, at various times during a campaign, feel they're under attack and no one is fighting for them, that they've been abandoned, that they're alone. It's a very normal thing that happens in a political campaign. When you're sitting there getting hammered for four days, psychologically you want to know that somebody's out there defending you. We gained a huge advantage by being able to report to the candidate, "We had a press conference today. This was in the media and this was our response, this is what we're able to do." I do think this was a big confidence-builder for Bill Clinton.

The week before the convention the Republicans did something very foolish. In front of a GOP National Committee gathering, Rich Bond said, "Advising Bill Clinton on every move is that champion of the family, Hillary Clinton, who believes kids should be able to sue their parents. . . . She's likened marriage and the family to slavery."

My initial response was basic, old-fashioned chauvinism: "Let's hit the pavement, boys, and settle this stuff. Leave the women and children out of this." I wanted to go down to Houston and hold a press conference and slam them.

But that was kind of stupid. If there's a human being in this world who doesn't need any protection it's Hillary Rodham Clinton. She can take care of me and ten like me. Then it just dawned on me, this thing was doing nothing but blowing up in their face. It made them look petty and irrelevant, just a lot of people going down to Houston and getting all wrapped up in each other and wanting to see their name in the paper. It showed a lack of discipline. They were trying to rally the Republican right. They had plenty of time to rally the Republican right, and you didn't have to alienate everybody else in the country to do it. It was ludicrous.

The message I took to Governor and Mrs. Clinton was, "We don't need to defend her. It's not me that they're attacking, but I can assure you that we don't want to do nothing to stop this."

Mary

As chairman of the Republican National Committee and a well-reputed politician, Rich Bond was entitled to rally the troops without having his text vetted by anybody. Everyone assumed we were singing off the same song sheet. He delivered his remarks in red-meat rhetoric appropriate to a partisan RNC meeting.

Red meat we wanted. What we were concerned about was that Bond had done what the Clinton campaign had been unable to do: make Hillary a likable character. She had been trying to re-craft her image as a tough and strident career woman by baking cookies and handing them out at the Democratic convention, by softening her hairdo, by staying largely out of sight, and, when she was in the public eye, doing the Nancy Reagan stare at her supposedly dominant husband. Maybe it was working. But Bond turned her into a martyr.

We weren't there to slash away at Hillary. We were convened in Houston to pump up George Bush and deflate Bill Clinton. We'd been having enough problems breaking through without this distraction. My first thought was, "Oh, no, another fire drill." It was one of those situations where you've got to cut your losses. Even though Bond was quoting one hundred percent from Hillary's past work, if the campaign defended him it would kick the story another day. Of all the things going on, the press glommed onto it and the campaign didn't respond, in the process unfortunately cutting Bond off at the knees.

Between the conventions, when we should have been thinking about general election strategy, we were stuck on immediate tactics. I arrived in Houston ten days before the convention and shuttled between the Astrodome, where the convention was being held, the platform committee meeting rooms, and our makeshift offices the entire time. We had punching bags that went "Yay!" when you smacked them, and every day as CNN showed Clinton's 20-point lead in the polls, we'd throw paper wads at the TV and slam these bags. "Yay!" My specific pre-convention assignment was to prevent a floor fight over the issue of abortion.

There was a strong pro-life plank in the 1988 GOP platform and it was going to reappear, exactly, in the 1992 edition. That battle had been going on for four years and the issue had been decided.

When Lee Atwater took over the RNC in 1988 he began working on what he dubbed "big tent" language, an attempt to make the party more inclusive and accessible to people who had difficulty accepting the pro-life strictures but who agreed with us on many other important issues. Lee was big on, and good at, bringing the many factions of the party together. One guy he turned to often in this effort was Dan Quayle, who had close ties to the more conservative elements.

Lee and I would regularly go to Quayle's Old Executive Office Building office for doughnuts and coffee, and kick around political ideas. Though the Vice President was firmly pro-life, he also wanted to stop alienating the pro-choice Republicans. He helped us reach out to the Lifers, and early on they tentatively indicated that as long as the party was firmly pro-family and pro-life, we could add "big tent" language to the plank.

These discussions were not negotiations, more like vapor talk. But word got out that we were supposedly backing off the pro-life position, and the ground troops of the pro-life movement went absolutely nuts. They drew a line in the sand. Under no circumstances would they accept even one word changed. Nothing. They remained suspicious of George Bush's pro-life credentials, even though every piece of pro-life legislation that went up, he got passed. Now, with pro-life guardian John Sununu gone, they were even more nervous and completely unmovable in any kind of negotiation. They were a loyal, hardworking, and critical component of our coalition. We decided to accommodate them.

Of course, this raised mega-problems from the pro-choice faction of the party. Elsie Hillman, who was an original Bush backer and leading national committeewoman from the important state of Pennsylvania, refused to run a pro-life campaign in her state and threatened to quit. Our constant refrain was "You can be like a number of people who are pro-choice and supporting the President, like Lynn Martin. Let's focus on the things that unite us." It was a tough sell, but ultimately she and other pro-choice leaders like Massachusetts governor William Weld, Maine governor Jock McKernan, and California governor Pete Wilson—only out of diehard loyalty to George Bush, the man—grudgingly went along.

The acrimony between pro-choice and pro-life Republicans is palpable. It's a ferociously personal issue and I've never seen anyone on either side persuade someone on the other. It has also changed the face of the Republican party. Pro-life activists began to make alliances and coalitions with the party's other conservative factions and began taking over county, local, and state organizations. The abortion issue became a rallying point to gather all the conservatives into one camp, and they would wipe out regular, moderate, establishment Republicans. They would then use the state party to forward their agenda, which was broader than pro-life.

Not only were their power base and agendas diminishing, moderate Republicans also didn't like the way they were being treated. Far-right-wing forces rarely hold their nose and vote for somebody who disagrees with them; they'll sit on their hands rather than compromise. The moderates, less fueled by moral indignation and more grounded in the give-and-take history of practical politics, were consistently being asked to put aside their individual beliefs and vote for someone simply because he or she was a Republican. They did it, but they were feeling very abused in the process. This was their biggest beef. The big-tent plank of the platform was only the latest example.

The members of the platform committee are chosen, one man and one woman from each state, by their states' delegations. The campaign's need, strongly stated to the state leadership, was to make sure two people were elected who were loyal to George Bush. We didn't really care if they were pro-life or pro-choice, as long as they were pro-Bush. We let the word go out that if people were pro-choice and could not bring themselves to vote for the pro-life plank, we wouldn't notice if they simply went to the bathroom during that particular vote.

When the whole platform committee convened the week before the convention, it turned out that not only on the abortion issue but across the board they represented the most conservative faction of the Republican party. These people had a political agenda that encompassed more than simply the abortion issue. They started all these fires we hadn't expected. They proposed platform language revoking the 1990 budget deal, and wanted to codify "No new taxes." It was spontaneous conservative combustion.

The few moderates on the platform committee were getting ticked off about having all these strident planks ramrodded down their throats and we ended up having to precariously navigate each one. Charlie Black managed this process. He had more convention experience than anyone in the party, was a skillful politician, and had bona fide conservative credentials from his leadership roles in Reagan's campaigns. To monitor all the problems and try to put out brushfires, he assigned a state delegation to each field rep.

Our firefighters almost missed a three-alarm blaze.

The bar at the campaign headquarters hotel is one huge ongoing central clearinghouse where reporters, operatives, and delegates gather to drink, exchange information, and gossip. It's a very productive workplace and inspires a necessary camaraderie. In 1988 I lived in the bar; in 1992 I hardly ever saw it. The one and only night I did get there I was chitchatting with Ann Devroy.

By eleven o'clock she was kind of tipsy and I was wiped-out, loaded, and exhausted. I walked her to the front of the hotel to get a taxi, and when one pulled up who got out but Charlie Black and his wife, Judy. Charlie gave me that look: "Come with me." Charlie never gets disturbed—Lee Atwater used to say he had the best bedside manner in the business—but I could see on his face something was doing. Ann also saw his face and her reporter's antennae went up.

"What's going on?"

"Nothing, Ann. Get in the cab." He hustled her out of there.

"What's the matter?" He was making me nervous.

"We have to talk."

"I can't talk. I can't see."

"Round up the boys. Let's go."

Through our pager system we called everyone to our little office with the punching bags, which quickly became the quintessential smoke-filled room. (Everybody in campaigns smokes.) We were APBing people all over town and they were rushing in.

Charlie had run into a formidable pro-choice contingent at a CBS dinner. "Those guys have enough states to reopen the abortion issue and raise it on the floor," he reported. It was now around midnight on the night before the whole committee was to vote on the platform. Everybody thought the issue had been settled and was out celebrating. No one who was there was quite on their game.

"Which states? Maine? Vermont? California?"

We were stunned. We thought we'd had everyone covered. If this was true it meant they had a sophisticated communications system outside of our observation or earshot. It meant our intelligence had major holes in it. Who could we trust? We were flying blind, going off Jock McKernan's cocktail chatter that they were going to blow our socks off the next day.

We stayed up till morning, calling our most trusted state delegates in the middle of the night. "What's going on? Are you guys going to bolt?"

By six in the morning we were in total freak.

Charlie assigned the biggest mouths to the most potentially troublesome delegations. I hadn't had a wink of sleep when I went over to speak to the caucus *most* likely to cause trouble, Connecticut. With me were the regularly scheduled speakers that morning, Small Business Administration head Pat Saiki and Congressman Jim Leach of Iowa. In the holding room, Congressman Leach started haranguing me about the absence of "big tent" language and the inflexibility of the right-to-life plank. He strongly supported George Bush but he didn't know if he could go through with his pep talk to Connecticut if we weren't going to budge on this issue. He was fighting with his conscience. He was the next one to go out and rev up the troops about the need for harmony, and he was on my case big-time.

In my exhaustion I got very defensive about it. "Look, you've just got to submerge this. We all can do whatever we want in '96, but this is one issue. We cannot let the whole convention blow up over this one issue."

Saiki made her pitch and then Leach came on. He was red in the face and almost hyperventilating, and gave a terse "Let's give a hand to George Bush" speech. It was clear that he was opposed to what was going on, but his loyalty took over. His message was that disrupting the convention is going to hurt George Bush in immeasurable ways, that we can't let this happen. Then it was my turn.

I blasted Connecticut with all the scary statistics about Clinton: failed governor; a liberal wolf in moderate sheep's disguise; an old-time tax-and-spender. Rabid stuff. Real red meat to get them off being mad at us and onto what they were supposed to be mad at: the Democrats and Bill Clinton. I was shouting and jumping all over the stage. Even though the Connecticut delegates thought I was a traitor for being pro-choice and supporting this plank, at the end of my spiel they started clanking the cowbells and other noisemakers convention-goers carry around. Their leader, Joan Rader, got up and laid it out: "I don't like what you're doing, but you're right."

Whew. I hugged her. Without Connecticut, there wouldn't be enough states to reopen the abortion issue.

Charlie Black extracted a bargain from the pro-choice forces that if they didn't have enough votes to bring the issue to the floor by eleven that morning, they would hold a press conference and say so. They agreed to tell the press they were going to support the platform, and unlike at the Democratic convention, they would be able to air their opposing views.

I don't know if anyone ever told the President this mêlée was going on.

We weren't sure if we'd stymied enough votes, and we all lined up at the press conference to find out. Eleven o'clock came, they didn't have the six states they needed, the press conference went off, and we had what seemed from the outside to be Republican harmony.

Between 1988 and 1992 there was a technological explosion that changed the way conventions get covered. Though there were some in 1988, by '92 a veritable fleet of local TV satellite trucks rolled into town, which meant we needed more people and more time to get our word out. The campaign communications division set up a media outreach program to book GOP spokesmen with the networks, print, and local TV and radio stations.

We generally worked until midnight and then at four in the morning I'd get up and start my assigned media rounds. A car would pick me up and either shuttle me to the convention center, where all the nets had makeshift operations, or they'd drive me to a local affiliate.

The first morning they sent me out, the driver got lost. I was going on the air live, which meant that if we arrived late I missed the free media time. He was circling all over predawn Houston, speed-dialing the car phone, which, of course, kept breaking up. He was sweating; I was screaming at him, "Didn't you advance this? It's supposed to be five minutes away!" Finally we got there, they rushed me in, miked me up, stuck an earphone in my ear. I'm still not awake, and as they were doing the countdown—"Thirty seconds . . . fifteen seconds . . ."—some kid ran in with a blurry fax in his hand and said, "Oh, yeah, Harry Smith is going to ask you about this front-page story in the *New York Post*." All I could see was the headline. Jennifer Fitzgerald? A tryst?

". . . ten, nine, eight . . ."

"What? Give me that!" Allegations that Bush had had an affair with his longtime aide had been around for years and never been proved. I had six seconds to scan the article, and I was hyper-pissed. No one in the communications division had briefed me.

298 ■ Mary Matalin and James Carville

". . . three, two . . ."

"Good morning, Mary."

"Good morning, Harry. How're you doing?"

I started blabbing as fast as I could, wouldn't let him get a word in edgewise. I was in overdrive and he was actually laughing. When he finally did ask me about it I gave my pat answer: "It's Democratic trash. We've been through this before—it's absolutely not true." I didn't know what I was talking about. For all I knew, this was grand jury testimony. However, I *did* know that George Bush was innocent. The press had pursued the Jennifer Fitzgerald story through the entire 1980 campaign and again in '88. When they want to find something like that, they find it.

James

The Washington rumor mill had been going around with that for a gazillion years. Hillary mentioned it in a *Vanity Fair* interview, when she thought she was off the record, as a way of fighting back when we were being shellacked, but she never did it again and it certainly wasn't the policy of the campaign. We forbade everybody even to use the name. That's not some overwhelming sense of decency; I've wasted more time with that kind of foolishness than anybody in the world. It just never works and it's a colossal waste of time. Our message wasn't a rumor about George Bush and some woman that the media had spent God knows how much money tracking down. (And, believe me, if they could have made the case, they would have.) We were talking about having focus and staying on message; you can't say you've got to have discipline and then chase down every off-the-wall jackass rumor that comes up.

Mary

On my next A.M. assignment, same thing. Five in the morning, we're backtracking and circling the greater Houston metro area, lost again. I came running in to NBC, they sat me down and showed me a front-page *New York Times* story charging President Bush with escalating activities in Iraq for political reasons.

It's one thing not to have been briefed on a *New York Post* story, but *The New York Times*? Another speed-read. I was clueless.

Of course it was the first thing they asked me about on the air. I told them, "I haven't talked to anybody on the campaign about this."

"What about anybody in the White House?"

"No, I have spoken to no one about it. I only know what I read in *The New York Times* about it."

"So you haven't been told to prepare a spin on it or anything like that?"

"Well, a spin? This isn't a political issue."

When we got off the air they came running off the set. "You didn't know about Bush and Iraq. Your campaign didn't know about it. They didn't tell you about it!" They weren't asking, they were telling, and they were aghast.

They didn't care if *I* had been hung out to dry; the larger issue to them was incompetence: The President was being accused of major political dirty dealing and his campaign had sent a spinner out without a line of defense.

The media arrives at its conclusions by observing exactly this kind of behind-the-scenes activity. They could use this incident as an index of how mechanically screwed up we were. It certainly wasn't "Poor Mary"; it was "They can't get their act together enough to have a line on Iraq."

I stormed back to the eight o'clock convention/campaign senior staff meeting, beyond livid. "This is not working," I fumed. "You can't wind us up and put us out there on no sleep and not brief us. It's bad enough we don't even have the convention talking points for the day to set up the media. But you've got to give us the late-breaking stuff. If you don't we're going to go out there and screw something up big."

"You should have just said it wasn't true," said a communications wonk who never had his butt on the line.

"I don't know if it isn't true. I know George Bush would never escalate for political reasons, but how do I know they're not escalating for *real* reasons? I can't say it's not true, I could start an international incident."

This is how campaign-in-disarray stories develop.

We *were* in disarray, and it was because we were still working with a dysfunctional White House. The rumor about James Baker coming back had been making the rounds since June. We had a daily campaign mantra: "He has to come back. We can't do it without him." The White House could not get into campaign mode, they could only operate in governing mode, and you don't govern during a campaign year. Jim Baker is the only guy in the interplanetary system who could be a governing politician, and by all accounts he desperately did not want to do it.

For some people, campaigning is a profession. People like me and Carville do it as a career and love the ups and downs. Others get involved because they're the only smart friends a candidate has. These guys hate campaigns, it's like taking medicine, and they get through the job with their noses held and lumps in their throat because the only way you get to govern is to get elected. Campaigning is the ugly price they pay for the opportunity to practice statecraft.

Jim Baker never liked being cast as what the media called him, a handler. He loves policy and substance, and was a brilliant chief of staff to Ronald Reagan, a brilliant secretary of the treasury, a brilliant secretary of state. George Bush got him into Texas politics and they have been like brothers ever since. All of us assumed that Baker saw the reelection going up in flames, and even if Bush didn't ask him, would sooner or later volunteer. President Bush did ask him, and on August 13 announced that Baker would be White House chief of staff and special counselor to the President.

Someone brought a tiny television into the pandemonium of our pre-convention offices and we watched as Baker gave his farewell speech to his people at the State Department. The room was usually a total cacophony, people yelling, phones ringing, faxes screeching, copy machine humming. It went from volcanic decibel levels to total E. F. Hutton–esque silence as everyone gathered around the TV.

When he finished people cried. We were so infused with the notion that Jim Baker was going to make things right. He was an honorable, eloquent man coming to give shape to the cause.

The minute his speech was over the phones started ringing again, the faxes whirred into overdrive, and everybody went back to being crazy. I'm sure nobody in the country cared or understood the significance of this event, but to the entire convention—left, right, and center—it was manna from heaven.

James

Jim Baker won two presidential races—the 1984 Reagan "Morning in America" reelection campaign and the 1988 "Read My Lips" Bush campaign. I don't think there's any doubt that in the pantheon of presidential campaign strategists the man stands alone. In this business, Jim Baker is the gold standard.

What civilians forget but consultants know well is that he was also a player in what most of us consider the best race ever: Ford, '76. He took the guy who pardoned Nixon, had no political skills and a fairly weak economy, and started 33 points down—and he came within Mississippi of winning the presidency of the United States. That race is legendary among political professionals.

Our people who had worked against him in '84 and '88 were totally Baker-obsessed. As the race developed, Jim Baker got credit for everything that could possibly happen in the world. A reporter would ask a question and our guys would say, "Baker planted that question." He was larger than life. When you're pitching and the first two times you've faced this guy he's taken you over the center field wall, and now you've got to go up against him again . . . Jim Baker was the Babe Ruth of political operatives.

We wanted to keep him on the bench, in the White House. Knowing that when a guy like that comes in there's going to be a certain amount of friction—my sense was that Bush and his family didn't feel too good about all these stories that Jim Baker was riding to the rescue—we did everything we could to pile on.

"Here comes Jim Baker to save George Bush from himself." "Who is really the President here?" "If Jim Baker is the solution, George Bush is the problem." We were doing a lot of spin, cracking a lot of jokes, trying to aggravate what we thought—and I believe we were correct—was a sore subject.

I'm sure it wasn't doing Jim Baker any favors. Every time he tried to increase his visibility we'd take a shot at him. The whole idea was to make him keep his head down, to make his life inside the campaign as difficult as possible.

Mary

After a week of pratfalls we went into the convention exhausted. Getting through the major events and hourly minutiae of a convention is murderous in the best of times. If you're distracted in even the slightest way, things fall through the cracks. You're staying up later, you're getting tired, the cracks widen, you're making worse judgment calls.

I have some culpability here. I had the feeling weeks before the convention that, in terms of the message we wanted to deliver, the campaign and the convention operation were totally out of sync. They were focused on cultural issues, we were focused on the economy. I specifically mentioned this to Teeter, who told me to dig into it.

To dig into it would have been to dismantle it. The *whole* third night was being devoted to *family*. It was an important issue, but (a) we had been spectacularly unsuccessful in defining it—we always ended up sounding exclusive, intolerant, and sanctimonious—and (b) it was one whole night we weren't talking about the economy.

Further assaulting my political senses was the fact that Family Night was also Women's Night. Our *women* were going to represent the family. This was too much. It was worse than the Democrats' ridiculous Year of the Woman.

As it turned out, that third night did cause us problems, but only because we'd already lost control after opening night.

Opening night was designed to solidify our base. Between Perot peeling off our anti-tax, anti–big government voters, and Buchanan capturing the more conservative factions, we had a lot of outreach to do. But we had the cure-all for any conservative ailment: Ronald Reagan. Reagan was going to be our base savior/healer and all-round inspired Great Communicator.

The strategic concept was to get everybody back on the Republican bandwagon right off the bat, so the rest of the convention could be devoted to advancing Bush's economic agenda and demolishing Clinton's. Reagan would take us a long way toward our objective, but a threshold imperative was getting Buchanan's endorsement. Buchanan would precede Reagan and get his troops in line, and then Reagan would move everyone forward in unison.

As necessary as Buchanan's endorsement was to our candidacy, Teeter was always suspicious of giving him a coveted prime-time spot on *any* night, let alone opening night. We had been playing cat-and-mouse games with him since April, when we'd accumulated the requisite number of delegates for the nomination. Buchanan had reduced his anti-Bush rhetoric but refused to endorse us. Teeter was afraid he'd pull some stunt on TV.

Teeter dispatched Jim Lake to negotiate the terms of an endorsement. Everyone trusted Lake, for good reason: In all his presidential campaigns, he had never screwed anyone, a pretty rare phenomenon. Teeter was still wary and insisted on seeing an advance copy of the speech. Buchanan complied. When Teeter, Lake, Charlie, and Craig Fuller received the early text, all they were looking for was the endorsement. They were not analyzing the remaining contents in the context of the pre-convention ad hominem attacks on Hillary, the divisive platform hearings, or any of the atmospherics attendant to Houston.

The first time I saw the speech, it was on the Associated Press wire immediately before Buchanan gave it. I also read it only with an eye toward the endorsement we so desperately needed. I read further, to where Buchanan said, "There is a religious war going on in this country . . . for the soul of America." It was a pretty inflammatory phrase. Maybe it was taken out of context? It was a pretty ominous harbinger, but . . .

So Buchanan gave his conservative call to arms. I didn't even listen to it. He endorsed us, we were happy.

For many people in the public, and even some inside the party, this was the first exposure to vintage Buchanan. His speech was highly partisan red meat, Buchanan on the edge. Read in a vacuum, there were strident passages that attracted attention, but it was nothing he hadn't said before.

But Buchanan is an acquired taste. In the context of a week of moralistic rhetoric on abortion, to the world at large it seemed harsh. We tuned out the harshness and concentrated on the endorsement. We had a tin ear. We wanted Buchanan to speak to his constituency, and he clearly was doing that. Because our hearing was attuned to him and not the public, we dismissed it. That was a mistake.

We should have been more cognizant of how Buchanan in full rhetorical flourish could sound extreme, how his words could be used against him, because we'd done it to him ourselves. We'd had tremendous success against him in the primaries, and we should have known the Democrats would go right at him. We missed it.

We were ecstatic over Ronald Reagan's incredible eloquence. The press had made a big deal about his looking aged, and his tripping coming off the plane. Was he going to get through the speech? All the hot-air talking heads were predicting he wasn't going to make it.

I'd never been on a convention floor where utter bedlam wasn't standard, but all of a sudden the forty thousand people in the Astrodome all stopped dead in their tracks and were riveted by President Reagan.

Reagan's speech, which we presumed the press would focus on since they made such a big deal of whether or not he would actually be able to give it, in conjunction with getting what we'd wanted early in Buchanan's remarks, distracted us from realizing how the Democrats could distort and misinterpret Buchanan's speech, and, more important, the media's shift in focus to it.

Every night after the convention recessed we would group up in a trailer behind the stage and go over the day. Ten percent of the conversation was about logistical screw-ups and the rest was spin. All we talked about was Reagan's speech. I don't remember getting spin on Buchanan. We did not understand the impact of that speech that night at all. In fact, we missed the impact of it during the entire convention.

We were divorced from reality beyond the Astrodome.

My friend Grace Moe, a veteran of presidential campaigns since Ford '76 who had special expertise in convention communications, had a big job at the State Department and so sat this election out. She watched the Houston convention on television. Grace is my most conservative friend; she and her husband, Ron, are intellectuals; their conservatism is not emotionally based. After Buchanan's speech, she turned to Ron and said, "We are going to lose the election."

James

This was one of the few times I saw Governor Clinton really angry. Buchanan had twisted one of Hillary's scholarly articles into some trumped-up charges and told the convention, "Well, Hillary believes that twelve-year-olds should have the right to sue their parents. And Hillary has compared marriage and the family as institutions to slavery and life on an Indian reservation. Well, speak for yourself, Hillary."

Governor Clinton was watching at the governor's mansion, resting, getting ready for the general election. We were having a meeting and the television was on.

"Can you believe what they're doing to my wife?" He was all for getting out and doing something. We briefed him on our rapid-response team and how we were going to pick our spots.

I thought the Buchanan speech was sort of mean-spirited. Just like there is an optimistic and pessimistic tradition in the Democratic party, the same thing exists with the Republicans. Pat Buchanan is in the pessimistic tradition: protectionism; there's a religious war; there's a constant fight; things are terrible; people are having sex; they're getting pregnant; there's abortions around us everywhere; everything that we walk, talk, breathe is being taxed; unless we rally the troops for Armageddon and march resolutely all is lost. Some Democrats will tell you, "There's disease, ignorance, poverty, and crime everywhere; people in this country go to bed hungry and cold at night; we're losing jobs—they're being moved to Mexico and Malaysia—and our government sits idly by; people are being discriminated against. How dare anybody speak in any optimistic tone?"

The truth is, you go through life and you've got to be a little bit of an optimist. These kinds of problems are always going to be with us, and people want to believe, in the end, that things are going to get better. They want leaders to believe it. They don't want dark, depressed leaders who talk about limits. Just remember Jimmy Carter versus Ronald Reagan.

The whole tenor of that first day was pessimistic. I thought that was good for us. I also couldn't believe how they were highlighting Pat Robertson. And the TV cameras couldn't stay off Jerry Falwell. It's hard to explain just how bad that guy's polling numbers are, but every time he showed up on screen we picked up votes.

At one point Jerry Falwell was pretty much the most unpopular man in the state of Virginia. One of the great campaign professionals I have known was a guy by the name of George Stoddard. In the 1981 Virginia gubernatorial race, he was Chuck Robb's press secretary. Jerry Falwell endorsed their opponent the day before the election, and George started calling all the radio stations in northern Virginia, asking them if they wanted a reaction to the Falwell endorsement. "Haven't heard it? Let me fax it to you with our response." So the Monday before the election it's all over drive-time radio. Robb, of course, won.

That taught me two valuable lessons: First, you can kick a story and increase an opponent's negatives by demanding media time to react to their bad events; second, Jerry Falwell is just remarkably unpopular. In fact, Falwell is much more of a symbol of outright intolerance to people than Pat Buchanan is. I kept saying, "I wish they could just stick on him more."

The Republicans were saying that the government was promoting homosexuality, promoting a lifestyle. How does a government promote a lifestyle? When I was thirteen years old, the first time I stuck my hand down a girl's blouse, the government was neither encouraging me nor not encouraging me to do it. People's sexual business is hormonal in nature, not governmental. Governments are singularly unsuccessful at affecting something as basic as people's sexual orientation.

I would love for a gay person to stand up and say, "You know, I was really thinking about it, and this government policy sort of pushed me over the edge and I decided to be gay." Or: "I was teetering on the brink of being a homosexual, but because of the Republican convention, I got the message loud and clear. I recommend that every eighteen-year-old get a lecture from Pat Buchanan and Pat Robertson about the pitfalls of homosexuality and the virtues of heterosexuality. Thank God I found out in time." It defies imagination, it's just that stupid.

I didn't watch the Republican convention gavel to gavel, but it was on the monitor in the War Room and I'd stick my head up and see what was going on. The short-range impact was twofold. Number one, they set out to consolidate their conservative base. You've got to say they succeeded in that. Problem was, they didn't expand it. Number two: The myth is that they alienated a lot of people. All the elites immediately rushed to the conclusion that the Houston Republicans were turning off massive numbers of people. They were: all of the liberals, who weren't going to vote for them anyway. In actual fact, the massive numbers that appeared in our polls were all voters saying, "What are these people talking about? This is not my life."

In reality, the Republicans missed a huge opportunity to define themselves economically. They were screaming about homosexuality and religion while people were sitting at home saying, "My biggest war is to pay my bills and save my job."

We had an entire rapid-response operation down there, headed up by Ron Brown, and were generating a lot of paper. We couldn't spin directly on their convention site, so Ron held a press conference each morning to get in the stories and respond to what had happened the night before. We were knocking the crap out of Bush on the economy and at the same time sending a message to the media, the Republicans, ourselves, and our candidate: Four years have passed; there's a new regime here; these ain't your daddy's Democrats.

Betsey Wright was another prominent player down there for us, and very early on I got a phone call from Ron Brown. His voice was cracking. "Man," he said, "you've gotta do something. I've never seen anything like this. I'm sitting there whacking Bush on the economy and all of a sudden Betsey Wright grabs the microphone and says she wants to debate Mary Matalin one on one. She starts screaming, 'I'm the one who came up with the phrase "bimbo eruptions," it wasn't her. She's stealing my phrase!' You've gotta do something, somebody's got to talk to somebody."

Rich Bond, in response to an interviewer's question, said, "We are America; those other people are not America." That was not a smart political thing to say, and it was damaging to them and probably helped us. I got kind of emotional about it.

Mary

This was one of the few substantive things James and I talked about during the campaign. He was so mad at Bond he started ranting. Not fake ranting this time, but biting off his words with his serpenthead ferociousness. We were on the phone but I could just see his face scrunching in anger. "You guys make me sick! How dare you say that? Who the hell does he think he is? I'm as American as anybody else." James took it extremely personally. Then he went into a diatribe about "You guys hate Southern men."

That was it for me. "Get a grip. It was just red meat, it wasn't some personal attack on Cajuns."

James

I told the media, "I don't need Rich Bond or any other Republican telling me what kind of American I am. And, frankly, I think you could go through an entire election without discussing somebody's patriotism." We'd been through that in 1988 with flag factories and idiotic Pledge of Allegiance insinuations. "If we're going to vote for the guy that has the biggest flag, the guy that owns the used-car lot would win every election." There's no question that patriotism is a powerful image, but this was way out of line.

Mary

They picked one target and stuck with it. No matter what speech they were asked to respond to they showed up each day with the same line: The Republican party is crazy, it's been taken over by the right wing. I was furious and insulted at Carville's demagoguery. He took all these disparate elements and put them into one sound bite and it was everywhere. I thought, "This is such flagrant insanity and he knows it. I can't believe his audacity. I hate his guts." But it came out right on paper. I stared at *USA Today* and said, "This guy is just too good. Just too darn good."

They were in our faces every day. Even though we always send an attack team to the Democrats' conventions, usually the other side doesn't get in the stories. You hold your press conferences and try to get in the local ones, and sometimes you succeed. But because the

Democrats didn't take their candidate down during our convention, which had been the custom, the national press was picking up their full-fledged attack every day. It was unprecedented.

People who work on conventions don't really watch them, unless the nominee is speaking. You try to catch some on TV in the trailers, but there are people running in and out with problems to be solved and you're too distracted shouting into walkie-talkies, making sure the crowd applauds on the applause lines and holds up the right signs at the right times.

Conventions are scripted to the minute, and Stud Muffin Carney was the maestro at command central, perched over this little folding chair. The expanse of his body filled about half the trailer and he was hooked up by headset and wires to a switchboard that connected every operative inside the Astrodome. Nothing ever ran as planned, and Stud Muffin was always shouting orders and flapping his arms. "Start the spontaneous demonstration now!"

Monday evening, the convention was running two minutes ahead of schedule. To run off the time, Carney sent out the order for the crowds to start cheering. Just after the crowd got going, however, convention chair and minority leader Bob Michel gaveled the convention to attention. Carney, temporarily oblivious of his considerable size and not at all pleased, tried to lean over one of the monitors and cover Michel's face with a piece of paper. This way, Carney figured, at least he wouldn't have to watch the guy gaveling down his demonstration.

Suddenly every walkie-talkie in the place went blank. Operatives started screaming into dead receivers—we'd just lost all internal communications, our only link to controlling forty thousand people.

It turned out that in his moment of apoplexy this huge behemoth that was Carney had flipped over backward, the wires wrapped around his neck, and he pulled the entire internal communications system out of the wall. We thought maybe the world had ended.

Most of what we did in the trailer was monitor closely what the media was saying about the speeches, which for our purposes was more important than what was actually being said from the podium. At some point, of course, we had to know what was being said so we could rebut whatever charges the Democrats would be making. But sometimes we missed stuff.

One thing I really missed, and the whole campaign missed it, was Marilyn Quayle's speech. Mrs. Bush's speech was the evening's highlight, and we focused on it much the way we'd been focused on Reagan's when we missed Buchanan.

The third evening of the convention was Family Night, Women's Night, the main speakers being Mrs. Quayle, Lynn Martin, Pat Saiki, an HIV-positive woman named Mary Fisher, and Mrs. Bush. I was not in favor of Women's Night. First of all, it's incredibly sexist to assume that the main speakers in behalf of the family should be women. Second, I loathe trotting out women simply because they're women. It's degrading. I hated it when the Democrats did it and I disliked it even more when it was us.

This parade of Republican femininity was so transparently a defensive response to the Democrats that it appeared to me we were conceding their point that women didn't play significant roles in our party and our administration. They were wrong, of course; women were everywhere, doing everything. But it was clear to me that the other side had already defined the issue and that we were not going to be able to redefine it, which didn't concern me since it was inconceivable that anyone would be so stupid as to think women were the exclusive province of Democrats.

The press hated Mrs. Quayle's speech. One of the objections was her delivery; some thought she looked angry and pinched, making a mean face. Her staff told me the problem was she couldn't see the TelePrompTer. To which I say, "Do you have a pair of glasses?"

Marilyn Quayle is an articulate, smart, dynamic woman who kind of got boxed in—and stayed loyally boxed in. She was a lawyer who chose to leave her job, stay home, and work as a mother. She told the convention, "Most women do not wish to be liberated from their essential natures as women. Most of us love being mothers and wives, which gives our lives a richness that few men or women get from professional accomplishments."

The press and the Clintonistas said Mrs. Quayle was putting down every woman who didn't make the same choices she did—which is a great twist on their demagoguery, women who don't work are lesser beings.

I understood where Mrs. Quayle was going. She wasn't the only one sick of the long-winded liberal demagoguery on feminism.

The feminist movement is in its third generation now, but in its initial stages it was hostile to men. "A woman needs a man like a fish needs a bike." Well, I need men. I love men. My father was my idol. Most of my mentors were men. I'd be dead without men. So I was put off by early feminism on the anti-man element, but worse was the intolerance toward women who chose to stay home and raise families. It has left a terrible inferiority complex on half a generation of women.

It is no less liberating to choose to be a mother and homemaker than it is to choose to be an investment banker or an attorney or a politician. Liberation is the freedom to make any choice. Which I think is what Mrs. Quayle was trying to say.

When Mrs. Bush expressed a similar sentiment in a Wellesley College commencement address—which, paraphrased, went: In the twilight of your life you don't look back and say, "Gosh, I wish I could have gone to more meetings"; you say, "I wish I could have spent more time with my family"—everybody loved it. Since this is what we thought Mrs. Quayle was trying to say, and we agreed with it, we couldn't believe the press reaction. I think the press attack on Mrs. Quayle was really an objection to our pulling that stupid copycat Woman's Night stunt. The press doesn't like unsophisticated tactics at the presidential level.

In any event, to us in Houston her remarks that night were eclipsed by Barbara Bush's. Mrs. Bush is the epitome of class and grace. You can never be bad or rude in her presence. She makes you have better posture. Her speech to the convention was healing. It was also coherent, cohesive, and low-key, an understandable list of the Bush administration's accomplishments and a discussion of things left to be done. We were getting some traction on the abominable record of Bill Clinton, but we had never laid out in any sustained way why people should vote for George Bush. Her speech told you why you should vote for George Bush.

In the midst of the ongoing chaos, every day we were trying to get President Bush's acceptance speech written. You might wonder how, between three mega-organizations—a campaign, a White House, and a convention operation—we had no acceptance speech for the President of the United States. Well, we had no speech precisely *because* we had three mega-organizations. No one and everyone was in charge. We had no speech, but our cup ran over with speechwriters, all of whom were playing tug of war over the rhetoric, and policy wonks, who kept butting in with "new" old ideas like a taxpayer deficit fund.

Getting the speech just right was tricky business. We didn't want too many rhetorical flourishes, too much poetry in it, because we didn't want a repeat of 1988 and everyone saying, "This is not George Bush, this is Peggy Noonan." (I always thought that was patently unfair; Peggy got criticized for being so good.) The decision was, it had to be Bush; in some ways it almost had to be flat, no glitter, a substantive speech. It also had to inspire thoughts about the awesome significance of the office of the presidency. The comparison we were setting up was between the young and insubstantial flash of the Democratic ticket and the real solid statesmanship of President Bush.

Easier said than done.

I wasn't involved in this nightmare, I only saw the aftermath. Steve Provost, the President's chief speechwriter, was the ringmaster of the speech-construction circus. He was locked in a room trying to incorporate the disparate components delivered by a veritable army of Bushies: Baker's guy, Bob Zoellick; Dick Darman; Bob Grady from the Office of Management and Budget; our guy on Clinton, David Tell; Teeter; Skinner; Fuller. People came in and screamed at Provost and then left. He'd write a draft, show it, get told, "No, that's wrong," and have to go back and change it. The gang was breathing down his neck, wringing their hands—"Where's the speech? Where's the speech?" But it was kind of like, "Where's the soufflé?" You can't rush inspiration, you can't rush the wordsmith—particularly a guy who is sleep-deprived and having fits of delirium, being pulled every which way by policy wonks. So no one wanted to bother him because they were afraid of a meltdown, but everybody wanted to get their fingers in the text. They wouldn't let him sleep. Then they'd make him go to sleep and just stand around and pace the halls for hours at a time like expectant fathers. The big guys were all naturally obsessed with this effort. They weren't available to spin back the unpleasant images the Clinton forces were building up about us every day. Up to the last minute, they were crazed, pondering the possibility that the President of the United States would have to go out there and wing it.

At five in the morning, the last day of the convention, Steve and his assistant, Christina Martin, were in such a state of delirium they were singing the speech to each other. Crooning.

> This nomination is not for me alone
> it's for the ideas, principles and values
> that we stand for. . . .
> Just pause for a moment to reflect upon
> what we've done.
> Germany is united, and a slab of the Berlin Wall
> sits right outside the Astrodome.
> Arabs and Israelis now sit face-to-face and talk
> peace.
> And every hostage held in Lebanon is free. . . .

Their phone rang, they picked it up and kept singing.

> Black and white South Africans cheered each other
> at the Olympics.
> The Soviet Union can only be found
> in history books. . . .

"Hello?"
It was the President. "Can you come to my room? I want to look at my speech."

James

What really scared us was the possibility that he'd dump Quayle. Clinton didn't think Bush would do it, but it scared us anyway.

If I had been advising Bush I would have said, "We've got to do something. We've got to say something very definitive that the next four years aren't going to be like the last two. And changing Vice Presidents is the most definitive statement we can make."

Quayle could have helped by falling on his sword. If he had said, "The most important thing is to maintain the market system and to keep Bill Clinton and his big-spending ways out of the White House. Whenever one thinks he's more of a hindrance to the President than a help, he should get out of the way. Unfortunately that is what has happened, and today I am resigning so that the President can get on with the important business of moving this great nation forward. . . ."

Quayle was there to help with the conservatives. Bush didn't need any help with conservatives: In the end they were going to be with him, they had nowhere to go. Dumping Quayle would have given him a chance to shake up the equation. Bush didn't, I suspect because he is a loyal guy. But you ain't loyal unless you're in office. If I'd been advising him I'd have moved quickly and decisively to someone else.

South Carolina governor Carroll Campbell would have been a possibility. He would have moved them a little bit more toward center, which is where a presidential race is won, and would have meant they would probably have carried Georgia. Arlen Specter would have given us fits. He was a moderate, Jewish former prosecutor who would have cut into some key states in the Jewish constituency. Could have taken Pennsylvania. Would have been viewed as an unorthodox choice. Probably couldn't do it because the conservatives would have been infuriated, but he had gotten into their good graces by taking on Anita Hill. I'm sure you would have had the feminists buzzing, but it would have scared me.

Former New Hampshire senator Warren Rudman's name could have come up. Jeane Kirkpatrick was a former Democrat, a good spokesperson, good on national security; she projects a strong image and would have shaken things up; people would've said, "This is different."

The basic flaw in the Republican strategy was just to defend their record and tell people, "It isn't as bad as you think." They should have said, "Look, what difference does it make how we got here? I say it's the Democrats' fault, they say it's my fault. I'm saying let's move beyond that."

We were always afraid that Bush would concede a big point to make a larger point, that he would say, "I've got to get my plan through. I'm willing to give in on capital gains to get this economy moving again." This was an ongoing fear, that he would call Congress back into session and concede a major point.

Every day we'd try to think like they could. We were mortally afraid they would say, "Bill Clinton is going to tell you he won't raise your taxes. He probably doesn't mean to, because he's too good a politician to want to raise your taxes. But he's such a politician that he'll never be able to say no to any spending, so it'll keep going and going, and eventually you're going to have to pay for it." That tack would have worked very well.

We'd have had an answer—"The spending has gone up under George Bush's administration, who's he to talk about . . . ?"—but it was an attack that would have hurt us. We were always afraid he would hit us harder than he did on spending and taxes.

Mary

I was sitting on the wooden stairs outside Charlie's trailer smoking a cig and making my ever-present stomachache worse, when a Bush aide came up and said, "The President wants you to be on the podium during his speech."

This was an authentic piece of history. They escorted me to a carpeted holding room beneath the podium, where some Bush comrades and longtime friends were waiting to go up. We all hugged. I got all choked up. Even the guys were crying. It was one of those rare campaign moments when you actually have the presence of mind to understand the gravity of a presidential election.

We moved single file up the staircase, out to the podium and looked out on the pandemonium of forty thousand waiting for the high point of the campaign so far.

The atmosphere on the podium was just as charged. The entire GOP hierarchy was up there, but my thoughts were with the Bush kids. They were all so proud of their father and had worked like dogs on all his campaigns. It was their moment, too.

I looked out into the Astrodome and back to the tiny TV monitors displaying what people at home were viewing. There was no comparison. There is no political event as gripping as a convention. TV cannot begin to capture the collective spirit and excitement in the hall.

The speech was so late in coming that I didn't know exactly what was in it. I was on my tenth roll of Rolaids when the President walked out. I could tell by the way he sort of sauntered to the podium that he was fine, it was going to be good. I would have been an utter wreck if I didn't get a speech until the day I was supposed to deliver it to forty thousand people, a nation, and the world. And by everyone's expectations he had to give the speech of his life. But he just walked out and began.

". . . I'm proud to receive and I'm honored to accept your nomination for President of the United States."

Delegates are the kind of people who live and die for conventions, and this is what they come for. You could feel it in the room, the pinnacle of the frenzy; they couldn't wait to go crazy for this man.

I started crying for real. My throat was constricted and tears rinsed down my face. I turned and the man sitting next to me, Tim McBride, who has been the President's "body man" since before time, was crying too. There was majesty and magic. Even the press stopped and watched and stared.

It sounds corny, but this was the man and these were the words that so many people had worked so hard for, the living embodiment of what it is to be an American. He walked out there and he was larger than life. He was the President of the United States.

It was a great speech and he delivered it well. It was vintage Bush, everything he wanted it to be: not flighty and glittery, but magical and serious. What really got to all us jaded campaign hacks was the part about the historical and wondrous office of the presidency. We all knew this came from the President's heart. He always thought of the presidency not as a person but as a glorious institution, peculiar to our democracy and roots.

The speech flashed by, and when it was over everybody was hugging and kissing and waving American flags. All my favorite people in politics, my buds, were up there. The customary balloon drop ensued, except this year the convention-meister added giant medicine-ball balloons in with the regular ones, and we were bouncing them back and forth into the crowd. It was a huge party. They were using a new brand of environmentally safe confetti this year, smooshed into gargantuan plastic bags on the ceiling in preparation for the finale. It was hot-hot-hot in the Astrodome in August, so the air-conditioning was turned way up, blowing cold, wet air. I was waving from the stage, tears streaming down my cheeks, when this huge, one-pound chunk of stuck-together politically correct confetti hit me right in the face. Kind of broke the moment.

Of course, it was never going to be more than that, a single, solitary moment. Within minutes of our climbing down from this magic perch, the hordes were upon us.

Because President Bush's speech wasn't finished being written until literally the last minute, advance copies were not made available to the press. Of the 128 convention speeches, advance copies were distributed for all but the President's. It was bad enough the press had to listen to it in order to cover it; they didn't even have a hard copy to work from in order to get their stories into their final editions. Bush's speech was late and long. In a major blunder, we violated press rules 101 and 102; we inconvenienced them and made them miss their deadlines.

They took it out on us in their coverage.

The press wasn't even remotely moved by Bush, the speech, or us. Their instant analysis: Unlike in 1988, Bush did not give the performance of his life (and, believe me, if he had, they would have pundited that we were "all package and no substance"); the speech was a disjointed laundry list of foreign-policy accomplishments and domestic-policy objectives. (Of course, we'd have gotten killed if we'd given a speech long on rhetoric and devoid of specific achievements.) You could argue the merits of the speech, which, being hyped up from my podium high, I did. But you couldn't argue with how badly we screwed up the mechanics.

James

In 1988 Bush had delivered a hell of a speech, and we were worried that he'd do it again. He didn't. I think, to a person, after the Bush speech there was a sense of relief in the campaign. His speech was even longer than Clinton's. He said it had been a mistake to go along with the tax increase, and promised not to do it again. He called for a tax cut. We were happy with that; we could really hit him for being a panderer. And with him hitting us, it would be a good comeback.

We wanted to answer Bush's speech before it was finished. If this rapid-response team was going to work, it had better start working right now. We had people all over Houston and we sent someone to fax us an advance copy, which is handed out to the press and pretty much anybody who sticks his hand out. We assigned people to read and research different sections, so that if Bush said job growth in Oregon was such-and-such we could fax something out to the nets saying it wasn't, and get in the original story rather than the follow-up a day later. We did this (a) to show the press that we had the research and resources to do it; and, more important, (b) to show ourselves we could be in the mix.

The tone of bitter, angry zealotry coming out of the Republican convention certainly energized our supporters. We didn't take the mean-spiritedness personally, the way many other Americans did. We were pretty unanimous in the belief that they were being zealous to shore up their base, and that they had gone further than they'd had to and had damaged themselves with the voters. When you're in a campaign you're not devoid of emotional or political feelings, but you're trying to assess the potential for damage. We looked at it as a political move. A bad one.

We started the week with a 20-point lead and ended it up by 8. We thought we were in good shape.

Mary

The 1992 convention will go down in political annals as the most overanalyzed and least understood event in modern American presidential politics. The continuing question is, How was the right wing able to dominate the convention of a moderate candidate, and why did we let them take over the party? The fact that no one believes the truth is a testament to (a) the power of the press, and (b) the discipline of the Clinton campaign.

It is true that one of the convention objectives was to solidify our base, an effort that is usually undertaken immediately after the primaries. But in 1992 Perot and Buchanan held the conservative segment of our coalition right up to the convention. We had to get the Buchanan Brigade back in the tent as well as appease the more significant antitax, anti–big government segment that was still ticked off over the 1990 budget deal. No one envisioned, and so no one was prepared for, Buchanan's setting the tone for the whole convention.

I realize that I am flying in the face of conventional wisdom, but I do not accept the view that the entire convention was intolerant and hateful. There were 128 speeches that week, encompassing a vast diversity of philosophies. Some speeches, like Phil Gramm's, were magnificent. The press totally missed that one. I've never heard a more substantial or eloquent statement of the differences between Republicans' and Democrats' view of government. Lynn Martin's nominating remarks outlined President Bush's accomplishments spectacularly. Pro-life governors had their say, and other governors who had tackled and were solving difficult domestic problems, like welfare, detailed winning GOP approaches.

Yet even the most informed political observer remembers mostly an atmosphere of intolerance, anger, and exclusion.

Because we were in the middle of reviewing all 128 speeches, we missed the myopic focus of some of them. We all knew Pat Buchanan. He is not and never was intolerant or hateful. His views are premised on *individual* freedom, *individual* rights, responsibility, and initiative. While he does wrap his philosophy up with moral overtones, he speaks to the government's role in encouraging lifestyles or diminishing individual freedom.

If you say you're for *individual,* as opposed to *group* rights—which diminish the individual and discriminate against nonmembers of whatever group is currently in political favor—opponents charge that you're anti-gay, or anti-woman, or anti-minority. This is not an easy concept to grasp. Conservative ideas are harder to articulate, or in the alternative, easier to distort than liberal ones.

The Clintonistas claimed moral outrage over Bond's "We are America" remark yet daily hurled charges of homophobia, bigotry, and misogyny at us. When they stoked up that crass nonsense after our convention we grated at their utter hypocrisy and blatant demagoguery. We never thought the American people would be persuaded by it.

We underestimated the power of emotionalism over logic. Democrats have always been pandering purveyors of empty emotionalism. It always works.

So here's the lesson we never learn, and the essence of our problem in Houston: Since liberals are always going to find intolerance in what we say, it is incumbent on conservatives to be overwhelmingly circumspect and temperate in articulating our philosophy. Strident rhetoric just feeds into their strategy. You can't use phrases like "religious war" and "moral jihad." The overwhelming majority of Americans are conservative, religious, and moral. But attack phrases strip the virtue from those values. The trick is to appeal to the right values with the right words. Though many thousands of right words were spoken in Houston, between the press's and the Clinton camp's focus on the strident ones, the convention was defined by their distorted image.

Their definition of our convention was "hateful and intolerant." We have worked with the religious right for years. The last thing they are is hateful and intolerant. They're churchgoing, family-oriented, patriotic folk who are scared, just like everyone else, by the cultural breakdown they see all around them. As is the case with every single voter group from the far left to the far right, it is only ever the extremists who grab headlines and, unfortunately, come to define the whole constituency. This was a real blind spot for us. Because we knew it wasn't true, we never effectively rebutted the charge.

We did succeed in solidifying our base. Unfortunately, in the process, we alienated swing voters, who make up the margin of victory.

And this was a real failure of our convention. From night one in Houston, we lost control of the spin. Though it wasn't reflected in poll numbers, the Democrats' negative definition of our party in Houston lingered on through the fall. It was a fallacious definition, but in the absence of our getting out a better one, theirs stuck.

Our failure to control our own image was bad enough, but even more debilitating to our reelection bid was the fact that this distracting internal feud totally fogged up the focus on an economic message.

In the ten days after we left Houston, the proponents of jihad rhetoric were claiming the convention had been a rousing success because we'd gotten a bump in the polls. They were afraid, because of the way the press was spinning it, stressing the strident tone of some of the speakers, that we were going to pull back from cultural issues. The jihadists were attributing the bump to the fact that these issues had been discussed. History, however, demonstrates the bump is always GOPers coming home.

We missed a wide-open opportunity. The 1992 election was about the economy, and despite the overwhelming number of convention speeches dedicated to the subject, no one heard a word. The American electorate was no more clear on the Republican message after the convention was over than they were all year long. The Democrats made sure they were real clear, however, on a distorted cultural message.

CHAPTER 17

Mary

Since I was tied up all through the primaries and the convention with White House coordination problems, out-of-the-blue crises, unending media needs, and general bedlam, Carney was really doing my job—the daily care and feeding of the field division. He was so good there was no need for me to stay at headquarters. Once Baker and crew arrived, they immediately eliminated my major distraction—White House bumbling.

Baker hit the ground running. He was better than we thought was possible, given the late start. Teeter finally had the monkey of the White House off his back and could now concentrate one hundred percent on the campaign. The first thing Baker did was bag the meeting-marathon mode we'd been in. Now he and Teeter had a streamlined decision-making and implementation process. We all felt the difference from day one.

Even though the campaign and White House were now in lockstep, both Baker and Teeter wanted a campaign representative on Air Force One to double-ensure communication coordination. They put me on the plane. Rather than having to spend all day on the phone with the media, now I had to deal with them twenty-four hours a day face-to-face. I boarded immediately after the convention.

I had done my days of living out of suitcases, waking up in strange hotel rooms, schmoozing with voters till my eyes glazed over, but I really wanted out of D.C. I just couldn't get a sense of the real campaign through the filter of media impressions and field complaints. And I thought I could do more for George Bush attacking and defending on-site. Teeter was a good guy and a good manager to let me out there.

From my direct contact on the ground, right away I could see we were in trouble. I complained to the campaign, and, now that I was in his daily presence, to George Bush, that we were burdened with the negative impression created in Houston. The Buchanan wing was in my face; they thought I just didn't get it. "You're a moderate, you're misreading the convention. This is what the country is all about. You don't understand the complexity of these issues and you are hurting George Bush by not supporting it completely." I resented their blind eye to the *perception* they'd created; I resented their labeling me a squishy moderate. I totally got it and was getting it every day—right between the eyes.

For ten days this battle went on. They were saying, "We won," and I was saying, "We've lost."

There are three targeting factors to consider when you're scheduling a candidate in a national election. First, if the candidate is an incumbent, you have to show up at least once in each state for appearance's sake and so as not to offend any constituency; but in the end you really only work the swing states, the ones that are up for grabs. You essentially ignore the states that you know you're going to win and the ones you are definitely going to lose.

Second, you are constantly trying to send a signal. Geography counts, and every trip has more than local significance. For instance: Because the presumption was that by picking Al Gore as a running mate Clinton was trying to break the Republican lock on the South, we scheduled our first post-convention trip through Mississippi, Missouri, Georgia, Alabama, and Texas. We wanted to send a clear signal that they had no chance of picking our lock.

Third, groups and constituencies often represent broader support than their presence in the state itself. A cop event in Detroit, for instance, says more that you are supported by the forces of law and order than that you are welcomed by the Midwest. Meeting with a group of local evangelicals also reaches a larger constituency.

Of course, overlaying all targeting decisions is the media reach. You hunt where the ducks are. You send the President to the major media markets; the VP to "B" markets; and all other surrogates to local markets.

James Baker took control of the White House two days after the convention, but the first week's general campaign schedule had been set before he arrived. The second day out, after buzzing through Georgia and Alabama, the President was scheduled to speak at nine P.M. to a convention of evangelicals in Dallas. Given what had just happened in Houston, it was a scheduling blunder extraordinaire, but to have pulled out at that point would have caused a national sensation and been even worse.

The President's stump speech was tinkered with daily to keep it fresh and topical and to add some local color. In this script, President Bush was to criticize the Democratic party platform, saying it "left out three simple letters: G-O-D." Steve Provost, the President's chief speechwriter, who traveled with us on the plane, saw it and raised the issue of whether this was an appropriate phrase to include. It sounded to him a little incendiary. The consensus on Air Force One was, "It's past deadline, nobody will cover it, this is our audience, they'll love it."

The President saw the line and asked, "Is this all right? Are we sure this is all right?" I don't think he or any of us at the time fully understood the negative perception left by the convention; Bush was just generally uncomfortable politicizing God. Episcopalians are very reserved in practicing their faith. The guy had just gone from a grueling convention to a tightly scheduled five-state campaign swing, everybody was tired, he asked the right question. It was a late-night event before a partisan crowd, way past everyone's deadline. He got the wrong answer.

To this day everybody's running around saying they had nothing to do with it.

Up to that point we had been about 50–50 beating the press back about the convention. I had been adamantly and consistently saying, "There were a hundred and twenty-eight speeches and you fools have listened to them and reported on them. You're being manipulated by the Clinton campaign. We have not been taken over by extremists. Unlike the Democrats, we were letting every faction of our party speak. This is unfair. How about some balance? You should be ashamed of yourselves." Blah, blah, blah, blah, blah. So Bush said it, and of course it blew up.

That event, more than the convention, turned regular Republicans against us. It precipitated a steady stream of howling from our local organizations. My gut feeling was that a lot of Republicans who tuned in had been put off by the extremism at the convention, or, more precisely, the subsequent bashing in the press, but didn't associate it fully with the President. They could listen to him and Mrs. Bush and still feel that at the head of the ticket and the nation were kinder, gentler Republicans. But when they heard it come out of President Bush's own mouth, that was it for them. Detachment from the candidate was gone.

James

I suspect that God's feelings would not be hurt if He or She was left out of an American political party's platform. I also don't think this was a particularly significant event in the campaign. Some people saw this as a microcosm of the Republicans and what they stood for. Sure it was. So what? It didn't drive voting behavior much one way or another. The people who were knocking down four buildings to vote for us were outraged. Good. It might motivate them to get out and work for us, or at the very least talk it up. It was probably calculated to do the same for the fundamentalist voter.

Of course we whaled them with it, but I don't think we did a lot of damage.

Did it drive me crazy personally? Yes. Since when is a party's platform the Lord's Prayer? I'm kind of Jeffersonian in that regard; I believe in the wall between church and state. The whole country was founded on the idea of religious freedom, and here they were demanding orthodoxy. But did it bother me as a strategist? No. Bush is a high-church Episcopalian, I just thought he looked kind of silly, and I was glad he said it.

I don't think religious beliefs have anything to do with who's a better person. I also have known very few people who have a better understanding of religion and God than Bill Clinton. Anybody who has talked to him for more than fifteen minutes would draw the same conclusion. He knows more about Catholicism than I do, more about Judaism than a lot of Jews. He knows a hell of a lot about the Bible. I have absolutely no doubt that he is a person who has thought more about God in his lifetime than 99.5 percent of the people in this country. No doubt. He understands what faith is, he understands the contours of it, the power of it, the contradictions and limitations. He'd be a year's study away from being a theology professor. Now, do I think that qualifies him to be president? No.

Americans have very complex views of religion. Some people look at it like I look at LSU: They wear it like a university sweatshirt.

That's their right. But for me, you shouldn't equate your religion with your football team.

As far as I was concerned the more substantial strategic issue, from August on, was the presidential debates.

During the Republican convention Mickey Kantor had brought in Tom Donilon, a Washington lawyer who had worked on the Mondale campaign, and said we should start preparing for the debates. Donilon is a good guy, I basically liked him, but as soon as he showed up I said, "Aaah, they're just bringing in some Mondale people here, it's going to be the same old stuff." Just me being reflexive, forming an opinion first, thinking second, not knowing much about what I'm talking about. We were ahead, I was kind of cocky.

They said, "We're going to talk about how we're going to do the negotiations."

The Republicans had always done well in the negotiations over how many debates should be held, where they should take place, how they should be formatted. But this year a bipartisan Commission on Presidential Debates, participated in by the national committees of both parties, had been set up specifically to make those kinds of arrangements. In fact they had just announced the sites and times for a series of three presidential and one vice-presidential debates.

"Stop," I said to Tom and Mickey. "We shouldn't do negotiations. This commission has made a recommendation and we should say we're showing up. Everybody agreed when they went in that this commission was going to set up the debates. That's it. That's just the way we're going to do it. We'll say, 'Fine, we'll be there.'

"Don't get me in a room with Jim Baker. That's all they can't wait for us to do. That is their whole life, is getting us in a room and negotiating debate terms. We'll have a huge debate over debates. To hell with that."

"We've never done that before," they said.

"Well, we're going to do it now."

It started out, I was for it. The next thing you know, I was for it and Hillary was for it. The next thing you know, I was for it and Hillary was for it and everybody else was for it.

The Republicans hit the bait. They said, "No, before we will debate we have to have direct negotiations between the campaigns." Well, they could only look like they didn't want to face us. Here was a legitimate commission that they had participated in, established specifically to iron out all these details beforehand, and they were backing off. You can run but you can't hide.

The commission had set a specific date for the first debate, which gave the public and press something to focus on. Governor Clinton said he'd show up, President Bush said he wouldn't. It was very clear. The question then became, How can the President of the United States refuse to come before the American people and explain his policies? What's he got to hide? We could embarrass them endlessly.

This went on for almost the whole month of September. We wouldn't come to the table and they couldn't make us. The signal I think the voters picked up was, "These are Democrats who are tough and mean. These are not people coming to beg." The Republicans sent us a letter saying that if we didn't negotiate they would assume we didn't want to debate them. On the same day, the bipartisan commission threatened to cancel the first session if Bush didn't accept the conditions. All they looked like was scared rabbits, and our numbers rose from an 8-point lead after their convention to 19 points on September 29. I kept saying, "How much longer are these guys going to keep taking this pounding?"

Mary

Though the Democrats and the press were having a field day, the prolonged negotiations were too inside for the general public to focus on. All our data indicated that the electorate believed there should be and would be debates. The nuances of the silly negotiations did not register with them, and so long as they didn't care, we didn't care how macho the Democrats were acting.

James

Hershel Gober, Arkansas's director of veteran affairs, wanted us to go to the American Legion convention in Chicago. We were hoping that if we went and got a decent reception we could put an end to the draft story, the story from hell.

There is a rule of thumb in political consulting: What a candidate thinks really matters. Only in extreme circumstances should you ever try to talk your candidate into doing something that he doesn't want to do. Almost never do that. And seldom should you try to talk a candidate out of doing something he does want to do. Certainly you can get into arguments about which television spot to run, or which ending a TV spot should have—that's our job—but you can't move him around like furniture. The main deciding factor was that Clinton wanted to go.

Bush was also going, and there was no question but that he was going to be better received than we were. But the draft issue was a fundamental part of this campaign, and neither I nor Bill nor Hillary Clinton thought the governor could get elected President of the United States and not go before this group and address it.

We got a polite response. What most of these veterans groups care about is their benefits. They are patriots, but they really want to protect the benefits of the people they represent. We thought we had taken a big step in putting this issue behind us, that we had, in effect, stepped into the lion's den and come out unscathed.

Labor Day is the traditional start of the campaign season. We had been before the American people since the previous January and already had our team operating smoothly, but Labor Day was like the beginning of the NBA playoffs.

In the National Basketball Association the casual fan starts to tune in about game five of the first round. Hardcore fans who watch exhibition games have been there the whole time, but now more media is showing up and the crowds are getting bigger. As for the team, your roster is set; the role players know their roles; your best plays have been worked over till you know what works; you pretty much know when you're going to your big man and what your strategy is for three-point shots. The game is played a little crisper and a little better, it's more deliberate. The championship is on the line.

There's another analogy. Think of the electorate as a county waking up, and the campaign as a day. Farmers and construction workers and people who have to commute long distances, they get up at four in the morning. These are the reporters and the political junkies, C-Span people; they never sleep, they're taking Dexedrine or drinking coffee. After that you've got the working moms with kids, got to get them dressed and up and off to school. Then there are the white-collar people, lawyers and bankers and accountants, they're getting up a little later. Then you've got the retirees who want to go fishing or go down to the mall, they get up a little later still. After that there's the college kids and the unemployed, who can get up any damn time they please. Labor Day is seven o'clock in the morning. Some people are already awake but the majority of the alarms are going off all over town. Folks are kind of groggy, only got one eye open. The problem is, sometimes they get up and you've got them and then they fall back asleep on you and wake up with a different attitude.

Labor Day weekend the governor went to a stock-car race in South Carolina. That was a stupid scheduling event; there was no good reason for us being there, we were never going to carry South Carolina, but former governor Riley wanted him to do it and we said okay. So Governor Clinton got booed.

Mary

When President Bush was at the Firecracker 400 he went out into the crowd, went down in the pits, drove the pace car, and everyone loved him. So when this Southern, populist Labor Day crowd booed Clinton we thought it was great. We also thought maybe one of us had something to do with it. A light plane had circled the track towing a banner: "No Draft Dodger for President." My mind went instantly to Dave Carney. It sounded like one of Stud Muffin's stunts.

The President saw the story on the wire and asked me, "Did you do that?"

"No."

"Did anybody on the campaign do it?"

"No."

"Okay."

I called Carney and said, "Tell me you didn't do this." I didn't even say what it was.

"I didn't do it. I don't know what you're talking about."

"Who did?"

"I don't know, and I don't know what you're talking about."

There is a cast of characters in each state who can get things done without implicating the local organizations. Sometimes they screw up, sometimes they get it right. If you *are* going to get involved in this kind of campaign terrorism you have to maintain plausible deniability; you do not want to know. Your implicit message is, Do what you gotta do. It's got to be done without fingerprints; if anyone on the campaign gets caught involved in this kind of activity it's grounds for firing.

"Ask around," I told him. "I need to know because I've just told the President we didn't have anything to do with it. If the press thinks we did, Marlin is going to get questioned and we're denying it. You can't lie about this. So find out how much we *didn't* do."

It made all the papers the next day. The fact that Bill Clinton had gotten booed by this populist crowd was a very significant event to them.

Carney checked his network and found that the banner was funded by some local businesspeople who had a crop duster and just went up and did it. We were all delighted that the incident occurred and even happier that it was an independent action. That way we could imply that we were in some way the masterminds who got away with the scheme without getting in trouble for it. We got political points for Clinton's embarrassment having happened, bonus points because they figured we did it, and double bonus points because they couldn't tie us to it. The press kept saying, with noticeable admiration, "You did it. You did it," and we told them we didn't, with a face that said, "We did but we're not going to tell you." Are we juvenile, or what?

But there is such a thing as going too far. When something similar happened not long after, Carney and I had to issue a memo *on paper* to all the states, saying in essence, "The following events happened and this campaign had nothing to do with them. Neither did the states. You are to disavow them, and under no circumstances are any campaign funds ever to be spent on such activities." I wanted it on paper because I was afraid that somebody was going to go out there with a chopper one day and drop a smoke bomb on one of Clinton's events. People do get crazy in the heat of battle, they lose their sense of proportion, get detached from reality, and weird things happen.

James

On Labor Day itself, Governor Clinton was in Independence, Missouri, at Harry Truman's house. This kind of day is absolutely illustrative of what drives campaign strategists up the wall.

President Bush had been trying to hitch himself to the coattails of Truman's reputation, which we thought was pretty absurd to begin with, and we wanted to squelch that quick. We had a good speech written. Governor Clinton told the crowd, "We gotta go beyond trickle-down economics—not back to tax and spend, but ahead to invest and educate and cooperate and compete and grow, putting people first."

We got the report from the road: "Man, he gave a great speech in Independence. It was the perfect backdrop, the perfect event, talking about 'Invest, educate, move away from past policies.' Then he goes to the rope line and it all goes to hell."

At the rope line, reporters asked once again about his draft record and the governor told them they should be checking out Bush's record on Iran-Contra instead. The draft thing "does not amount to a hill of beans," he told them. "There is a memorandum of a conversation between two cabinet members"—it was in the press—"which, if true, would call into question not only the President's veracity but his support for illegal conduct."

Now, what do you think is going to get on TV? Do you think in your life it'll be "Not back to tax and spend but ahead to invest and grow"? Of course not. The Beast don't want to report the stump speech, they hear it all the time; the Beast don't care about the economy, that's boring to them. The Beast likes the draft story, the Beast likes the Democratic nominee saying the incumbent President's "veracity" is in question.

"Ladies and gentlemen, this is Randolph Smith of Channel Whatever with the presidential campaign in Independence, Missouri. Democratic nominee Bill Clinton, under attack for his draft record, lashed back at George Bush today in an effort to divert the dialogue away from his conduct during the Vietnam War and toward Iran-Contra. Clinton is continually plagued by questions about the draft and now it seems to be a personal tit-for-tat between Bill Clinton and George Bush. Meanwhile, there's very little talk about the economy out here in America's heartland. Back to you, Joyce."

Meanwhile in Little Rock, campaign strategists are kicking trash cans.

I flattened myself against the wall and started screaming into the telephone at the Road Warriors. "You people cannot keep him away? What is going on out there?"

They don't say much, but I know they're thinking, "It's easy for them to sit behind a desk saying, 'Don't go to the rope line.' But the Beast was all over. . . ."

This is why when you watch the news, you will often see a candidate glide right by reporters without stopping. We're happy then. If the candidate doesn't say anything else but what he's supposed to, the media don't have anything to run but what he said. Or they'll say, "He refused to answer questions and returned to the themes of his campaign." That's fine. That's the point. Our guy can say, "Gee, it's nice to see you. . . . I'm in a hurry, let's blow this pop stand. . . . Thank you." That's a whole hell of a lot better than creating controversy and stepping on your own story.

But there's this huge myth, which the media perpetuates, that candidates do what they're told. They don't. The press wants to write, and the elites want to believe, that everything in a campaign is scripted and contrived and organized. The truth of the matter is that a lot of it we *try* to contrive and organize, but very little of it ends up that way. A candidate sees a rope line. You might have twenty people telling him, "Don't do it!" but he goes to the rope line. You tell him, "Man, we blew our story by going over there," and he tells you, "Some people say we ought to do it, some people say I shouldn't do it. They were asking me questions."

So little of this stuff is contrived, and so much is accidental. So little of it is Machiavellian, and so much is actually human.

Mary

Two days later we were on a mega-trip in Pennsylvania and New Jersey. It was one of those exceedingly long days where we would fly in on Air Force One, get into a motorcade, take a helicopter, get out of the helicopter, get in another motorcade . . .

Every day you try to do a substantive event, which deals with policy, and a color event, which revs up the crowd and looks great on camera. The color event is usually the one that ends up getting covered. We did a wonderfully successful Ask George Bush and a single-issue education event in Pennsylvania, and a color event in New Jersey.

It was brutally hot that day, the kind of hot where you think you're going to faint. The Pennsylvania events were indoors and air-conditioned, but when we got to the Jersey color event it was outside in the peak heat of the day. We were so hot and thirsty we were all walking from the cars like little Stepford people. I had thought the stage would be shaded, but it wasn't; I stepped out on it and got blasted like I was walking into Hades. I thought, "How is he going to get up there and give a stemwinder? I can hardly breathe."

President Bush got up there with a jacket and tie on. The sun was right in his face. He was working through his standard speech and trying to rouse the crowd. And he was doing a pretty good job.

By this time of day, even though we should always be paying attention, nobody in the press or the entourage really is. We've all heard the speech a hundred times, it's a stock speech, only the poor candidate has to get up for it every time. So I was listening out of one ear when President Bush said, "I found out the hard way, I went along with one Democratic tax increase, and I'm not going to do it again. Ever. *Ever.*"

The second "Ever" was ad libbed.

Even in my sweat and fatigue, it registered. I looked across at Marlin Fitzwater, who always looks laid back, whether he is or not, and it had definitely registered with him too. On the way back to the motorcade he and I bumped into each other and said, at the same time, "Ever. *Ever,*" acknowledging that we'd noted it, hoping that nobody else did.

Well, they did. One extra word made the promise more definitive than the President had been on the subject this campaign. And it wasn't a major policy moment, it was President Bush at a color event, going off text, trying to push some emotion into a speech he'd given a thousand times. Which required Marlin to go out and respond to the press, who were asking whether this was in fact a new pledge not to raise taxes. Had President Bush just said, "Read my lips" again? Was the President "taking the pledge"?

This is a classic case of political jargon conflicting with human jargon. To humans it meant what it looked like; he said he refused to raise taxes. To us, the "tax pledge" is a term of art, it doesn't mean what it means to normal people. It refers back to a specific fight during the 1988 New Hampshire primary over "taking the tax pledge." Marlin said the President did not "take the pledge," meaning, in political-speak, he refused to commit to *not* raising taxes.

It was all very confusing. Marlin was responding in politicalese and the press played it, rightfully, as policy. "Bush backs off pledge not to raise taxes. . . ."

James

On TV he looked almost like he was laughing when he said it. It was a silly sound bite, and then they had Fitzwater saying it really wasn't "Read my lips." Then the networks went back and showed the original "Read my lips" from the 1988 convention, the promise he broke and that they'd been trying all election to run away from. That was a bad day for Bush. They could not have been happy with that.

Mary

We all now had a new operative phrase. When the Air Force One steward came around I said, "May I have a red wine? And I don't want a beer. Ever. *Ever.*" Everyone was doing it. It was funny but not funny.

Despite the daily snafus, the big picture was falling into place. Under the leadership of Baker and his team, the White House was speaking our language. The Baker team, all assistants to the President, included his alter ego, Margaret Tutwiler, who had done campaigns going back to Gerald Ford, for communications; my White House counterpart, Janet Mullins, for political affairs; Dennis Ross for policy planning; and Bob Zoellick, deputy chief of staff, who also oversaw speeches. We at the campaign never had to look over our shoulders again. No more double-checking events or having our own people on the ground; the scheduling was right, the events were right, everything started running smoothly.

They also recalled Sig Rogich, the best political ad man around. Sig was one of those Horatio Alger stories—raised by his mom, made great . . . . The standard joke was, His shoes cost more than your mortgage. He had a great home and business in Nevada, but was so devoted to George Bush, he left them to join the White House as the all-around image guy. He was extraordinarily talented, which is probably why Sununu started picking on him. By the time the campaign started, he had left out of frustration with the White House. The one guy we needed. Margaret lost no time getting him back, and he lost no time cutting spots. He could create, script, produce, cut, and distribute a spot in twenty-four hours.

My initial job was to tell Margaret and Janet, as fast as I could, everything I knew about Clinton, his economic plan, his tax hikes, his abysmal Arkansas record. Working at the State Department, they had been out of touch with American electoral politics for three and a half years. But they were real smart. Out of this mass of data they keyed on the one truly valuable piece of salient information, which we had gotten some traction on when the plan first came out: the fact that Clinton's figures didn't add up. They figured how to turn it into a TV spot and get it on the air. This became "Truth in Taxes." We were starting to get some traction.

One thing we knew from our data, and just from being alive, was that people did not think George Bush had a plan for the economy;

they weren't convinced he had any kind of domestic interest whatsoever. At Jim Baker's direction, Zoellick pulled together all the disparate
parts of Bush's previous economic-recovery packages, legislation, and
ideas, and put it on paper in the form of the Agenda for American
Renewal. It had a camera-friendly cover and was one page longer than
Clinton's. Now we had a plan.

The President delivered his plan for the economy in a speech at the
Economic Club of Detroit, and we bought five minutes in prime time
on ABC, NBC, and CBS.

It was a great speech. The future of this country, the President said,
and the very quality of life of every American, depends to a great
extent on our ability to compete and succeed in an increasingly competitive world. Although geopolitical concerns are not gone completely, he told them, we need to dedicate our energies and talents
into maintaining the country's leadership role in a world now gov-
erned increasingly by geocommercial boundaries. It was a beautiful
articulation of the connection between foreign policy and domestic
policy, encompassing our original campaign strategy.

With much pre-hype, including a definitive press backgrounder by
Zoellick, we got off with a big bang. The initial press reaction was
very positive. It was just the kick-start we needed.

Too bad there wasn't any gas in the tank.

To get a message out there you gotta stay on it. One set of five-
minute spots does not resonate. We should have roadblocked the
Sunday shows as well. We should have had every administration
heavyweight on point. We didn't. Baker was too closely associated
with it, so he couldn't, but we had no heavyweights pushing the
speech. Bush was a voice in the political wilderness.

James

We were very scared of this one. This is where we went into
what we called DefCon Five. We had our people ready to analyze and
scrutinize and tear that speech apart.

We were always afraid they were going to start talking about the
economy with repetitiveness. "Bill Clinton is a traditional tax-and-
spend Democrat. I have a new export-driven, market-oriented plan
to drive this country forward to the twenty-first century. . . ."

There had to be some economic distinction coming. We thought
for sure they were going to use their five network minutes to do a

plan spot, take excerpts from Bush's speech, and do what we did in New Hampshire: say "Write to this address and we'll send you George Bush's economic plan for America." We were absolutely convinced of it. There wasn't any other possibility. We were convinced that this was really going to help Bush, and we were panicked.

Bush gave a damn good speech—it seemed to have Baker's hand all over it—and then it just went away. No write-in. No toll-free number. And the next day they were back talking about the draft.

We were startled, but we weren't asking questions.

Mary

We did not make it clear to the press that this was our defining moment of the general election. When they didn't see any concerted follow-up, they treated it like any other one-shot deal. Though Bush gave a shorthand version of the Detroit speech repeatedly, the press never came back to it. I carried copies of the plan around with me in a big tote bag so that every time someone said to me, "George Bush has no plan," I could grab it and say, "Here it is. Now get out of my face!" I handed out these things at the events and media people would look at me like it was a live kidney. We never broke through with the plan.

James

Baker himself was going to give an economic speech at Harvard. I couldn't believe they were so colossally stupid as to allow that to happen. It just cried out for some Democrat to ask the question, "Is George Bush President, or is it really James Baker? Who's the monkey and who's the organ grinder?" I had no problem asking it. If Baker was on the stump making policy speeches, it was a tough one to answer.

The public doesn't care if Jim Baker is campaign manager—it's hardly a vote issue—but the press does. It becomes a story about the takeover of the presidency. So I called Ann Devroy and told her, "If campaign managers are out there giving speeches, I want to give the Carvillian view of the economy." She called the Bush people to get a response to my threat.

Almost immediately, Baker canceled his appointment at Harvard. After that, he never left the White House. Hell, I think personally, if

I was Jim Baker, the last person in the world I'd want to be compared to is James Carville. I'm sure Baker was a great secretary of the treasury, and he probably did have interesting things to say about the economy, but it was the President's job. George Bush sending a surrogate to make a major domestic speech just played directly into our hands; here's another example of George Bush not being involved in the domestic problems of America.

The media pushed the idea that Jim Baker stayed low the entire campaign because he was trying to distance himself from Bush and a losing effort. That is just plain stupid. It was the only thing he could do. If he'd have stuck his head up, we'd have shot it off. He made a totally rational political decision. Frankly, I think the man's a genius.

CHAPTER 18

Mary

I loved the people in the campaign—they were my family. I had had too many run-ins with the White House crowd and figured they didn't like me. Now I'm on Air Force One, I've got to be depressed with a bunch of people who hate me.

I'd been on the plane before, during the primaries, and I figured I was in for trouble. Their culture was to be tight-lipped and serious. Everyone had to be serious. They all looked the same to me: serious, serious, serious. Part of what they didn't like was the looseness of campaign culture, and I was the epitome of looseness. I believed it was a big part of my job to keep people loose, to make them laugh. Forget that horsing around was a very natural part of my personality, I did it because everyone was depressed all the time. We were down 10, 15, 20 points on any given day; we still were getting no traction; nothing was going right. People get more creative when they're looser. When people get depressed they quit doing their job, they just choke. I was bound and determined to loosen up the plane.

Although, you have to be careful about transplanting a campaign personality into a White House environment. Obviously, the decorum gets more highbrow as proximity to the President increases. I could have been more deferential. George Bush, Jr., told me that initially the White House women had been opposed to my getting the job as deputy campaign manager; they thought I was decorum-challenged.

I think we had a dress code problem, too. There is no dress code on campaigns, but the White House women weren't even allowed to wear pants suits. White House people dress for protocol, campaigners dress for convenience.

My convenience garb: one short black skirt with interchangeable blouses for dress-up events, and jeans for get-down campaign days, one all-weather jacket. Most days I wore men's ties to spunk up the otherwise repetitive outfits—which everyone made fun of until President Bush gave me a tie a supporter had given him.

The plane is run on a tight hierarchy, seating is power, and the first way the White House ostracized the campaign was to put the campaign's person—me—in the guest cabin. I didn't have contact; I could come up and sit on the arm of someone's chair but I was out of the loop. I needed to be with the speechwriter and the advance person and the White House political guy.

I blew a gasket, said, "I *have to* be in the staff cabin." I first bitched to Teeter, who called Margaret Tutwiler, who got it done.

Much to my amazement and delight, the atmosphere lightened. I think it was the difference between Skinner's White House crowd and the crew Jim Baker brought in. Not only did the Baker bunch understand how to work with the campaign, they knew how to play with us. Everyone started loosening up. People finally started wearing their cowboy boots and taking off their ties.

I thought Air Force One was going to be a palace, the White House of the air, and I was kind of excited to get my first look at it. Major disappointment. It's no work of art. It's decorated in hideous California PC decor, earth tones, wheat and gray. It was sterile, which maybe shouldn't have surprised me but did.

On the other hand, from the fully stocked kitchen to the state-of-the-art office equipment to the conference room with the big-screen TV and excellent stereo system, it sure was efficient and self-contained.

The first cabin, with two large side beds, a desk and chairs, TV and VCR, dressers and closets, belonged to the President. The next was the President's doctor's. Air Force One had a full hospital. I don't think any previous Air Force One had surgery facilities. (I wouldn't take that to mean President Bush was more concerned about his health than his predecessors were; Nancy Reagan built the plane.)

Then came the senior staff: National Security Adviser Brent Scowcroft, Marlin Fitzwater, James Baker, longtime Bush aide David Bates. Everything was very spacious. Then there was the kitchen. (I loved all the stewards; they were very good to me. They had a fully stocked bar and you could get them to make you anything you wanted to eat.) Then came a huge conference room with an always-polished conference table, a phone at every seat, the walls lined with couches.

Then came the senior junior staff, whom I called the kids. My room. We sat at work modules, pretty much staring each other in the face. Now how could you be distant when you're working at such close quarters?

Then came the White House photographers, then a total office setup with a high-speed copy machine, fax, and word processor. There were bathrooms every couple of feet, with every conceivable tidy-up device known to mankind. Then the cabin for guests and junior junior staff, then the Secret Service and then the media, who had their own hierarchy.

In the kids' cabin were my seatmate, White House political director Ron Kaufman; speechwriter Steve Provost; Christina Martin; advance people and military guys; and the head paper-pusher, assistant to the President and staff secretary Phil Brady, who had among the most demanding and critical White House jobs.

The guy who manipulated the paper manipulated the presidency. Darman held this post in the Reagan administration. When time permitted, Bush was pretty accessible; he'd send for the speechwriter or policy wonk to clarify a point he was studying. But in all events, any policy paper, speech, correspondence—any physical facet of the office of the President—was Brady's responsibility. If Bush didn't have everything he needed at any given moment, he beelined for Brady. Brady, appropriately, was completely anal-retentive, never without his briefcase, very much a lawyer, an unbelievable paper machine. President Bush was a stickler for details, and Phil Brady was his key link, so when the President would come down the aisle and keep going past us, we would all breathe a sigh of relief because we were off the hook and he was going to Phil.

The bespectacled Brady was always and forever going through his briefcase, nerdily working on his papers, and I took it as my personal task the struggle to distract him in the most annoying way possible. I would challenge him to eat three pieces of key lime pie, I'd have beers sent to him, I'd burst out singing really loud in his face. His unrelenting diligence just cracked me up.

Steve Provost was on my wavelength; things would strike him funny for the same no-reason. He was a perpetual college kid, always rumpled, ripping off his tie, forgetting his shirts, or pulling all-nighters. He was about thirty, looked kind of like Dennis the Menace at nineteen after a twenty-four-hour game of poker. He had, in a previous career, dressed up as Kentucky Fried Chicken's Colonel Sanders and crashed Elizabeth Taylor's wedding. After the last event each day, when the deadlines had all been met and there wasn't much work left to do, the stewards would bring me a glass of red wine and him a gin and tonic or a beer and we'd start singing the speeches or telling Bush jokes. Poor Phil would be sitting there, trying to concentrate, going, "You guys. You guys," and we'd do goofy things to try to get him to laugh.

Brady never thought I was stupid, but everybody on the plane thought I was kind of brash. One day he was sitting there trying to write something, eyes a little glazed, asking the air, "What's another word for, you know, 'explain' or 'shed light on'?"

I said, "How about 'illuminate'?"

"Wow! 'Illuminate'! What a great word. How could *you* think of that?"

"Phil, get a grip. I got all the way through high school. 'Illuminate,' it's a cool word."

He ran around telling the whole plane, "Mary Matalin came up with this word: 'illuminate'!"

Jeez, you guys, grip out.

Ron Kaufman and I had known each other for over a decade. He was a Massachusetts Jew who went from bagging groceries to presidential politics overnight. We had worked together in so many incarnations there wasn't a political person in the U.S.A. one of the two of us didn't know. Ron was one hundred percent political, which is to say pretty loose. I never wanted for a fellow prankster when Kaufman was around. A lot of the White House staff thought we were both sophomoric, but the reality was you need some levity in pressure-cooker campaigns. Ron and I only got depressed with each other. To everyone else we were the court jesters. And that plane needed some jesting. For most of the general we were 15 points down.

Bush liked to talk politics with Kaufman and me. Ron had all the gossip, and I was notorious for knowing too much about Clinton's every utterance, a result of the continuing Clinton Lie-a-Day fax research. Before the debates, President Bush asked me to come to the front cabin and watch videotapes of Clinton's speeches with him. Know thine enemy. I would sit there and make disparaging noises, tell the President, "He's lying right here," or "That's a flip-flop." I was always kind of spirited in my political loathing for Clinton, and Bush just thought I was funny.

James

In a lot of campaigns there's real bitterness between headquarters and the road. We didn't have anything like that. We were long-time partners, different cultures. But whenever the Road Warriors would come to town it would be disruptive. They would come to the War Room, they didn't have a desk, they didn't have phones, they were not in their element. When some of the War Room people had to go on the road with them, we had the same trouble, we were in somebody else's house. In the War Room everybody was everywhere, but on the plane who sat where meant a lot; if three people high on the War Room pecking order got on board, three Road Warriors had to go to the back of the plane. It made a difference. We didn't understand the way they did business, they didn't understand the way we did business; they didn't know our rituals and we didn't know theirs. As long as they were on the road and we were in the War Room, it was fine; otherwise we were all inconveniences to each other.

Inside the War Room the guy I spent the most time with was George. I had heard of him before the campaign but never really knew him. He and Paul worked for Congressman Gephardt, the Democratic majority leader, and I would always hear about how George ran the floor of the House of Representatives and brought bills up and understood the legislative process. Paul would tell me, "Oh, that's George, he's a Rhodes scholar, he's the smartest guy on the Hill, he knows where every body is buried in the House." At first, I never could remember what his last name was. Once I met him and we started to work together he became one of my closest friends ever and I found him to be just a spectacular person.

George's daddy is the dean of the Greek Orthodox church in New York City and I guess you can't grow up the son of a cleric and not have some of that rub off on you. He goes to Mass every Sunday, he's very cognizant of the holy days, he's got no sense of hubris. As much as anybody I know, George wishes people well. He's almost shy. I'd hate to think what would have happened if I'd been thirty-one and had the women available to me that he could have had available to him.

George, having worked for the majority leader, defined success as Getting It Through. That's how deliberative bodies work; you find a way. That was George. George knew every position we had, every issue, what we'd said in every interview. You could ask me a question on politics and I would know the answer, but you could ask me a question on policy—"Was that in the budget agreement of 1990?"—and I wouldn't have any idea. You could ask a policy person and he wouldn't know the politics of it. George would know it backward and forward. He was swinging from both sides of the plate. He had an unbelievable wealth of information, and he knew how Bill Clinton thought. George could read the governor as well as anybody, which was a tremendous asset.

His biggest strength was that Clinton trusted him. Time and time and time again, that was a huge strength. They hadn't known each other very long, but George had proved himself. I didn't ever talk to the candidate without talking to George first. Most every time I saw the candidate during the campaign, I was with George. I suspect that most times George saw Clinton, he was with me.

In the War Room, George always had too many phone calls to return. He was always slightly disheveled, and he had a strong grain of pessimism to him, as if disaster was just around the corner. I always thought he was very Catholic in that sense, which may be why I liked him so much. He'd always be saying, "There's a story going to come out that's going to bust this thing open." Or, "I don't like the way it feels out there." People would ask how we thought some piece of business was going to work, and they'd be told, "George is dark."

"Well," I'd say, "George is always dark. What the hell's new here?"

Any bad news, he would take it and magnify it. "The *L.A. Times* is working on something that's going to knock us out of the race." "Bush and those guys are going to do a spot that's going to knock us out of the race." It got to be a joke with us. We couldn't allow ourselves to get too far in front of ourselves, because this was too big a deal. "You mean we're going to win this thing? Naw. You can't even think of that. That's too big, it's too much to think about." So we would sit and have these conversations about how we were going to be the idiots of the world when we lost.

"You can survive it," he'd say, "I can't. I was head of the rapid-response team in the Dukakis campaign, and not only did we not respond rapidly, we never responded."

We'd work out elaborate scenarios. "We came back, we led by twenty points in the polls, and we're going to lose. We're going to be the standard of political ridicule in America."

"Yeah," I'd say, "I can feel it crumbling out there."

"You really mean that?"

"Man, I've seen it a thousand times."

Sometimes I'd do it just to torture him. "Man, you know, there's this one guy I was in the service with, he ain't never wrong on anything, and I talked to him and he told me he thought it was slipping a little bit out there."

He'd say, "I know. I feel the same thing myself."

But George would never act it out. He kept pushing forward. He stays focused, with greater intensity, than anyone I've ever known.

He's also outstandingly smart. He knows things. I can't tell you the number of times I'd read a reference I didn't understand in the paper and say, "What does this mean, George?" and he'd tell me. I never saw him where he didn't know. "I've forgotten, George, what was the Glorious Revolution?" "Re-explain this existentialism to me." "How do you spell . . . ?" It was sort of amazing to have your own encyclopedia that you didn't even have to open.

I'm nowhere near as religious as he is, but I'm a pretty good Roman Catholic, and every now and then we'd discuss life and morality and what you're doing. The kind of stuff that people have talked about in political campaigns since day one. Is there a righteous side? Can you employ less than righteous means to achieve a righteous goal? Things that were always coming up in the course of a campaign, things I had long since reconciled. We were like baseball players discussing whether or not to intentionally spike somebody.

Like, if there are two sides to a story and you're hitting your opponent, are you obligated to present the other side too? If we said, "As governor of Arkansas, Bill Clinton cut taxes forty-eight times," were we under an obligation to say that he raised them thirty-four times?

George would actually go morally along and say, "Maybe we ought to point that out."

I'd say, "To hell with it. Let them do that. We're going to say it this way."

Mandy Grunwald was another War Room figure. I first met her in the Wilkinson race in Kentucky in 1987. She was our lead media person, had a lot of creativity, and her spots were very clean and crisp. Even when I'd been in other races I'd call her to get her opinions and see what was going on.

Getting spots made and on the air is a huge job, and we would fight a lot. She could meet forever. She always wanted to sit and talk about options. "We could do this, or we could do that. But if we do this, then we've got to do that."

"Come on, man, just slow down. We ain't got to do any of that."

She was very disciplined. She had spots that had to get out at a certain time in order to air in thirty states, and she was always advocating to move things along. "I've got to have these decisions."

"Okay, let's do this."

"Well, if you do this, then you can't do that."

After a while when we'd see her coming we'd start up, "Hey, here comes Mandy. 'If we do this, then we got to do that. But if we do that, then we can't do this. . . .' "

We were good friends, so I could scream at her. "Look, goddammit, there's too many options here. You're driving me crazy with all of this."

"Well, if we don't do that, then we got to do this."

Mandy was insult-proof. She was as hardheaded as I was undisciplined. I could say, "I am sick of this shit. I don't want no more meetings. I can't concentrate no more. I don't want one more fucking option. You understand? Not another fucking option."

"But if we don't do this, then we've gotta do that."

Her attitude was "Look, I've got a job to do. I've got to get it done. If what it takes for me to get my job done is having you blowing up every twenty minutes, so what. We've got to get the job done. So when you get through blowing up, then come back."

The truth is that Mandy had the toughest job on the campaign. She worked with seven ad agencies and fifty media markets, and was responsible for spending somewhere between two thirds and three quarters of the campaign budget. After working with her for over seven years, in a variety of different circumstances, I can honestly say that I know of no one in the field of political advertising, Republican or Democrat, man or woman, who has her combination of talent and tenacity.

Mandy brought in Mike Donilon from Doak and Shrum. Mike had done the polling on the Wofford race with me and is easily the most underrated political strategist in the country. His desk was right next to mine in the War Room. Mandy would sometimes actually get irritated; Mike was totally unflappable. He would always bring the conversation back to, "Okay, that's good, we know all of that. But we've still got to ship a spot by five o'clock. Which one do we ship?"

The way the system worked, we strove for consensus. Me, Mandy, Stanley Greenberg, Donilon, Mickey Kantor, Eli Segal, David Wilhelm. And Clinton, he wasn't exactly a passive candidate. So many times I just got exhausted. "I can't make another decision. You-all got to do it. Just decide it. I'm for whatever anybody's for. I'm out. I'm thought out, I'm decisioned out, I just don't have it left in me."

When you're making a thirty-second spot there are five or six decisions you have to make. What voice do you use? What's the tag line? What's the content? We would argue over individual words. Whether to put "Read my lips" in a spot three times or two. When we're doing a spot on Bill Clinton's record as governor of Arkansas, do we mention welfare or not? Or do we put it in a separate spot? Thirty seconds is a very contained amount of time; you've got a lot you want to say; ads are expensive. The temptation is to load them up with everything you're about.

But the less you put in a spot, the more likely people will remember what you say. The more you put in, the more they'll hear but the less they'll remember. Also, the faster you speak, the more you can say; but the slower you speak, the more people will remember what you said. It's a constant conflict.

And what about the opening? And the visual. Do we make a spot on spending and taxes, or do we expand it to a job spot? Or do we do a spot that's a job spot *and* income-growth spot?

What do we have up now? What do the internals on the polls show vis-à-vis taxes and jobs? And what is Bush going to be hitting us on?

The easiest thing to do is put both jobs and taxes in the same spot. "We can do both."

"No, you can't do both. To do both is to do none. To do one is to do one."

"Oh, okay."

Then Hillary calls in and says, "Bill really thinks that we have to keep Bush on the defensive, and that all we do is respond." That was a big road criticism of the War Room early on. The candidate was talking to a friend of his from Yale who told him, "You're just being too nice to Bush. You've got to hit him. The whole campaign is good at responding, but it can't set its own agenda."

In our meeting we say, "We've got to talk the governor into this because he thinks we're just responding."

I kind of kept wanting to shoot the messenger but Mandy was very good at (a) aggravating the hell out of me, and (b) coming back and saying, "We've got X amount of time and money, what do you want to do? . . . I can do that, but if you want anybody to remember it, you've got to do it this way." That is the mark of a good media person. A bad one will let you roll them.

Stan Greenberg, our pollster, is probably the gutsiest person I ever worked with. He'll say "Good-bye." We had a big flap about a questionnaire that had been set and approved, and then people wanted to come back and change it. He said, "At two o'clock, if you have some changes you want to make, I'll try to make them if they're consistent with good methodology. If not, I'm gone."

Pollsters are in a very time-sensitive business. They've got to reserve a phone bank, train their workers, start making their interviews at a given hour, fax up the questions; someone has to go through the questions and then the answers. And if the thing doesn't start at two o'clock, he can't do it. Forget 2:01.

"James," he'd say, "last night I said we had to have a poll meeting, you said you couldn't go to it. This morning I handed you a questionnaire. At ten o'clock this morning I came back and said you had to make a decision. Now, I am sitting here with this whole phone bank reserved, and I'm not going to cancel it because you're too scatterbrained, after five requests, to look at the thing."

One of the ways our system worked was that we'd get things ironed out before we went to the candidate with them. We'd flush it out pretty hard. Greenberg, in particular, is very persuasive. But everybody was willing to concede something to present a united, confident front. There's nothing worse for a candidate than to have his campaign advisers in a big argument in front of him. If we had a big enough split we would acknowledge that we had an internal difference. "Well, governor, George and I think this but Stan and Mandy disagree with us." But that didn't happen often.

Another major personality in the campaign was Paul Begala, my partner. Paul spent very little time in the War Room; he was a supreme Road Warrior. Paul is the single most honest person I know. I think it bothers him that he takes a home mortgage tax deduction. People refer to me as a populist; I ain't close to Paul.

Nor do we think totally alike. His cultural values are much more conservative than mine, and his economic values are more in tune with what's good for the middle class. I think I have a pretty good sense of what middle-class people are thinking, I think I'm a pretty good defender of them, but I pale in comparison to Paul.

Paul always believed that the best way to define Clinton—better even than being the agent for change or getting the economy moving again—was as the champion of the middle class, the people who played by the rules and got left behind. He felt they always got the short end of the stick. What could be done to right that? In our meetings we'd say, "We've got to talk about the economy and trade, how we can get it to grow and expand." Paul's consistent theme was "But we've got to show how the middle class is always getting shafted and this is going to benefit them. Not just the people on the top and the bottom, but the folks in the middle." There were several message tracks in the campaign and this was most fervently Paul's. The images he evoked and heroes he used in his speeches for Clinton always came from and were aimed at middle-class people.

Paul can work harder, more creatively, and at more unbelievable speed under pressure than anybody I know. He can sit at a word processor and write a speech or a statement, or do research at one-thirty in the morning with twenty people around him and a national audience only a couple of hours away. He writes the words you want to hear. The guy is incredible.

CHAPTER 19

Mary

When *Newsweek*'s Howard Fineman called me at six o'clock Friday night I knew something was up. The newsmagazines' deadline is Friday at noon. If one of their reporters calls you a minute later, something's breaking.

He said, "Bush is going to rip Clinton's face off on the draft issue." Or words to that effect.

President Bush was scheduled to address the convention of the National Guard Association in Salt Lake City the following Tuesday. The subject of Bill Clinton's draft status might be expected to arise.

I told him, "No, he isn't."

Up to that point the President had not directly attacked Governor Clinton on his draft record or his attempt to cover it up. The campaign had gone after him, and it was beginning to pay off. Polls showed that Clinton was being hurt by the issue—not by his refusal to go into the military, but by his lying about the circumstances. Carville was right: It was not a draft problem, it was a Slick Willie problem.

Insiders, pundits, and the media in general were saying that if we didn't keep the issue alive, we'd lose it. It was the one issue that really drove the Slick Willie negative. Here's another cardinal rule: If you want to mount the most effective attack, forget surrogates; get the candidate to do it. A lot of people in the campaign were advising—urging—President Bush to go out to Utah and bash Clinton.

I thought it was a really bad idea. I thought it was beneath him. I also thought, even if he was going to attack Clinton, it was bad tactics for us to telegraph it. Some speeches, like the Agenda for American Renewal, you want to build up. Others, built up, do not meet expectations. If President Bush was going to slash Governor Clinton, I certainly didn't want to diminish the effect. Let them wonder.

I didn't know what the President's plans were, but I denied the story for both reasons.

Maybe they'd been hashing it over in campaign headquarters, but I was on the plane now. So much of what goes on in campaigns doesn't actually happen in meetings, you absorb it, and I was out of their osmotic circle. I thought, "I can't believe these guys actually think Bush would do this." But sure enough, the next day in *The Washington Post* there were all these anonymous White House sources saying, "Get ready for Salt Lake City."

I got on the plane the next morning and the President called me forward to his cabin for his normal political briefing. "What's happening on the ground? What's going on?"

"The press thinks you're going to go lowlife and attack Clinton in Utah."

"I haven't decided what I'm going to do in Utah," he said. "Why are they saying that?" I told him about Fineman's prediction. He had seen *The Washington Post*.

"Who said that? What's the matter with you people? I haven't decided what I'm going to do. What's the campaign's thinking on this?"

"I don't know," I said. "Let's call Teeter."

"What do *you* think?"

"This is your audience; be spellbinding. You're the commander in chief, you don't need to do this."

The President was upset that a course of action had been laid out in the press when he wasn't certain which way he wanted to go. He called Teeter and Baker, who said they were working on an "intellectual" speech about service and country that would also draw some Arkansas blood. So we had a two-day running debate in which we on the plane were saying, "Don't do it," and they on the ground were saying, "Do it."

While it hadn't been decided what direction the speech would take, we weren't letting the press or the Clintonistas know we were conflicted. On Monday, still undecided, we put out the word that we were, indeed, going to rip Clinton's face off. We wanted Clinton to get all hyped up and write a response speech. That worked. The press was telling us, "He's ready, he's not going to take it, he's going to give it right back."

Good. In that case he's got to come to Utah.

There was no reason in the world for Bill Clinton to be in Utah. It was our number one state. Every time new poll numbers came in we'd get an updated electoral map, and Utah was consistently number one, for many weeks one of only about ten we were winning. If Clinton didn't think Bush was going to bash him, he wouldn't have gone there to defend himself. And in anticipating the showdown for four days preceding the event, the press re-raised the draft problem repeatedly. Pick up any paper and you'd find lumped together the words "Clinton," "draft," "evasion," "confusion," "Slick Willie." That was another part of my argument: We didn't have to get ugly because the press was going to regurgitate the whole story all the way through the event. The tension was a great story, and it kept feeding on itself.

Steve Provost, speechwriter and my comrade in crime, agreed with me. He worked with the President to craft the non-attack remarks Bush would deliver to the National Guard. But when we got the ground's prepared text, the night before the Utah convention, it really was a masterpiece. After a full day's campaigning, we were all mainlining caffeine, huddled in a hotel hospitality suite over the one copy. Provost was either moved or sleep-deprived. "I like this speech," he said. "I've changed my mind."

"You cannot change your mind." It was two o'clock in the morning; the President was doing this event at nine. "We're not going to rewrite the speech. We're going to give the speech that you wrote."

"I'm going to incorporate this."

"No, you're not."

Now both the D.C. campaign and the White House were saying, "Do it." The President didn't want to, and Provost was the man in the middle. He had to read his reconstructed speech back to the White House. First he pretended he couldn't find a phone, which is impossible, there's a White House phone drop every three feet anywhere the President goes. Then, knowing his fate would be death or worse if he didn't, he got on with D.C. and was being persuaded that going negative was the way to go.

It wasn't only that I thought I was right; if this had been just any attack, I would have been wrong. I wasn't. I knew what Bush was thinking. We had discussed it often. His concept of the commander in chief is a very lofty one. His handlers were telling him to politicize the issue, but he felt that would undermine the dignity of the office. There is also a unique chemistry among military service people; Bush respected the National Guard and didn't want to use them as props for a political ploy.

He did not want to do it. Another cardinal rule, which applied especially to Bush: If your guy isn't doing something like this from the heart, it ain't gonna work.

Plus I happened to think he was right. Plus Provost had written a beautiful speech. Plus Bush had had a big hand in the speech. And the biggest plus: The damage had already been done; Clinton's ham-handed response had kicked the story all week.

Before dawn, the President called Provost to his room. Provost, of course, had stayed up all night. He was a wreck, as always; his hair was sticking up, he'd got his shirt buttoned wrong. And they went over the speech. No one knew what Bush was going to do. He had two speeches.

We motorcaded to the convention center. There were extra people on this trip, and in the holding room they were all trying to get face time with the President. Right before he went onstage, he motioned across the room. "Mary, come over here." He had his speech in his hand.

"What are you going to do, sir?"

He gave me a mischievous smile. "Don't you ever think I don't listen to you." He walked out and gave the non-attack speech.

I was so proud of him. Against the advice of every handler and pundit, President Bush had done what he wanted to do. And it was a spectacularly moving speech.

Clinton was forty minutes late. Photographers caught him sitting in his limousine in the garage at the event, doing a rewrite, taking out his counterattack. He ended up giving the same speech he had given to the American Legion in Chicago.

This was a big victory. The press had been lying in wait, they were going to trash our butt big-time for going lowlife. Now they couldn't do anything but report our smashing success, taking the high ground in front of a very receptive pro-Bush crowd. We disrupted Clinton's schedule, we jizzed them up, we wasted their time and got their entire campaign off message for four days solid. It was the coolest strategic fake-out we did in the entire election.

After having revved up the press—they were going to stand up to Bush—the previously macho Clintonistas pooh-poohed the whole thing. Though we both knew the event mattered little to the general populace, we knew and they knew we knew, they'd been tied up and strung out for four days. A little psychological warfare goes a long way. We'd got them, we'd sucked them in.

James

It was a huge chess game, a grand chase, a thirty-phone-call, minute-by-minute day that only amounted to four votes. If we didn't make an appearance, he'd go and say we were backing down. The National Guard people were calling. Clinton had a pretty good record with the National Guard in Arkansas, so they were saying we should go. So we went.

Bush didn't attack us; we didn't attack Bush. It was one of those standoff dates. I suspect they felt like, "We got him out in Utah when he could have been in California or Oregon." They probably viewed that as sort of a success. We were telling ourselves, "Well, he didn't attack us because we were there to defend ourselves. If we wouldn't have gone they'd have said, 'He didn't show up here and he didn't show up in Vietnam and he won't show up for the economy.' " Cost us a day or so.

I'd rather talk about Chicken George.

When Bush refused to debate us, a campaign worker in Michigan named Derrick Parker dressed up in a chicken outfit—yellow feathers, big beak, webbed feet—and heckled him at one of his events. "George Bush is chicken to debate." He was wearing a sign that said "Chicken George." I'd been saying, "We've got to get somebody out to really give them hell," now here he was. Chicken George was born.

The idea took off. Chicken George was kind of like Santa Claus. There's a Sears Santa Claus, a Macy's Santa Claus, a JCPenney Santa Claus; well, there was a Michigan Chicken George, a Mississippi Chicken George, a Tennessee Chicken George. At first we recruited them, but real soon all the local people wanted to do it. Everybody wanted to be Chicken George. It was the way to get on TV. At War Room meetings we'd get a Chicken George report.

It had to be embarrassing for the President of the United States to be compared to a chicken. I know it got us a lot of great bites on the news. The cameras showed the President and a chicken, the viewers got the message. We never gave the Chicken talking points; Chicken George wasn't audio, he was strictly video.

Finally, the Republicans started to clamp down. In Mississippi, a Chicken George got arrested. In Shreveport, Louisiana, they weren't going to let our guy through, but he showed them a sign, "Poultry Workers for Bush," and got in. Once inside he turned it around and it said, "Chicken George."

What I never understood was why George Bush kept talking to the chicken.

Mary

Our first response, in the cocoon of the ground campaign, was that it was pretty damn funny. I didn't think the prank was going anywhere, but nonetheless I reported in to Carney in D.C., "We're being stalked by this chicken."

And it is true, George Bush did love that chicken. He thought it was hilarious. He'd find the chicken in the crowd—"Where's that chicken?" he'd bellow—and he'd tell fish jokes to the chicken. He had a whole arsenal of original fish jokes that he'd made up about Clinton's environmental record: "It's so bad in Arkansas, the fish have to walk on water"; "The environment's so bad in Arkansas that the fish glow in the dark"; "The baby fish can find the mama fish because they're glowing in the dark."

The cue, in his mind, for Bush to tell the fish jokes was the presence of the chicken. That evolved into his sending advance guys out into the crowd to see where the chicken was so he could specifically address the chicken. To us on the road it was an absolute riot. I'd always make sure I was standing next to Steve Provost, whose Elvis jokes were routinely rejected, and say, "Let's see what fish joke is going to beat you today." We'd all mill around and wait and then give the President high fives when he came off. "Great fish joke!"

It was bound to happen. Sooner rather than later, President Bush's conversations with the chicken ended up on CNN.

Teeter called me on the plane. I was making my endless argument, which everyone was ignoring, which was "We have to debate."

"Well, we don't have any data that say we have to debate," he told me, "but we have to stop talking to that chicken. Tell the President to stop talking to the chicken."

"Why?"

"It's all over CNN. The President of the United States is talking to a chicken."

"But it's working out here." It was. "The President and the Chicken" was a real crowd-pleaser at the events, the President was getting the best of the exchange, and the chicken ended up embarrassed and slinking away. (Which wasn't easy, since the chicken was as big as Jabba the Hutt.)

Here's the difference between the plane and headquarters. People on the plane knew it was George Bush's hook to the audience; the crowd would make fun of the chicken and love the President. The press missed the good humor, or chose not to mention it, and covered the event as "George Bush is losing it." It didn't feel as adolescent while he was doing it as it appeared after the fact. Headquarters only read the papers and watched the news.

"I don't care," Teeter told me. "It's not working on TV, and it's stepping on our story, and he's got to stop talking to the chicken."

"With all due respect, I am reluctant to tell the President of the United States to stop talking to this chicken. He likes it; the crowd loves it. And if we'd announce our debate plan we wouldn't have this chicken problem."

We were in the middle of a presidential campaign, we were 13 points down, and Bob Teeter was all atwitter because we've got to beat this chicken. We were discussing it seriously but we both just had to laugh. When you're 13 points down you have to find events like this to laugh at.

Stud Muffin Carney was Weird Events Central. I would only report the need for a weird event and he would somehow get it done. Because the Democrats refused to come to the bargaining table and negotiate the time, place, and format of the debates, we were accusing Clinton of being chicken. Ours was a more circuitous argument than theirs, but the wildlife concept was the same. What did we care about his overstuffed fake fowl? We had our own silly pet tricks. For instance, at one event where Clinton had lost his voice and Hillary was about to fill in for him, we released a bunch of live ducks that waddled across the stage. They were waddling and squawking like crazy, and our supporters were prodding them on with duck calls. Our point, of course: Clinton had ducked the draft.

Clinton got really ticked off, stormed off the stage, and yelled at his advance guys for allowing such a scene. It was a big local story. All these ducks were loose and then the Clinton people in the crowd started beating up our people with the duck calls.

So a few days after Teeter's entreaty, Carney called me on Air Force One. "You're not going to believe this. I've got my Clinton's-chicken-to-debate event all set. I've got two hundred live chickens ready to go in Madison, Wisconsin, and Teeter just called me from Baker's office and said, 'Do you have the chickens?' I said, 'Yes.' 'Well, we want ducks.'

" 'I don't have ducks. I have chickens.' "

" 'We don't want chickens. We want ducks.' "

This was chairman of the campaign Bob Teeter calling Mr. Weird Events from White House Chief of Staff Jim Baker's office. Carney could hear Baker in the background, going, "We want ducks."

It was now an hour before the event. "What am I going to do?" Carney whined. "I've got chickens and they want ducks."

"Call Janet Mullins. I can't believe Teeter and Baker are sitting in there arguing over chickens and ducks."

So Carney called Mullins. Then I called Mullins. She said, "No, it's true, we want ducks."

"We got chickens!"

"Well, you're just going to have to get ducks."

"We can't let these chickens go loose in Madison, Wisconsin, the bastion of liberalism. We'll get an ASPCA rap."

Carney improvised. He sent our guy on the ground to the local sporting goods store for duck calls. We released chickens, but over the sound of two hundred duck calls, who could tell?

Teeter thought he was so cute. He called the same day. "If the President won't stop talking to the chicken, we've got our own strategy."

"What is it?"

"I'm not going to tell you."

"Does it involve Carney?"

"Yes."

"I know what it is. You're going to get ducks."

"How did you know that?"

In subsequent conversations about the need to debate, I did say to the President, "And, sir, the campaign is concerned that there is footage running of our talking to the chicken."

He just started laughing. "I love that chicken!"

"It is my job to inform you that the press is making much ado about our talking to the chicken."

He was the President, he could do what he wanted. He did not stop talking to the chicken.

James

He could keep on talking to the chicken. In fact, as far as we were concerned, he could just keep on talking. They kept denying the obvious, that the economy was the issue. As long as they were insisting that everything was all right, we were all right.

We hit them with the first negative ad, President Bush saying three different ways that things were just fine, with the tag line "If George Bush doesn't understand the problem, how can he solve it? We can't afford four more years."

Three days later they slapped back with a negative ad on Clinton's Arkansas record. No one likes being under fire, but having a negative ad up against you is, in a way, fun. They're attacking us. It's like you're in a submarine and the alarm sounds and everybody runs to their battle stations.

"Hey, Bush has got a negative spot up. Stand by. It's on the Arkansas thing. Get to the Arkansas record people. Stand by over there. Somebody be sure that we got the fax machines cleared. Get me my call list for the reporters. Somebody find the governor on the road so they hear it from us first." There's a protocol.

"Why can't we get a copy of it? Somebody please, *please*, get on the phone, see if they can satellite the thing, see if they can ship it down. See if we can get a script faxed down here, at least. Get somebody to describe the spot, people. Let's move, let's move, let's move here. Somebody get our satellite people, see if we can pick this thing up. What state's it running in? Get me a copy of the spot."

It's on Memphis TV. "Can we get somebody down there to tape the spot on Memphis TV, get it up here? Is it a national buy? Find out something. Quickly, quickly. Come on, let's go, let's go, let's go over there. See if we can find something wrong. Let's try to blow a hole in there. Will somebody get moving, please, please.

"Where's my call list? Where's Mandy? Find her, somebody, if it's not too much trouble. Think we can get 'em, huh, quickly? What states is it on?"

"We don't know yet."

"How could we not know? Somebody find out. Please, please, please, please."

Everybody is scurrying. "Where's the fucking spot? I know it's a tax spot. What taxes? What does it say? Don't give me that shit, that's not any good. We're coming up against a deadline. George, are the nets going to do anything with this? Is he going to get some free god-damn airtime off of this goofy spot?"

Somebody tells me, "The satellite people are picking it up now, they'll have it for you in just a second. They'll be in George's office, James. Calm down, calm down, we're moving as fast as we can."

Then you get it and you look at it.

Mandy had worked with a firm called Sawyer/Miller, and Scott Miller did the Mean Joe Greene Coke commercial that made every-body cry. I asked him, "What's it like when you do a spot for Coke, when you show it to them?" Thinking that they had all this sophisti-cated marketing wizardry. He said, "You show it to the president of the company and he calls his secretary in and asks her what she thinks." It's a little like that in a presidential campaign. Somebody's walking by and you say, "Excuse me, look at this spot. What do you think about that?" It's not real scientific.

"Is Celinda doing focus groups? Stan, where are we tonight? We're in what, Denver? Okay, can we get the spot to Denver? Let's show it, see what we're doing. What've we got, college-educated women, men, what? How soon can we get something up?"

Sometimes you can satellite it from one place to another. Other times you just put a cassette on a plane.

"Call somebody in the field. Have the Denver people go to the air-port. Stand by, right there, okay? When it comes off the plane, get it from the airline, then take it to this address. No, I'll tell you what. Go downstairs, get Simon Rosenberg, tell him to come up here to my desk. Right now. This minute. Got that? Get him, I want him right here."

Simon shows up. He runs state operations. "Okay. Simon, this is what I want you to do. I'm gonna put this in your hand. I want *you* to go take it to the airport. I want *you* to call the best person we got in Colorado. I don't care if it's the campaign manager. I want *them* to go to the airport. I don't want them to send somebody, I want *them* to go to the airport and I want them to take it to *this* address and I want them to put it in Geoff Garin's hand. You got that?

"And I want to know, at every point, *when* this is happening and *who* is doing it. Because if it doesn't fuckin' get there and they don't see this fuckin' spot, it's going to be your fucking ass, you understand? *You*. Personally. If that thing doesn't get there, if that plane is late, it's gonna be your fault. If there's a thunderstorm, it's your fault. If that fucking thing crashes, it's your fault. Okay? You got that? Now go do it. Get out of my sight and then come back and tell me when I know it's there."

That's the way campaign people talk. If you don't, you get excuses. "Oh, I told somebody to do that." Or the guy they sent got lost. "James, it was a volunteer that really wasn't from Denver. Went to Haverford. He was from Ohio and he got in rush-hour traffic and couldn't find the focus group place. They wouldn't let him in the building. It was on the wrong floor." All of these things go wrong. You say, "Meet me at the Denver airport." Well, *where* at the Denver airport? The Denver airport is bigger than half the cities in the United States. If you want something done you've got to take your best people and do it right. If you don't do it with repetitiveness, specificity, simplicity, it just ain't gonna get done.

All that day you're trying to find more information. You trust your instincts only so much; then you want to verify. Campaigns do not like to answer these spots because we're up in rotation, we don't want to take down one of ours to answer it; but we don't want to leave one of theirs up that can hurt us.

Then there's Mandy on the phone with options. "I understand that. If we choose to answer this spot I have to know by . . ." And "If we don't do this, then we can do that."

"How much is it going to cost to answer the damn thing, Mandy? What, three grand? Let's answer the spot like this. Talk to Stan, he said this is the best answer. Get the thing done. We don't have to ship the goddamn thing until we see what the research says, until we get a better sense, until we talk to Clinton about it. Okay? Just go make the spot."

"But if we do that, we gotta do this. If we do this, we gotta do that."

I can't take another option. "George, talk to her. I can't go no more. I can't come to another fork in the road."

So you make the spot and you want to test the answer.

Campaign research is like firecrackers on the Fourth of July; it can be nice, it can be entertaining, it can blow up in your face, and you've got to be a pyrotechnician to fool with it. You've got ten or twelve people in a focus group, and one likes a welfare spot, another one likes an economy spot, one more likes an attack spot. They grade them. One gets a 7.5 and one gets a 7.3. Well, gee, let's do the one with the 7.5. It becomes the tyranny of the focus group. But groups change, we're all over the place and we're out of message all the time. That's why you have the sign on the War Room wall.

If they made a rule outlawing focus groups, I would be happy.

How do you know whether to answer a negative spot or not? The elites and the media say, "Why doesn't the candidate just go out and say what he thinks, and to hell with all of this?" Well, your opponent, who's trying to politically eviscerate you, has a charge up. Do you let the charge go? Is that their idea of brilliant politics? That's exactly what they all attacked Dukakis for doing. Said he was inept. That sort of stupid drivel is enough to make you puke.

CHAPTER 20

James

The Republicans were probably sent running to their battle stations when all this Iran-Contra stuff started to come out in mid-September. Bush had said continually that he was out of the loop on the arms-for-hostages deal, but here was General Richard Secord saying Bush was in the loop, and NSC aide Howard Teicher saying he told Bush in 1986 that the U.S. was trading with Iran, arms for hostages. I had a debate appearance on TV with Lynn Martin and said, "Madam Secretary, there ain't five people in the country outside the Bush administration think George Bush is telling the truth that he didn't know what was going on there." I don't think there is a sane person in America, that wasn't paid by George Bush, who doesn't think he knew it was an arms-for-hostages deal.

I think I clearly know what happened with Clinton and the draft. I think I clearly know what happened to Bush in Iran-Contra. Clinton was against the war, he didn't want to go, and he used the means at his disposal to stay out. I think Iran-Contra is very simple. Bush was told what happened. He was probably doing ten other things and didn't think about it very much, but clearly he knew what was going on, acquiesced in it, and went on to another meeting. That was in 1986, he was probably trying to put a presidential campaign together. Somebody asked him about it and he said, Well, I'll just deny it. That set in motion an untenable position that he couldn't back off. "That's my story and I'm sticking to it." And people knew that he knew. It's the old example of, If the first step of the equation is wrong, then no matter how good you are later on, you're always going to come up with the wrong answer. Bush had the wrong answer from the start.

I think he was lying to protect his own man, President Reagan, which is not the most unusual thing that ever happened in politics.

Reagan's friends did a really good job of spinning him, that he was so naïve, he just wanted to believe that it wasn't true, ergo it wasn't true. That's a nice one, I always loved that. Fact is, there's no rational explanation other than that they engaged in bad policy and lied about it. They violated something we said we wouldn't do—we wouldn't trade arms for hostages—and then they covered it up. You think the draft was the story from hell; the Iran-Contra scandal had been dogging Bush since 1986.

But my view was that the American people didn't want an election about Iran-Contra or about the draft; they were interested in paying their bills. Iran-Contra was a godsend only because every time the Republicans would bring up the draft they would get Iran-Contra right back in their face. And by a huge margin, more people thought Bush was not telling the truth than that Clinton was not being candid.

The next day *Time* magazine came out with a poll: 40 percent of the people thought that Clinton was lying about the draft, 37 percent thought he was not lying; 63 percent thought Bush was lying, 22 percent thought he was not lying. I rest my case.

Mary

That's more Carville spin, and the Clintonistas got no traction with it. We laughed every time they used Iran-Contra as a draft defense. It came out as another limp, evasive, "Slick Willie" answer. The public discounts issues they've already thought through, and they were done with this one. Yes, Bush was required to respond to the charges, but even the press was tired of it by then.

Iran-Contra had been a dog in the '88 campaign, but Bush handled it deftly and got a big boost when he defended himself against an aggressive interview by Dan Rather. In the fullness of time he had complied with every request for material, given countless interviews, and negated the issue. Lee Atwater used to say, "People's capacity to focus on politics is about the depth and breadth of their thumbnail." This election was about the economy; Iran-Contra was an old story. Bush never did change his story: He was out of the loop. The Democrats were dreaming if they thought this was in any way a defense to their incredibly changing draft dodge.

Late in a campaign, to maximize your coverage and save money, you usually take the President only to major media markets. Fly in, land Air Force One, walk onto the tarmac, hold a rally in a hangar right there or motorcade to the nearest gymnasium, then retrace your steps, get back on the plane, and go somewhere else and do it all over again. It shows up that night on TV across the region.

That's the most effective tactic, but there are drawbacks. First, those trips get old fast. After a while they weren't inspirational to the President, and they didn't mean as much as they might to the towns you visited. The decision was made to try something different: an old-timey train trip.

In late September, with us down by about 14 points in the polls, we embarked on a two-day train trip through Ohio and Michigan and at every stop took after Clinton on taxes. The train adventure was Margaret Tutwiler's idea and she brought on additional advance people with "train experience." We'd pull into small-town stations and there'd be cheerleaders and bands and local dignitaries and *thousands* of citizens. It was personal politics, a throwback to Harry Truman's whistle stops. Bush was at his best, every stop a home run. I can't remember getting any good stories or TV coverage of these fabulous events.

It's all in the way the press covers you. When Clinton and Gore jumped into an RV and toured suburbia the media could have said, "In a highly choreographed, tacky, phoney-baloney, doughnut-ridden cross-country bus trip . . ." But, no, they chose to portray it as Bill and Al's Excellent Adventure. When we got on board they could have said, "In a trip recalling the historic roots of the American political tradition, President Bush rode by rail through small towns and big cities, meeting thousands of cheering voters and bringing his message of . . ." But, no. Instead, the press kept asking, "Why did you avoid Toledo?"

Okay, this was too much. "Are you people crazy? We're on a T-R-A-I-N. We're following the *tracks*. What do you want us to do, stop at the station before Toledo and walk?" They had it in their heads that for some nefarious reason we were blowing off a major Ohio city, and they didn't want to be bothered with the fact that the tracks didn't go there.

The trip was designed to be a showcase of Americana, and it was. We didn't stop at every crossroads, but we did pull into towns that had never seen a President. If the advance guys hadn't knocked on everybody's door, they had let people along the route know that the President was coming, and folks turned out with handmade signs and posters mixed in with the ones the advance guys had mass-produced.

We'd pull into the station and the whole town would turn out, and President Bush would speak from the back of the train with one of these wireless microphones that looked like some kind of karaoke implement. He'd deliver an excellent speech about taxes, and people would cheer and the bands would play, and then the train would roll on for an hour or so and we'd stop at another town and do it all again, about six a day. Each night there would be a huge fireworks display. It was like an endless string of Fourth of July events.

The President loved the train. There wasn't much to do between stops—the phones on the train were difficult to use—so we'd sit there and rock along and stare out the windows at this beautiful country.

The President always stayed outside on the platform of the caboose as the train was rolling through the countryside. People whose homes backed onto the tracks would stand in their yards, waiting and waving. I rode between cars and would wave and point to the back of the train. "He's back there!" Some held signs—"Women for Bush," "Willie is Slick." Some brought out their kids for a look. He'd be standing there with his microphone. "Hey, how're you doing?" People would jump back, shocked that the President was talking to them from the back of a speeding train. I was concerned because the President was getting sick and losing his voice, but he wouldn't come in. He felt the people would be disappointed if they were standing there and missed him.

He called me into the back car, had something he wanted to tell me. "I've been mooned, I've been mooned!"

"Oh, my God."

He thought this was incredibly funny. "Yes, an entire family. Mother, father, and the children. Can you imagine?" We got into a big conversation about what kind of parents would let their children moon anybody, let alone the President of the United States. I was aghast, he was laughing away.

He stayed out there. It was raining. I said, "Please come in." He said, "No. We will never come this way again. They may never see a President again in their lives. That's what this country is about."

We were sitting in a station waiting for the press to file. The President was on one side of the train, looking at the handmade signs, I was on the other, looking at the crowd.

I said, "Look at these people." We were out in the country and there was a group of eleven guys with farmer tans, totally grubby, you could tell they'd just got off work; filthy hands, filthy, faded blue work clothes, blue baseball caps; some of them with no teeth. "This is great."

"Bring 'em on up here," he said. "Let's get a picture with them."

President Bush brought them all in and had their pictures taken with him one at a time.

Of course, their reaction was total shock and deference. They had come out to see a President. To meet him was impossible; to have their picture taken with him was the farthest thing from their minds. The first guys just stood there, kind of quaking, having their picture taken. But one by one they got bolder and by the end of the line one asked respectfully, "Why did you raise our taxes?" Another said, "I don't like that Clinton guy, there," and another, "That Perot, he's got something to say."

It was so cool to watch these people loosen up and say whatever they wanted to say to a President. We sat around and guffawed with them for a while. I loved it, and President Bush loved it too.

I don't want to sound too patriotic and geeky, and the President didn't sit around and get goofy about it, but he really did appreciate this trip and loved this kind of campaigning. It was one of those times when the insider's take-it-for-granted cynicism got dissipated and I really, truly got a sense of what people feel about their President. Not just George Bush. What it means—to the people and to the man—to be President of the United States.

James

Clinton liked retail campaigning. One of the reasons he was always behind schedule was that after each rally he would stay and shake hands and talk to people. He felt, with some justification, that pressing the flesh had helped turn it around in the New Hampshire primary. Now, of course, you're not going to shake every hand in America, but he's the kind of guy who, if you wait a long time to see him, figures he owes you a handshake and a pat on the back.

A lot of politicians, after they give their stump speech, want to go on to the next stop. That will back up on you. If you're not a good retail politician, the press will write stories about how people stayed out for hours to hear you, you were late, you gave a speech and left them there. They'll go interview people in the crowd who'll tell them, "Gee, that guy was kind of a bum. We drove fifty miles to see him and waited in the rain for three hours, and he never came by and said hello or thank you." That was never going to happen to Bill Clinton.

For some reason the War Room was getting sort of lethargic. I couldn't put my finger on it, but staff morale was slipping just a little bit. I pulled out a $100 bill and said to Meeghan Prunty, one of the more visible War Room twentysomethings, "I'll make a deal with you. I'll give you a hundred dollars if you let me crack three eggs over your head." I took the bill out in front of everybody. "See this? A crisp hundred-dollar bill." She said, "Oh, okay."

Seventy people in the War Room started to gather around. "No," she said, "I don't want to do it. You're up to something."

"What could I be up to?"

"Nope. I don't want to do it."

So Gene Sperling, who had a sense that there was a guffaw here, said, "Okay, I'll do it."

Here you had the chief economic adviser and the chief strategist, and somebody went down to the store and brought back a dozen eggs.

I told the assembled multitude, "I am going to crack three eggs on Gene's head." I took the first egg and . . . *thwack* . . . there was egg going all down Gene's head, down his neck, and people were howling and screaming.

"Y'all understand the deal here. When I crack three eggs he gets a hundred bucks. I've already cracked one."

So I cracked the second egg. *Thwack*. There's slimy whites and yolk following down where the first one hit. I took the $100 bill and said, "Okay. When I crack one more egg this is Gene's hundred-dollar bill." I paused.

"You know, it's a kind of perverted guy that would give up a hundred bucks just to crack three eggs. But you know something? I just don't feel like cracking that third egg."

Everybody started screaming.

"But I'll tell you what I'll do. I'll let Gene crack two over my head."

So Sperling cracked two eggs over my head and we all kind of got picked up.

I've done that more than once and I've had people almost want to fight me when I've done it to them. But campaigns need rituals and moments, and that's always one that works well and is fun.

You did what you could to avoid the bunker mentality, because that's a dangerous feeling, but you spent so much time in the same room with people that sometimes nothing else mattered.

Very central to what the War Room was about was that you constantly monitored what was happening so you could immediately respond. One day Danny Reich—a college kid, a War Room regular—missed something big. Bush had a press conference on the issue and we didn't get in the story. Danny Reich really fucked up. I went ballistic.

"How could this not happen? We're spending all this money, we have this whole thing geared up, this is one of the main reasons that we're here is to have instant access to information, and you're not there." I was screaming.

The next morning at the War Room meeting I told Danny in front of everybody, "You no longer have a name. From now on you're just 'you.' You let everybody down. Everybody who wants change in this country isn't going to get it because you are just a fuck-up. You're a nothing fuck-up, you ain't got a name."

I was merciless on him. Every time something came up I would single him out and berate him. I refused to call him Danny. "Where's that fuck-up, that sack of shit? What's he doing now, that worthless waste of skin?"

People came to me and said, "Don't you think you're being a little tough on this guy?"

"Ah, he'll make it. But, you know, he fucked up bad."

That night we were in Doe's restaurant and I saw the kid there, eating with some of his friends. I said, as I passed by, "Well that's good, you got time to eat supper. The whole goddamn campaign's falling apart while you're supposed to be monitoring the news."

George, who was there with me, said, "You ought to lay off the guy. The Jewish holiday was the reason he wasn't at work."

"Are you kidding me?"

"That's it."

It was Rosh Hashanah.

"Jeez. And the kid never used it as an excuse."

I felt just awful. Terrible. The next morning I said, "Come here." He walked to my desk. "Why didn't you tell me that you weren't at work that day, it was a religious holiday for you?"

He said, "I figured it was my responsibility, and that if I took a religious holiday I had to see that my replacement knew what to do. He didn't know what to do, so I figured it was my fault. I thought you were hard on me, but I didn't want to make an excuse."

I said, "Danny, in the pantheon of Carville campaign heroes, you have an exalted place."

A week later it was Yom Kippur. We had a War Room meeting that morning. I said, "Look, if there's one thing that Clintonism and Bill Clinton is about, that is 'Don't disrespect or dishonor your traditions.' If there's anybody here that I catch working that would normally take a holiday off, I will fire you. If I am told that you normally take the holiday off and you're here working, I will fire you. Now, if you're a heathen like Stan or Mandy, that's different. If you've always been a heathen, you can stay a heathen. But if you've never been one, you ain't gonna start now."

Sara Ehrman is the Jewish grandmother of American politics. Her legend extends beyond my little community. She said, "You know, James, I've been working in campaigns for thirty years and this is the first time that I've ever heard a campaign manager tell people they ought to take off for the holidays." I didn't tell Sara that one of the reasons I did this was I was mortified that I had taken this kid's head off. To this day she probably thinks I'm the most respectful campaign person toward Judaism in America.

I'm not saying that I wouldn't have done the same thing without prodding, but I was really panic-stricken that somebody's mother would call and find out that their kid hadn't taken off for the Day of Atonement.

"Why? You've never missed it in your life."

"I was scared that James Carville would bite my head off."

I had this vision that I would be some kind of impediment to people's religion. And think, if they'd found out about it, what the media would have done with that one.

I wrote Danny Reich a glowing letter of recommendation to Yale Medical School. And I'm sure that Sara Ehrman is out there telling people, "That Carville's a real mensch."

CHAPTER 21
_____

James

On September 28, the giant sucking sound you heard was Ross Perot drawing all of our people and all of Bush's people down to Dallas to kiss his ass.

Perot had said he didn't know if he was going to run, so he was going to let representatives from both campaigns come and meet with the volunteer state coordinators of his organization.

I didn't go. I said, "Look, I don't much like him, and these people are volunteers as much as I'm a volunteer. But I understand that if we don't go down there, probably Bush will and there will be a huge story that we don't care about his supporters." Had somebody called from one campaign to the other and said, "We won't go if you don't go," and they'd said, "Fine," it would have given Perot the chance to say, "I've given them a chance to talk about the issues that matter and they didn't come." It would have helped him. We had to go. "So as long as we're both down there," I said, "I guess it don't matter." It was the most sane of the options.

It wasn't a pretty sight. Mickey Kantor and Lloyd Bentsen and Mary and Bob Teeter and Phil Gramm all went down and Perot stood there with his pants down and his ass in the draft and everybody was kissing it, and he was clearly enjoying it.

As far as being a man of substance, he wasn't that much of a man. But I think he had a pretty crafty short-term political message. "Let's just fix it." He had that can-do aura about him. Let's face it, the guy made millions off of Medicaid and Medicare. He had about the most aggressive lobbying programs of anybody in the country. He builds businesses, rescues hostages, he's a can-do guy. I don't dispute his view that he's a patriot, and I think that he's a skilled political figure. But he's just wacky, and very deceitful, and about as politically dishonest a person as I've ever run across. As we say in Louisiana, he's got a mouth like a catfish, he can talk out of both sides of it and whistle out the middle all at the same time.

All that summer and fall I was having ongoing conversations with former Texas governor John Connally. Connally would talk to Perot a lot. He told me, "James, Ross is just stone-ass crazy. He's a friend of mine, but no one knows what the hell he's going to do."

I asked whether or not we should go to this thing, and he said, "I don't know. You can't predict what he's going to do; he is the most unpredictable man there is."

Governor Connally was one of the people on my call list that I'd bounce stuff off of every now and then. He couldn't stand Bush. I'm not exactly sure why, but he really wanted Clinton to beat him. In a campaign, information is power, and I was trying to find out if Perot was going to get back in or not. We thought Texas was a Republican-leaning state, and at one time I thought if Perot got in the race it might knock it down enough that we could take it. But Governor Connally was pretty consistent in his counsel to stay out of Texas. You never know if somebody's giving you false advice, but I don't think his counsel this time was Machiavellian.

I'd call and Connally would say, "Looks like he's gonna go." I'd call again and it was, "Looks like he's having second thoughts." After about the third call he said, "Hell, just go do what you gotta do and don't worry about him." I pretty much took that advice. Predicting what Perot was going to do was like trying to predict what the weather is going to be in Oklahoma; wait ten minutes and it will be something else.

Some Democrats can be so stupid, they always want to talk about how stupid people are for voting for demagogues like Perot and Reagan. They always want to deny the obvious, but you can't. You have to learn from the obvious. First you have to acknowledge the obvious, then you have to learn from it. You have to give Perot his due. As an independent candidate he got himself on the ballot in fifty states and took 19 percent of the vote. It's a major political achievement. Perot has a pretty good political instinct and he has a way of being full of hot air and convincing people that he's talking straight. Which, given the current political environment, ain't a bad skill. It's probably as good a one as you can have.

Mary

Everyone thought it was idiotic to go down and kiss Perot's ring, but we had to. Our delegation was impressive: Brent Scowcroft on foreign policy; Jack Kemp on domestic issues; Phil Gramm on budget and economic issues. Teeter outlined our campaign strategy, and I was there to weave the Perot people into our organization, on the off chance that this might be a real meeting.

I was late, since I had been on the road with Bush and had had to catch a last-minute commercial flight. By the time I arrived, we had already gone through most of our presentation and the "volunteers" were pummeling us. I just sat there, revolted by this nightmare. Tom Luce, who was chairman of the Perot Petition Committee, and the Perot crowd denied that the organization was all *paid* volunteers, but I recognized them from the states. I knew that they were paid guys and all the questions were planted, and they were just making speeches and literally yelling at us. To Phil Gramm's credit, no one yells at him; he was the most loyal and articulate about the President's program, and didn't let any of these guys get in his face.

Afterward our delegation went to a holding room with Perot to discuss how the press conference to follow was going to work: who was going to say what, where everyone was going to stand, what questions were likely to be asked, and what were the answers to be. This is what you normally do before each press conference, so you don't look like the Keystone Kops up there.

We were standing in the holding room in kind of a circular huddle, and Perot, who's about as tall as my bellybutton, kept standing with his back to me. I would shift around to talk to Teeter and he would get in front of me again. All I got was his back. He talked to everyone else in our group, he thanked them for coming to Texas to see him. Me, nothing. He didn't thank me, he didn't shake my hand, he didn't do anything other than stand in front of me with his back turned.

I am not easily insulted and I am not a sensitive female type, but this was gross sexism. It was clear that he thought I could not conceivably have any part in this discussion.

The press conference went off as planned. Perot pulled his good ol' boy routine for the media, Teeter tried to look dignified. We were all standing on the press platform like the dopes we were, except for Kemp, who claimed he had a plane to catch. We were mortified standing up there, Perot's play-toys. As we were leaving Perot thanked everyone again—except for me.

Walking down the hotel corridor we were assaulted by a bevy of lights and still cameras and TV cameras and reporters trying to get us to say something more real than the obviously scripted presentation. Teeter hates to walk and talk, he's very contemplative and measured, not an off-the-cuff kind of guy. The cameras were on us. I said to him, "Watch this."

He gave me a look and said, "Matalin, don't do it. I don't know what you're going to do, but don't do it."

I went up to Perot, and in my most disgustingly sugar-sweet voice said, "Oh, Mr. Perot, you're my father's hero. He just loves you so much. Can I please have your autograph?" I shoved a piece of paper into his hand. "Oh, please. His name is Steve. It would mean so much to him."

He stared up at me. Never said a word. He took the paper, scribbled his name, turned on his heel, and left.

That afternoon the office tracked me down. Perot had had some newsie call the campaign and ask if my father's name was Steve and did he live in Indiana, and did we know what his voter registration was. I quick called my father, who thought Perot was a disgrace and a nut, and told him, "Look, if you get any weird calls, don't answer." We were all shocked to see Perot's paranoia in action.

Teeter stood there and said, "I can't believe you did that, I just don't believe you do things like that."

But Perot deserved it. The little twit was too self-absorbed to be embarrassed. He missed the sarcasm completely.

The next Thursday, Perot was back in the race.

We watched his press conference and sat there saying, "God, what a blowhard. What a phony, what a jerk." Carney got on the phone to make sure none of the Perot people we had converted were going to jump ship. (None did.)

We misread the Perot campaign and his entire candidacy from the start. We were wrong about the reaction the electorate would have to his spending his own money to buy the race; thought it was a negative, the polls registered a positive. And we definitely thought people would see right through him.

There had been a lot of Washington cocktail chatter about why Perot was doing this, why Perot hated Bush. The question was privately put to him by one of Bush's closest Texas friends about the purpose and/or motivation of his candidacy, and Perot sent word back on three things he objected to about George Bush. One, Bush had messed up his daughter's wedding. Two, Bush had known of an Iraqi assassination plot on Perot and had restrained the CIA from informing him. Three, Bush had been complicit in an incident in which Black Panthers had been plotting against Perot. Five alleged armed terrorists had supposedly been chased off Perot's lawn and been bit in the butt by his dog.

This was all absurd. We all figured once those kind of wild delusions became known, that would be it for his candidacy. We were one hundred percent confident any normal human being would think, "Okay, so George Bush broke his 'No new taxes' pledge; he would never mess up anyone's wedding!" It would seal Perot's fate once and for all.

Never, ever in our wildest imaginings did we think voters would actually believe the crackpot. The Democrats had laid the groundwork that we were negative campaigners so well that polls showed the public gave some credence to his ludicrous charges. "The Republicans, dirty tricksters, are capable of anything." It was stunning. A state chairman actually called and asked me, "Did we have anything to do with his daughter's wedding?" It was the single most insulting question I got during the entire campaign.

James

I had to laugh when I heard that one. I loved it. How do you screw up a Texas wedding? Show up sober in a sedan? Leave with the woman you came with? I said, "Man, ain't nobody going to believe that."

But we did a focus group of swing voters in Atlanta, and Stan Greenberg's partner, Celinda Lake, told us, "Hey, they believe Perot." People did think that Bush was capable of most anything.

Mary

Our spin was "This hurts Clinton"; voters frustrated with Washington who wanted change now had two places to look for it. And the initial numbers did look that way, so our spin matched reality temporarily. We obviously were not happy to have Perot back in the race, despite what the numbers were showing. He was attacking us but eroding Clinton's strength; it was one of these campaign paradoxes we didn't know how to deal with. But we also knew that the Perot candidacy was all about trashing Bush, and sooner or later it would start to hurt us. Perot would provide for Clinton what he had provided earlier: He would attack us, which would leave Clinton unfettered to push out the Democratic message.

Perot was a truly remarkable political phenomenon. People believed that Perot believed what they believed. He was the anti-establishment; anything they didn't like about Washington, they looked to him as the answer. He didn't say much of anything, he was stunningly short on specifics, he just became a vehicle for their frustrations. They would imbue him with whatever they felt.

He had a plan, a ghostwritten book, but for a while nobody in the media took his candidacy seriously enough to dissect in any way what it was about. It never got the going-over that either Clinton's or ours did. It was enough that he had one.

Still, his second time around the print media did finally kick in. Say this for them, at some point they do recognize the magnitude of what it is they're covering. From off-the-record conversations I got the impression that finally these guys were going to get serious about Perot's candidacy and were not going to let him skate, they were going to call him on his multiple inanities.

We didn't have the time, inclination, or resources to work on Perot. We were having enough trouble beating Clinton. When reporters called, mostly we just steered them to Texas. People who had had dealings with the man there were hard not to trip over.

Despite stepped-up scrutiny, Perot was still getting a free ride on the talk shows and TV morning shows, where he was able to manipulate the format. He'd go on the air and dominate the conversation. They let him get away with anything. It was like watching *Hee Haw* every morning.

James

My theory on Perot is, After you're worth $3 million nobody will tell you no. Perot is the guy who went from $3 million to $3 billion without ever being told no. That's fine. You got $3 billion, I'll guarantee you, every word you say, you've got fifty people hanging on it, agreeing with it, telling you how smart you are, what a genius you are.

So he ran for president. And all of a sudden every word he said, somebody was going back and contradicting him or looking it up. Ross Perot couldn't remember the last time somebody disagreed with him. You run for president, every day somebody is contradicting you or disagreeing with you. It's very irritating, and he didn't like it.

But it's the scrutiny, more than anything else, that gets to a first-time candidate. In everyday life, in everyday conversation, if you exaggerate a little bit, who cares? If someone introduces me and they say I was a sergeant in the Marine Corps when I know I was a corporal, and I don't say anything, it doesn't matter. But if I'm running for office and I let someone believe I was a sergeant when I was merely a corporal, then the press says that's a character flaw; I was trying to inflate my military record and therefore my standing in the political community. "If you can't believe Carville about something as public and vital as his military record, what else can't you believe about him? What else is this man exaggerating?"

When you step in the political arena you've got people like me, with three or four people behind us, going through every word you've ever said. Then you have all the reporters, who would like nothing better than to make you answer their feisty questions in public and eat your words in the pages of their papers. It makes you look foolish and it makes them look like a star.

I saw this the first time Perot got himself in hot water, in July, when he addressed a national convention of the NAACP and talked to them about "you people." Although I believe he meant well, I had never seen a politician more out of touch with an audience. It was a pretty amateurish performance. The conventional wisdom at the time was "So what?" Offending a group of blacks wouldn't hurt him with his base of voters.

But I made some calls and found out different. I have a kind of rolling focus group of people I knew from school, or family, regular folks around the country that I call and get their reaction to things. After the first three or four calls I usually pick up something, and what I picked up was, "He's a buffoon. If he doesn't know how to talk to some black leaders in Nashville, Tennessee, how's he going to be able to do anything with the Japanese?"

It was like what people thought about Tsongas. Just because people don't like politicians, it doesn't mean they don't want their politicians to be good at their business. Americans are torn; they want you to be a different kind of political figure, but they want you to be politically adept enough to guide things through the system and get things done. It wasn't so much that they were offended by Perot's behavior as it was a statement that the man just didn't have any political skills.

CHAPTER 22

Mary

A group of British Conservative party strategists and members of Parliament, including Sir John Lacy, was making the rounds of conservative political circles in Washington, talking about how they had pulled out their election that past spring. Prime Minister John Major, who'd looked to be a political goner, had staged a remarkable comeback and won reelection. There were definite parallels to our situation. Both men had followed charismatic and strongly ideological leaders; their popularity had risen after taking a tough stand against Iraq; and the economy had gone downhill while they were in office. Jim Pinkerton, special counsel to Bob Teeter, and I received an inquiry as to whether we'd have an interest in chatting with these MPs and hearing what they had to say.

I was on the road and couldn't, but Pinkerton set up a meeting attended by junior campaign staff and our communications people. The ranking members of our staff present were Pinkerton and issues director Jim Cicconi. If there was anything to be gleaned, Cicconi was the gleaner.

The British Conservatives talked specifically about how they had defined the differences between themselves and their opposition, the Labour party. They'd made taxes and trust their key issues, one of their main thrusts being that Labour was going to raise taxes. As part of their presentation they brought samples of their advertising and election materials. The message was very pointed, very sharp, not understated in any way, certainly not as subtle as one might have expected, given the stereotype of the British character. It was also very timely.

There had been a hot debate within the campaign, going on since the middle of June, over how we should deal with the tax issue. On one side were people who simply didn't want to touch it, in large part because it evoked the President's reneging on his "Read my lips" commitment. These people had supported the 1990 budget deal and had a stake in preserving it, and thus not making taxes an issue. On the other side were all the political people, who felt we could not afford to lose the one issue that most distinguished us from the Democrats. Republicans have been winning against tax-and-spend Democrats for decades.

In June, when Clinton released his budget plan, Cicconi had analyzed it. He'd found that when you added in all the promises and commitments, like health care, the Clinton plan on its face called for at least a *$150 billion* tax increase. Clinton was going around saying he was going to cut middle-class taxes, and there, in black and white, his own plan said he was going to raise them. With Cicconi's data, we'd been pounding the press, telling them: This guy can't be believed. We weren't breaking through too good. But now these senior British politicians walked through the door, carrying the same message: In a very similar political atmosphere, where the public was seen as wanting change after many years of conservative government, they had won because they were able to sharpen the divisions between the two parties on the issues of taxes and trust.

Now, was this some nefarious link-up conspiracy against liberals between the great Western conservative parties? Hardly. No one had really heard of the individuals involved. We recognized what they had accomplished in Great Britain, and were interested intellectually in hearing how it had been done. The presentation itself wasn't confidential; it was almost a seminar on how they'd won. Cicconi says it could have been made at the National Press Club.

One of the things that did strike Cicconi was the way the Tories had focused on *individual* taxpayers. We had calculated the increase in taxes for the entire country, which was astronomical and hard to grasp; the British had broken their calculations down to the tax hike for the married electrician, with two kids and a mortgage, making £13,840 a year. They brought it home in human terms.

Under the headline "In come Labour. Income Taxes," their print ad read, "Labour has made billions of pounds' worth of promises. But they haven't told you where the money is coming from. Because they suspect you won't like the answer." Then they listed taxpayers by profession and income, and how much more each one would have to pay if Labour won.

It wasn't like light bulbs went off in our heads. It's Campaign 101; they were reminding us of our own basic Republican themes, which we'd run on in 1980, '84, and '88. But the breakdown by individual was a very good idea and it spurred Pinkerton and Cicconi, unsanctioned, to create their own. They used the British presentation as fuel for their argument. Cicconi would have loved for the British to have gone over and met with the President personally; they were carrying a message he himself had been focused on for months.

It helped. Cicconi's staff came through with the figures, and the pooh-bahs on the Hill and in the Treasury Department (on their own time) double-checked them to satisfy themselves they weren't putting George Bush's reputation in the tank with the calculations. Finally, the first week in October, we got an ad on the air saying, "Here's what Clinton economics could mean to you." Cicconi quite consciously copied the British approach, and directed his staff to prepare the statistics. Instead of the crane driver, salesman, engineer, and personnel director who appeared on British TV, we used a $40,000-a-year steamfitter, whose taxes would go up $1,088 a year; a $55,000-a-year scientist, whose taxes would increase by $2,072; a housing lender, and two sales representatives. It was a great spot, and it worked.

Did the British have a decisive influence on the themes of the campaign? No, they just give us heart that our philosophy was a winner and one that would prevail, despite our opponent's consistent lead in the polls.

The meeting with the British centered almost solely on economics. The Major campaign had gotten very personal with the Labour challenger, Neil Kinnock. Cicconi doesn't recall any discussion of Kinnock's character at the meeting in our offices. Whatever we said about Bill Clinton was our own; we had no shortage of material.

James

Frankly, I didn't give a damn how many Conservative MPs Bush met with. It wasn't going to have an effect on the election any more than if John Major met with Republican members of Congress and then went home and tried to run on their advice. It seemed like a colossal waste of time.

We were not unaware of the British election. The Labour party had been ahead, they were supposed to win, and there had been a late swing away from them. I always worry about a late swing away from us, so, sure, I was aware of it. We wanted to know what had happened and what lessons we might learn. Hillary, independently, was worrying about similar problems. She urged that we look into the British campaign.

Philip Gould, a consultant who had been the Labour campaign's communications and polling adviser, contacted Stan Greenberg, who invited him to Little Rock. Gould stayed several weeks. At dinner one night he, Stan, George, Mandy, and I went through the late-in-the-game Tory strategy and how it had undermined confidence in Labour.

There were some similarities. Democrats had not held the highest national office for a long time; neither had Labour. As Stan said, in advanced market economies people get nervous about center-left parties and their ability to assure prosperity. The fear was that once people got near the voting booth they would get cold feet and doubt the ability of the Democrats to manage the economy, as they had with Labour. The Tories had massaged those doubts and we wanted to make damn sure the Republicans didn't do the same thing.

One of our researchers, Bennett Freeman, also worked up an exhaustive report. He consulted with Yvette Cooper, who had worked for shadow chancellor of the exchequer John Smith, and Geoff Mulgan, who was the top adviser to shadow trade and industry spokesman Gordon Brown. The report listed the campaigns' similarities and differences, and noted trends that had developed in the last ten days of the British campaign, which we would be well advised to look out for: Major's energized campaigning, Kinnock's overconfidence, the Tories' distortions on taxes, Labour's lack of focus on message, the broadcast press focusing on the horse race and not the issues, the conservative press scaring people into thinking that Labour would actually win. Labour had not responded to the Tories' campaign. If we were going to make any mistake, it wasn't going to be that one.

Freeman's report also gave us a list of "British Warning Signs to Watch For":

> The pandering "all things to all people" image that began to stick to Labour generally and to Kinnock personally in the final days of the campaign.

Stepped-up late, direct personal attacks on the opposition leader as untrustworthy, smug and slick—all charges flung at Kinnock.

The tax issue that only came to the top of the list among voters' concerns in the final few days.

Misrepresentations, distortions, and outright lies on taxes beginning to stick just when it was too late to correct the facts and undo the perceptions.

Large polling shifts every few days . . . that revealed greater volatility than the fairly constant top-line national numbers.

We had concluded early on that the situations were not analogous, and the report, while noting the parallels, backed us up. In fact, when the Bush campaign ran the TV spot that was almost a direct replica of the spot the Tories ran in Britain, we were ready for it. Freeman had written, "Once we see the Tory TV ad, we may find we're on firm ground to charge that an imported copycat campaign based on lies and distortions just won't work on this side of the Atlantic. They're exporting our jobs—but importing their campaign ads."

When the Republicans ran the ad we attacked its credibility. The Tories had lied; chances were the Republicans would try the same thing. We checked their claims of what our plan would cost. Based on nothing we had said, they told the public we would raise taxes. In fact, we had proposed a cut in taxes. We told the press, and they pretty much maligned the spot as just a rehash. It was not a successful spot, nowhere near as successful here as it was in Britain. It didn't run for long.

But the biggest difference between us and the Labour party was that we responded. They never did, and they got beat.

We did get word back that the Tories had gotten a British civil servant to rummage in the files over there. The rumor—totally goofy—was that, while he was at Oxford, Bill Clinton had petitioned the British government for citizenship. I don't know what British law is, but I don't think the Conservative party is very pleased that somehow or another they got dragged into an American election. It was such an incredibly stupid thing for them to do. I hit the ceiling when I heard about it, but any anger I felt was at our own government, not theirs.

I'm not a British citizen, but if I were I'd wonder why in the hell the Conservative government wasn't worrying more about fixing the problems in Britain and less about Bill Clinton. I thought the British government came across looking like a gofer for George Bush. It was not, as one Briton would have said, "their finest hour."

Mary

We continued making the case that you couldn't trust Clinton. On *Larry King Live*, the President laid out our position. "I'm just saying, level with the American people on the draft, on whether he went to Moscow, how many demonstrations he led against his own country from a foreign soil. Level. Tell us the truth, and let the voters then decide who to trust."

The reference to Moscow created a mini press frenzy. They played it as red-baiting campaign strategy, just because Congressman Bob Dornan and some others had had a White House meeting in which, it was reported, they urged us to press Clinton for details on his Moscow trip. And there *were* many holes in Clinton's original story.

It was absolutely not a campaign strategy. The Moscow element wasn't even discussed within the campaign except insofar as it dovetailed with all Clinton's other evasions; this was yet another story that this guy couldn't get his facts straight on. If it had been a strategy, we would have presented it much more tightly and not left an opening for the press to call us red-baiters.

No one told the President to include Moscow in his litany of Clinton evasions, and when he did, Marlin and I made some more eye contact. We knew the press would never believe this wasn't an intentional strategy, that this one came from George Bush's heart.

James

California congressman Bob Dornan and all these right-wing guys had a meeting at the White House, and they were all over this Moscow trip. They convinced the President to imply that there was some nefarious purpose to Clinton, in his early twenties, visiting the Soviet Union. I mean, we were playing them in basketball!

I can't tell you how silly I thought Bush looked in that whole thing, and I'll never understand why he let himself look that way. To everyone to the left of Jesse Helms, the whole thing looked awfully stupid. I mean, talking about some college kid traveling, and where did he stay, what hotel did he stay at. As if Clinton was going to remember. What difference did it make?

Reporters called me and said, "You're not going to believe what President Bush said." I told them, "These people have lost all their marbles." The implication Bush and them were trying to impress on the voters was that Bill Clinton was somehow working for the KGB. Now, why would a kid from Hope, Arkansas, be working for the KGB, and what the hell could he do for them? I guess they were trying to say that maybe they'd programmed him over there and now Governor Bill Clinton of Arkansas was some Communist mole running for president. Who knows? It just couldn't have been a goofier, sillier thing, and it was nothing but a bunch of nutcakes putting stuff together. We were laughing about it.

It was one of those times where you don't get in the way of an opponent who is self-destructing. We didn't say much about it unless we were asked. The next day, Governor Clinton said, "It is now obvious from the press reports that far from speaking from his heart, he was speaking from a prescribed political strategy cooked up in the White House by Robert Dornan and other extreme right-wingers. He turned the Republican convention over to the far right for a few days; now he's apparently going to turn his campaign to that. It's very sad."

Mary will tell you that it wasn't about Moscow, it was about "I can't remember"; she was doing her best to make it seem like an evasion, a "Slick Willie" rerun. My own sense is that she had to be profoundly embarrassed by something that stupid.

Mary

That night at a speech in Houston the President said, "I can't understand someone mobilizing demonstrators in a foreign country when poor kids, drafted out of the ghettos, are dying in a faraway land. You can call me old-fashioned, but that just does not make sense to me." (While he was at Oxford during the Vietnam War, Bill Clinton had organized anti-war demonstrations in England.) On *Good Morning America* the next day President Bush said, "I just don't think it is right to demonstrate on foreign soil, or mobilize demonstrations against your country's policy, on foreign soil. . . . I make quite a distinction in my own mind—going to a foreign land and mobilizing demonstrations against your own country. It has nothing to do with patriotism; it has a lot to do with judgment."

The President felt very strongly about this. I'm not of his generation and I didn't understand. People at our events, however, understood exactly what he was saying. He got great response whenever he raised this issue. In private conversations, only some of the older press guys who had served in the military would say, "Yeah, there is a difference." One supporter from Illinois called my office and quoted Winston Churchill on the matter: "One should never criticize one's government when out of the country, and never cease to do so when at home." I carried the quotation with me everywhere.

Apparently foreign demonstrations had been an issue in another era that missed a lot of us. It clearly was a serious one to the President, and he left it in the speeches. There were some subjects on which, whether or not they were right politically, he didn't care, he was going to make his feelings known. One morning he had me join him in his car on the way to an event and we had a tête-à-tête about it. I was saying that the issue didn't really resonate with me, that what was more important was the fact that Clinton couldn't ever get his facts straight. "You've got to stick to the issue of veracity of his ever-changing stories," I said, "or lack thereof."

He understood politically what I meant, but this wasn't politics to him. President Bush was very passionate about it. I am paraphrasing, but the essence of what he told me was that the whole world looked to America for leadership, and the notion that while some Americans were putting their own lives in harm's way for their country, someone would be speaking against his own kin was repugnant to him. The fact that it was done on foreign soil was of particular significance; there was something especially disloyal and unpatriotic about that distinction. The President never voiced strong opinions about demonstrating at home. My impression was that that was a free-speech issue, and he respected people's freedom to be against the war. But to take that disagreement visibly and vocally to another land, he felt, was particularly hurtful and disparaging to soldiers and their families.

James

Bush was of the generation where if you didn't serve it was hard to get elected. (That started basically after the Civil War; if you didn't serve in the Great War there wasn't much sense in even getting into politics.) Somehow they thought they'd found the magic bullet. But times have changed. I don't dispute George Bush's patriotism, but people were not voting for him because of his patriotism; they were more interested in his sensitivity and judgment, that was the problem. And the Republicans never would come to grips with what their fundamental problem was.

Mary

We knew what Bill Clinton's fundamental problem was: He was incapable of telling the truth.

I was on my way out the door to do a talk show against some Democrat one evening when Rhonda casually said, "You know, one of the volunteers was watching Clinton last night and she said, 'If you can't believe anything he says about his past, how can you believe anything he says about our future?' " That stuck. I went and said it on the air, and it stopped the Democrat cold. He just didn't have an answer. I started saying it on the ground every chance I got. It encapsulated the draft issue, it was a really good hook, and it was a temporary distraction from the red-baiting accusations. "Why didn't he just say he was trying to avoid the draft?" I asked. "No one is questioning that; they are questioning why he always prevaricates on these issues. If we cannot believe anything he has said about his past, how can we believe anything he is saying about the future?"

It was around this time I made another terrible, hideous mistake. We were still getting the faxes out every day, but I was on the road, so other people would write them and I would Mary-ize them before they went out. They sent me one with the headline "Back in the U.S.S.R.," which largely made the same points about "Where was he and why doesn't he know?" that weren't being well received. I knew it was the wrong tack, definitely overkill. But it was one of those frenzied campaign days and I just said, "Fine, let it go."

It was a horrendous mistake. The title alone was enough to give the press fodder for what they wanted to write anyway, which was another campaign-in-desperation story. I was stepping on my own lines. I was out there every day saying the point was he was a "pathological prevaricator," while putting out releases focusing on his Moscow connections.

It was a campaign lesson I already knew. You've got to stop and take a breath and think. The days are longer, harder, and more frenetic; the nights are shorter and you can't sleep anyway. The combination of those factors makes for increasingly bad judgments just when you need the best judgments. And that was a very bad judgment. It was the one and only fax I regret.

James

To paraphrase Samuel Johnson, there's nothing that focuses people's attention like a hanging every fortnight. The political corollary is, There's nothing that focuses voters' attention like a debate every fortnight.

The first debate was scheduled for Sunday, October 11, in St. Louis. It would be Clinton, Bush, and Perot. Our polls were showing that Perot, while he was making a dent in the campaign, would have very little, if any, effect on the outcome.

We would always do a two-way and a three-way, and the conclusive result was that the spread between Clinton and Bush was always within a percentage point of being the same with Perot in the race or out of it. If we were going to win by 7 points going head-to-head with Bush, we would win by the same 7 in a three-man race, with Perot running third. He was taking a more-or-less equal number of voters from both of us. It looked like things were going to stay that way, which was fine with us. As a result, we weren't that concerned about Perot. We were much less absorbed with him in October than we had been in May. Hillary always thought he would do well, and Clinton felt Perot was on to something by expressing the voters' frustration. But there was no reason to exclude him.

We began our debate prep in earnest about a week before. At first we thought we'd stay in Little Rock, but the phone would be ringing all the time with the governor's business, so we decided to go somewhere else. In St. Louis, we figured, there would be less privacy, more press. So we ended up in Kansas City, a decision that was based a lot on the kind of hotel we could get and the rooms we could have to prepare for the program. We all got in to Kansas City Thursday night and had our first mock debate Friday morning.

We worked in the hotel conference room, with the exact kind of podium they would be using, in the exact physical positions the candidates would take. There were TV monitors in the back of the hall and others in another room for taping. The senior campaign people and senior policy advisers sat at a big conference table in the back of the main room about seventy-five feet away from where the candidate was speaking. There were the usual suspects: me, George, Paul, speech coach Michael Sheehan, Mickey Kantor. Tom Donilon was responsible for the overall pace of the proceedings. We had the room miked back to Little Rock, with a fax machine and a phone right next to the

TV monitor so they could be involved. Our fact-checkers, foreign-policy people, and economic people sat in an adjacent room and took notes on any factual errors the governor made.

We decided that we would just walk in and have a debate, first thing. No practice, no nothing, we'd just start asking questions. We knew who the questioners would be—PBS's Jim Lehrer, ABC's Ann Compton, *The Boston Globe*'s John Mashek, and freelancer Sander Vanocur—and we had people try and talk like them. Research went back and found what kind of questions they'd been asking on their shows, what stories they'd been running, what they were interested in, what we could anticipate from each of them.

Then we looked at the questions. We said, "There's an eighty-five percent degree of probability that there's going to be a deficit question. There's a fifty percent chance there's going to be a question on Bosnia. There's a one hundred percent chance there's going to be a question on taxes." It wasn't that difficult to home in on what the questions were going to be, and we crafted our answers.

The part of President Bush was played by Washington lawyer Bob Barnett. He showed up with briefing books a couple of feet thick on every question Bush had answered and everything he'd said.

The mythology was that Bush was a stumbling, fumbling political figure who couldn't speak straight. He wasn't. You've got to give George Bush his due. People would talk about his goofy speech patterns, how he would mangle the English language. Some folks found him kind of amusing. When I run against somebody, I don't find them amusing. I very seldom find anything an opponent says or does amusing. I didn't think George Bush was a particularly funny man. He can be very tough, very aggressive, and he plays the expectation game like a pro—you don't expect anything out of him and then he sneaks up and whups you.

We'd started the whole debate process by looking at tapes of the 1988 debates, kind of like football players watching game films, and he was impressive. Bob Dole is supposed to be real mean; George Bush decimated Bob Dole, just out-toughed him. He was in against Pete DuPont, another guy who was supposed to be hard. Called him "Pierre." Just went right up to him, cut him open, dropped his guts on the floor. He kicked Dukakis's ass all over the state. If you look at those tapes you have a healthy, healthy respect for George Bush.

Ross Perot was played by Congressman Mike Synar of Oklahoma.

The governor was coming in off the road. He walked in Friday morning and we said, "This is what we're going to do. We're gonna run through this thing one time, walk right in and scrimmage."

What the candidate didn't know was that we had primed both Synar and Barnett to be relentlessly aggressive in their attack on him. Clinton was coming in cold, but the other guys were prepared to the gills.

Our strategy was to cream him. The theory being that when Clinton got slaughtered in rehearsal we'd scare the hell out of him and everybody else. From then on we'd all have a real sharp edge. If there was any temptation to take George Bush lightly, it would be gone. If we'd gone through the debate the first time and we'd creamed them, we would never have had the necessary killer anxiety it takes to win a presidential debate on national TV.

It worked.

Compared to past strategy sessions, this was surprisingly restrained. There was no den of screaming advisers. The setting was kind of intimidating, and you didn't think of interrupting the proceedings any more than you would the real debate. There wasn't a lot of blurting out "We oughta do this" in the middle of an answer; people were on pretty good behavior.

We went through the whole debate, and the thing that became startlingly clear was that Perot was going to do well and it was going to be hard for Bush to win.

We were ahead in the polls by 18 percent. Bush didn't have a very good rationale for why people should vote for him; he had no other choice but to attack Clinton. And any time he went after our guy, any time there was a rift between them at all, Perot could come through with his rhetoric, dismiss them both as ordinary pols, and counterattack.

Synar did a really good job. An Oklahoman, he's a neighbor of the Texan Perot and was on the money with the sharp, quick, nasal imitation. "See, that's the problem with Washington. Y'all two fightin' with each other, we're not fighting the problems of this country. I don't want to go to Washington to fight with you, I want to go to Washington to fight problems. And you got the same ol' way of looking at things. It's just like you take a ol' dog and it goes out there and it sticks its nose up in a trap and gets it bit. Well, it don't stick its nose back in it. Y'all keep stickin' your nose in the same trap 'cause you never learn. I want to go to Washington, I'm 'onna be like a mechanic, I'm 'onna get under the hood, I'm 'onna fix it."

Any question that he would get, if they asked him about taxes or the like, he'd say, "He says 'No new taxes,' then he raises taxes. Him, you can't go in Arkansas, they tax the air you breathe there. We gotta have a new way of doin' things, a different way. I'll raise taxes, but I've told people what it's gonna be, we're gonna have spending cuts, it's not gonna be the same old way."

We had all of the research on Clinton, we knew the types of attacks that we didn't want to get, and we had Barnett deliver them ferociously. "My opponent said such-and-such on this day, then he said such-and-such on that day. Let me read to you what he said. . . ."

Clinton walked into this headfirst. In fact, we didn't know he'd get creamed as bad as he did. When we ended the debate—"Thank you, President Bush. Thank you, Governor Clinton. Thank you, Mr. Perot. This is Jim Lehrer wishing you all a good night"—everybody went, "Gee, well, we got a lot of work to do." The general feeling was that it was good that we'd done it this way.

We always thought that Bill Clinton practiced better than he played. It happens with lots of candidates. He had had some good debates in the primary, but we had seen some staggering performances in the locker room and there was a feeling that he would sometimes leave his game there.

We worked all day Friday and Saturday, and he got a lot better fast. By noon of the second day we knew we were moving in the right direction. We were making our points a lot more relentlessly and in the allotted time frame. We were solid on when to look at the candidates, when to look at the press, when to look at the camera—the basic things you have to execute on television.

In a debate, the protocol I try to emphasize is, Answer, attack, explain. It does matter that you answer every question. People understand if you don't answer the question, so do it first every time. Then attack your opponent, do some damage. Then explain your position. If you get cut short, you're cut short on the explanation, not the answer. If you leave the voters feeling like you didn't answer that question, you lose a lot.

Say Bill Clinton was asked, "As governor of Arkansas you raised taxes a hundred and twenty-seven times, by your own admission. And now you're going to be President of the United States. Is there any assurance you can give anybody in America that you won't immediately start taxing everything? Isn't the reality, Governor Clinton, that your first solution is taxation?"

Answer number one is, "I didn't raise taxes a hundred and twenty-eight times, as my opponent says; that includes things like extending the dog racing season. I might add, why didn't you ask me about why I *did* cut taxes sixty-two times.

"My opponent gave the most devastating broken promise in a political campaign: 'Read my lips: No new taxes.' We just had the second-largest tax increase in American history. The problem when people hear that is, people lose faith in government. The question of taxation, how the government raises revenues, is serious. We have to level with people, we have to be honest with people. I'm not making any more 'Read my lips' promises. But the American people in the last twenty years have had declining, stagnant income. They can't afford any more taxes, and the government can afford more cuts. . . ."

The tendency is to explain first, but when you do that, sometimes the answer gets lost. Answer, attack, explain.

Another major training technique to learn is how to say everything in one minute. It's particularly tough for Bill Clinton. In fact, if you can answer in less than a minute—if you can answer in a word—do it, then talk about something else.

"Do you favor the death penalty?"

"I do." And then have a light go on in your head. "Beyond that, and one of the things I want to talk about—I do favor the death penalty—but I want to talk about crime in general. Under my opponent's regime . . ." Then explain. You don't have to go into a history of the death penalty. You say it, then you move on.

I learned that lesson in a Texas Senate primary. Lloyd Doggett was against the death penalty, which was not the popular position in Texas, and of course we got the question. We had this long, involved answer about how he'd voted against it in the Texas legislature but in the U.S. Senate there might be different circumstances that could . . .

We were running against Kent Hance, and Hance turned around and said, "Lloyd, you fer it or agin it? Which one?"

Not every question lends itself to a yes-or-no answer, but if it does, say it—"Yes." "No."—then move on, attack, explain.

Another thing you practice a lot is how to change the subject.

"Do you favor the death penalty?"

"I do, but I want to take my forty-five seconds to say something about what my opponent over there said just before . . ."

Or, "I do, but I got beat by the clock on that last question and I want to explain further . . ."

In the middle of all this preparation, George came in and said, "I got to talk to you." He has a way of putting his hand through his hair that, when you see it, you know there's trouble.

George said he'd gotten a call from a major newsweekly reporter, who had gotten a tip from someone from the National Security

Council, who said that someone had gotten into Clinton's passport file and there was a passport that had been issued to William Blythe, or William Jefferson. (Clinton's father's name was Blythe; Clinton's middle name is Jefferson.) The implication was that sometime in the sixties Bill Clinton had tried to renounce his citizenship.

We called the reporter back. "What are you talking about? How can you say this?" Then we went to the candidate. He said, "Yeah, I believe I lost my passport one time when I was in England and might have reapplied for another one, but I can't remember more about it than that. What you all need to do is stop worrying about this, there's nothing to it."

George was dark.

We even put it in the debate prep. We were always practicing for the Big Bomb. The truth of the matter is, there's never a Big Bomb; debates are won and lost on fundamentals. But that didn't stop us from having our mock George Bush reach into his pocket and come out with a piece of paper. "I have a letter written by you, sir, dated June the fourteenth, nineteen hundred and sixty-nine, in which you state unequivocally to the Consul General of the Swedish Embassy . . ." Clinton looked at him and said, "I don't know what's in your hand, sir, but it isn't any letter I ever wrote."

This was one smoking hot big-time rumor. The newsweeklies, which were really pursuing it, called and started talking about where the staples were on the passport file. It was getting that specific. We were getting press calls: "I've got a source in the CIA, I've got a direct line. I understand there are two pages missing." Supposedly, a lawyer in Williams & Connolly talked to somebody in the White House who had actually *seen* a copy of a letter written by Bill Clinton either renouncing his citizenship or seeking political asylum—something. It depended on what hour it was.

Everybody knew about it and everybody was talking about it. "Where's the letter?" It was swirling around internally, in the media, in the campaign, in the back of the plane, everywhere. It became an article of faith: Somebody saw the letter on paper, in the office, in the White House. They'd given out numbered copies and then picked them up.

Clinton, of course, said he had never written any such letter. We told him, "Look, man, this thing is really out there. You're sure that you never wrote something . . . ? Couldn't be selective recall? Could someone have written a letter and you not know it? Did you show up at the embassy one day? Is it possible that you had a drink with someone from the embassy? Anything?"

"I can assure you," he told us, "there was never any such letter."
But that didn't stop the rumor mill from grinding.

Mary

We heard this rumor, of course. All the press kept saying was
"You have the letter, you have the letter!" We also heard that the
Democrats were actually freaked. We knew we didn't have this letter,
but it got to be a running joke in our campaign. We were going to
have a folded piece of paper sticking out of President Bush's jacket
pocket at the debate, and have him slip it in and out every once in a
while during the debate, just to keep Clinton off balance.

James

When a political rumor hits, it has great authenticity and force.
But give it time. When we asked people and started to cross-examine
them, it got to, Well, they didn't really see it, they talked to somebody who saw it. But they did talk to that person.

"Well, call and find out . . ."

Actually the person he talked to didn't see it, but the person that
guy said he talked to said he saw something.

When I was a kid you'd pick corn and you'd run it in the house and
boil it right away, because right after you pick it it starts to lose some
of its sugar content. My grandpa would tell us, "Go over there and get
ten ears of corn and then run 'em back in here so your grandma can
cook 'em." As soon as the corn came in, man, it was so sweet.

That is just like a political rumor. If the corn sits there, two hours
later all the sugar's gone out of it and you got nothing but starch left.

You're always having to deal with rumors. In political campaigns
you just don't have an affair with somebody, you have a baby. It's got
to be compounded. It's like Old Faithful, every so many days it kind
of gushes up.

At the same time, you can't just let these rumors sit and get
starchy, you have to deal with them—because the press calls. And
they're scared. "Somebody tells me something, I don't print it, somebody else does and there's something to it, I look like shit." It's a
competition, and as competition increases the whole thing keeps
escalating.

Mary

There are rumors and there are rumormongers and there are moles. I got a call from a stranger around this time that I paid attention to. My calls were screened, but this guy knew things only I knew about Lee Atwater, and said he had important debate information that he would only give to me, so he got through.

His firm, he said, was nonpartisan, but some Democratic activists in it had been commissioned by the Clintonistas for debate prep and he could give me inside information about their activities.

Some of his facts were true, some were worthless. Some were true *and* worthless. He said they had dyed Clinton's hair but it had come out too dark and they'd spent all Saturday trying to undye it. Sure enough, when Clinton came out for the next debate his hair was a different color.

James

This is the first time I've heard that one. The only person I'm absolutely certain dyed their hair in this campaign was Gennifer Flowers.

Mary

He claimed he had two critical pieces of information. The first was about the citizenship letter. His contribution was that the Democrats really were concerned that we were going to whip out some document in the middle of the debate. The second was that the Democrats had a mole in our campaign.

I took this mole business very seriously, because there were lots of volunteers who came in and out, and security was not as tight as you'd think. Somebody ripped off my Visa card and charged $1,100 worth of clothes and stereo equipment. Another time somebody stole $200 out of my purse on my desk. We had code locks on every door, but the doors were always either propped open for air or everybody in the world knew the code. We had security badges that nobody ever wore. People were forever roaming around; they could get into your computer files without much difficulty. It's very easy to infiltrate a campaign, and I'm surprised it's not done more often. His information was not out of the question.

The mole was supposedly a woman in our opposition scheduling department, the people who keep tabs on the opposition's itinerary. In fact, the Clintonistas did always seem to know which events we were going to bracket—bracketing is coming in right before and after their events—and were always prepared to bracket our bracket operation. It could have simply been smart thinking on their part. The only thing this person knew about the supposed mole was that she was dating someone in the Clinton campaign and that all the boys said she was ugly but had big breasts.

So I was the one who had to call the head of bracketing and say, "I know this is a weird question, but . . . do you have an ugly woman with big breasts in your operation?"

He hesitated. Was this a trick harassment question? "I don't know. I'll check it out."

Carney and I and the guy who ran bracketing planned a counter-terrorist strategy. We had no idea who the mole might be—there were a lot of ugly people there, and we didn't exactly know how to go about checking out breast measurements—so we left fake information around to see if it got back to the Democrats. To this day I don't know if we had a mole.

I have known of moles at various levels of political campaigns, so you always have to take that possibility seriously. In fact, it is wise to maintain an observant outlook in general. Once at the RNC we found a telephone bugged, and thereafter had to sweep the joint regularly. Another time Atwater had a strange feeling he was being followed. He hired a private investigator, who discovered Atwater was indeed being tailed by some reporter goons. (Lee lured them to a gas station, and while they were busy keeping an eye on him, had his aide stick a banana in the guys' exhaust pipe.) On many occasions when we were on the road, our makeshift hotel staff offices were broken into.

No campaign heavyweight goes out and hires a mole, but it happens. No one on the organization chart is assigned to "mole," but sooner or later someone just emerges as a person who is adept at it.

Sometimes moles just pop up. Some supporter in the state who has been a volunteer for the other side will arrive and the state chairman will pass him on. Whoever discovers the connection becomes in charge of it. At least, that's how we worked. I have heard of campaigns where it is a specific assignment.

My thought when I heard it was, That's pretty smart. The worst place to find a mole, and the best place to put one, is in the research operation. Researchers are typically intellectuals in real life, policy wonks and computer hackers, the kind of people you have to go out and hire, not ones usually hanging out in campaigns. No one really gives them the CIA once-over. I bet if you asked Carville, he is probably the kind of guy that specifically ran them. I don't think there's anything unethical or wrong with it. It's an article of war. Industrial espionage.

You're always trying to find out information about your opponent. We had all our TVs hooked up to the bird and we were constantly trying to find out what their satellite coordinates were so we could pull in their ads and interviews. I was always on the lookout for Clinton to say something different from one shot to another; he was notorious for that. We'd always hope he'd say something embarrassing when he thought he wasn't on the air. That's not really sabotage, that's technological opportunity. I think the press did it, too. If they didn't, they should have.

We used to joke around about scrambling his signal and knocking him out of the sky. But it would be so easy to get caught it wouldn't be worth the risk, and the press would go absolutely crazy if they found out.

So here we were on the eve of the first debate, and on top of everything else, I'm thinking about scrambled signals and ugly, big-breasted moles. What a job.

Most everybody in politics starts out sane, but even though you've been through it before and you swear it won't happen to you again, by the end of the campaign you're paranoid about everything. You think your phones are tapped, your computers are rigged. In the last few days before the election I started using pay phones only and talking in code. It's a psychological breakdown that just kind of slips up on you.

James

We would put ads on the satellite that we weren't going to run, just to freak them out. Fake spots, so they would have to put some time and money together and respond to it. We thought they were going to attack us on health care, so we sent out one to attack them to try and keep them on defense. There was a whole Star Wars thing going on. That cat-and-mouse game reached its zenith when the Bush folks actually sent a health care spot to the stations and we sent an immediate response. Neither spot ever ran. The missiles stayed in their silos.

The fax machine has taken unsolicited espionage to new levels. A page from a strategic document could just come in over the wire, you didn't know if it was real or not, you didn't know if they were sending it to you just to throw you off. We got a lot of mysterious faxes. I never paid much attention to them.

Mary

Our debate prep was dignified and formal. It must have been humiliating for the President of the United States to rehearse in front of all these little staff weenies. The President had been given several three-inch-thick three-ring binders crammed with material, and the early sessions were more like briefings with policy experts and Clinton record aficionados.

In fact, they gave him too much material. George Bush was meticulous about studying everything he was given, which then came out of his mouth sounding like policy gobbledygook. During an Air Force One flight I was called up to his cabin and found him knee-deep in study mode. He was being overwhelmed by superfluous junk he was never going to be asked about but felt compelled to memorize. I told him he didn't need that, it diminished his own good instincts.

The final debate prep session, the day of the debate, was held in an auditorium in the Old Executive Office Building. With podiums, speakers, panel, and audience, Roger Ailes had the whole place set up as closely as possible to what the real event would look like. He had a guy on the clock so the President could get accustomed to making all his points in the allotted time. By the time he got to St. Louis, he was ready.

Except for dress rehearsal, which Teeter was nice to let me attend, debate prep was not my job. On-site spin was. A lot more goes into it than meets the eye. All the public ever sees is a bunch of goons propagandizing; they never see the behind-the-scenes pandemonium. You had to move your best research guys out to the debate site from Washington. Their computer system had to be hooked up to home base in D.C. for the purpose of holding Clinton accountable for his every word. As Clinton was making each statement, a research wonk would pull up his exact previous statement on the topic, highlight the discrepancies, and run it in to the spinners, who would all be in a separate room glued to the debate as it progressed. Charlie Black, a cool head, was in charge of this operation. He would sign off on the response, staff would get it typed up and to the copy machine, and then run into the pressroom and hand it out while the debate was still going on.

The wire reporters file continuously during the debate, constantly updating their pieces. By the end, their stories are already done and running. They are the first ones out, and most of the rest of the print guys follow their lead. This has been true for twenty years. Time for reflection is at a minimum. Reporters could go back and do their own research, but that's not how debate coverage works. It's really like a sports event; whatever happens while you're there is what gets covered, period. They rely on their memories and on what each side gives them. We would get big points if we got there first with the facts.

This was head researcher David Tell's finest hour. He was a big brain, he could never download all of his information, but he knew everything and he knew exactly where to get it. He and his crew were the Clinton experts. Put me to shame. Jim Cicconi, our invaluable issues researcher, and his crew were the Bush experts. Between them we had this two-pronged attack. If Clinton lied about Bush or Bush policy, which he was wont to do, Cicconi's end of it would whip out the facts. If Clinton backpedaled on something he had previously said, Tell's operation would crank out the truth.

You never know if it's going to work before the real event. You have a technical run-through to see that the computers are hooked up and the copy machines can handle the speed and volume. God forbid you blow a fuse, you have hard copy backup. The gigantic brains were in St. Louis with their most trusted aides hooked up to the computers at home, but dress rehearsal is never like the real thing.

Fact correction was phase one. Phase two was political spin. As the candidates began their closing statements, Charlie would gather all the spinners together and give us marching orders. We were not responsible for memorizing the fact sheets already distributed; our job was to put a positive spin on our guy's performance, and to denigrate the opposition:

"President Bush clearly demonstrated tonight the breadth and depth of his knowledge and experience. He is a proven leader. Leadership is what this election is all about, and we're thrilled the voters have had this opportunity to compare the candidates and focus on their choice."

That's verbatim. I said it so many times, it's burned into my memory.

Then Charlie would give us a rally cry like in a football huddle, and we'd run to the pressroom. As soon as we entered we were surrounded by reporters, microphones, cameras, and tape recorders. After the beat reporters got their fill, our advance men, one assigned to each spinner, would move us to the satellite station. The local print press subscribe to the wire services. The local newscasts used to take network feeds, but with the advent of satellite now they've got us live. It was very effective message dissemination.

Deputy communications director Leslie Goodman, our technician extraordinaire, got to be very good friends with her Democratic counterpart, and between them they got the satellite stations set up. She hooked up and pre-scheduled satellite tours for dozens of spinners. The obvious suspects, like me and Charlie, were always on hand. Then they broke it out by topic: We'd have Phil Gramm there for budget issues; Lynn Martin for domestic issues; Brent Scowcroft for foreign policy. As the debates progressed, depending on where we were we would have the appropriate surrogates: the senator and governor from the state the debate was in, senators and congressmen from the surrounding areas, and a lot of cabinet members.

James

The morning of the debate I was on *Meet the Press*. Tim Russert asked me, "Mr. Carville, the deputy campaign manager for the Bush-Quayle campaign, Mary Matalin, said that Governor Clinton is guilty of pathological deception. Does she have a point?"

Mary

I was always saying that. We never wanted to call Clinton a liar, so I had Rhonda go through the thesaurus and give me every other word for it. I liked "prevaricator"; it was alliterative with "pathological."

James

I said, "Well, I think Mary Matalin has got a good career in fiction writing when this is over." I was missing her but I wasn't going to let her get away with that kind of cheap, whiny political rhetoric. Russert asked me, "What's the best thing you can say about George

Bush?" I said, "Anybody that Mary Matalin likes as much as she likes George Bush can't be all that bad."

We all went over to the auditorium on the campus of Washington University, where the debate was going to take place. It was a carnival atmosphere, like there was either going to be a game or a hanging. Satellite trucks were moving in, technicians were running wires, student volunteers with green and yellow and red badges were moving things around. It was the ritual in preparation.

Yes, you're committed to what you're doing. And, yes, you try to stay focused on the important things at stake. But, yes, it is fun to play this game. All kinds of aspects of the game are fun to play. Paul and I got up onstage and stood behind the podiums, me in Clinton's spot, Paul to the right of me in Perot's. It must be like what you would feel if you walked out to the mound at Yankee Stadium the day before a World Series game and tried to hum a few over the plate.

"My fellow Americans," I began. "The basic question this election is a choice. It's a choice of whether we can take four more years of George Bush or do we need change, and we need change now. Do we need to move away from trickle-down economics and toward investing in our own people. Investing in people so we can build a greater America. We're a country that is coming together again, not one that is falling apart. For the past twelve years we have ignored such fundamental issues as rising health care costs—" I started laughing. I could recite the stump speech by heart.

"Y'understand what I'm sayin'?" Paul began like a machine gun. Paul, mind you, does a wicked Perot. "It's just about time to open that hood and fix the darn thing. Let's just git to work."

"Well, sir," I responded, "I think that you have some good things to say there. I also think while you're under that hood you gotta do something about health care costs, and while you got that wrench out you gotta stay under there because you know if you got out the hood might fall on your head." We laughed ourselves off the podium.

Mary

I was in a terror going to St. Louis that day. I hadn't seen Carville since a one-hour dinner on my birthday, almost two months before, and there he was going to be. The first thing I did when I got in was call him.

But it was just another point-of-contact call. I had a ton of things to do to distract me. The small hotel lobby was stuffed with supporters to schmooze and press to spin. I hooked up with Teeter and went to the debate hall to get the lay of the land.

James

Back at the hotel for one last hour of prep it was a madhouse. Everybody wanted to see the practice. A senator is in town, some big contributors are here, supporters, FOBs. Everybody had some kind of credentials, we couldn't kick them out, so they would just come in, they wanted to be part of the scene. And Clinton likes to see his friends.

In the middle of all these people milling around we were saying, "Let's go over the closing statement one more time. Don't forget, when you talk about Bush you've gotta turn this way, look that way. Now, these are our objectives: We want to stay focused, we want to bring it back to 'Can we afford four more years of the same?' 'It is time to change.' We want to continue talking about the economy and invest-ment strategy. Watch out for Perot, because if you get too enmeshed in what's going on with Bush, you leave an opening for him."

I started to get antsy. "Now, look," I said, "don't talk about every-thing; we already got too much on there. If you want to add one issue, you've gotta take one off. You leave the goddamn room and y'all put something else on the plate."

Then we had the traveling throat and voice physician, Dr. James Suen, saying Clinton's voice was about to go. "He has to stop, he can't talk any more. If he talks any more he's not going to be able to talk tonight." But, hell, in a campaign nobody listens to a doctor, you've got to suck it up. The campaign doctor—me—said, "No, we gotta run through this one more time." Then Hillary came in. "That's it." Okay, that settled that. On to the next one.

It got to be time.

We had kind of a ritual. George and Paul and I usually arrived with him to a debate. The reason was, we could occupy space and say nothing. Everybody has a tendency to want to overtalk it. George and Paul and I could ride in a car with the candidate and get five or six words in, maybe. "Gee, look at those people out there." "Man, there's a lot of signs along the way here." Prep time's over. It's like when you take an exam: Either you're ready or you're not.

We got out of the car and into the locker room. People were making him up; then you had the final people putting the mikes on. It's a little like you're going into an operation and they're prepping you.

When you're a presidential candidate you've got to get acclimated to it, you get handled a lot. Physically. "Wait, let me brush this back." "'Scuse me, Governor, can you just talk into that? We got this remote on you in case the other mike goes down." "Governor, I'm sorry, they're going to need you for five minutes in there with somebody. . . . Where is he?"

"Well, he's gone to the bathroom."

"Goddamn, we gotta get out there on the stage."

"Well, you know, a man's gotta piss. What the hell can you do?"

Then there's always somebody in the campaign that walks in and feels the compulsion to say something at the last minute: "Don't forget the—"; "Mention—." You see a presidential candidate, some people just feel compelled to give advice.

We made a little gangway for Clinton as he headed for the stage. High fives, a lot of chatter—"Yeah, yeah, yeah, come on through. Go get 'em"—like the heavyweight champ entering the arena or the Dallas Cowboys running onto the field.

Here comes the champ.

We watched the debate in an office at the auditorium. We were also hooked up to a dial group in Dayton, Ohio. The people were turning the dials and Greenberg was on the phone calling off the numbers. Dial numbers are like the weather: 50s are kind of cool, 60s are comfortable but nothing memorable, 70s are good and warm. Anything over 80 is truly hot. Clinton was talking and getting strong response.

"Seventy, seventy-one, seventy-two, seventy-five, seventy-eight, seventy-nine . . . seventy-five, sixty-nine. Shit, what's this? Why's he saying that?"

Mary

 Clinton wasn't in the 70s. He never got over the 60s in our dials.

James

Maybe we had different groups, I don't know. You could see Perot was doing pretty well. And we were doing pretty well. Bush was doing a little less well.

Greenberg was calling out the numbers, I was talking to the screen. "Come on, Governor. Six times we practiced that. Six times, man . . . Oh, that was great, he improvised there." I'd just fall on the floor. "How could they ask such a stupid goddamn question as that? Where's Mickey? How'd we let that dumb son of a bitch get on the panel, Mickey, huh? Goddamn."

A lot of it was just worthless nervous blather, and some of it was that I was kind of expected to entertain. It's fun.

Mary

It was nerve-racking. We sat there, and as we were watching, pollster Fred Steeper was deep into his focus group dial-a-thon. He would give his dial numbers to communications director Will Feltus, who had previously been a pollster. Feltus digested the numbers and ran in every ten minutes with a list of topics and how each man was doing in them. Anything over 70 was hot; the 50s were boners. For instance, President Bush, in his discussion of health care, always emphasized doctor choice and malpractice reform, and it got us off the charts. He got a couple of good shots in.

Charlie Black synthesized, in his mind, the high and low points and constructed for us no more than four or five talking points for the media. The rule of thumb was that the total talking-point package had to fit on half a page of paper; anything more and you couldn't get it out the way you needed to get it out. And everybody had to say the same thing.

Fifteen minutes before the debate was over Charlie pulled all the spinners together and, via the dial-a-thons and his own thinking and the ambience and tone of what was going on, gave us a set of talking points. He lined us up and handed us this piece of paper and we rushed into the spin room.

We were too early. The press ignored us. We stood there like dopes and watched until the very end. Then, within an instant, the assault was on.

You never know; these things aren't over till they're over. I was told the story of Lee Atwater (who called himself a junkyard dog; he couldn't wait to spin for his guy) going out early in one of the Reagan debates and missing some last doofus comment by his candidate, out there spinning away and making a total jerk of himself, which could happen to any of us. Plus, another part of you wants to see the debate.

Forget about what your job is; you want to see the whole thing. And the press didn't want to hear from us too early; they wanted to see how this show turned out.

The spin room is now a campaign constant, and the concept of hordes of reporters and media personalities screaming at operatives and spokesmen has entered the mainstream. But it hadn't been done at this level, at this volume, until this event. Spinning took the great leap forward at Washington University that night.

The spin room was in a cavernous gymnasium filled with long tables and folding chairs, where each member of the press sat typing away on a laptop. At the far end was a phalanx of camera stations with their battery of lights, each with a little director's chair in front of them. When we walked into that room there was an instant frenzy of cameras and microphones and people just shouting at you.

It feels like you're being spun like a top. Simultaneously terrifying and invigorating. It never got routine. You have to think so fast on your feet, and in every single instance I dreaded going in. There were people you'd see on TV who weren't necessarily on the campaign, and that would be intimidating. I got used to the national television press who traveled with us, but these were new guys who I didn't know and didn't know how to appeal to. I was always nervous about the press covering Clinton, because I thought they were pro-Clinton. Plus, there were local guys and everybody was screaming.

There was no protocol whatsoever. On campaign trips, reporters are usually kind of orderly; one will ask a question, then do a follow-up, then someone else will have her turn. You walk into one of these things and it's like the attack of the locusts. You feel like there are bugs all over you, picking at you. Everybody's pushing, and they've got these giant boom mikes that swing around and literally get in your face. People are all screaming at the same time and you're trying to answer all their questions, and then someone will refute you and the tone is hard and aggressive and nasty. It's just so intense, and you get totally involved.

You can't move. Every two steps another circle of reporters would form around me and there'd be another confrontation.

They would go from Republican to Democrat, comparing answers and demanding comments. The whole campaign has come before them in one room. They like this madhouse.

How'd we do? "I thought the President was exceedingly and clearly more relaxed, more experienced, a leader. Governor Clinton set out to be boring because he thought that would be a victory, and in being so cautious and so tentative he proved what he is, another politician. You had a nice, folksy guy up there in Mr. Perot; and you had clearly a leader, an experienced, steady leader, in George Bush; and you had a cautious politician spewing a lot of statistics. I almost passed out on account of how boring he was. Governor Clinton, compared to the relaxed and experienced George Bush and the folksy Ross Perot, came in third. So we are very happy with what happened tonight. Very happy."

They'd come back for the second round and say, "Well, Carville just said—" My favorite response to that was "What does he know?" As if Carville were the oracle. I told them, "It is not unknown for Carville not to be exactly correct on every single statement that he utters." They always thought that was a hoot. Their little joke was to try to bait me on Carville, and I'd always be ready.

James

Right before the debate we had all the congressional people in for a briefing. We said what they would say after the debate, before the debate. "Now look, when we go out, this is what we're going to say." About five minutes before it was over we got together again to focus it even further. Then we hit the ground running.

George and I were charging down the cinder-block corridor to get there. "All right, what are we going to say?"

"That Clinton clearly showed command, he was very relaxed, he kept control of the agenda. Exactly what we wanted to do. We couldn't be any happier with his performance. This was a great win. Bush needed a win; not only did he not get it, he actually had a loss. This is devastating—"

We knew we had done well, and after years of creating political patter those lines come out of a strategist naturally.

"All right, fine, go on."

The spin room is the presidential-campaign equivalent of the locker room after the big game. But it's a locker room where you don't know the score. In fact, if you work hard enough, you can tell them the score.

Everybody is claiming they won.

"Mr. Carville, why did you think Governor Clinton won this debate?" I was asked.

"Well, I mean, he made the most sense." I laughed. "I think that people looked at him, they wanted change, and I think they looked at him and said, 'Is this guy gonna bring the kind of change that I want?' and 'Is he somebody that I want as president?' And, I mean, I'm only a political consultant, but projecting from where I sat I thought that both answers were in the affirmative."

"Do you think the President lost the debate?"

"Yes."

George, who was standing right next to me, said, "Yeah, Governor Clinton won the debate in the first ten minutes. He confronted President Bush and said, 'Mr. Bush, you've had your chance. We tried it your way; it didn't work; it's time for a change.' That's really right where people are right now.

"President Bush has based his whole campaign in the last week on questioning Governor Clinton's patriotism. Governor Clinton said, 'No more. It's beneath you, it's beneath the presidency.' "

That's all one hundred percent pure, unadulterated, unrefined, unfiltered spin. And everybody knows it's spin: us, them, the world. In a pool of thirty cameras and people screaming, wanting answers, one guy asked me the best question I've ever heard in a spin room. He said, "Does any of this do any good?"

I said, "No."

"Why do you do it?"

"Because if I didn't do it, you'd say that we lost and we were scared to come out and defend our candidate. So we just come out here because you're here. Am I going to change your mind with any of this? No. Are you going to change my mind with any of this? No. But we've got to do it because it's expected. Anyway, where else can you go and have forty people with cameras asking you questions?"

Mary

My major terror was that I was going to see James. Even walking into this mayhem I was thinking, "I'm going to see James Carville and I don't know how I'm going to react but I know it ain't going to be good." Which was very stupid for me to think going into an attack situation.

I was tormented over this relationship. Ninety-nine percent of my being, my brain, my breathing, eating, sleeping, waking was the campaign. But there was a very weighty 1 percent that was him, that was ever-present. I didn't know what was going to happen to the relationship, and in alternate minutes I hated him or I loved him.

This was not your typical kind of relationship conflict. George Bush had been down 15 points for a month, and I was not in the best frame of mind. And in my personalization of the situation, I was blaming it on Carville. The reason Clinton was winning was because of Carville. The reason we were losing was because of Carville. All the bad things about the campaign were because of Carville. I was having a difficult time separating the nightmare of the campaign from the nightmare of James Carville.

I was standing in a circle of cameras, and right behind me was another circle of cameras. This was not in itself unusual; there were knots of reporters around everywhere. You never look who's in the next frenzy; who cares? But I could see this one boom mike going back and forth like a tennis match, so I glanced behind me.

There was this shiny dome, instantly recognizable as the Carville serpenthead. We were three feet apart.

It was an instantaneous peripheral glance and I didn't miss a beat. No visible reaction whatsoever. I just kept hammering away at Clinton, noting almost subconsciously the weirdness of spinning back to back with the love of my life.

James

Out of the corner of my eye I caught Mary. "Wait a minute, that's not—" I did a hard double-take. Maureen Dowd of *The New York Times* caught me at it and wrote in the paper the next day that it was "so violent, onlookers worried he might have wrenched his neck." I don't know about that. I do know that I almost started crying. My heart jumped in my chest, I had this instant hole in the pit of my stomach. I got all clammy.

I got flustered. These sessions are mostly bullshit, but say something stupid and they'll get you in trouble. Thank God it was near the end of the spin cycle, I don't know how much more of being near her I could have taken. I couldn't talk to her; I think I would have broken down. People were looking at us for a reaction. I mean, you haven't seen somebody you're in love with for almost two months, what do you say to them in front of forty TV cameras, "How's it going?" It took the breath out of me.

Mary

I really did not want to talk to him. I couldn't and I didn't, and it was not painful not to. We stayed away from each other. His presence was more the enemy than James himself. Which was also a little disconcerting. I was hoping that wouldn't be the reaction, but in that mode, at that time, he was the enemy.

I did the satellite tour and by the time I got back to the office the guys had taped the spin scene from C-Span. We kept playing James's head jerking back and forth twenty times in a row, and we were on the floor just dying, it was so Carvillian.

James

Then I had to go through this gruesome satellite spin. We had a whole team of surrogates on the air. You've got to do it—there are cities and states that are yours for the taking and you've got to get in front of their local cameras and say the same thing to a half-dozen different individual newscasters and keep it fresh.

You sit on a stool and the communications guy in charge of getting this right hands you a list.

"All right, this is Sam, he is the anchorman for Channel Whatever in Sacramento. Do we have him hooked up yet? Wait, stay right there, James, don't move. Okay, here he goes. . . ."

"Hey, Sam, how's it going out in Sacramento? All right."

"Well, what did you think about tonight, Jim?"

"I thought the governor gave a very good account of himself. He was very focused on the economy, the need for change in this country, about bringing about a new message of hope and optimism."

"What did you think of Bush?"

"Well, I thought he was a little off his game, he seemed a little nervous, a little unsure of himself. But he had a very difficult job trying to defend his last four years, or twelve years, whichever way you want to look at it. I mean, this has been a tough go for him."

"What did you think of the question on the draft?"

"Well, that's not what people are worried about. I mean, what they're really concerned about, Sam, is this economy. And I think that's what the governor talked about. As we get closer to election day, people are really sort of focused on what's important to them."

"Thank you very much."

"All right. Good. Tell everybody hello out there in California."

Red light goes off. "Where are we now?"

"Betty in Beaumont. Okay, ready. . . . Hold on just a second, we can't get this thing hooked up. We're going to go now, what do we have over here? We have Corrine in Cleveland."

"Why am I doing Cleveland? Why isn't George doing Cleveland, he's from Cleveland, he could have sat on Cleveland TV, he's a Cleveland native. Why in hell do you have me in Cleveland and not him in Cleveland? You probably got him in New Orleans and not me. What the hell are you people doing? I mean, you can't think past your—" Red light goes on. "Oh, hey, hey, hey, how's everything in Cleveland? God, I love that city. Okay, what do we have over here?"

Everybody's trying to hook up, and they're trying to get some satellite to phone in and catch something here and bounce off this.

"Hurry up, we gotta cut short, we got you live. Hey, we got James live in Syracuse."

"What? That's not a target state. Shit. Why don't you have me live in Louisville, Kentucky?"

"Because Senator Ford's doing that."

"Oh, okay, good, cool. Where are we? What town are we in now?"

Mary

As the evening wound down I'd grab a beer and sit there and schmooze off-camera, or what I thought was off-camera. I don't think anybody ever displayed me slugging down a long-neck. They held up a sign for my next satellite interview: "Seattle, Dave." In my most snotty, annoyed, end-of-a-really-hard-day voice I complained, "What the hell am I talking to Seattle for? Washington is off the map. We're losing Washington. Why am I doing this?"

Of course, the camera was rolling. They skipped my entire interview and kept running that particular piece of tape over and over. It made its way into the Seattle papers, and from there to *The New York Times*. This time it wasn't life-threatening, we had no chance of winning Washington, but if it had been a close state I would have created an issue. You can't say stuff like that; it was really unprofessional. Loose lips. The point being, as the candidates will tell you, always consider your mike open.

James

All this time somebody's handing you data. Everything is instant. ABC, who won the debate? CBS? "Well, ABC says that Perot won." "Yeah, but right here CBS says we won."

"It's Andrea Mitchell. She needs two minutes with you on camera."

"Can she talk to me while I'm hooked up here?"

In the midst of this I was having a good time. We'd had an okay debate. If we'd had a bad debate I probably would have felt different; you never have a good time losing. But it don't matter as long as you win.

CHAPTER 23

James

Senator Gore knew he was in a tough position when he was going up against Quayle in the vice-presidential debate. So little was expected of Quayle that he couldn't help but win the expectation game; the only thing that would have met expectations would have been if Quayle had spelled something wrong or done something stupid. I knew that Quayle would be well prepared, that he was a better debater than people thought. I didn't want to say it to Gore specifically, but if we tie, we lose; if we win by a little bit, we lose. Everybody knew it. Marlin Fitzwater knew it, all the Gore people knew it, Gore knew it.

George said, "The senator wants you and me to go to Atlanta and work on debate prep." I was very flattered that he specifically asked for me.

There's some truth to the old saw that the campaign is a reflection of the candidate. The difference between Bill Clinton and Al Gore was immediately clear. Gore's prep was very methodical, very organized, very to the point. Ours was more emotional. If you didn't see faces but just heard the sounds and saw images, each one would be instantly recognizable; they're the ones with the mineral water and fresh fruit, we had the real Coke and real Pepsi and cheese and crackers. They would start on time and be specific; ours had a lot more screaming and yelling.

I don't think many presidential races turn on vice-presidential debates, but they can help or hurt. Lloyd Bentsen certainly made his reputation against Quayle in '88. I think Bob Dole didn't fare very well, got his reputation for meanness, in his debates with Mondale in '76. Mostly they are momentum creators, and because we were definitely going to lose the expectations game, I thought this one had potential for disaster.

Usually what happens in a debate is that most of the people that like you think you did fine. Most of the people that like the other guy think *he* did fine. So if you start with more people liking you, you'll do okay. What you really want to know is, How do the people that like both of you feel? What are the people who don't know how they feel about either of you feeling? And, Do the people who liked you still like you?

Mary

Quayle got hammered by Lloyd Bentsen in '88, and he was absolutely not going to let that happen again. Bush's performance in the first debate had been criticized for not being hearty enough, and people were still saying the President wasn't being aggressive enough on the campaign trail. Well, Quayle was a pit bull.

Where the first presidential-debate spin room had been a hard sell because each group could make a claim that their man won, this one was a tad more relaxed for us because we had clearly taken it. The expectations for Quayle were so low that the press was shocked when he got off a couple of good riffs. Everyone thought he did a great job, not only in substance, tone, tenor, and feistiness, but also in taking the offensive.

With minimal urging from us, the press picked up on the fact that every time Quayle attacked Clinton, particularly on the "Slick Willie" issues of character and veracity, Gore did not defend him. That alone was enough for us to have a happy face going out there.

I cannot tell you the difference in spinner attitude when you can dance out onto that floor.

The environment was a lot less hostile than it had been two days before in St. Louis, and I was chatting away, being a wisenheimer in the middle of a clutch of reporters and cameras, when I felt something at my ankles. Felt like a cat. I looked down and there was this man—a very good-looking man, as a matter of fact—with long hair and a video camera, shooting from the ground up. From where I was standing it looked like he was shooting up my skirt.

I screamed—"Oh, my God, it's crawling up my leg!"—jumped back, stepped on him, we're knocking over cameras, the whole circle were slamming into each other, cameras were crashing, boom mikes were banging, there's a domino thing happening.

I only missed one beat with this guy—stepped on him, stepped over him—then went right back to the cameras and kept on spinning.

The entire circle burst out laughing. Even they couldn't believe I was such an obsessive spinner that I didn't even take a breath to yell at this guy for shooting up my skirt, just kept spinning away.

James

Gore went in with a message he wanted to deliver—change—and came out very well. There was a lot made of his not defending Governor Clinton against Quayle's attacks. That was something the press manufactured. Gore went in with a good strategy: Don't let the opposition knock you away from making your important points. He supported Clinton all the way, and anyone who doubted that was an idiot; what the media was looking for was headlines from an event that didn't really produce any of its own.

Of course we had to respond. By chance, the next day the story on the GOP's searching Bill Clinton's passport file broke, and it was the perfect time for Al Gore to charge to Clinton's defense. Gore would defend the governor against dirty tricks and we could soar above the political fray on the issue of the economy.

Mary

So, of course, the next day, because Gore was taking such heat for not defending Clinton, Gore takes after us for supposedly expediting a search of Bill Clinton's passport files. *The Washington Post* was reporting that, in response to Freedom of Information Act requests by some news organizations, U.S. embassies in London and Oslo had been ordered to search their records for information on Clinton while he was a student in England. Gore said that President Bush had ordered the searches as "part of a McCarthyite smear effort." It just wasn't so.

Way back during the Democratic primaries the press had called David Tell, wanting Clinton's State Department files, presuming we could get them. They said they thought something was there, might have to do with citizenship. In the same way that we would always report press trends to each other, Tell reported to me that an inordinate number of press people were calling about these files, what should he do? I said, "Tell them to eat doggie-doo and die. Do not call the State Department under any circumstances, or you will be fired. If they want anything governmental they can get it through the Freedom of Information Act."

I said that for two reasons. One, even though they were asking for this dirt, if we supplied it we would have taken the heat for being dirty tricksters. Two, I knew Jim Baker. I'd worked with him on the '88 campaign and I knew him by reputation. He did not mix politics and government. And the State Department was his crown jewel, one of the shining monuments of the Bush presidency, he would not tarnish it in any way.

"If you even return these calls," I warned Tell, "you're crazy." He would have been burned at the stake for everyone to see. For a while the issue went away.

Newsweek was the next place I remember hearing of it. I asked Teeter and Charlie Black, "What is this?" Nobody knew, and certainly everybody had enough sense not to ask. You don't drink and drive, you don't rifle State Department files.

What I think happened, and I've seen this happen before, is that people on the ground, who love the candidate and are occasionally in unique positions to do something about it, went off and did it. They thought they were being helpful. This was a very bad version of some locals renting a crop duster and flying over Clinton's stock car event. We did not tell them to do it.

Elizabeth Tamposi, a neophyte Bush operative from the '88 campaign who was now at the State Department, got the FOIA request. An experienced hand gets this kind of request from the media all the time, knows that in these cases the reporters don't usually know what they're looking for; they're fishing. You also know you can do serious damage, even innocently, by helping them in their search, so you just put them off. I can see where someone with less experience could get these calls at her office, get all juiced up thinking there was something there, and thinking if she'd be helpful in finding it she'd be a hero. Because this information was relevant to this election, because the FOIA requests were active, she probably thought she'd be helping the President by acting upon them with dispatch. No one—I repeat, on my mother's grave, *no one*—called her up and said, "Expedite this stuff."

That is my theory on her mind-numbing naïveté.

Although no one from the White House called her, she contacted the White House. There was a great hoo-hah over this call *that was never returned*. The computerized, under-penalty-of-law-never-to-be-falsified phone log of Margaret Tutwiler indicated she did not return Tamposi's call. No human beings ever employed in government service are more learned and disciplined in government regulations than the Baker bunch. They all know how counterproductive and damaging it would be to get involved in that deal.

I know for a fact that no one from the campaign had anything to do with it, and I can state with one hundred percent confidence that the White House had nothing to do with it. Loyalty aside, it was personal survival. They have watched friends like Lynn Nofziger and Mike Deaver and Ed Meese get tied up in court for many years and countless dollars over technicalities. Nothing is worth doing that to yourself.

Strategically, it would not even have been the right move for us to provide this information. There are many times in a campaign where one side's providing evidence diminishes the quality of, or even discredits, that evidence. You want your most damaging info to be gotten independently by the press. And the press could get it by themselves, through FOIA or their own nefarious sources. They have sources all over the place. They got great stuff on Perot that we never had an inkling of. They dug up all Clinton's draft information. Our research banks consisted almost entirely of press clips, voting records, and public documents—pretty dry stuff. We relied on the bulldog aggression of the free press to dig up the dirt. We were sure if dirt was to be had, they would have it.

James

My original thinking was that maybe they thought this was helping them in some kind of strange way, and that this would accentuate and kick the draft story. I went to lunch thinking, "I wonder if this is hurting us. I wonder if, instead of talking about this weird search that was going on, people would say, 'Gee, is there something there?'"

Clinton had told us the whole time that there was nothing in his file that could be noteworthy. But I was concerned they'd put something there. If somebody's going to go to the trouble to look, and you've got all these government people getting their hands in there, who's to say? "I'm going to look in your glove compartment. Oh, gee, look what we found in here—some cocaine. Step out of the car." Here you're getting people willing to go out in the middle of the night to some government records place out in Maryland; how do we know what they're going to do once they get there? You're right in the middle of a presidential race. You don't have control of the document, they do. They could put in a notation. Anything.

It was definitely a major distraction. We weren't getting our message out because the press was asking about this passport file. Of course, neither were they. Then they went through the governor's mother's file. I think the press let them off easy on that one.

How did the rumor get started in the first place? Who said there was anything in Clinton's passport file worth finding? How did something start that (a) obviously didn't have a grain of truth to it; (b) consumed probably a good five hundred person-hours of a presidential campaign; (c) rolled up a million dollars in legal fees, and meters, if not miles, of newspaper space?

We were befuddled, but you could see pretty quickly that this thing was starting to turn against Bush. I tend to think it was probably more political stupidity than criminality involved. And they paid a pretty good price for it.

Mary

The second debate was held in Richmond, Virginia. It was an audience-participation show performed in front of 209 undecided voters selected by the Gallup organization. The questions were to come from the audience, not the usual panel of journalists.

The Clinton people didn't think we wanted to do this, that this was their event. We weren't worried. George Bush had been doing town meetings since 1979, and he loved and did very well at our Ask George Bush affairs. With the press expectations down—they all said we'd lost the first debate and were convinced that Bushspeak would work against us—we thought we were going to do very well.

At debate prep, Steve Provost played Perot. He had the little runt's voice, manner, and answers down impeccably. He was so good he actually caused problems; every time Provost opened his mouth we all cracked up. No laughing allowed, but even the President lost it. Dick Darman played an awesome Clinton. He knew every answer the Democrat had given in his entire political career and, of course, he knew more about Bush than Clinton ever would. Darman is by nature an aggressive, go-for-the-jugular guy, and he got in Bush's face. He was much better than the real Clinton.

The President, however, was not a happy camper. He knew he was a good debater, and these "performances," played to the handlers, irked him.

To make sure we covered all bases, Janet Mullins had given each "audience member" a topic area but had left the manner of questioning to our own theatrics. My topic was health care. When it came my turn I stood up and said, "Mr. President, my name is Sherry. I am a single mother with three kids and no health care. I can't make ends meet, and you don't seem to care." It was mean-spirited and took the President aback momentarily. Maybe he thought the "audience" was going to be polite. Fat chance. But he recovered in a nanosecond and responded with substance and compassion. Though it wasn't allowed, we gave him a round of applause.

We got to the hall hours early to check out the computers and see the setup. We picked our chairs in the holding room and put our little turkey sandwiches on them to save our place. In the studio the moderator, ABC News's Carole Simpson, was warming up the crowd. A few of us wandered out to listen to her.

Carole Simpson is a good person and a serious journalist, and President Bush likes her. Ed Fouhy, the producer of the debates for the Commission on Presidential Debates, says she was pre-locating the questioners so the cameras could practice finding them during the telecast, but it certainly appeared to us that she was pre-screening the questions. Which is valid; you want to make sure you have a diversity of questions, or that a person is not too shy to get his/her question out. However, in front of all the cameras and lights, and in the presence of TV personalities they never see up close—like Brit Hume and Andrea Mitchell and Carole Simpson—normal people want to be told what's acceptable behavior.

One man stood up and said, "I have a question of Mr. Perot, but I don't want to push the President."

I remember her saying, "Well, you push the President. That's what this is about. This is about getting the answers. You just push him."

The audience laughed. The way they took it, and certainly the way the questioner took it, was that it was okay to harass the candidates. It was immediately apparent to all of us that she had given the entire crowd, whether she meant to or not, permission to be disrespectful to the President.

We ran back to our room and began screaming about it to each other, just to get prepared. Charlie Black called Bob Teeter in the President's hotel suite and said, "She's gunning for us."

James

We ran a poll using the same criteria the Gallup people used in selecting the audience, to see if we could determine what the audience might be interested in. We went in with some degree of confidence.

This would be an event where the candidates would sit on stools in front of a semicircle group of voters, and there's nobody better in a room full of people than Bill Clinton. The reason is, he *likes* people. So often, particularly in a presidential race, which happens over a long period of time, the truth emerges. The truth is, Bill Clinton can listen better than anybody I've ever seen. Whether it's something he came by naturally or it was something he acquired, I couldn't say for certain. But he can be engrossed in people's stories.

Our preparation for the Richmond debate was different from the one in St. Louis. The big thing here was, Use the questioner. The TV audience would view this as if they were asking the questions themselves, so this was our opportunity to make personal contact. We couldn't turn away from a questioner the way we could turn away from a reporter if we thought we were being led somewhere we didn't want to go. In the scheme of the audience, reporters are Big People and as long as you aren't cruel to them, the press conference/spin room/interview battles are Big People going after Big People. This was the average person, and he or she had to be paid individual attention to.

We had great respect for George Bush as an aggressive debater, but we all felt this format was much better for us. We felt like, "Let's go back to the fundamentals in New Hampshire," where the candidate was in with the audience. "Just let Bill Clinton be Bill Clinton."

Our big concentration was to play off the question. "Even if Bush attacks you, don't talk to the camera. Don't talk to anybody but the questioner. In talking to that person you are, in effect, talking to the audience."

We did practice having the governor get off his stool and walk down to make contact with the man or woman asking the question. In New Hampshire, even when we were rehearsing for our own events, we would always remind him, "Go talk to that person. Be engaged in what he has to say." But by this time Bill Clinton didn't need that reminder. The main thing I wanted to stress here was "We've got to answer the question."

The most worrisome thing was that the enemy was Bill Clinton. I'd seen him spend fifteen minutes answering one question for a fry cook in Peoria. While he had to be engaging and do all the stylistic things that he normally did, he still had a limited amount of time to get the thing across.

Practice wasn't as organized or methodical as it had been in St. Louis. Rather than run the security risk of having strangers participate as crowd members, we recruited campaign staff and told the Virginia Democrats to bring some people. We couldn't simulate it as well, because the questions were all over the place. We didn't seem to be quite as crisp.

The final practice had more of the standard staff lack of discipline than I would have liked. Nobody had their game face on. But Clinton didn't seem particularly flustered by it. I was the one who was nervous. We were sitting there with a 10- or 12-point lead and I knew something was going to happen. He's going to have his fly open, something. I try to stay calm but I've learned to expect disaster; there's a point at which it knocks on your door.

Once I saw the room and the site I felt a lot better. I said, "Man, this thing looks like Bill Clinton."

Mary

Our performance in the debate wasn't as bad in the happening as it was subsequently reported. There were many cheap shots taken. A woman asked President Bush, "How has the national debt personally affected each of your lives? And if it hasn't, how can you honestly find a cure for the economic problems of the common people if you have no experience in what's ailing them?"

Everybody in our room was saying, "What's the question? What is she talking about?" We had the same reaction President Bush did, which was literal. To us, "national debt" was an economic term of art, a concept we dealt with every day. Beyond the Beltway, normal people mentally translated "national debt" to "recession." We didn't.

"I think the national debt affects everybody," said the President.

"You personally," said Carole Simpson.

"Obviously it has a lot to do with interest rates."

"She's saying, 'You personally.' You on a personal basis. How has it affected you . . . personally?"

James

The woman said "the national debt"; she meant "the recession." Everybody except Bush knew she meant "the recession." I very rarely fault another campaign, because I'm sure they could find a gazillion faults in any campaign I've been in, but if there's one thing I would fault Bush and his campaign on, it is that one question. It was the one question I feared the most.

Clearly Bush's biggest problem was that people thought he was out of touch. That he just sort of had some rich friends and didn't understand what real people were going through. If I had been running the Bush campaign I would have said, "That is the one question we want." I would have *paid* to have that question asked.

It's like you teach an infielder in baseball: Every time that pitcher cocks his arm back, the thought has to flash through your mind, "Hit the ball to me." Every system in you has to say, "Just smack the most amazing line drive, the toughest short-hop grounder, anywhere near me, I'm going to gobble it up." The minute you shy away from it, the minute you're not on the balls of your feet, the minute you're not concentrating, the ball's going through your legs.

If I had been in the Bush campaign I would have told him, "Any chance you get to explain and tell people that you care, that you understand, is a chance you want." It's the riskiest course, because what if you blow it? But if you don't blow it, you have answered the basic reason people have for not voting for you.

If I were Bush, this is how I would have answered that question: "You know, there's no question about it, I have grown up more fortunate than most. But there is nothing—nothing short of sending troops to war—that bothers me more than to know that this is a stagnant economy and that people like yourself are working harder and earning less. I cannot sleep, I cannot rest easy knowing that we have people like yourself, and people in this audience, who are working hard and having a hard time. That's why I've not been afraid to take on the tough fights. Because, however tough it may seem for me, I understand that every day, in every way, and all over this country, people are struggling a lot harder with their checkbooks than I'm struggling with these Democrats in Congress.

"The mail that I get every day . . . Let me just relay one, just pick one letter out from the millions of Americans who write their President hoping for their American dream to come true." I would have a real piece of mail. "Mrs. Gerasowski from Des Plaines, Illinois, sent me a letter, and I think she was saying the same thing that you are. And this is what I wrote her back, and I would say the same thing to you." I would read the letter. " 'I hope you understand that because I've been lucky, because I've grown up with more than most, the problems of this country bother me more. That's why I want to fix them.' "

In Des Plaines, Mrs. Gerasowski would already have been contacted. She would be up to the media onslaught. I would have tried to speak very haltingly, from my heart. And, man, I would have had that letter in my pocket before I went out there on that stage.

Now, why didn't they do that? I'm sure they were thinking of it. But there is also the very real possibility that the criticism is valid. That they were well-off white guys who were saying, "The markets are fine. The price of long bonds is actually up a tick or two." The very real possibility is that Mary's the only person in that whole campaign who ever bounced a check or got a dun from the Visa people. Until you've been chased around the block three or four times by some bill collectors, to a lot of people you ain't lived. Until you know the trick to call the bank people back at noon, when they've all gone to lunch, you may not be able to understand.

Mary

Maybe she was nervous at this big event, or just trying to do good TV, but at one point Carole Simpson told Ross Perot, "Mr. Perot, you have an answer for everything, don't you? Go right ahead, sir." She was in Phil Donahue mode. Someone asked an education question and she asked Bush pointedly, "Who would like to begin, the *Education* President?" She says it wasn't meant to be disrespectful. We all groaned: "What a cheap shot."

Simpson was doing an adequate job of controlling Perot, who kept defying the time restrictions, running on, butting in. But she seemed especially attentive and accommodating to Bill Clinton's body language. Whenever Clinton appeared to indicate that he wanted to follow up a question President Bush or Ross Perot had answered, she seemed to be aware of it immediately. I don't know if the President was out of her sight line or what, but George Bush was just about charging off his stool and she rarely came back to him. She all but ignored his body language, which while more reserved than Clinton's jumping-bean act, was not invisible. She never missed Clinton's. At one point the President of the United States had to raise his hand like a schoolboy and ask could he please have a comment on that. When you're watching in the holding room, that's the kind of stuff that curdles your blood.

While Clinton was going on and on, as we knew he would do, President Bush looked at his watch. In our room we all understood that signal. It was directed at Carole Simpson: "Are you going to cut him off? There are rules here, are you going to make him comply with the rules?" On the air and in the next day's papers the press implied that Bush was so bored he wanted to get out of there. It was patently false, and they knew it—the President even had the classic Bush mischievous half-smile on his face—but they couldn't restrain themselves from taking the truly cheap shot.

James

The one thing you didn't want to do in that debate was look uninterested. I said, "I'll bet you they're throwing up over there now."

The next day, Bush got heckled on a college campus in New Jersey and got irritated. He'd probably been hearing about how he wasn't aggressive enough in the debates and got tired of it. He told the crowd, "I wish these draft-dodgers would shut up so I could finish my speech." He didn't look too good doing it.

You have to understand his mind: I am George Bush, youngest pilot in World War II, ambassador to China, chairman of the Republican National Committee, director of the CIA, congressman, Vice President of the United States, President of the United States. Why am I having to go through this? I am running against a failed governor of a small state, a man who didn't go into the military—and I'm losing. I'm losing in the polls, I'm losing in the debates. The papers are saying I'm losing, the commentators are saying I'm losing. People are saying I'm losing.

George Bush is a very, very competitive man. The Iran-Contra deal goes out of his mind. He doesn't deal with the fact that he switched his positions on taxes and abortion. Nobody in polite company reminds him, and he doesn't remind himself. He was frustrated. He was losing.

Mary

After the second debate, the President was angry. He was very ticked off, as we all were, about the cheap shots he'd taken. He also got annoyed at the steady stream of sycophants on the plane who would come up and tell him, "That was a really good performance. You've done so well. Good job."

"Why do you keep saying that?" he said. He'd seen CNN and the rest of the media pulling him apart. "Why are you saying that when they're saying this? How can you tell me the numbers are so good when they're saying they aren't?"

He was still in the midst of a post-Richmond crank attack the next day when he let it rip at the hecklers at the New Jersey college. It was the only time I saw him lose it on the campaign stump.

The third debate was only three days off. If we didn't win that we could just pack it up. There was a lot of staff infighting—"To book or not to book?" The White House policy wonks dragged out their huge three-inch three-ring notebooks full of everything you ever wanted to know about anything. The President looked at them and shook his head. "Yeah, these have been a lot of help."

The prep mock debate was held the day before the real one, in an auditorium in the White House, room 450. The lights were dimmed on the theater-style seats to simulate the more formal staging of the third debate. Everyone was on edge. Steve Provost, who was playing Perot again, could usually lighten things up, but this time nothing was breaking the ice. I was asked to play the part of United Press International's Helen Thomas. The President thought this was pretty funny. I love Helen Thomas; she's tough but always asks fair questions. The dean of White House reporters, she is beloved by the many presidents she has tortured over the years. Bush doesn't like softball questions, so you were supposed to hit him with your best shot. But when someone asked a wonk question—"What are the thirteen points of your economic plan?"—Bush just rolled his eyes and moved on. He wasn't in a mood to fool around with us.

You've got to know your man. Some candidates are capable of absorbing and spewing back voluminous data bits, others can manipulate the dialogue to get in the perfect setup line and then deliver a practiced answer. But often, having a prepared phrase can be distracting; if you're thinking about the setup line you're not thinking about your larger purpose. All these guys have got the substance down. I've always thought the most important part of a debate was tone and tenor and attitude.

President Bush was very tense. And who wouldn't be? No matter what we did, we were getting trashed. His Richmond performance had been roundly criticized by the press and he was sick of these handler charades. About halfway through he said, "That's enough," and walked off the stage. He had the material down cold but he had a bad attitude.

This is when the *real* important preparation comes in. Only one man could get Bush in the right state of mind: Roger Ailes. He was the President's shadow that day, joking, encouraging, keeping everyone else out of his face.

The way to prep George Bush was to sit down and talk to him. Go over the big picture, go over strategy; the President lapped that stuff up. Ailes sat with him and reviewed Clinton's record. The general theme: During his governorship in Arkansas, Clinton doubled state spending; he increased taxes 128 times; and for all his tax-and-spend policies, in no category has there been an improvement in quality of life—in fact, the quality of life has gone down.

Ailes always played to Bush's strength, which was counterpunching. He devised comeback lines for every attack we expected from the Democrats. He wouldn't tell us what they were because (a) he wanted the President to get the credit, and (b) he knew some scum would leak them to the press.

We got on the plane and everyone was walking on pins and needles. The President called me to the front cabin; he wanted a riff on the worst aspects of the Arkansas record. When I got in there he was in a perceptibly better frame of mind just for having Roger around.

I figured I'd brighten things up more. I told him the rumor that Clinton dyed his hair—"No," he said, "men don't dye their hair"—and that they'd tried to dye it darker but to leave it gray at the temples, which is a very hard thing to do unless you're Christophe. And that they'd botched the job. "As a former beautician," I said, "it is obvious to me that Clinton has, in fact, done it recently. You can tell by the color of his scalp, you can tell by the way the light bounces off it. Just look at Clinton's hair."

Mrs. Bush said, "Oh, Mary, don't even say things like that. That's so silly."

The President said, "Don't tell me that. I'll just start laughing when I look at him."

James

When we got to East Lansing, Michigan, for the third debate, it was pretty clear that we didn't have the same fervor we'd had for the first two. We'd had a little explosion in the polls, we'd done real well in Richmond, and we were cocky. We had lost some concentration. It showed up in odd ways. For instance:

It gets cool in Michigan in October, and at our previous stop, Ypsilanti, I'd gone down to the hotel gift shop and bought a University of Michigan sweatshirt to run in. So, the afternoon of the debate, engrossed in a presidential campaign, I left my hotel and hit the streets for my daily run.

There were a thousand people outside the lobby, waiting to get a glimpse of the candidate, and they all started booing me.

"What'd I do, man?"

"You got a goddamn Michigan sweatshirt on!"

You'd think I'd know better than to walk out a couple of blocks from the Michigan State campus in Michigan maize and blue. "Well, the hell with it. It ain't that cold anyway." I stripped it off and threw it in the air. The crowd cheered.

Bush had the same thing going for him in Michigan that Quayle had had down in Atlanta: If he did any better than average they were ready to give him the win. The expectations game. And he did perform better than he had in the first two, and we did get a little cautious. As a result, we made a classic error: We pulled up at the sixteenth pole, not the finish line.

Usually the audience for the first presidential debate is the biggest, and it goes downhill from there. What I found significant was the level of public interest in these debates and in the campaign in general. This wasn't going to be an election day where people sat on their hands; the numbers got larger from debate to debate, and more people watched the last debate than watched the first.

Mary

We were all in a funky mood, braced for the worst, and President Bush was fabulous. He hit Clinton hard on trust and taxes and the Arkansas record. He gave no ground. But more than anything he actually said, it was a feeling that from here on in we were into take-no-prisoners mode.

We were so happy we went running into the spin room after this one, leaping, laughing, giggling, it felt so good.

"This is not a sports event," I told the press. "People don't get out their peanuts and popcorn and rate these things. They focus on the choice between these candidates and their philosophies. And we have tried to do that in each debate. We're not trying to create drama. We are not a made-for-TV candidate. Yes, Governor Clinton won on Geraldo-like activities. That's his shtick; he's a performer, he's a phony. I mean, he walks into the audience. He puts Geraldo to shame. That's not our gig. We are a leader. We are mature. We have a breadth and depth of experience that's unrivaled on that stage and that's all we've ever tried to do, and have been very successful in each of these debates doing it."

I was so happy for the President I temporarily forgave James. I went right up and gave him an electric-blue winter parka I'd bought for him. He told me he was taking me on a trip after the election; he wouldn't tell me where. I was actually glad to see him.

The next morning, CNN had us 18 points down. Didn't matter. We were cooking with gas now.

On the plane after the debate, President Bush came back to my seat. "You're not kidding," he told me. "His hair *is* darker and I almost started laughing."

Mary

You had to hand it to them—the Clintonistas were really very cagey. We were the President of the United States; events of international significance happened around us all the time. We were in the practice of giving the media, who always traveled with us, ample time to research, write, and file their stories. It amounted to about an hour of down time. If you didn't give it to them, they'd rag Marlin mercilessly.

The Clinton operation, the challenger, was under no such constraint. They never provided enough telephones, typewriter/laptop facilities, or time to think about stories so reporters could include analysis or interpretation. What they did was tighten the schedule so that there was no time to write anything other than what the reporters had just seen or been told. Not by accident, there was also no time to call us for any reaction. All these years we had refined the art of accommodating the press's needs, and the Clintonistas did it backward.

That, in combination with the media's dwindling resources for research, made it very difficult for the press covering Clinton to compare what he was saying today to what he had previously said. It allowed the Clintonistas to get into print, in a very organized way and with minimal interpretation and no counter-opinions, what it was they were doing each day.

I gave them big credit for that. They'd do their event and get back on the plane while reporters scrambled for a phone. When we complained, the press admitted they were writing one-sided stories, but their first line of defense was "They don't give us enough time to let you in." They wanted to include our point of view but were mechanically unable to. Meanwhile, I'd watch reporters attend our events and then go out and find some disgruntled citizen for a man-on-the-street counterpoint. It was really discouraging.

Ultimately Torie badgered the folks covering Clinton so much they gave us a way in. "Call the desk," "Here's my beeper," "Call my counterpart covering your campaign and give it to her." Torie Clarke and deputy director of communications Alixe Glen went on a numbers binge, collecting home phones and beepers and fax numbers from everyone in the Clinton press entourage. They'd get fifteen minutes to file and we'd call and get in their face. And every time they'd print a story without returning our call, we'd get on the horn and rag at them. It was only through constant vigilance and aggressiveness that we started getting into Clinton's stories. The Fax Attacks had by now petered out.

We were simultaneously ticked off and—professionally—begrudgingly admiring. We never begrudged the other side's being good. What ticked us off was the fact that we were playing on an uneven field. We couldn't get angry with them; we'd do the same thing if we had the opportunity. In fact, we'd have thought they were idiots if they hadn't done it.

Of course, our stories weren't safe, either. Carville or Stephanopoulos or Begala or Greenberg would call Ann Devroy or any of the other people covering Bush right after our events and get in them. They knew where they were and they knew they'd have time to talk. This had been going on for weeks. There would be a Clinton counterpoint in every Bush story. We were the first to know how rapid their rapid-response team really was.

Reporters are as wary of our spinning them as we are of their burning us. When you meet a new guy, there's always a kind of journalistic dating ritual until you figure out whether they're legit. Mostly I worked with print people, but they all had their tricks. You knew the trick with network reporters was that in order to get in the broadcast, they had to take a harsh angle on their story. If it didn't have a hard edge, forget it; they wouldn't get on the air. We never held it against them; that was just the deal. Plus, I didn't really build the same relationships with them that I did with the print people, because all they were going to get was a one-minute story, and mostly what they were looking for was pictures. Marlin was the TV guy; they all loved him.

Local reporters always get standard fare. Nothing muscular. They're not getting national exposure, you don't know who they are, and while they may be more accommodating, they're still reporters; you don't trust them. They don't care, because for once they're getting a primary source.

Reporters understand that partisans are always only going to give them a one-sided view. When a partisan goes out on a limb and presents a warts-and-all analysis of an issue, reporters emphasize the warts and splash those negatives all over the front page. I've made the argument to journalists: "Why would your sources want to give you an honest assessment of things if you're going to single them out and they will then get criticized for having embarrassed their President?" Reporters don't have a compelling answer.

They love rumors and they're tremendous gossips. At any given moment there is a busload of unverified stories careening down the information superhighway; everybody's got the real goods on everybody else, but no one's got the three sources to get it into print or on the air. The level of informed cynicism is overwhelming. All my juicy stuff I got from them.

I am going to resist lumping the entire press corps into one category. Though studies have indicated 80 percent self-identify as Democrats, they will tell you they're not liberal. Or they'll tell you they *are* liberal but they don't bring their bias to their stories. Or they'll tell you they're apolitical and just contrarians. However they defend themselves, few disagreed that there was a definite pro-Clinton bias in 1992. There was a young, conscientious reporter for *The Wall Street Journal*, John Harwood, and in one of our unguarded, off-the-record moments we actually got to talking. I said, "You don't like George Bush, do you?"

He said something like, "It's not that we don't like George Bush"—I was asking him to speak for his age group, and he did—"it's that we really do like Bill Clinton. We like the energy of the campaign. We relate to his generation. We relate to his raised consciousness." He explained there was a group of younger reporters who were simpatico with Clinton. Bush was like their father. That was why some of their coverage had more energy and flair than ours did. (Right now I'm burning him by repeating this off-the-record conversation, so let me add that in his case, his feelings did not affect his coverage.) It was a very honest thing for him to say and an important insight for me to have.

I, of course, subsequently twisted that conversation into a media diatribe about "This press loves Bill Clinton. They're all in this together." I'd get out there and trash the media and then have to get on a plane with them. No one took it personally. I don't think as individuals they liked being attacked as a group, but they understood why we were doing it. There was a real honest-to-God feeling that the coverage was biased and skewed.

Someone sent us a bumper sticker: "Annoy the Media, Reelect Bush." Maybe forty of them. They caught on. There is, among liberals and conservatives and just normal folks out there, the widespread feeling that they're not getting all the news or an unbiased account of events from the mainstream media. Both sides had their own examples to bitch about, but we felt particularly chagrined. We contacted the guy and said, "Print up a gazillion." I always carried a bunch in my purse. Then Bush started incorporating the line into his stump speech, and the crowds went wild. Well, anything that works with a crowd is going to get repeated, and since we were getting trashed more than Clinton, it worked better for us.

It actually began to get a little dangerous at the events. Before the President came on, an untamed herd of television camerapeople and light and sound guys with camera stands and boom mikes hustled into position. It was kind of scary to watch, all these technician guys toting heavy equipment on their shoulders, stampeding to get the best spots and camera angles on a rickety makeshift press platform. There were no reserved positions; they had to fight it out each time. Then the reporters themselves, with their little hand-held tape recorders, got settled in and took their notepads out.

As the campaign got more heated, and these bumper stickers got real popular, the crowd began to boo as the media came in. At one event a woman actually spat on a reporter. People always had little American flags and they began poking the press with them. I was walking alongside saying, "Cut it out, knock it off." We were in a big, hot, smoky barn somewhere, and the energy level that usually builds in anticipation of seeing the President was taking a hostile turn. I had the feeling that if the President didn't get in there soon there was going to be a rumble with the press.

Bush calmed it down, and thereafter he always led with, "Amnesty for the boom guys!" It became an event mantra. Unlike the reporters, the technicians all seemed to like Bush.

James

We call them "the Beast." Paul came up with the phrase, and it is perfect. You can just see the media in a pack, howling for raw meat.

The few times I traveled on the plane, the first thing I'd do in the morning was walk to the back and see what they were thinking. It was no great secret; you could tell what their mood was that day by the questions they'd ask. First thing we'd check: "What's the Beast up to?"

The last thing they want to know is what the campaign was really about: message. They hear the message every day, they're sick of it. We didn't get into a lot of intellectual discussions about the future of America; they'd never ask you about what Bill Clinton was trying to do for the country, they'd want to know how he was going to get there. What reporter wouldn't rather report on strategy than message?

They'd find three or four different ways of phrasing the question "Why are you going to Missouri today?"

I'd try and give them message wrapped up to look like strategy. "Our strategy is, Missouri's been hard hit by the devastating policies of the Reagan-Bush years and they're susceptible to hearing our message of change and the fact that we've got to do something about getting health care costs down and incomes up. That's why we're coming to Missouri."

They'd gag. They understand that a campaign wants to act in what it thinks is its strategic best interest. (It very often does not do so. A lot of times a campaign doesn't even know what its strategic best interest is. It is not some sort of monolithic, brilliant, intelligent being that always does the right thing.) And they think we're bullshitting them.

"You've got a poll that says you're in trouble in Missouri."

Now, in fact, the polls may be down. Or it might be that some congressman wants you to go and you got rolled into doing it. But generally, you're going because it's a swing state and you need it.

"Look," I tell them, "we poll all the time in different states; this is meaningless. This event was set five days ago, has nothing to do with that. Why do you always want to cover process? Nobody out there cares what our polls say, they care about their jobs." Pick any one that you want from that list.

A lot of times there's a dance that goes on between reporter and strategist. They try to position us and pin us down and get us to admit to something we can see will result in a huge and unflattering headline in the next day's paper, and we just will not be led down that path. You can see their case building, and the skilled thing to do is dispute the premise. "That's your opinion of what happened, but I've got to tell you there's a different view of what actually went on. But the real question here is not your premise or mine; the real question is people's incomes have declined, their health care costs have gone up, the economy is stagnant, and the federal government does nothing about it. That's what we should be talking about, not arguing over some kind of premise."

The other option is "Why are you asking me this? Why don't you go ask our opponent?"

The press always likes to cross-reference a candidate. "In Michigan you said this, but yet when you went down to Florida you said that. Now, how do you reconcile the two?"

You're not going to say, "By God, you're right. They're two important states and we're out there trying to carry them. We're in a political campaign and we had to say something." You tell them, "Oh, you know, you can nitpick anything that you want to and find something wrong with it. But the real issues are . . ."

You know instinctively, when you're asked a hard question, you attack. You attack the other side, you attack the questioner, you attack the premise, you attack something—but you keep it moving along.

I can deal with the hard questions. If someone said to me, "Clinton's position was this; now it's that," I could attack the premise and come out looking good. A question you wouldn't want to get would be "What is it about Bill Clinton that causes people to perceive that he has a position here one day and there the next?"

Now, I could answer it. I would say, "That's a perception that's been set by the media because they don't want to acknowledge the fact that . . ." Boom, boom, boom. But that's a better way for a reporter to ask a question and have a shot at getting it answered to his satisfaction. Tim Russert asked David Duke, "What did you find so objectionable about America that you thought Nazism would be preferable?" He had the answer down pat about "It was in my past," but for this one he had to struggle a little bit harder. Hardballs you're ready for; you've gotten them before and you know they're coming. It's the softballs that can throw you way off.

Sometimes the most startling thing you can do is agree with people, it just takes the wind out of their sails. They say, "Well, you know, your candidate has had three different positions on that," and I tell them, "That's true. But the question is, is it the correct position now?" If a candidate switches his position on abortion, the voters don't care what your previous position was as long as you have what they want now.

My favorite all-time reaction from a reporter, and it's happened several times, was "Aaah, you're just saying that because you want to win the election."

"Of course! What do you think I'm doing here?"

I am a political professional. I am paid to win races. Without breaking any laws, or lying, or appealing to people on the basis of bigotry, I have one agenda: to win. Let me say it again: The cause and purpose of a political campaign is to win the election. I will represent the interest of my campaign and my candidate as ferociously as I can, and I'll be equally aggressive in defending even the things I don't think are too good about him. The bottom line is, My guy is better than the other guy. If you're looking for somebody objective, don't talk to me.

It is not my job to be disloyal. Only in Washington do they respect disloyalty; the media loves to encourage someone who will trash their own party or their own candidate. To hell with them; I won't do it.

Some people come to work on campaigns with a specific agenda. An individual cause, say, like abortion or anti-abortion. The cause may be noble, and they try to get the campaign to do what is in the interest of the cause, as opposed to the interest of the candidate. If their candidate doesn't live up to their expectations—if, on a scale of one to ten, she and the voters take a position of seven when the worker's agenda is at nine—the workers will trash the candidate even though she is paying them and is, on balance, a better choice to represent the people than her opponent. I disagree. The cause has to be the candidate. I don't find these people contemptible, I just think they have a very limited place in a political campaign. And the press, always looking for controversy, abets them.

I also cannot stand the self-righteous cultural-elite types who constantly carp that political campaigns are worse now than they were twenty, fifty, a hundred years ago. I've taken my last lecture from those people. The amount of information available to the public now is higher than it's ever been. And all this goofy, ignorant slobbering about the tyranny of the thirty-second sound bite. Did "Tippecanoe and Tyler too" represent a well-thought-out campaign strategy?

The press's main fuel, and a campaign's main source of power, is information. The campaign-press relationship is a continuing mutual supply operation. There's been a lot of talk about leaks and spin, and I thought I'd spell out the differences.

One of the things people should understand is that the whole idea of leaking information and talking to reporters is good. It ain't bad for democracy. It's very much a function of what reporters should do, which is ferret out things people don't know, and what campaigns ought to be doing, which is putting their candidate before the public. We're giving them facts, leads, directions to take, things to go on.

Most of the time you leak to good publications. They have the resources and the reputation to follow up on the story. If you leak to the *Star*, it ain't gonna matter. If you leak to *The New York Times* it's quite another thing. The quality of your information weighs heavily in your ability to leak stuff; you're taken much more seriously if you have some substance or reason for your call than if you're always just spreading stuff that can't be checked out. I wouldn't say I do a lot of it, but I do it when it's necessary.

The opening line is normally, "I understand X newspaper or Y network is getting ready to run this story. I figure you're all probably on top of it, but . . ."

It's our job to put out information good for our side and bad for the other side. We got a videotape off Brazilian television showing a huge printing press running Bush-Quayle material, and relatively reliable information that their campaign was getting printing down there because the cost was cheaper than it was in the United States. Think of it: With millions of Americans out of work the President of the United States was taking his business to South America, undercutting American jobs. Is this the man you want in charge of your economy? Is this a man who understands the plight of the American worker?

I called Susan Zirinsky at CBS News and said, "Look, I've got this tape." Leaked it like a sieve. Ultimately the Republicans weaseled out of it by claiming that some independent operative did it himself, which to this day I don't believe.

I got a call from a source saying that a doctor at the National Institutes of Health had seen Bush's medical record, and that the President was on an excessive dose of some kind of thyroid medication.

"Who's the doctor?"

"You can't use his name, but this guy is legit."

It's always like that. The hottest leads usually come without credible ways of verifying them. The ones that can do you the most good are the ones that can do you the most harm. Of course.

I had taken temporary leave of my senses. "Well," I told the guy, "I might just leak this, or say I heard it on the grapevine." I called Howell Raines, Washington bureau chief of *The New York Times*.

Raines was in Ohio at Johnny Apple's daddy's funeral. He returned my call several hours later. "How's Johnny?" I asked him.

"You're not going to believe this. He filed today." (When I talked to Johnny later and mentioned it, he said, "My daddy would have kicked my butt if I hadn't.") "What's going on?"

In the couple of hours since my original call, better sense had gotten hold of me. "I forget what I called you about." You can spread rumors about people getting fired, or campaign infighting, but talking about people's ailments has a way of coming back at you. Plus, I didn't really have the goods, so I let it go. And Bush is still fine. They say God watches drunks and fools, so I always figure I've got double protection.

But there was plenty of other stuff I heard and repeated. You're not just passing it along; you're trying to accelerate it, you're kicking it. A lot of times it comes on the phone. I was talking to Congressman Dan Glickman of Kansas. He mentioned in passing that you never see Bob Dole with Bush these days. I'd never thought about that. I turned around and called Dan Balz at *The Washington Post*. "You know, when's the last time you saw Dole and Bush campaign together? I think Dole wants Bush to lose, so he can be more popular when Clinton wins." Now, is that going to get you any votes? No. But if Balz runs it and the Dole-Bush split becomes an issue, maybe you can start a little brushfire and make Bush waste time and money by going to Kansas, which is a state you figure he's going to win anyhow. A lot of times you're just playing, you want to cause some mischief.

Those are leaks. A spin call is completely different. When you're spinning a reporter, you're telling them how to look at a story. Or you're telling them they're covering it wrong. For instance, everybody said Clinton's economic numbers didn't add up, that we added 50 and 50 and came up with 104. I'd call and say, "Y'all say our numbers don't add up, but Bush says 50 plus 50 equals *104,000*. Our numbers hang a lot closer to the truth than his do. You people have become part of a pack mentality. You're not watching what Bush is doing, all the things that he's proposing spending for. And on top of that he's for a balanced-budget amendment. . . ." That's a spin call. You're giving them perspective. George did it for us. He was great. Mary did it for them and she was as good as anybody. It's what I call working the pipes.

We don't work in a large community. Bob Shrum told me one time that the Renaissance wasn't but fifteen hundred people. A presidential campaign, including staff, operatives, and reporters, is about the same number. If I placed ten thousand calls over the course of the campaign, they were probably to fifty different people.

I'd make anywhere from three to ten spin calls a day. More on Friday. Friday is a big, big spin day. A lot of the wrap-up shows are on the weekend, the programs that establish the mindset for the coming week, and we want them to have our perspective. Also, a lot of reporters are calling us on Friday, getting ready to be on these shows, wanting to know our strategy.

The mental state of the press is very important. You can call three or four of them and take a swab test. I'd tell George, "Well, I stuck a thermometer up his ass, this is what came back." There's constant chatter flowing. People like to do this, so they want to talk about it. They like getting calls, it helps newspeople do their jobs better, it helps campaign people do their job better. It's also flattering. Means that they've got clout and our attention. They can say, "I talked to the Clinton people today, and from their perspective . . ." I can say I know what they're thinking.

My contact with the media was more on a reporter-to-person basis than on an institutional basis. I don't like *The New York Times*, *The Wall Street Journal*, *The Washington Post*, or the *Los Angeles Times* institutionally. I do, however, have enormous affection for most of their reporters. Is that contradictory? Yes, but it's not unlike the way people hate Congress but like their congressman. After a while you know who are the people you can talk to, the ones who shoot straight, and you tend just to deal with them. If someone burns you, or isn't honorable, you become very guarded in what you say, and you talk to them only when you have to.

Reporters are individuals, and their organizations are not monoliths. I'm not in the business of glorifying the press, but I could always get Howell Raines on the phone, and you could always make your case to him. That's all that a guy like me is looking for. I never thought, "I'm speaking to *The New York Times*"; I'd think, "I'm speaking to Robin Toner." And at the *Times*, Robin Toner had an entirely different perspective than Maureen Dowd or Gwen Ifill or Michael Kelly. Robin was doing political analysis, so you would talk to her on Friday for Sunday's paper. Maureen Dowd wasn't extremely interested in covering basic politics, you knew that going in; the *Times* let her do pieces on what kind of guy Bill Clinton was in high school. The *Times* wouldn't cover the Gennifer Flowers story but they'd run seven draft articles in one issue.

At *The Washington Post*, I have a close relationship with Ann Devroy. I had known columnist Maralee Schwartz for a long time, and her column, "Politics," was very influential. Dan Balz was a first-class person and a first-class political reporter. David Von Drehle and David Maraniss, along with Maureen Dowd, were probably the best writers on the campaign, and did the funniest, most interesting pieces.

It's also important to recognize the separation between news coverage and the editorial page. At *The Wall Street Journal*, to my knowledge, it is total. Their editorials exist as a consistent mouthpiece for the conservative cause, but their day-in-day-out coverage of the campaign was as good as any of them, and I talked to Al Hunt, the *Journal's* Washington bureau chief, on a regular basis.

The *L.A. Times* distinguished itself in this campaign, and *USA Today* was very influential.

The media has gone from covering what the candidate says to covering what the media *says* the candidate says. The networks, in particular, have tried to make their reporters as important in a political campaign as the candidates themselves.

ABC's character was that they were the Big Guy, they spent the most money covering the campaign. A CBS producer told me in May that ABC had spent more than CBS and NBC combined. Mark Halperin spent more time with Governor Clinton than any other media person on the face of the earth, and during the campaign, *Nightline* was certainly the most influential show. I don't know who would even have come in second. Ted Koppel has a gold-plate reputation; if he airs a show it's generally thought to be fair.

I had a good relationship with producer Susan Zirinsky at CBS, who brought a lot of energy to their coverage. They wanted to make a niche with Eric Engberg's "Reality Check" analysis of campaign ads. Dan Rather had the "Feisty Insiders," he'd have me and Charlie Black on together and see what we could ignite.

At NBC, it was the Cult of Russert. Tim Russert had a lot of influence and used to work for Pat Moynihan, so he understood what we were doing. He would listen to our pitch and say, "That makes sense," or "That doesn't make sense." I didn't agree with everything he did, but it would be hard to think of a more straight-up guy to deal with. I started the campaign sort of cool on Andrea Mitchell and ended up feeling she was a lot better reporter than I'd thought.

CNN's influence reached far beyond its viewers.

My Friday list generally included Russert at NBC, Susan Spencer at CBS, Jeff Greenfield at ABC, Robin Toner or Howell Raines at *The New York Times*, Al Hunt and Jeff Birnbaum at *The Wall Street Journal*. John King at the Associated Press, Kit Seelye with *The Philadelphia Inquirer*. Bureau chiefs are easy to get because they're always at their desks and not out in the field, like Jack Nelson with the *L.A. Times*. David Lauter, Ron Brownstein, and Cathy Decker were in the field covering the race.

One of the great arts in this business is what we call wiring up the event. If you are about to stage a major event, there's nothing that can help you more than to anticipate who the media is going to call to comment on it, and get there first. You call a guy and say, "Look, I just wanted to let you know what's coming down the pike. We're going to do this today. This is the reason for doing it." That person is flattered. They are a group of people we call Quote Sluts.

I have a Quote Slut list. People available by the phone, ready to be called. Let me say I have probably qualified to be on that list myself; there's nothing wrong with it. The list varies. Whether it's a congressman; whether it's John Sasso, the very talented guy who ran the Dukakis campaign; whether it's Bob Beckel or Chris Matthews, they're going to have some intelligent things to say and you can count on the nets to contact them. You want them, when they're called and asked, "What do you think of this?," to say something complimentary.

Those are political Quote Sluts. The economic team has a list of economic Quote Sluts.

You try and guess who the reporters are going to call for a comment and get there first.

"Who do you think they're going to call?"

"Well, they're going to call So-and-So at MIT."

"Call and wire him up."

These people are human beings. They like it. So when the press does call and ask them, "What do you think of the latest Clinton move?" they may well say, "The Clinton people were very smart to do this." The smart thing we did was call them.

Do they know they're Quote Sluts? Do they know they're being flattered? Yes. Do they like it? Yes. Is there anything wrong with it? No. If you call someone and say, "I want to tell you what we're doing and why we're doing it," you're making a statement that says, "You're somebody important." People like that. I like that. I'm as susceptible to flattery as the next guy.

Sometimes you'll be watching the tube and someone will have something negative to say about us and the first words out of my mouth will be, "Aw, man, why didn't we think to call that guy? How stupid of us."

There are even times when you've got to wire up an event within your own organization. If you call and explain your plans and your reasoning, people will tend to be more supportive than if you just spring it on them. That goes for people inside the campaign, it goes for reporters, it goes for people in everyday life. It's better to tell somebody ahead of time and get their support than to tell them afterward and try to change their mind.

Bill Clinton is not the kind of guy who says, "Well, four people in the campaign say I ought to do this, I guess I'll ride along." Sometimes he'd call people, and we had to know which FOB to wire up. Knowing who the candidate will call for advice or an opinion can be very useful to a strategist. It would be fair to note that this is often effective because an advance phone call is a form of ultimate flattery. If it was a Democratic Leadership Council issue like reinventing government, you'd call Al From. If it had to do with worker training, you'd call Bob Reich. If it had to do with a black event, call John Lewis or Mike Espy. And when in doubt, call Hillary.

Sometimes you call because you want to hear what the guy's got. Very often you go back and say, "I just talked to Al From and he's got a very interesting thing to say about this." Sometimes you run little trial balloons. You may want to know media reaction. "You know, one of the things I've been kicking around, I can't seem to get much support for it, is if we did this." The reporter might well tell you, "Boy, if you did that you'd really eat a story about it being in conflict with this."

Your mind is always racing. "I haven't gone to Clinton with this yet, but . . ." The reporter feels that his input is going straight to the candidate. There's a very pleasing element of power to that. An even stronger gambit is when you call and say, "Look, we're getting ready to propose this and I know that the governor is going to want to know what you think." That'll ring them up pretty good.

CHAPTER 25

Mary

The numbers weren't moving.

When you're in a hole like we were you focus on something else. On Air Force One, the President and I were focusing on the individual states. Carney had them categorized by poll numbers: minus 10, minus 5, even, plus 5, plus 10. There weren't very many in the plus 10 column. What we were looking for every day were states shifting from one column to the next.

It's human nature. When the day is completely rotten, you can't look at it. You concoct a reason why the data is bad and you stick with it. Why torture yourself? I'm not into self-flagellation, if I looked I'd get depressed, so I convinced myself that the data was unrepresentative of the electorate's ultimate vote behavior. I was in total denial.

As far as I was concerned, the polls continued to reflect anger at Washington, and at the President for sitting at the helm in Washington. But that could not last the entire election; when the final vote was cast, I felt—we all felt—it would be cast on a comparison of the candidates, not anger at the President. And that was part of our strategy: to move people away from their anger and toward reflection on the next four years, and who they trusted to lead them. As the focus shifted, we all convinced ourselves, the numbers would shift with it. That was our spin, and we believed it.

We just refused to believe the polls. At one point *The Washington Post* had a 10-point screw-up, and we hung our hat on that for the rest of the campaign. In 1988 we never did get accurate readings on Pat Robertson, for instance, so I always hung on to the theory that people didn't always tell the truth to pollsters, and the corollary that people were becoming increasingly sophisticated about polls. People were simply not admitting that they were going to vote for George Bush. I had all sorts of similar notions that allowed me to ignore the polls and not get upset by them.

I paid attention to Carney's state chart because some of the minus 10s were moving into the minus 5 category. We could actually see some closure. It would have been better if the minus 5s had been turning into dead heats, but any movement was good movement.

Then we counted electoral votes. Carney and I would spend endless nights recounting. "Let's go over the states again." This was our psychotherapy. "Okay, there's no way we can lose New Hampshire. There's no way they're going to win Colorado, Connecticut, Kentucky. We've got a shot in Michigan. We've got a shot in Montana, even though it's a labor state. We could take Ohio. Pennsylvania we always say we're going to lose, and then we won it in '88. Tennessee . . ." It was an endless mind game, going through the list of states and telling every piece of political history and stories and tactics and past successes, thereby reinforcing our belief we could win each of them. We'd go over the electoral map until we found the 270 votes we needed to win; then we'd quit. This was not just psychobabble, it was also the way you drive your scheduling, your advertising, your finite resources. Everything is driven by the electoral college count, not the total vote count. Besides, we were down in the probable vote count by 15 points.

Faced with imminent disaster, you've got to have faith in the cause and a way to cope from day to day. Campaign coping mechanisms take strange forms. Take, for example, the day Bill Clinton said the United States of America ranked down there on the scale with Sri Lanka. That was so patently absurd that everyone else ignored it. But absurdity was a staple for me and Steve Provost. We went back and forth, "Sri Lanka, didn't that use to be Ceylon?"

"What is Sri Lanka? Who knows where Sri Lanka is?"

We ran a contest, went all through the plane offering cash prizes. "Who can say where Sri Lanka is?" The White House guys rolled their eyes. "*Now* what the hell are these nuts talking about?"

Provost went into a creative terror, busy writing away, his tie askew, hair wild, nose three inches from the paper. I always knew to stay out of his way when he was really in the grips of one of these creative spasms. Finally he looked up, grinning. "I have it. The masterpiece."

"Finally, a decent speech, Steve."

"No. It's the 'Sri Lanka Conga.' "

He had four verses:

> *Some say our country's like Sri Lanka*
> *I say that's just a bunch of bunka*
> *Sri Lanka, no!*
> *America, Yes!*
> *We're not second-rate*
> *We really are the best!*

Every verse was equally inspired:

> *That sounds as stupid as Paul Anka*
> *I say you're drinking too much Sanka*

We typed it up and made copies, constructed a melody, and insisted that everybody in the cabin practice and sing it with us. We had to do something before everybody killed themselves.

Steve was going "A-one and a-two . . ."

Here was this whole crowd, the advance guy who never laughed and the military guy and one of the doctors, and I looked around and they were singing, "*Some say our country's like Sri Lanka!*"

We made "Sri Lanka—Not!" posters and *Ghostbusters* posters with a circle around "Sri Lanka" and a big red line through it, and taped them to the walls of Air Force One.

I made all of these guys get in a "Sri Lanka Conga" line and we conga'd through the whole plane. We were losing miserably and we conga'd into the media-pool cabin, and we were singing all the verses, ending with a rousing "SRI LANKA, NO! AMERICA, YES!"

The press pool was just stunned. Cameras flipped on. I heard some guy talking into his tape recorder: "Some say the Bush campaign is losing, but spirits remain high on the plane. . . ."

We were conga'ing back to our cabin when we ran into President Bush, who was wondering where his entire support staff had gone to.

"Ready?" I said to the line. "Hit it!"

"*Some say our country's like Sri Lanka . . .*"

We were waving Sri Lanka posters, singing, clapping, dancing. The President was, needless to say, speechless.

"Sing along, President!"

"*Sri Lanka, no! America, yes!*"

Toward the end of the campaign he started coming back to our cabin regularly because there was always something happening.

I dubbed our bosses—Teeter, Baker, Malek, Mosbacher—the adults. And, believe me, President Bush was plenty happy when the adults came on the plane for the last ten days. But he played along with me. He would come past our cabin and mock-whisper, "The adults are here." They'd all be hunkered down in serious meeting mode in his office cabin, and the President would come back and joke, "I'm just trying to get away from the adults." This was one of the many ways President Bush dealt with the "aura."

There is something about the aura of the presidency that makes everyone more respectful of the person who is the President. Once he is elected you cease to perceive him as the person you know—as one of your pals, as a guy you've played cards with and talked politics and yucked it up with—and commence treating him as The President. People clean up their language around him, they prepare their comments, they watch their posture.

Everyone, including his inside circle, which usually consists of his lifelong friends, behaves and speaks in an unwaveringly reverential manner. The protocol, the linguistic circumlocutions, are intimidating at first, then become like a second language. It's not the way anyone would talk in real life. For starters, the man in the front cabin was no longer George, never George, I'd be surprised if even behind closed doors his lifelong friends still called him George; he was Mr. President. Then there's a constant effort to find the most comfortable, most ear-pleasing, most stomach-soothing conversation for the Chief Executive. By constantly being treated reverentially, the man who is President becomes accustomed to hearing news, suggestions, and advice put in their most palatable form.

He also doesn't hear a lot of bad news. When reporting to the President, you put on a happy face. That's the politics of politics. Nobody wants to be the bearer of bad tidings. You've either got a happy face to cover your butt or a happy face because, in your presentation, you have just saved him from a near-death experience he never knew of in the first place. So the President receives positively streamlined information. He is spared the gory details and always given the bottom line; how we are getting things done is rarely a topic of his concern.

I was raised with a blue-collar awe of the presidency. I know a little something about American political history from what I studied in college and picked up on the job, but what I feel about America is what my family taught me. Every time I walked into the Oval Office

I got a lump in my throat and goosebumps. You walk in there and start thinking about Abraham Lincoln. Combine that with the real love that I feel for George Bush, and every conversation felt like a once-in-a-lifetime experience.

George Bush always seemed conscious of the "Presidential Presence" phenomenon, and went out of his way to put people at ease. The comment heard most often from folks who had just met him face-to-face was, "He's so normal. What a good guy." Reporters consistently commented on how good he was one-on-one.

It never ceased to amaze me how Bush could win people over, or how patient he was with the literally thousands of people he had to make feel like his buddies. Even more amazing was how he always stayed upbeat. I mean, it was *his* presidency, but he never liked when *we* got down. And I swear he was happier for us when good news came in than for himself.

We finally got some good news.

The President spent a week on the road and we were breaking through. Clinton's lead shrank to 11. Then on Tuesday, October 27, a week before election day, the CNN/*USA Today*/Gallup tracking poll changed its polling methodology from registered voters to likely voters and the race closed to a 6-point gap.

The Clintonistas squealed like stuck pigs—"They're changing the rules in the middle of the game!"—but we loved it. You go out there and keep hammering and at some point your mind shifts over; you start believing your own spin. Now we'd been proved correct. Our polls showed the race closing, and now the public polls verified what we'd been saying all along, that the numbers would close when voters began to narrow their focus. You always get different numbers between registered and likely voters, and there was historical data to support the premise that Republicans are more reliable voters than Democrats. We always looked at likely voters; we thought they made for more credible data.

The adults hit the plane in full force.

James

First thing I said when I saw the CNN poll was, "What the fuck? Where is Greenberg?" Pollsters all talk to each other. The only pollsters who don't communicate directly are pollsters for the opposing campaigns, and they probably talk through intermediaries. "Where's Stan? What the hell is this?"

"This is what they did," Stan said. "They switched the sample." He had a whole technical explanation about the nature of sampling, but the bottom line was that he felt our numbers—our lead was about 6—were holding steady. I got nervous for a second, but his evidence was clear and he was pretty convincing.

The race did start getting closer. Bush always thought he was going to win, and now that the polls were a bit better and he was being vindicated, he was out attacking. He had a good week and we saw the national number start to drop.

You start out with a convention bounce that puts you ahead 15 points. Well, you know you're not going to win by 15, you know you're going to fall, and we had that built into our calculations. But it's one thing to believe your calculations, it's another to see points come off the board.

Governor Clinton got to talk to us twenty minutes a day, and he was pretty testy. He said, "I saw this. What's going on?" Stan tried to explain it to him, but the governor said, "I'm telling you, I'm telling you, people are coming up and saying we're losing ground."

"Governor, we're going to hold steady. We've got to stay focused here."

You meet some nervous Nellies on the road, and they were getting to the candidate. Plus, as he was going from one place to another he would see politicians and Democratic party officials—if you light a firecracker under them they think it's a nuclear explosion.

Hell, I was sitting there with probably the most complete and sophisticated data ever available in an American presidential campaign, and it was everything I could do to stay calm. I kept saying to Greenberg, "Hey, man, tell me not to panic."

"James," he said, "don't panic."

We lost 14 points in Ohio in one night. Bush spent the whole day there. Scared the hell out of us. Then we showed a huge drop in Pennsylvania. We went back and polled in both of them and we bounced right back in Pennsylvania, but the Ohio drop was legitimate. Clearly we needed these two states. We had a scenario where we could lose Ohio, but never Pennsylvania.

Our overall strategy was to stay focused on change and the economy. "Change versus more of the same." It was probably best encapsulated by Al Gore when he talked about waking up the morning after the election and moaning, "Four more years." People felt that in the past twelve years government had become removed from them and tended to favor the powerful and special interests over ordinary people. The health care issue was a vehicle to show our concern with people's everyday lives.

Our electoral strategy was state-specific. We would buy TV, and spend our time, only in those states we thought we had a chance to carry. David Wilhelm and Paul Tully—Tully was DNC liaison to the campaign—did the yeoman's work on developing a detailed chart and formula for this. We had five categories. Some places we knew we were going to win: West Virginia, District of Columbia; we were way ahead in California. Some we had no chance in: South Carolina, Indiana, Utah. Some states we *thought* we were going to win, but still had to spend money in: Pennsylvania, Connecticut, Oregon. Some we kind of flashed our armor but really weren't going to spend a lot of money contesting: Texas, Florida. Some we would fight for and hold to the death: Louisiana, Ohio, Georgia.

Because they were behind, it wasn't enough for the Republicans to move the South Carolina number, the Ohio number. Bush had to buy national spots in order to move the national number. They needed to close the gap in California—not to win the state, but to show voters that their guy had some momentum.

Usually you can dismiss polls as a strategic device, apart from the fact that you like to be ahead, but in this race we felt they had some strategic imperative. Part of our strategy was "validation," that because there were a lot of other people for Clinton, it was okay for you, the individual voter, to be for him, too. "Validation" was a word you would hear a lot in Clinton strategic doctrine. On the other side, the Bush people were looking for polling results they could use to tell voters, "As your neighbors are looking at Clinton they're finding him wanting, so shouldn't you?"

Greenberg was very good. He took me through the country state by state and showed how and why we were winning this election. "What we're seeing is states where we were ahead by fifteen points, we're now ahead by seven. But we're a solid seven points ahead. It's that other eight that's dragging down the national number. States where we were even, that we knew we'd never carry, we are now fifteen points down. But when you do a state-by-state analysis"—which we would do to double-check ourselves—"you will find that we're right on target."

It's impossible to give Stan too much credit here. We had a way to project the national number based on state polls. With our national poll showing the lead at 6 points, we'd take all the data from the thirty states where we were polling, and combine it with the twenty media state polls we thought were the most reliable—we made a point of using the most pessimistic—and the simulated number would come in at 6 or 7 every time. So we knew right where we were. States that had been blowouts for us were getting a little closer, and close Republican states were turning into blowouts for Bush. None of it was fundamentally changing the scope of the election, it was just Republicans coming home. Stan's basic point was that there was nothing happening internally that should cause us to change our tactics, strategy, or message. In fact, to change would be the worst thing we could do.

"Don't worry," he told me. "Don't force yourself to do anything different. Just stay where you are, trust your instincts."

I was jumpy. I was damn jumpy. I had sat on a lead the last two weeks of the Dick Davis race in 1982 and lost; I didn't want to do that again.

Clinton thought Bush was attacking him personally, and he wanted to make it personal back. He was pretty heated about it.

"I'm telling y'all, he is eviscerating me. He is attacking me personally. I know y'all want to stay on the economy but I think we've got to hit him back."

Wednesday, six days out from the election, after delivering his stump speech about changing the direction of this country, Clinton blew a gasket. He told a rally in Louisville, "The very idea that the word 'trust' could ever come out of Bush's mouth, after what he has done to this country and the way he has trampled the truth, is a travesty for the American political system."

We'd tried to prevent it, but now character had become an issue. You knew what the news was going to be. The press was sick of the economy and health care and change. Now the Beast had some red meat.

Mary

We loved it. I'm sure the Clinton people didn't do that on purpose. There's nothing cooler than getting the other guy on your turf. Their strategy had been to stay on the economy, and we'd had to go there. Now we had Clinton where we wanted him.

Despite two months of stagnant numbers, the unsolicited comments coming from our focus groups vis-à-vis Clinton all revolved around trust. And his negatives were increasing nightly. The trust side of the draft issue resurrected in people's minds all the amorphous things they didn't like about the man. We called answers to open-ended questions "verbatims," and the verbatims re Clinton were "You can't trust a guy who lies to his wife"; "You can't trust a guy who says he didn't inhale."

Women in focus groups told me, "He's like that kind of boy in high school that you're attracted to that you just know is bad for you and is going to do you wrong. You can't trust him." And everybody would go, "Yeah, that's right!"

I don't know what Carville could have been thinking, but I'm sure they didn't want Clinton talking about trust. The trust factor is intangible, it's like trying to get your arms around smoke. People couldn't really verbalize why they didn't trust him, which made him even less trustworthy. They just had a feeling about it. It came in the form of "He's just like my first husband."

There's public trust and private trust. Private trust goes to the nature of the man. People trusted Bush. They had already factored "Read my lips" into their opinion of his public persona, and those who weren't going to vote for him because of that issue had already been factored out of our equation. But no matter how bad our overall numbers got, we never lost ground on the issues of honesty, likability, trustworthiness. No one thought of George Bush as a liar.

So when Bill Clinton himself brought up trust we were rubbing our hands together in glee.

James

There is one thing that Bill Clinton does that drives me and most people around him crazy: He repeats the charge. He says, "They're going to say this about me. But let me tell you . . ." It makes a story every time, and he loves to do it. It's part of his makeup, he's a very competitive guy, and he feels you've got to answer everything.

But the worst of it is that he repeats a fifteen-second charge and answers it in fifteen minutes. So what you see on the news is him repeating a Republican attack sound bite and then you get fifteen seconds out of his answer that no one can understand. It's what I called the Clinton vaccination, the idea being that if somehow you took the charge and you said it yourself, that would immunize you against the charge itself. In my opinion it never worked, but I never achieved any real success—nor did anyone else in the campaign—in convincing him.

He'd say to me, "I'm telling you, James, I'm telling you. He is out there saying I'm an untrustworthy person. I am going to stand up there and I'm not going to take it. It is *me* that they're saying this about. And I am going to stand up and I am going to tell people that I am not untrustworthy."

The mythology of political campaigns is that everything is all well greased and organized and happens as a result of careful consideration. Hell, we had seven different people saying, "Don't, *please* don't go out there and say that he says that you're untrustworthy." I was just waiting for him one day to go out and say, "They say I'm a draft-dodger. . . ."

By mid-week I was going in four times a day and saying, "Greenberg, tell me not to panic. People are telling me terrible things, tell me not to believe it."

The other media polls and pundits—and some in our campaign, as well—would have us believe that we were in some kind of free fall, that there was a dangerous shift going on, that it called for changes in our strategy. What changes? Answer the charges. Step up our attacks on Bush on the issues of trust or character or Iran-Contra. Should we get out of the game plan that we had developed, to accentuate change and the economy and twelve years of trickle-down and investing in people? Was our message going flat on people? Was it not resonating? Was Bush breaking through?

Most campaign professionals are, in and of themselves, action people. If we were doctors and a patient showed up, we'd start cutting them. Let's do something different. Let's go negative, let's put up some Iran-Contra, let's hit him hard. Why don't we attack Perot? That'll show people.

I was within a week of fulfilling my ultimate professional dream. I was scared. If we lost, the analysis in all of the TV postscripts and newsmagazines and books would be, quite correctly, that we'd run a very stupid campaign; we'd had information that we could have acted on with six days to go, we'd chosen to ignore it, laid back and got cold feet, got very cowardly, and lost the race. It would be major public humiliation.

And not inconsequential was the fact that, deep down inside, I and most of the people on the campaign were really good Democrats. We wanted to win because we wanted to win, and it was good for us, but we also believed it was for the good of the country. I'm sure the Republicans believed no less in their candidate.

There's a great myth that people in politics don't believe in anything except getting elected. We do believe in getting elected; it would be goofy to deny that winning elections is important to us. But it's just as goofy to assert that you can't believe in what you're doing and believe in winning at the same time. I've never had much trouble reconciling the two.

I was asking Stan for reassurance. He kept telling me, "James, don't panic. We knew it was going to tighten." His basic reasoning was that if anything was hurting us it was the fact that we were not disciplined and focused enough; instead of changing our original strategy we needed to buckle down and get back to more of the same. More on the economy, more on "Putting People First," more on health care.

The truth of the matter is, I basically agreed with him. But I needed to hear him say it. Our internals, our feelings thermometer, the projected job performance, were all showing that there had not been a fundamental structural change in the race. The shift in numbers was just a question of some Republicans coming home; among the voters we needed in the states where we needed them, things still looked real solid. When we surveyed the electoral map we got even more confident of our direction. We kept telling each other, "We knew this would happen. We've always said during the campaign, 'Look, when this happens we've got to remind ourselves, *Don't panic. Don't panic.*' So now, what we said would happen is happening. Let's don't be stupid because we were prophets."

I always thought, and I think Stan agreed with me, that the more people talked about Bush having a chance to win, the more it helped us. They may have had reservations about Bill Clinton, but if they really thought that Bush might be reelected, they'd go, "No, that's not really what I want." In fact, it got to be a catch-22; we felt the real danger was that people might think we had a lock on the race and would lose their fire and not turn out at the polls, and Bush would sneak up over the weekend and storm by us on the final day.

Most political campaigns have an accordion effect: They open up, get close, stretch out, and get close again. The Democratic convention coming first, we always get a bloated bounce coming out. Carter was up by 33 after the Democratic convention; he won by one. Dukakis was up by 17 for a week. In a statewide race, the challenger starts out far behind and closes in the end; in a presidential race the incumbent starts out farther behind and then closes.

So, once you went beyond the fact that we had dropped 5 points in a week, things looked pretty good.

Mary

A lot of states on Carney's chart were moving daily. The "even" states column was getting longer and the negative states were getting shorter. At that point you start paying attention to the polls. We were not confident by any means, but we were ecstatic anyhow. The people on the road were walking on air. What we had been saying was going to happen was actually happening.

People were gasping. We were breathless. I would wake up at five in the morning and have to wait until seven for Mary Lukens to get to the office to give me the overnights. She would torture me. "Now, don't get excited." Gave me a five-minute walk-up. We had numbers for every state and every manner of polling document available to mankind, and on Wednesday, less than a week out, we had it 39–39. A dead heat.

On the plane, the highest man in the hierarchy gets the numbers. When Jim Baker was there, he got them. Even when they're bad, it's the most critical piece of data you can have. When they're good, it's like you're handing the President a piece of gold.

Even the press got into the spirit. When their home base gave them new numbers, they were happy to call us and pass along the good news before the numbers came out publicly. So that morning I had a whole bevy of new numbers from *The New York Times.* And I'd got it first.

I went sprinting up the aisle as the plane was taking off, running uphill, sliding backward, tripping, banging against the walls, and hurled myself into the presidential cabin of Air Force One. I stood there breathless, panting, *"The New York Times* has—"

The President looked up from his desk and said, "I don't want to hear the polls. I don't care about the polls." Then he laughed. Thought we were all crazy. I presume he liked the fact that everybody was doing the jig on the airplane, but he refused to look at the figures. Maybe he did out of my presence, but he told me, "I didn't care when they were down, I don't care when they're up. I know I'm going to win and I know why I'm going to win. It has nothing to do with these numbers."

Bush had been through many campaigns, winners and losers. He was less reactive to day-to-day movement. He kept his eye on the long view. Plus, his opponent did not exactly fit his view of the office of the presidency. He had steeled himself against bad news and was not going to let his guard down for good news. By that stage of the campaign we were going to five and six events a day, the crowds were absolutely crazed to see him, and he was drawing strength from them. He had his speech totally down, had stopped using note cards and had begun speaking from his heart about the points of his economic plan, and the difference between the candidates, and what the presidency was all about. He was almost serene.

We, of course, were going nuts. We would run off the plane, couldn't wait to get to the next rousing event. And when a campaign catches fire, the press gets into it as well. It breaks the humdrum. On Thursday, October 29, we roared into a community college in Warren, Michigan.

President Bush was sick. About a week before, the White House photographer had gotten ill, and Ron Kaufman had gotten so sick the doctor had had to quarantine him. He gave Kaufman shots in the medical room and wouldn't let him out. I was so mad. They had come on board sick and had passed it around. It was like going into a house full of children when you've got a contagious disease; you just don't do it. These guys were not trying to be irresponsible; they were trying to do their jobs. But you can't take any risks at that stage of a presidential campaign; there's no margin for error. By that time we were running on four hours' sleep per night; we were all rundown and exhausted. The last thing you want is for the President to get sick.

In the holding room before the event he was sniffly, had big circles under his eyes, was about to lose his voice, no energy, just depleted. I looked at him and he was gray as a suit.

Michigan governor John Engler had the crowd juiced up to new highs, and as I watched President Bush walk from the holding room to the stage he went through an amazing transformation—from Gray Man to Candidate Man. He began his speech and the crowd went wild. The high-ceilinged hall's acoustics were thunderous and the President got the jolt.

"The only way they can win," he declaimed, "is to tell everybody everything isn't worth a darn. They criticize our country and say we are less than Germany and slightly better than Sri Lanka. My dog Millie knows more about foreign policy than these two bozos. It's crazy."

The crowd went gonzo, the governor was guffawing and slapping his knee, everyone from the plane was laughing.

"If you listen to Governor Clinton and Ozone Man . . ." the President went on. The crowd roared. "You know why I call him Ozone Man? This guy is so far off in the environmental extreme, we'll be up to our neck in owls, and out of work for every American. This guy's crazy. He's way out. Far out, man."

It played a lot differently on the news that night and in the papers the next day than it did as we heard it. The press reported that President Bush was getting desperate, and that in his desperation he was resorting to unseemly and inappropriate displays of language and emotion. They made it seem like he was having a meltdown.

But it wasn't a meltdown. In the context of the speeches he was giving and the crowds who were receiving them, it was a verbal up, one of his highest moments of connection with his audience and one of his highest moments of campaign happiness. I don't know if it was from being exposed to his grandkids all the time, or to the lunatics on the plane, but this vernacular was not foreign to him. It wasn't anything we would have put in his mouth or taken out of his mouth. He knew it was contrary to the Bush persona, but that's exactly why he knew it was funny. I'll say it again, it was funny to hear George Bush say, "Far out, man." And it was a winner, the people absolutely loved it. The press was there and clearly knew the context, they could have reported it accurately. Instead they made it seem like he was having an acid flashback.

I totally missed this one. As with the fish jokes, or talking to the chicken, it was the difference between being on the ground and on the plane, one more time. They got "bozos," we didn't. We heard a real crowd-pleasing zinger; they heard something less than presidential. The ground told us immediately to cut this out, that it was cutting against us. But because the crowds were reacting right in front of us, we thought we were more in touch with the mood of the people. We'd get back on the plane and tell him it was hilarious.

We were wrong. The Bush campaign was trying to reaffirm in the voter's mind the fact that our man was more mature, more elevated, more presidential than this pot-smoking, draft-dodging, womanizing Baby Boomer. You don't do that by saying, "Far out, man." In that context, this kind of language was incongruous.

You do get into a cocoon of craziness on the plane, and this was part of it. There were papers fanned out all over the place, Coke cans and posters, people running around, the place a mess. Kaufman had a boom box and was blaring Lee Greenwood's "God Bless the U.S.A." over and over. It was getting to be like a pajama party, and I think we ill-served the President.

Of course, the President loved these lines. He said them all day.

Barbara Bush knew better. She is the kind of woman who makes you sit up straighter and use better table manners. She would walk onto Air Force One, which had begun to devolve into a zoo plane, and it was like being in the presence of the Mother Superior. She is wonderful and maternal. There's nothing pompous or officious about her; she could not have been more supportive of people, and she had great political instincts. She knew George Bush better than anyone else. She wasn't intimidating, she was just never wrong. I do not know how often, or in which events, she proffered an opinion privately. I do know that nobody ever disagreed with Mrs. Bush.

The story goes that it was she who got the President to rein in his speech. I think he may even have said at one stop, "Barbara doesn't think it's a good idea that I call these guys 'bozos,' but I'm still going to say 'Ozone' . . ."

James

Calling Clinton and Gore bozos was a huge error. A mistake of the first order. They had run TV spots that massaged people's doubts about Clinton's record in Arkansas, and there had been some closure in the race; whether it was natural or not, things had begun to tighten. But that night that's all you saw on TV: The dog knows more about foreign policy. . . . Ozone . . . And that night it stopped. Our focus groups picked that up instantly. People said, "That's not fair. Bill Clinton and Al Gore are not bozos." People had seen Bill Clinton destroy George Bush in two debates, they had heard him, they had seen him answer questions on *Larry King* and all the shows. They knew he was a Rhodes scholar, they knew he'd been a governor for twelve years. No one thought Bill Clinton was a bozo; it was a charge that was just patently absurd on its face. They had seen Al Gore. Al Gore is the personification of stability. They make jokes about how stiff he is. And George Bush calls him crazy. "Ozone Man," I think is probably acceptable in the political rhetoric scheme of things. "Crazy," no.

This was more evidence that Bush was nuts than that we were. You could make a very good case that the President was losing it. People have a sense of parameters and boundaries about politics, and they'll give you a lot of leeway. If Bush had said, "You can't pin this guy down," that would have been within people's realm of credible things to say. And it works both ways; if we had called Bush "crazy" it would have hurt us bad. But clearly this "bozo" deal was counter to everything the voters knew about Bill Clinton. It didn't add up, it didn't make sense; all it did was make Bush look silly.

Assuming that he had momentum—and he certainly had natural momentum going, the incumbent taking back some of his flock—well, that's it. He's out. It's the Thursday night before the election and he's not talking about economic distinctions, he's not talking about the Arkansas record, he's not talking about stature or experience, the natural concerns that people had about Bill Clinton. All he's on the news talking about is "crazy" and "bozo" and "Ozone Man."

I was delighted.

Mary

Friday is bad-news day. If you ever have a bomb to drop on a campaign, you do it at a time when there's minimal opportunity to respond, and Friday afternoon is it. The Friday night newscasts are the last ones people pay real attention to until Monday. Weekends are big news droughts; there's a reason Saturday newspapers are thin. Make a big splash Friday afternoon and you can ride that wave all through the weekend.

On Friday afternoon, Independent Counsel Lawrence E. Walsh announced new counts in the Iran-Contra indictment of Reagan's secretary of defense, Caspar Weinberger. Among the papers released was a Weinberger memo suggesting that, in his opinion, at a White House meeting in 1986, Vice President Bush had been in favor of trading arms for hostages.

It was a technical addition to a previous indictment. There wasn't anything in there that wasn't already in the *Congressional Record*. But go try explaining that to the American people in a reactive sound bite four days before a presidential election. There was no reason whatsoever in the interplanetary system for Walsh to drop this thing on that Friday, except one.

President Bush had been disparaging Walsh's investigation. There was no restriction on its duration or the amount of taxpayer money being spent on it; after six years, thousands of documents, and over $40 million in taxpayer dollars, they didn't have anything. And now here we were, four days out from the election, and Lawrence Walsh sucker-punched us.

I have been told since that the Walsh office had called the news organizations the day before and alerted them to get ready, something was coming. I am not in any way suggesting that the Clinton people asked them to do it, but it's clear to me that the Clintonistas knew about it. (Some DNC kid bragged to David Tell: Buckle your seat belt, the big one's coming. When subsequently questioned about it, the DNC guy denied it.) It was just in the vapors, they had this unwarranted air of confidence. The press, too, was on pins and needles, waiting for something to happen, and now I know why. I have no doubt in my mind that this was strategically planned by Walsh. Why? To pay back George Bush.

This is how politics works. It's a very individual payback. It's Perot saying Bush screwed up his daughter's wedding. It's Walsh feeling disparaged by the revelation that he was abusing his office and taxpayers' money. This was his payback, and it was very effective.

Our historical voting behavior data showed that people were making up their minds increasingly later in the election cycle, and particularly with Perot in the race and an unusual set of choices, they would be doing it over the final weekend. This was perfectly timed and perfectly executed. It stopped us cold.

We were trapped on a train trip, we knew the logistics and timing would prevent an effective response, and everybody knew it was Walsh. Rather than focusing on the substance of the charge, we were consumed with the fact that he had pulled the ultimate act of political treachery. Charlie Black was the first to receive the wire story. He kept the piece of paper, circled the time, and saved it. He knew on Friday, October 30, 1992, that we had lost.

Not that we said it out loud, or even consciously acknowledged it. If we'd been truthful with ourselves we all would have agreed that was it, there would be no coming back. But we couldn't afford to look it square in the face. Marlin Fitzwater went out and told the press that all we were going to lose was a day's news, which wasn't a particularly appropriate response, but you can't really blame him or anyone; our first reaction was shock.

After the shock came the funk. We tried to deny it, but you just know in your stomach. We'd quit tracking at this point because by the time you could poll and respond to poll numbers, it would be too late. We had our final weekend course already plotted and we had no effective way to deal with this bombshell.

Back on Air Force One, George Bush, Jr., said, "This thing is over."
I looked at him. "You don't mean, 'It's *over*,' like we're going to lose."

That wasn't what he meant. He just stated the obvious: "There's nothing more we can do."

James

It came in at one o'clock. I was sitting on the sofa taking my little relaxation and Danny Reich, now a hero, handed me this thing that came in over the wire. I immediately took it into George's office and said, "They got some problems over there, big time." We spent the rest of the afternoon on the phone, George with the nets, me with the papers, stoking the story.

You don't do a full-scale spin on this. You kind of do a little underspin. You start with, "We're getting all the final arrangements here for Tuesday night. When you're here be sure you come by. . . . Man, you see this thing just come over the wire? Walsh and Bush and Cap Weinberger's notes? Ooh, man, I tell you, I feel sorry for Mary. I understand CBS and ABC are going to lead, and NBC's still toying with it. Big story out there." You look stupid spinning it directly, you have to go under and express some sympathy.

They knew what I was doing, of course. They'd tell me, "Yeah, it's going to be a story, he's going to have to deal with it." They were asking about it out there, trying to get an answer. "Apparently the Bush people are kind of holed up, nobody can get to them."

"Oh, yeah," I said, "they're shelled back in the bunker. I guess they're trying to figure out what to say, I don't know."

"What would you say, if you were them?"

I was laying the bait out there. Stoking it. "I guess I won't be hearing from Mary this afternoon." The skill is to resist the temptation to pick up the phone and go, "Wow, look at this! Is this huge!" You just kind of float it, bleed into the conversation. But you immediately get up from your nap and start working the phones.

When something like this happens you're more likely to take the political calls coming in. If I was bullshitting with one of my political buddies and it's a reporter on the other line I'd say, "Hold on, I'll take that one. . . ."

"Hey, what's goin' on, anything happening? Oh, yeah, I saw that thing over the wire. Yeah. Our polls, you saw the polls, seventy percent of the people think he's lying. I don't understand why everybody's covering the thing like it's the end of World War II or something. . . . Who y'all calling for comment on this?"

It's something of an understatement to say that this story hurt Bush and helped us. Anything he would try to do to make news over the weekend was going to get passed through the Iran-Contra filter. But you don't make a lot of news over the final weekend, it wasn't that big a story and didn't have much legs beyond Friday night's broadcasts. Bush was on *Newsmaker Sunday*, but I don't think a CNN show two days before is going to determine the outcome of a race. Our data, which was considerable, did not indicate that there was a Bush surge. And I don't think in any way, shape, or form that this thing cost Bush the election.

Mary

No emotion lasted longer than a couple of hours, but mostly we were in "Walsh is scum" shock. Jim Baker, who is not known for being a giggly kind of guy, repeated a favorite line of politicos: "Being called a liar by Bill Clinton is like being called ugly by a frog." We all loved it, of course, and the President went out and used it on the stump to rebut the Walsh accusations, which Clinton was repeating with every breath.

We were only temporarily dispirited, because we had been on a roll. We were still psyched by the polls closing, having been in a dead heat, about Clinton being on our turf re trust and character. With three days to go, the plane and the ground were all traveling together, which made for a real esprit de corps. The events were great. In fact, everything was looking spectacular. Unfortunately, we were in an emotional and political time lag. We had been hit but the shock waves hadn't yet reached the brain. We were more angry and stunned than comprehending or acknowledging what Walsh's bomb had done to us. You just cannot be that honest with yourself while you're in the middle of a closing campaign. You're in the deepest of denial.

We didn't really feel what hit us until Sunday morning, when the President was interviewed live on CNN by Frank Sesno.

We had made the tactical decision to do every free media interview we could get our hands on. George Bush hates doing perpetual interviews: They're tiring—the reporters grill you, they ask the same questions, and they're like little gnats. He didn't want to do any more. But TV has a broader reach than on-site campaigning, so he acquiesced.

Sesno grilled him. You can never get an ironclad agreement from these guys not to cover a topic, but there was some discussion that we'd hit Iran-Contra and move on. Well, Sesno hit it and hit it and hit it and wouldn't move away. After a while the President finally said, "Frank, do you want to spend the whole time talking about Iran-Contra?" and Sesno still pursued him.

It was a rainy, bleak, cold, ugly day. There were about thirty friends, family, and staff gathered in an equally bleak, damp, windowless basement holding room during the broadcast. I spent the time trying to keep up a happy chatter and polishing Bush's five-year-old granddaughter's fingernails. The people in the room kept sinking lower and lower, the sounds going from a depressed murmur to total silence except for this chattering child and me, doing her nails. President Bush came out of the studio and said, "I knew I didn't want to do that. I shouldn't have done it. I'm not doing any more of these. I want to campaign. I want to talk to the people. I'm not doing these anymore."

Campaigns do bizarre things to the people who are in them. If you're supposed to be happy, you can find a reason to be sad; if you're supposed to be depressed, you can find a reason to carry on. The weekend before the election in 1988, when we were about to swamp Dukakis, Rich Bond's back went out, he couldn't talk without throwing up, he literally went blind. This time Margaret Tutwiler was paralyzed, she had thrown out her back, couldn't move, she could only lie down.

It goes hour by hour. It's like an endless hangover. You're so over-adrenalized that you're not sleeping, you're not thinking rationally, you're giddy. It's like breathing helium. We didn't come back from the Sesno interview and overrun the president's doctor with "Give me a Valium," we catapulted into the next mode. We wouldn't let it get to us. We didn't have any new polls to read and we had other things to do, so we just kept pushing on.

When a campaign is peaking you bring celebrities along to the events. You've got thirty, or forty, or fifty thousand people who've been waiting hours for a twenty-minute speech; you've got to give them a show. The last weekend we were traveling with the great country music group the Oak Ridge Boys. All these guys in red cowboy boots and ponytails were hanging out in the Air Force One conference room. One of the few fine side benefits of a campaign is the chance to hang out with guys like these. They were cool.

Kaufman and I were back in the insane asylum cabin, guzzling black coffee, preaching to the choir just exactly how we were going to win, when a steward came and fetched us. "The President would like to see you." We went forward.

The President loves country music. He knew we did, too, since we were always bellowing along with Kaufman's CDs.

"Got any songs you'd like to hear?"

His small office was overflowing with the stewards and kitchen staff and attendants and military personnel who were assigned to the plane. They covered the couches that lined the walls, the President leaning back in his swivel chair, and the Oak Ridge Boys gave a concert.

The Oak Ridge Boys have beautiful voices. They stood in the middle of the President's cabin and sang four-part harmony a cappella. We were clapping and grinning and having a good time. The President said, "Let's hear 'Amazing Grace.' "

"Yeah, yeah, 'Amazing Grace'!"

The Boys hunkered down in a tight semicircle, facing the President, and began to sing.

I was sitting on a window ledge behind the President and to his right, my legs crossed, wearing cowboy boots. They started singing, my lip started quivering, and I began to cry.

The prospect of losing, which I had totally repressed into some other part of my body, had crept into my brain. This was the last weekend of the campaign; it was all coming to an end. I refused to believe that we could lose, but win or lose, this long haul was almost over.

I didn't want to cry in front of President Bush. It wasn't great sobs, just tears streaming down my face. I wasn't shaking. Trembling, maybe; that song always does it to me anyway.

I don't know how he knew, but President Bush reached back and squeezed my foot. He wouldn't turn around and look at me.

There was no applause, just silence. President Bush broke it. As soon as it was over I beelined to the bathroom, locked myself in, and sobbed.

CHAPTER 26

James

People started pouring into Little Rock like we were holding Mardi Gras. Contributors, spectators, the press. All the nets and papers had established bureaus there now. People were setting up tents and hawking T-shirts. It was like the weekend of the Super Bowl, with players in the lobby and fans saying, "That's George Stephanopoulos," "There's Carville."

After Friday, a strategist has very little to do. Truth is, you could probably go to the movies. The stage is set, you're not going to change your stump speech or your strategy with four days left to go. We were toying with a little last-minute advertising rotation, but nothing more. Nobody was going to put up any negative spots, there wasn't going to be a silver bullet. In fact, most of the action transferred out of the War Room and into the field.

The real work I had the last weekend was fielding press calls. I don't know if the public would be shocked by this, but when there's a story in a special edition of *Time* or *Newsweek* the day after the election, "Clinton Wins! Here's an analysis . . . ," somebody wrote that story on Saturday. When you see a quote in there, somebody gave that quote on Sunday. The huge post-election analysis in your local newspaper, on the AP wire, or in *The New York Times*, they didn't write that story Tuesday night; it was written before the election.

I'd get the calls. "I'm writing the story that you won." If what they think doesn't come to pass, they just wasted a story. Maybe they write it both ways. They say, "Assume that you won. If my story's buried, your quote gets buried with it." "We're going to air this thing the day after the election. Let's assume that you won, Jim, and . . ." Everybody does it. There's no way that you can't do it.

Starting Saturday it kind of got to be fun. Unless something unexpected happened at the last minute, I was going to attain my ultimate professional goal. Time, which had been in short supply starting the previous December, eased up a little. It was nice. People who I hadn't heard from in a while started calling. Someone I went to college with. A guy I knew in the Marines. "I didn't know if you'd take my call. My wife and I have been watching and she didn't really believe that I knew you."

The War Room got to be a tourist attraction. There was nothing of consequence happening there anymore, nothing that I knew or anybody knew that would be of any value. The thing that was happening was that it was a Happening. People were coming by, you couldn't kick them out. "Where's that sign that says, 'The Economy, Stupid'?" Contributors were coming in. The no-press-in-the-War-Room rule? That's gone. People wanted to have their picture taken with you. There was food all over the place. Vendors were sending tins of pecans, fruitcakes; people were coming up with bottles of wine and six-packs of beer. There were tours. They were taking school kids through! There wasn't much sense in stopping it. Hell, we could have let Bush in there, it wouldn't have mattered.

That's always the way it is at the end of a campaign. It's inevitable. If you're losing it's awful, nothing like the pain, so you laugh a lot. In the losing campaigns that I've been on there's been a lot of gallows humor. Here there was tension—"Could it go wrong? Could it break out there?"—but I had enough to do to keep it from eating me alive. On the road, Clinton and the Road Warriors were calm. If this had been a football game we'd have been up by eight, they'd have the ball on the fifty-yard line with a minute to go. Yes, you worry, "Geez, could we blow it? They could score, get an onside kick and get a last-second field goal." So you're keeping your eye on the ball. There's no high-fiving on the sidelines yet, but it's getting close.

Mary

We hit six states on Monday, starting in New Jersey and ending up in Texas. We didn't know where we were. We'd land, run to the tarmac, we'd scream, we'd go back up, we'd come back down. By the end of the day I'd grab a paper go-cup, get off the plane, stand on the fringe of the crowd, and smoke a cigarette and drink red wine. I could barely take it anymore.

You couldn't even get a buzz, there was just no way. You could have sat there and drunk three bottles by yourself but you were so numb that you wouldn't feel it.

Our last stop before Texas was a huge airport rally in Louisiana. It was late at night, I was standing there with my go-cup and my Marlboro Light, and all these people were going, "That's James Carville's girlfriend!" So I went over and they started naming people from the town of Carville. "I know Miss Nippy!" "Our sister works with his brother." They told me, "We're voting for Bush. We like James, he's a son of the South, but we're for your guy." All I remember thinking was, "I want to win Louisiana so bad I can taste it."

It was even later when we landed in Houston. Way past news time. Everybody was bailing out, not going to the President's final campaign event. You didn't have to: The national press wasn't going to report it, there was no spin to do, you could go back to the hotel if you wanted to. We were walking on stumps, the Night of the Living Dead, but a handful of us—Steve Provost, Phil Brady, Torie, Kaufman, the hardcore plane people—knew this was history. We huddled and said, "We've gone this far; we're going to the last event." It was a badge of honor.

Much more so than on election day, when you're frantically calling reporters and colleagues for exit polls and gossip, the last night of a campaign is when you peak. Every ounce of what's driven you, what you care about, your affection and loyalty for your candidate—everything you've had no time to reflect on while it was happening—comes into wrenching focus.

It was magic. There were ten thousand people in the hall, and more overflowed into the streets, another crazy, enveloping display of love for the man. I don't know where President Bush ever found the strength, but he gave a very emotional speech and we all got rejuvenated. We were hugging and crying and kissing. Then we stumped back to the hotel and tried to sleep.

I couldn't. I was in a fever pitch of hatred for Carville.

I called my sister. I called his sister. Everyone I talked to I told, "I hate him. I *hate* him. I never want to see him again." Of course, I was going to see him in about two days.

At the beginning of the campaign, every time James was on TV or the Clintonistas did something that didn't even involve him, my own people would come in and sneer at me. I thought this was so stupid. Why was I getting blamed for James? Why blame James—it's two campaigns going at each other. But by the end of the campaign, everybody liked James, including the President.

It took me the entire election to personalize the assault on my President in the body of James Carville. I had done a 180. Now I blamed everything on him. I hated his guts.

His sisters were so sweet. Toward the end of the campaign, they sent me a brass elephant necklace, which I wore all the time for good luck. I know they voted for Reagan and I know they voted for Bush in 1988. I don't know who they voted for this time, but they were so concerned about my feelings, and about George Bush and his feelings. James's sister Pat tracked me down that night, and I went into full-throttle I-hate-your-brother rant and she just sat and listened to it. I worked myself up into a real hateful snit.

James

Monday night was the final War Room meeting.

Generally I'd go into George's office and we'd talk for a few minutes and then walk in and start. That night you couldn't hardly get through, it was packed.

All our workers were there, of course, all the strategists, all these kids. ABC was doing a "72 Hours to Victory" shoot and had a crew. There was a whole pack of still photographers. D. A. Pennebaker and his partner Chris Hegedus were shooting what would become their Academy Award–nominated documentary, *The War Room*. And as soon as you walked in you could feel that this was something special.

The night before, Gene Sperling had given an impassioned speech about how much this campaign had meant to him, and how people would never know what it was like in the Dukakis campaign, where you could never talk to anybody and the doors were always closed; and how with us, everything was open. In most campaigns, he said, you got in trouble if you tried to go to a meeting; in this one you would get in trouble if you *didn't* go to a meeting. I was very touched.

The War Room was coming to an end. George and I were sitting on the floor, surrounded by the people we'd been working with for five months; it seemed like it had been years. George said, "Before I give him the floor for what I hope isn't the last time, I think we all know that, besides Bill Clinton, one person really gave this campaign focus.

And one person wrote what I call a haiku about five months ago: 'Change versus more of the same. The economy, stupid'—I think if you did a Nexis it would come up in about a thousand places—and 'Don't forget health care.'

"I was kidding James yesterday. I said that he was about to pass from a role of regular human being into the role of a legend, and I think he really deserves it, 'cause probably for the first time in a generation tomorrow, we're gonna win. And that means that more people are going to have better jobs. People are going to pay a little less for health care, get better care. And more kids are going to go to better schools. So, thanks."

I stood up. I didn't think I could say what I had to say sitting down.

What I wanted to tell each of these people was that they had done a good job, they had given it all, and I couldn't imagine something like this happening to people that young. I wanted to tell them to savor the moment, that they deserved it.

"There's a simple doctrine," I started. "Outside of a person's love, the most sacred thing that they can give is their labor. And somehow or another along the way, we tend to forget that. And labor is a very precious thing that you have. And any time that you can combine labor with love, you've made a merger.

"I think we're gonna win tomorrow, and I think that the governor is going to fulfill his promise and change America, and I think many of you are going to go on and help him."

These kids really were going to do it. My lip started quivering. For a moment I couldn't see real well.

"I'm a political professional; that's what I do for a living. I'm proud of it. We changed the way campaigns are run. Used to be there was a hierarchy. If you were on one floor, you didn't go to another floor; if you were somewhere in the organizational chart, there was no room for you there. Everyone was compartmentalized. And you people showed that you could be trusted. Everybody in this room. Everybody.

"People are gonna tell you you're lucky. You're not. Ben Hogan said that 'Golf is a game of luck: The more I practice, the luckier I get.' The harder you work, the luckier you are."

Who'd understand all of this? My whole jaw was shaking.

"I was thirty-three years old before I ever went to Washington or New York. Forty-two before I won my first campaign." I wanted to push on but the words kind of stuck. "And I'm happy for all of y'all. You been part of something special in my life, and I'll never forget what you all have done. Thank you."

I sat down as the whole room chanted, "One more day! One more day!" I tried not to cry in front of everybody. I don't know if I succeeded. There was this overwhelming sense that I had something to tell these people, that they were really counting on me, and I'd never got anything out. People were coming up and hugging and crying. I thought I'd blown it.

Mary

It was so weird to wake up the next day, there wasn't anything to do. It was the first time in months that I didn't have to get up at three-thirty in the morning to put my luggage outside my room for the Air Force One crew to pick up. We had the whole day to do whatever we wanted. We'd been going at three hundred miles an hour and now we were motionless.

People magazine had told my office they were doing an election-day photo essay on the two campaigns, so my day's only obligation was to hook up with this woman, which I really did not want to do. In the course of my conversing with her I got suspicious. "Who's doing this from the Clinton campaign?" I asked.

"Carville."

"Is this about 'Mary and James' or is it about the two campaigns?"

"Well, it's about the two campaigns, but James will be in it."

I knew it was going to be a Romeo-and-Juliet story, and I was plenty damn sick of them by then. Anything I could get mad about that day, I got mad. I called my staff and cussed them out good for letting the *People* people dupe them. All day long I was tailed by these two photographers.

I turned on the television and there was Alixe Glen saying we were dead even in Kentucky and ahead in the absentee ballots in New Jersey. I was stunned. If that was true, it meant we were going to win. I immediately quit being crabby. Minute by minute my emotions were going crazy. I went for a jog, secure in the knowledge that we were in the middle of one of the great election comebacks of all time.

We were staying at the Houston hotel complex where President Bush maintains his residence. As I was beginning my run I passed the President playing horseshoes with his sons Junior and Marvin. I run like Clinton, flapping around like a beached whale, and Junior, of course, shouted, "Pick it up, girl!" I shouted back, "We're even in Kentucky and we're ahead in absentee ballots in New Jersey. *We're going to win!*" I was really psyched, running fast.

The President said, "You're kidding!" He laughed. "Mary," he called, "we're always winning in your mind." And went back to playing horseshoes.

It was such a luxurious day. I went and got a massage, took a steam bath, got my nails done. Just to have that much time to myself was the queen treat you could ever have.

I got all done with these indulgences and walked out to the health-club lobby. The President was standing there with Mrs. Bush and Jim Baker, on the telephone. Everybody was in a funk. Oh, no. He was telling Congressman Bob Michel, "It's not good news, friend. We're not getting good news."

I flew back to my room and called the office. Rhonda tried to fudge. "We just got our first run of exit polls. It's still early so they don't really matter. . . ."

"Gimme the numbers."

She started going through the states, and we were losing everywhere.

"Transfer me to Carney." She did. "How could this be?" I asked him. "Where did Alixe Glen get that this morning?"

He said, "I gave it to her."

"Where did you get it?"

"I just made it up."

"What? She's on TV saying this? I told the President!"

"Look," he said, "we've got to keep our voters voting all day. What do you want me to do, send her out there and say we're losing?"

I'd been booked onto Larry King's show that afternoon and it was a total out-of-body experience. He asked me some touchy-feely question like "How does it feel?" and I said something along the lines of "I feel like it's been the highest honor to have served the most honorable, decent man that anyone could ever know, and to know what he's done for history. . . ." I then proceeded to do ten or fifteen radio and TV stand-ups, saying, "We're gonna win, we're gonna win. It's still early, don't quit, keep going to the polls. Don't listen to these exit polls; they were wrong in New Hampshire, they've been wrong all the way through. Keep going."

On my way back to the hotel I bumped into the Bushes, who now knew we had lost. Mrs. Bush gave me a big hug and the President said, "Matalin, we're winning!" This was now his running joke with me. I said, "We *are* winning. We're going to win." He just laughed and went on to his final reception.

James

Tuesday morning, election day, I had a panic attack. On Monday we had been up by about 10 points in the CBS poll, and now they were reporting us up by 5. When you factored in the mechanics of how CBS tabulated their numbers, that meant we had plummeted overnight, the vote had shifted, and we were actually going to lose the election by 15 percent.

Perot had bought airtime on all three networks and had sat there with his charts and taken shots at the Arkansas record. His points were convoluted, but he'd seemed authentic and had looked very good doing it. It was one of the more effective attacks I have seen in politics. It was too late to poll, but my gut instinct told me he had staged a pretty effective show. I remember looking at it and saying, "Geez, man, I wish this thing would stop." Perot is very astute politically, but he has a coordination problem: He can't talk and tell the truth at the same time.

On Monday I'd called the race 46 Clinton, 40 Bush, 14 Perot. After seeing that broadcast I thought, "He's taken a point away from us." That's a lot to do in an evening. "It's going to go down to five."

I went to George and said, "Look, man, I don't know how to say this, but we could be losing this thing. Let's get Stan and see could this have happened."

Stan said, "No, no, you're being ridiculous. Nothing's going to happen to change this." So he called CBS and they said, "Well, it's just one night . . . but it was a really off night. We still predict you're going to win the election."

George was darker than dark. "Paulie," he said to Begala on the phone, "I got up this morning, as I was driving to work I started to cry. I couldn't keep it . . . I just . . . I can't, I can't cope right now. Man, I'm scared. Because we're all going to have to jump off a bridge. Because, you know, because of the last two days. Yeah, it'll just be . . . kind of a mass thing. We can all just drink some Kool-Aid."

My superstitions had taken hold. In the Wofford campaign I didn't change my underwear for the last ten days. Washed them but didn't change them. In New Jersey I'd taken a strong liking to a pair of garden gloves and didn't take them off except to sleep. Before the Casey race in '86 I actually thought about saying, "I can't handle it. I'm going to leave and wake up the next morning, pick up the paper, and see if we won." This time I was onto the garden gloves again. I curled up, my knees to my chest, on one of the War Room chairs, and started reciting a concession speech for Bill Clinton.

"We tried hard; we came up a little short. To those who embraced our crusade, we say 'Thank you.' For President Bush, who's won reelection, we offer our full support, our prayers, and our hopes for a better America."

"Oh, God," George moaned, "shut up."

"Throughout this campaign I have endeavored to bring my message of change to the American people. And over forty-two percent of you embraced that message, and I am grateful to each and every one of you.

"Hillary and I will never forget you. The way you welcomed us into your homes, your towns, and your cities. It is not that we have lost this battle. It's whether we endure in a larger war."

Then I switched to press mode.

"In a stunning come-from-behind upset that shocked pundits, political professionals, journalists, people around the world, George Herbert Walker Bush proved his political resiliency beyond any doubt whatsoever. He was reelected today over Bill Clinton, garnering 274 electoral votes. Only four over. But as they say, it's not horseshoes and it's not hand grenades. George Bush will return—we repeat—George Bush *will return* to the White House for another four years."

Then the exit polls came in. You get your first one at about ten-fifteen in the morning, then two P.M., then four. It's a huge conspiracy between the networks, the campaigns, and the reporters that the results are a big surprise when the polls close. Sometimes you really do have to count the votes: Kennedy-Nixon, Nixon-Humphrey, Carter-Ford, the '86 governor's race in Pennsylvania. But unless it's a really close contest, everybody knows.

We'd won. Everybody was calling back and forth, the nets were calling the headquarters, the headquarters were calling the states. "How're we doing in Georgia?" I was scared to death we'd lose it. Governor Miller was way out front for us, the state was good to us in the primary, it was important that we take it for him. "How're we doing in Colorado?"

Mary

I followed the Bushes to the reception. Everybody was in suits and I was wearing jeans, so I only had one drink and left. Everybody was milling around and acting kind of chipper. You can't cry at that point; you can't do anything. All I kept thinking was "How can the President be going through this?" It was too shocking for your system to absorb, it was way past the point of an emotional response, so the only thing I could do was what I did: grab a bottle of red wine and head for the room where the middle-shots like Charlie Black and Torie Clarke, in a gorgeous skin-tight leopard minidress and holding a bottle of cheap champagne in each hand, and David Tell were watching the debacle on three different televisions.

We were screaming at the screens. John Sununu, now a notable talking head for CNN, was wind-bagging big-time. He said the problem with our campaign was that we never used the governors in their states. Our jaws dropped, since every one of our governors and former governors was a state chairman, except in *his* state, where no one would speak to him. It was the perfect opportunity to actually throw a shoe at a TV, which I did.

We sat there and rated the talking heads on their performances. Rich Bond came on, trashing the Democrats till the end. "Attaboy, Bond, keep kicking. And get a shave!" Phil Gramm was eloquent and never let up. When Dan Rather came on we threw pretzels at him.

Then came the time, as when somebody dies, that we had to start notifying people. I called my staff back in Washington and thanked them for doing a great job. I called my sister, hoping to get some support, and she picked up the phone and started crying. Then I got all quiver-lipped. I called my dad. "I've just left the Bushes. I can't believe we lost."

"Yeah," he said, "I can't believe James beat you." My dad had raised me to be competitive, but this wasn't a personal competition. It was such a weird thing to say that we both burst out laughing. Then he started ragging about, "It's that ass Nicholas Brady's fault." My dad had never gotten over the 1990 budget deal. As it happens, I was sitting next to Nick Brady, a sweet and loyal Bush friend. I was afraid Nick would hear his name coming out of the receiver. "I'll be sure to give the secretary your best regards, Dad." I cupped the phone. "Oh, Mr. Secretary, my dad says hello."

Charlie Black never lost his cool. He went immediately to analyzing what we could say, the spin. By this time it was about eight o'clock at night and he was focusing on the positives. "We won Florida, we won Texas. The Republican party is not dead. Let's not forget the underticket races." It was an exercise in futility because nobody takes spin on election night, and we weren't really required to go out and do it.

But Charlie wasn't doing it for the media. He wasn't doing it so that we could go out and deliver the message to the media. He was doing it, as he and he alone always did, to bring comfort and solace and cohesiveness to the group. He was always the guy you wanted to talk to when you'd taken one in the gut. He proved again that he has the best bedside manner in the world.

We were all pretty resigned and loose by this point. I took my camera and went into the pressroom, up to the front like I was going to say something. The place shut up. Usually they all glom around you, but everybody froze. I got out my camera and said, "This is a picture for history. You guys, hard at work as always." They all started laughing and gingerly gathered around. As opposed to even the day before, when they would have pushed and screamed and jostled, they were very sweet. No matter what I said, they wouldn't challenge me. I was full of remarkable banalities—"Sometimes the wind's in your face, sometimes it's at your back"—and they were writing down my drivel like it was important analytical perspective! I put my arm around Helen Thomas, and they took pictures of us.

Torie came in in her hot dress, toting her bottles of champagne. It was like a wake. You know how you behave when you're pretending as if somebody didn't die, and everyone is drinking and eating and telling jokes? That was us and the press. They got to be real human beings at the end.

I went to Margaret Tutwiler's room. Still in a state of paralysis because of her back, she was transfixed by Clinton's image on the four TVs in front of her. She just kept saying over and over, "I can't believe this man is President. I can't believe this man is President." Janet Mullins was with her and we had a little discussion about whether we should go to the concession speech. Of course everyone wanted to go out of loyalty to Bush, but in as much as moving was extremely painful for Tutwiler, I left her in the room with Janet and hitched a ride in the motorcade with the photo dogs.

There is an area between the stage and where the crowd is roped off called the pool zone, a buffer for the Secret Service and the press. Members of the media are rotated in and out of there. As the first rotation came through, the crowd started pushing and shoving and cursing and screaming at them. Punches were being thrown and a dangerous, full-scale rumble was in the making. The press guys weren't fighting back, just trying to defend themselves. I ran over and got between them and the crowd, screaming, "Stop it! Just stop this! George Bush has more dignity than this, he would never want you to do this!"

"Who the fuck are you?"

Some woman in the crowd recognized me—"*She knows George Bush!*"—and they pulled the guys off the media. There was a lot of murmuring, "That's right. George Bush would never want this. Too much dignity." There's the power of the press; my being a media big-mouth for once paid off.

All the Bush kids lined the stage, then Mrs. Bush, who looked like she'd been crying. Jim Baker introduced the President. Bush gave a short concession speech. He said he was going to "get very active in the grandchild business." I was ever respectful of the man's dignity, but I don't remember a lot of what he said. Your mind can only grasp so much. I was full of endless sadness, but happy at the same time that the President was surrounded by family and friends, who were crying, and a crowd that was still going crazy over him. I hoped that was giving him some support.

I stumbled back to the hotel and up to Margaret's room, where the four TVs were blaring. By the time I got there, Clinton was coming on to make his acceptance speech. Simultaneously on all three networks and CNN, about four people deep in the crowd in front of the stage, there was this turquoise jacket I had given James at the Michigan debate. There was this domehead on four channels at a time. There he was.

I was sick to my stomach. "I can't take it anymore," I said. "I can't watch this." I grabbed a bottle of wine and went back to my room.

It was a mess. Papers were tossed all over; my lunch that I hadn't touched was turning crusty on its tray; my clothes were lying every-where. I pushed everything aside and crawled into bed.

James

There must have been a dozen of us, staff and reporters, around the restaurant table for dinner at about seven that night. I was so nervous I stood up and said, "I can't take it no more." I got "Penny" Pennebaker and went over to some hotel bar and had a drink. Proba-bly had two drinks. Then I walked back to headquarters and watched the election returns with the campaign staff. Louisiana came in and everybody was whooping and hollering. Around nine o'clock it got to be time to go to the acceptance speech. The streets were such a cir-cus, the three-block walk took forty-five minutes.

I thought the whole acceptance ceremony was staged brilliantly. The only people who were actually on the stage were the President-elect and Mrs. Clinton and Chelsea, and the Vice President–elect and Mrs. Gore and their children. I was pleased with the decision, whoever made it. I hate those election-night onstage crowd scenes, with all the supporters in the background fighting to get into the TV picture. It's traditionally an ugly scene, the podium-standing thing.

The advance people had come and placed us in a little roped-off area in front of stage left. I was wearing the electric-blue parka Mary had given me. We were all pretty damn happy.

In his speech, the President-elect mentioned Paul Tully and Vic Raiser. Both men had died during the campaign, Tully of a heart attack and Vic in a plane crash. Vic had been a good friend of the Clintons', and one of our best fund-raisers. His daughter, Sky, was standing in the crowd right behind me. I turned around and gave her a hug, and she kind of went slack.

After the speeches, when the candidates and their wives were waving to the audience, the Vice President–elect saw me. He kneeled down at the front of the stage, reached into the crowd, and gave me a hug in front of 75 million people. That was, shall we say, a nice gesture, one that I'm not likely ever to forget.

People were partying all over Little Rock. Who knows how many drinks I had that night. But I couldn't help notice that something had changed in my life. Here I was, the chief strategist in a winning presidential campaign, there were probably three thousand available females out there, and I went home and went to bed. Hell, I must be in love.

Mary

In the middle of the night the phone rang. I was in a coma, overflowing with red wine and depression, waking up in a strange place and not knowing where I was or what time it might be. I heard James's voice on the other end, and I was indescribably, and from the bottom of my heart, as rude as I've ever been to anyone in my life. And meant every word.

"I cannot believe you could live on this earth and know that you were responsible for electing a slime, a scum, a philandering, pot-smoking, draft-dodging pig of a man. . . . You make me sick. I hate your guts."

I used every cuss word I could think of for him and his guy. Then I hung up. I don't remember him saying anything.

James

I didn't blame her. Change the details and she said about the same thing I would have said if we had lost.

Mary

The next morning I woke up with the adrenaline version of a hangover, and called James's sister. "I was really rude to your brother last night," I told her, "but I really do hate him."

She said, "No, you don't hate him."

"Yes, I do hate him. Well, I might not hate him. If you talk to him, tell him I might not hate him."

Then James called again. I didn't apologize for what I'd said, but I think I was calmer. I knew intellectually that it was irrational to hate him, but I really did. I didn't want to see him. My mind could not consider the possibility that Clinton was President, and I couldn't extract Carville from that Night of the Living Dead. He was Clinton, and I didn't want to see or talk to him.

He was talking about our trip, the one he had told me about in Michigan, and saying that it would be okay.

"I'll never get over this," I told him.

"Yes, you'll get over this. There wasn't anything more you could have done. He was a great President, he was a great man. Our argument was easier to make. . . ." He was being self-deprecating, and the more self-deprecating he became, the more I hated his guts.

He kept talking about the trip. "We're going to have so much fun. Don't you miss me?" The last thing I wanted to think about was resuming the relationship. On the one hand, for months all I'd been waiting for was to resume my life and patch up what was left of this thing and hope something actually was left. At the same time I hated him.

James

I am nowhere near as in love with victory as I am fearful of defeat. My overwhelming feeling the morning after the election was not "Thank God we won"; it was "Thank God we didn't lose." Not "Hey, look, I'm on the top of the world right now," but "Hey, look, I'm not on the bottom of the world." To me that was ecstasy.

At the end of a campaign, win or lose, there's a real sense that overcomes you that it's never going to happen again. You come to work the next morning not at seven o'clock but at eight, and on your way in you say to yourself, "I'll never walk back in this building again. These people, I'll never work with." It's been so intense, such an enveloping part of your life for such a long period of time, and it's gone.

During a campaign you are needed. People are coming up to you all day long, saying, "What do we do about this?" "So-and-so wants you on the phone." The media is calling. You are so central to so many people's lives. And then you're not.

When the campaign is over, for the first three, four, five days the phone's still ringing, people are calling, they're coming over to headquarters to write wrap-up stories or offer congratulations. And you say, "Man, I am going on vacation. I am gonna sleep, I'm gonna eat, I'm gonna have a good time." And you do. Then you get back and check your answering machine and you've got two messages where there used to be 250.

It must be something like if you have kids. You raise them and they do real well, they get high scores on the College Boards, they apply to three schools and get in all three. They're fine, healthy children and you're real proud when they pack up and go off to Harvard, or LSU. Then, about two weeks later, where there used to be kids playing around the house and food to fix and your family to take care of, there's just silence. You call them up and they say, "Hey, Dad, I'm busy now, I'll call you back." They love you, they appreciate you, but they've got other lives now.

One of my favorite titles was a book about the Civil War, by Bruce Catton: *A Stillness at Appomattox.* One day there's war. People fighting, screaming, dying; lead everywhere. The next day it's gone. There's a stillness.

Anybody who's been on a battlefield, whether it's a real battlefield or a political battlefield or a game, will know this: There's the smell, the odor, the feel that draws you back after it's done. They say in war it's the smell of cordite, of gunpowder. It stays in the air.

Same exact thing the morning after an election. All of that emotion and hollering, the shouting, the hugging. It stops. It stops and it don't ever come back. It doesn't peter out, it doesn't fade away. It's there; then it's gone. And no one needs you.

I think the reason most people get professionally involved in campaigns is that they like that intensity. I do. I like the short duration of a political campaign. I like the fact that it has a definitive result. They do keep score.

It happens all over America. You work on a church fair, all you do for months is organize it. You see that the booths are there, you worry if everything is going to show up, is it going to rain? What kind of food are you going to have? What kind of contest are you going to run this year? Who's going to be there? Everybody's calling you for these decisions, and you're making sure each one's done right. So you run the fair, and it comes off beautifully, and everybody loves it, and then they go home.

The day after, you walk out to the grounds and help clean up the bunting and crepe paper, and that morning no one cares. Folks wonder why it's always the same people volunteering; the person who does the church fairs is the one who does the United Way drive is the one who does the Heart Association picnic. It's because people come down from being a part of something, from being needed, and have to move on to something else to get that feeling.

There's a point after a campaign, it generally happens in early December, when I lose it. I just can't stop crying.

Mary

A lot of people flew back to Washington on commercial airlines, but the plane people had our last hoorah. Some were in tears, most were in shock, and President Bush walked back and told us, "There will be no bawl babies on this plane."

The President visited every cabin and told everyone to buck up, that things would be fine. He was supporting everybody else.

Bob Teeter, ever the professor, was going over what we'd done right and what we'd done wrong, what we could have fixed and what was beyond our control. His defense mechanism was to analyze the campaign intellectually. I started drinking Bloody Marys.

It was a drizzly, damp, overcast, gray day in Washington. We landed at Andrews Air Force Base, choppered to the Pentagon, and motorcaded in. Under normal circumstances we would all have just gone home, but I wanted to go back to the White House, where there was a group of loyalists on the South Lawn gathered to meet the President.

It was basically driving to the grave site.

We pulled into East Executive Drive between the White House and the Treasury Building. The D.C. White House and campaign staff, whom we hadn't seen much in three months, met us. All of us knew we were walking down this colonnade together for the last time. Every time I looked at anyone I started crying and they started crying. Nobody wasn't crying.

The military band was in tears. The White House staff and campaign people and plane people all stood under the balcony of the White House residence and sobbed and shook. The press took it all in. The President walked to a podium in the midst of this sea of people and said good-bye. He thanked us for all we'd done, for fighting the good fight.

This was far worse than the night before, and far worse than anything that followed. How he got through it without tears himself, I will never know. The Secret Service was crying.

Gracious to the end, the Bushes invited us back into the downstairs residence, but I just couldn't. There were cars going, but I began walking back to campaign headquarters. People came up to me on the street and started trashing Clinton and I snapped, "Just shut up."

They had cleaned out my office.

The way campaigns work is that you get paid up till the day of the election and that's it. So I walked back into my office and it was all empty, down to the bare walls, they had packed everything. I lay down on the floor and tried to take a nap.

That night we threw a party in Carney's office for the political staff, so now we were back in wake mode. Everybody told war stories and drank gallons of cheap wine and beer, and made fun of each other and took pictures, and tried to start talking about where we were each going to work, and tried to pump each other up. Meanwhile, Teeter's special counsel, Jim Pinkerton, was next door with a reporter, holding his own little news conference, telling everything that had gone wrong with the campaign.

The President's doctor had given me a sleeping pill. I had never taken one before, but I was desperate. I took it but I still couldn't sleep. I was beyond exhaustion, into utter sleep-deprived, emotion-overload, cried-out lunacy. I went home, I hadn't been there for weeks, and my house was a mess. Hell with it. I pushed all the newspapers and books and trash off the couch, made a little fetal-position place for myself, and flipped on the TV.

What, to my burned-out eyes, was the first image I saw but James Carville. Ted Koppel had done some sort of "72 Hours to Victory" special, and there was Carville's big giant serpenthead face filling the screen. He was crying—his lips were quivering—about *me*.

What an insult.

I got so mad. God was following me around trying to torture me in every conceivable known human way.

It was like a bad movie, or the Twilight Zone, where you're convinced that people are talking to you through the television. I was afraid to turn the channel. I was afraid he'd be on all the stations.

I turned him off. I couldn't read, I couldn't sleep, I stayed balled up on the couch all night long.

There was a last campaign meeting at nine-thirty the next morning, and Teeter and Malek were trying to console us. Teeter pulled out a big spread from a 1972 *Life* magazine showing them (pretty much the only ones who didn't get indicted) and the whole Watergate White House gang. He said, "I know it's hard to think you'll ever recover from this, and I know you think you'll never work again. . . ." He told us all he would personally do anything and everything to help us find jobs.

I'm sure I washed my face and brushed my teeth—I must have—but I didn't brush my hair, and I had on exactly the same clothes. I was in a fog. I went back to my office and lay down on the floor again. There were no couches, no chairs, no nothing. This time I slept for about two hours. Then I went home.

Carville kept calling. All he wanted to talk about was this damn trip. I couldn't bear the thought of getting on a plane with him. I didn't want to talk to anybody who wasn't similarly in mourning. I wanted to stay at the campaign forever.

We had a tradition; whenever James would come home I'd go pick him up at the airport. But this time he had the good sense not to ask me. I just went to bed. I was finally falling asleep when I heard his key in the lock.

James

I hung around Little Rock for two days. Wednesday was a lot of recapitulating and shaking hands and laughing. Thursday morning the President-elect called me himself and wanted to know if I'd meet him at his office in the Capitol and have lunch with him and Hillary.

"Well," I said, "I could probably arrange it. Let me check my schedule, probably move a few things around for that."

He was talking to some people when I got there. "Just sit in my office for a minute, James," he said.

I'd promised I would take some of the people in the campaign to lunch, so I told him I'd had a late breakfast. We sat around the little table where we'd had all those meetings, he had a bowl of chicken noodle soup and a glass of iced tea, and we talked. He said, "Go on get a soda pop out of the refrigerator if you want to."

"No, no, I can't."

The air changes when you're talking to a President. You know he's human, you know he's capable of mistakes and susceptible to disease and he's made of the same stuff the rest of us are. But now he's vested with 203 years of presidential history. He's going to take the same oath of office that George Washington took. He's a very important person now. It alters the way you behave around him.

A candidate is different. Bill Clinton was a good guy, a fun guy to bullshit with. A lot of candidates are all business, but he and Hillary were kind of a fun couple. During the campaign Hillary and Diane Blair and Susan Thomases would sit around with a bottle of some godawful white zinfandel that couldn't cost more than four dollars, and tell jokes. Clinton and I were the same age Southerners; we liked to have a good time. I had a pretty good handle on him, which made me able to say, when I had to, "No, goddamn, that's crazy, Governor. Shit, we can't do that!" There's something that prevents you from saying that to a President.

I was nervous. I noticed little things about him. I noticed what he was wearing, I noticed his fingernails, I sat there and watched the way he was eating his food. In a campaign you don't have the time or the interest. Table manners? Hell, we sucked down food. But this was now the President.

President-elect Clinton, Hillary, and I, just the three of us, sat around the table for about forty-five minutes, retelling campaign stories and talking about the future. Mrs. Clinton was very nice. She had spent fifteen minutes with my mother on election night and said what a character she was. It was all way more personal than business. "You know," she said, "I'm going to miss seeing you coming over here, and the meetings. We're going to sure miss Arkansas." A lot of "Hey, it's over." It was big-time over.

Mr. Clinton told me, "Both of us wanted to thank you, you put in a lot of work. We know you don't have an interest in working in the government, and we respect the fact that you like campaigns. We just wanted to tell you how much we love you, and love your mother, and how much fun we had. We enjoyed having you around and being in our house and helping us in this. We really thank you and appreciate it."

I told them, "You know, I do appreciate your inviting me here. It means a lot. This was the most meaningful job I ever had. I'll always consider myself part of the extended Clinton family, and I appreciate y'all for letting me in."

As exhilarating as it is to sit at a table with the First Lady-to-be and the President-elect of the United States, deep down inside I couldn't help but think of the kind of human beings they were. I come from a big, close family and I know a happy family when I see one. I can honestly say that from Mr. Clinton's mother, Mrs. Virginia Kelley, to the Rodhams to the President-elect to Hillary to Chelsea, their family was just as close as mine.

The one part of the human anatomy that is incapable of deception is the eyes. The mouth and the body have a hundred ways of being deceitful, but never the eyes. When people look at each other, or at their children or their parents, you can tell what's really going on. I could tell when the Clintons had been away from each other for a week or so; they'd see each other for the first time and it would change the chemistry of the room. And whenever Chelsea would walk in, their eyes would sparkle.

Hillary had taken some hits during the campaign, and much of the stuff that was said about her was true: She is smart, she is aggressive, she can be tough, she likes to bring things to a decision. That's the Hillary Clinton everybody in America knows about, and I know that Hillary too.

But the Hillary Clinton few people know is the woman who never misses a staff party, who knows the names of all my seven brothers and sisters, who never fails to stop and talk with my mother when she sees her. In a world where lots of people move great distances to get away from their parents, Hillary Clinton moved her mother and father from the north side of Chicago to Little Rock, where she and her family could spend time with them. Best of all, Mrs. Clinton has never in any way, shape, or form allowed her daughter to be used for any kind of political exploitation. My quarrel with the portrayal of Hillary is not that what people are saying is wrong, it's that there's a whole other side to her that isn't even being discussed. She's an admirable woman.

We did talk some business. They asked me who in the campaign did I think really shone, and I gave them some names.

They could not have been more warm or nicer, but I was kind of glad when it was time to go. This was now the leader of the world, I couldn't help worrying that I'd say something wrong, or feeling he had way more important things to do than talk to me.

Warren Christopher was coming in as I was leaving. He was the head of the transition team. We had a little chat. It was nice and I was flattered, but I thought, "Why is he talking to me?"

The press always has a camera assigned to the President. It's in case he dies, if he goes running and has a heart attack, they can't miss the story. I walked up to them and said, "Well, dammit, I didn't get State. That's it. I quit. I got nothing left to do with these people."

You want to know what the definition of status is? It's being the first person to eat a meal with the President-elect. Back at the War Room everybody gathered around. "God, what did it feel like? Did he look any different? What did he say?"

But it was too big a name even to drop. You could never say, "I had chicken soup with the President-elect today." It was beyond that. What most people in the War Room said was, "You know, James, it was so nice of him to call you over there. It was so nice of him." And it was. It was the single nicest thing anybody has ever done for me.

But politics is fleeting. A few weeks later I was on my way to Louisiana and went through Little Rock. They were in the middle of the transition, choosing people for the most important positions in the new government. I called up and said, "May I please speak to George Stephanopoulos."

"Who's calling?"

"James Carville."

"Spell that, please?"

I walked through the offices and everybody was happy to see me. "Hey, James, how you doing?"

"Anybody want to go eat lunch?"

"Oh, well, we're busy, we got . . ." People weren't rude or unappreciative, they just had a government to form. In the middle of a campaign, if I'd gotten the flu and been out three days, people would've been saying, "Gee, where is James? Get him out of bed and down here." After the campaign is over, if you aren't there, hell, who would care? If you're a cabinet secretary you're a much bigger deal than a former campaign manager.

It doesn't break your heart. You don't say, "What a bunch of ingrates." I just thought, "Damn, what am I going to do? Nobody needs me anymore. I'm not a needed person." There was a stillness.

Thursday night after the election there was a big party across the river in North Little Rock. Everybody in the campaign was in town. We had a band. I went to that, left at around ten. Greenberg had a private plane that took us back to Washington. We landed at Dulles Airport at about one in the morning. I caught a cab, went over to Mary's, put the key in the lock, opened the door.

"Honey, I'm home."

James Carville and Mary Matalin were married in New Orleans, Louisiana, on November 25, 1993. James continues as a partner in the political consulting firm Carville & Begala and is working on the reelection campaigns of Senator Harris Wofford of Pennsylvania and Governor Zell Miller of Georgia. James also serves as a consultant to the Democratic National Committee and periodically advises President Clinton on political matters. Mary is the conservative host of *Equal Time,* a Washington, D.C.–based political talk show, and is the Republican commentator on NBC's *Today* show. She continues to traverse the country, making campaign appearances on behalf of Republican candidates from sea to shining sea.

Index

ABOUT THE COAUTHOR

PETER KNOBLER has collaborated on the autobiographies of Governor Ann Richards, Kareem Abdul-Jabbar, Thomas "Hollywood" Henderson, and Peggy Say. He lives with his wife and son in New York City.